The Globalization
of Rural Plays in the
Twenty-First Century

The Globalization of Rural Plays in the Twenty-First Century

Alin Rus

LEXINGTON BOOKS
Lanham • Boulder • New York • London

Published by Lexington Books
An imprint of The Rowman & Littlefield Publishing Group, Inc.
4501 Forbes Boulevard, Suite 200, Lanham, Maryland 20706
www.rowman.com

86-90 Paul Street, London EC2A 4NE

British Library Cataloguing in Publication Information Available

Library of Congress Cataloging-in-Publication Data Available

ISBN: 978-1-66691-543-3 (cloth : alk. paper)
ISBN: 978-1-66691-544-0 (electronic)

♾™ The paper used in this publication meets the minimum requirements of American National Standard for Information Sciences—Permanence of Paper for Printed Library Materials, ANSI/NISO Z39.48-1992.

Contents

List of Figures and Tables

FIGURES

TABLE

Acknowledgments

This book is based on my PhD dissertation defended in May 2018 at University of Massachusetts Amherst, anthropology department. To this were added two more field trips in the area of Iași County, Romania and in Chernivtsi (Cernăuți) area of Ukraine, together with an intense work of more than two years of complete restructuring of the initial manuscript, editing and rethinking of some of its initial arguments. The early stages of my research were funded by the National Science Foundation's Office of International Science and Engineering, and by the UMass Amherst Department of Anthropology, through European Field Studies Program, Cultural Heritage in European Societies and Spaces—Multiculturalism, Migration, and Heritage in Europe. Besides, the Graduate School and the Department of Anthropology of the Massachusetts Amherst University offered six travel grants allowing me to take part in a series of cultural heritage conferences organized in the United States, Portugal, England, and Mexico, that broadened my horizons and improved my knowledge of heritage studies. The Township Hall of Helești also provided me with constant logistical support, without which this research could have never achieved all its objectives.

I would like to thank my PhD advisor, Dr. Krista Harper, for her intellectual guidance, insightful comments on my papers, for her patience and investment of time and energy into seeing the finalization of a project distant from the current trends and directions in Cultural Anthropology. Many thanks go to Dr. Jacqueline Urla for her suggestions, advice, and comments on my papers during many years in a row. I owe many thanks to Dr. Richard W. Wilkie who encouraged my creative thinking, and who believed from the beginning in my strength to accomplish a project that seemed difficult to comprehend during its first phases. I will always be grateful to my good friend and committee member in the first phase of my PhD dissertation, Dr. David A. Kideckel. He has constantly encouraged me to work hard, while at the same time making me aware that a few ideas and arguments in my dissertation, although self-obvious to me, could not be that clear for those who might read my work. I thank Dr. Ventura Perez, too, who gave me many valuable ideas in the field of the Anthropology of Violence. Several other professors from the University of Massachusetts Amherst, Anthropology Department, have given me their advice, comments and thoughts for shaping parts of this project. Among them, I would like to mention Dr. Robert Paynter, Dr. Elizabeth Chilton, Dr. Kevin Anderson, Dr. Michael Sugerman, Dr. Felicity Aulino, and Dr. Neal Silberman. In this list of professors, I must add the name of Dr. Cristina Amescua, from the National University of Mexico's Regional Center for Multidisciplinary Research. She was the organizer of several Intangible Cultural Heritage conferences in England, Mexico, Brazil, and Croatia where we had an interesting exchange of ideas on heritage themes.

I also owe my whole gratitude to Dr. Bogdan Neagota and Dr. Ileana Benga, two Romanian friends and collaborators, founders and members of the ethnological association *Orma Sodalitas Anthropologica*. Throughout my entire research, I had a fruitful exchange of ideas with both of them, and that helped me outline and clarify some concepts and theories of European Folklore and Ethnology. Bogdan was for me not only a simple friend and collaborator but also a spiritual master from whom I had learned enormously all these years. He is a man who created around him and his ideas a real school of ethnology and folklore in Cluj-Napoca city.

Two other mentors and collaborators from Romania that I could not forget because they marked my intellectual ascent are Ruxandra Cesereanu and Doina Jela. Dr. Cesereanu was my professor and mentor when I was a student in Romania and she stimulated me with advice and encouragement during the writing of this new book. Doina Jela was the publisher of my first important book in Romania and offered me a series of tips, advice, and critical comments that led to my intellectual formation over the following years.

I owe the same acknowledgment to two friends and collaborators from Indiana University, Dr. Elena Popa and Dr. Julian Carrillo (back then PhD students) who read various parts of my book and generously offered me their ideas. I have to add to this list the name of Dr. Monica Heintz, my friend, and collaborator for more than a decade. In December 2010—January 2011, we worked together in the villages of Heleșteni to make the filming of the documentary *Behind the Masks*. It was a fruitful collaboration that ended with a 44-minute film about *Pantomimic Mummers* in this rural locality.

I owe special thanks to my childhood friend from Jiu Valley region of Romania, Ioan Apostu, and also a member of *Orma Sodalitas Anthropologica*. Along with him, I started the first phase of my field research for this project. In addition to this, he has always helped me to systematize and archive my substantial video material collected from the field, consisting of videos and photos. Do not think your efforts will ever be forgotten, my friend! Also from the Jiu Valley area, I am indebted to three other friends and collaborators with whom I had numerous discussions and exchanges of ideas related to various topics of this paper. These are the freelancer Carol Gigi Nicolau, the journalist Marian Boboc and the sociologist Fulger Valentin. All these extraordinary friendships and fruitful collaborations proved once again that I was a lucky man.

I had an excellent cooperation with Elena Cărbunaru-Butușină, a professional translator and reliable collaborator. She was the one who struggled with translating some Romanian carols, wishes, and folk expressions into English. She also read my entire dissertation and often gave me her advice as a philologist and connoisseur of Romanian folklore when translating to English expressions and concepts from the local folklore of Romanian peasants.

My friend and collaborator Cristina Dragomir who was my colleague while we were students at Babeș-Bolyai University, philosophy department, now a political science professor at New York University, has provided me with valuable advice and suggestions during the last phase of my project. Comming from a field of study outside anthropology, her ideas helped me a lot to understand how my work will be perceived by scholars who are not anthropologists, folklorists, or ethnologists.

Also in the last phase of my research, I had the opportunity to exchange fruitful ideas with my colleagues at Franklin Pierce University, especially with Douglas Challenger, Sarah T. Dangelantonio, and Robert Goodby. The students in the anthropology department also gave me valuable feedback over the years. Among them I would like to mention at least some of them: Acacia Johnson, David Salvatore, Michaela Topham, Andrew Farley, and Isabela Niemi.

Professor Dr. Arlene Ash, although from a field of research other than the humanities, read a substantial portion of the manuscript, edited parts of it, and generously provided advice on the structure of the study, plus pertinent opinions regarding the usage of some political correctness terms throughout the book.

I owe a special gratitude to the entire Hâra family in Heleșteni: Constantin, Doinița, Evelina, and Dana. During my repeated stays in their village, they always hosted me and offered me the warmth and hospitality of their home and, above all, their expertise in the field of local traditions. Besides them, Florin Chiperi and his wife Andreea always offered me their unconditional support and knowledge in understanding local culture. I am connected to these two families not only through a close collaboration, but also through a friendship for life.

In Ukraine, I also owe thanks, together with my appreciation, to Mr. Gheorghe Stratulat and Ms. Olga Bruja Avdochimova, her son Victor together with their whole family. They impressed me with their hospitality, openness, and kindness. If all people were like them, we would all live in a better world today, without wars and conflicts.

Next to these close friends, I am also grateful to many people from Heleşteni, Ruginoasa, Cucuteni, Strunga, Crivești, Sticlăria, Bădeni, Iași in Romania, and Crasna, Carapciu, Pătrăuții de Sus, and Cernăuți in Ukraine. Their simple enumeration would cover almost an entire page. By their side, I experienced moments of intellectual satisfaction accompanied by the joy of understanding the rural world and the humanity of the people within it. Many of them generously offered me the hospitality of their home at least for a few hours. Some of them, especially the older ones, are now gone to the world of shadows, but I hope their voice will remain forever alive in the pages of this study. All of them have made me think differently and change from the one I was at the beginning of this project; thanks to knowing them, I am now a person with a broader and more complex vision of the world and life.

From my wife Florentina I have received constant moral and intellectual support, along with encouragements. She had spent many of her school holidays in a village in Western Romania where her grandparents lived; thus she became a good connoisseur of the rural world in that area of Transylvania, and was later able to provide me with pertinent advice on rural folklore and the way of thinking of village inhabitants, tempering my idealistic tendencies and hasty generalizations. A simple thanks would not be enough to express my appreciation for her help.

Last but not least, I have to thank my parents, Maria and Simion Rus, for their constant moral, spiritual, and material support over my years of study, and throughout the challenges I have been going through. I am convinced that there are few people who have the privilege of having such wonderful parents, so my gratitude will never be able to reward their efforts. My brother Octavian and his family (his wife Simona and children Mihnea and Ria) have always encouraged me in my struggle to complete this project. I want him to always remember the lyrics of a song we used to listen as children: "Nu există in lumea asta frate ca al meu/ Și la bune și la rele, e fratele meu!" (eng. "In this entire world there's no brother like mine/ To all good and bad, he remains my brother.") Finally, my eternal gratitude, appreciation, and esteem go to my grandmother, Elena Murarek, the one who helped, encouraged, and supported me with an abnegation worthy of all admiration. She was the one who always believed in my lucky star. Unfortunately, she passed away a few years before she could see the completion of this stage of my life.

Other members of my family were also close to me with their thought or presence while writing this book. These are my cousins Nora Maria Murarek and Iulian Murarek, my aunts Iulia Rusu and Susana Gorgan, my uncle Traian Rus and his family, my cousin Simona Rus and her family, Cristea family

(Andreea, Mirela, and Nelu), and also my godparents Cornelia Zara and Octavian Băban.

The intellectual formation of a person as well as the important ideas are frequently influenced by a series of meetings and friendships. My book is one about the transformation of rural culture under the influence of globalization. Living in the United States, I was fortunate enough to have friends from all over the world with extensive knowledge of our globalized world. They gave me the opportunity to exchange ideas and information based on themes from my paper. Among them I would like to mention: Carolina and Remus Ionete and their family, Mike and Judith Klein, Kendi, Penhia, and Harumi Okuda, Ştefania and Chriss Seith, Dan and Liana Mănescu, Ed Rizotto, Ann Rothstein, Morgan Ruelle, Elena Galeriu, Rosane De Oliveira, Rajive Rishi, Diana Cristea, Liliana Cristea, Phillip Glenn, Roger Langevin, Tania Catalan, Adela Popescu, Eduard and Eva Postol, Rafael Miranda, Adriana Otalvaro, Miriam Oliveira, Kreshnik Bezhani, Carmen, Dani, Marius and Gabriela Cîmpan, Ramona Dumitrescu, and Teodor Stan.

Introduction

A STORY OF A CHILDHOOD

This book is the result of my enduring passion for the people of rural communities, their stories, and the plays[1] that accompany their lives. My encounter with rural culture was due to a special event whose consequences I came to fully realize only decades later, when opening a new chapter in my life, as an immigrant in the United States. Only then did I realize that I had spent my childhood and youth in one of the last European countries where small-scale agriculture was still widely practiced.[2] This country is Romania, a land that, due to historical circumstances and to a special cultural context, maintained a well-preserved peasant culture until the end of the 20th century (Hobsbawm 1994). Although this rural culture is largely gone today, some of its features survived in the 21st century and I had the chance to study them in my research conducted between 2009 and 2020 in North-Eastern Romania, Moldova region, Iași County, one of the most ruralized areas of Romania.

One of my most vivid childhood memories of the rural universe is about an event that occurred at the end of summer vacation following first grade. There were about eight of us, children living in my apartment building. As we met on the playground the others related their experiences while visiting their grandparents in rural areas, since their parents were in the first generation of proletarianized peasants of Socialist Romania who had come to the Jiu Valley region[3] (Kideckel 2008). Although the industrialization of Romania started in earnest right after the Second World War, and the country's big cities had experienced the transformations of industrialization earlier, during the interwar period; in the early 1980s Romania's small industrial cities still had many peasants in the first generation of labor migrants. They had come to urban areas near the end of the 1970s, attracted by higher wages in the mining industry, but also by the promise of Romania's massive industrialization programs. I was the only one with no rural grandparents and no story to tell about my experience at the countryside.

However, back then I knew nothing about this history, and that evening I returned home with a heavy heart. "All the children in the yard were in the countryside! Why don't I have a countryside[4]?" I asked my mother. "Well, you're 'John with no country,'" my mother replied laughing, referring to the historical character John Lackland, King of England at the beginning of the 13th century. In fact, all my maternal and paternal grandparents had always lived in the city and worked as skilled employees in industry their whole lives. My mother finished the conversation saying: "I don't even know what interests you so much about going to the countryside. There is nothing special to see there!" This strange interchange aroused my interest in a type of life that I could only access through my friends' stories. So, I listened eagerly and became increasingly curious about a world that I feared I would never experience.

However, that winter my whole family was invited to the countryside in North-Western Romania, where my aunt's in-laws lived in a village. My family spent more than a week in that village, called Derşida, a place known for its wines, with its cellars dug inside hills. It was also known for its New Year peasant plays, which we were to experience. I vividly remember the experience of observing and playing freely with animals in that peasant household: chickens, ducks, turkeys, geese, pigs—even a newborn calf. My playing turned out to be a hardship for our hosts, because I had the costly habit of feeding the birds in the farmyard with food from our meals. After my parents admonished me "don't feed the birds with the good food we have for dinner!," I had to play this game secretly.

But the event that made the strongest impression on me happened on Christmas Eve, just two or three days after our arrival in the village. I had learned that early in the morning, on Christmas Eve, the *dubaşi* would arrive. The archaic word *dubaşi* especially resonated in my child's mind, stimulating my imagination enormously. I had no idea what would happen when those people came, making me even more curious. What I knew was that we had to get up very early, get dressed in our best clothes, and wait for the *dubaşi* to arrive. Although I usually found it difficult to wake up in the morning, before 7:00 am I was already dressed and ready to see what would happen. My father was ready early too, since he was used to a job that required leaving home every morning at 6:30 am, as were our hosts, who were accustomed to the rhythm of their domestic animals that had to be fed every morning before 7:00 am. My mother was the only one in the house who didn't wake up before 7:30, leading to a surprising event, I would never forget.

The village was suddenly aroused by the shrill sounds of drums, accordions and violins. About ten men abruptly entered our yard. My sleepy mother asked our hosts: "What? These guys enter without asking anyone in the household?" "Yes, that's how our *dubaşi* behave!" replied the head of the household with a serious mug. "And what am I supposed to do now?" my mother asked. "Get under the quilt quickly!" my father suggested. In the next moments the *dubași* were already in our living room, which was at the same time our bedroom during the stay there. "Happy to have guests, you host?" asked one of the men dressed in his holiday costume. The *dubași* seemed to be already dizzy from "the vapors of alcohol." "Happy, happy!" the hosts replied. After this brief introduction, the drums began to beat while the violins and accordion played. The whole performance lasted about 10 to 15 minutes, after which the head of the *dubași* asked with utter pride, according to the ritual: "Did we cheer you up, host?" "You did! You did!" the hosts responded immediately. "Let's say one more to cheer this host again!" decided the head of the *dubași* on the spur of the moment, leading to a new round of drum-beats and shrill sounds of the accordion. Then, following the *dubași* tradition, they sat down at the table, toasted a glass of wine with the hosts and took a small snack.

This ritual lasted about 30 minutes, after which the *dubași* went on to visit the next household, still sounding their drums. Only then could my mother come out from under the thick goose-down peasant quilt, which so effectively traps human body heat. Everyone in the house burst into laughter at the sight of her, red as a boiled lobster and with a sweaty face. I learned later that the *dubași* were supposed to be merciless to anyone who violated the strict rules of the ritual, such as being caught unprepared for the team's arrival or considered to be less than fully welcoming hosts. Indeed, my mother had heard two of the *dubași* sitting at her bedside, discussing with each other, "Beat well the drum so that she learns to be prepared when the *dubași* enter the house!"

This was the first time in my life that I witnessed this abolition of the daily rules of good sense and fair measure in a community, and saw them replaced by play, derision, irony, and mockery. All were part of a cultural landscape not encountered in the city, and it further aroused my curiosity about village life.

A STORY OF THE ROMANIAN COUNTRYSIDE

Indeed, the following year an unexpected event brought this rural world with its own rules and oddities even closer. My uncle on my mother's side married a young woman from Romania's rural south. After that, my grandmother and I would visit the village of Budieni in Gorj County for two or three weeks each summer.

My first memories are of the large agricultural lots that started right behind the gardens of the peasant houses. There were many kinds of crops: from corn and wheat to vineyards and fruit trees. Nearby, one would also find small lakes, hills, pastures for cattle and a stream. When visiting this village,

I would spend much time with my new friends, walking for hours in the field rows and the surrounding orchards and feeding all day on the fruits of the wild shrubs in the field and the fruit trees by the village streets, to the despair of my grandmother who was convinced that during such days I would die of hunger.

For me, all of this was part of a childhood universe where play and the exploration of the surroundings were the main elements of a new world. However, I would soon find out that play was sometimes severely restricted in the village. Especially children over the age of ten had limited access to it, given the fact that they already had precise tasks to do in their parents' peasant household. I learned this when, after a full day of wandering through the village forests, we arrived home late in the evening. We could not know that such a beautiful adventure would have an unhappy outcome for our eldest friends a 14 year old who, it turned out, had neglected his household duties. His father awaited him with a stick in his hand. There followed a fierce beating, accompanied by loud cries of the teenager. This event terrified me and made me look at the village world with different eyes. Until then, I didn't know that neglecting parental authority and harsh community rules could be punished so severely.

The next few days, our friend Bebe was given another punishment. He was required to shell the corn on the cob. Removing the kernel on the cob was done using a small iron tool with a blade blunt after a long-time usage, and whose use left you bruised all over the palm after only one hour of utilization. This two-days' chore was followed by another one, or maybe it was just another stage in the life of a teenager from the village—something I did not realize at that time. It consisted of taking the community's sheep herd to the pastures at the outskirts of the village. There, we could make sure that Bebe could continue to enjoy childhood games with us. So, we brought a soccer ball with us to the fields outside the village where Bebe had to bring the herd, so that he could join our games. And if the sheep moved too far while we were playing soccer, we would all help him get them back from the meadows where they had made their way.

In children's plays, social differences are often blurred, or may even vanish completely. However, when I was playing soccer, there was always a noticeable difference between me and the kids in that village that we had to bear in mind. All my friends in the village used to walk barefoot during the summer. I was the only one who stubbornly kept his sports shoes even in the muddy places on the edge of the village. So, before our soccer games started, I always heard a voice or two from the group warning: "Well, you guys wearing sport shoes, be careful not to hurt those barefoot!" Although the call didn't explicitly refer to me, it was more than obvious who the target was.

There were other events that revealed some of the fundamental differences between the rural and the urban worlds. During a torrid afternoon, when even the most diligent householders had ceased working in the field, our group of friends made their way to a village creek where we liked to bathe on such hot days. At one point, a long black snake crossed our path. After a first moment of surprise and terror I saw the boys chasing the poor creature with sticks. Within five minutes, the snake was almost dead, and spasmodic shudders had taken over its entire body. Neither of the boys touched it with their hands, but they raised it several times with their wooden sticks to convince themselves that the snake would soon die. And when they were fully assured, victorious shouts came out of their chests. They were convinced that they had killed a creature of the devil or even the devil's incarnation on earth. The biblical image of the serpent misleading Adam and Eve seems to have been deeply rooted in their minds.

I would later discover that Christian religion played an important role in people's lives, and that even children would make the sign of the cross when passing by a church or even by the roadside where big wooden crosses were placed. All this happened during a period marked by the official Marxist-atheist vision, when at least in the cities, making the sign of the cross on the street and talking openly about the events mentioned in the Bible was not seen with the good eyes by the Communist authorities (Leustean 2008).

In addition to these notable events, there were some memorable meetings I cannot forget. One of these was the meeting with Mr. Savu, an over 80-year-old man who spent most of his day on the porch of his house, resting on a pole, often seeking the opportunity to communicate with the villagers walking nearby. I listened to his first stories on a gloomy summer afternoon preceded by a few days of heavy rain that had kept us all indoors. Such rains made the village roads unpleasant, especially those from the agricultural lands in the hilly area, where we spent a lot of time. That afternoon, when the day already seemed compromised and nothing special was announced, one of the children came up with the idea: "Let's go to Mr. Savu and ask him to tell us a *moroi* (ghost) story!" I had never heard the word *moroi* before. However, I instinctively followed the group to Mr. Savu's house.

"Mr. Savu, could you tell us a story about *moroi* (ghosts) or *pricolici* (werewolves)?" "Did I tell you about Toader's ghost?" "That's what you told us last time!" one of the children replied. It seems that Mr. Savu had his own set of stories that the children in the village had already heard, but sometimes they liked to listen to again. Thus, I witnessed a set of negotiations between the group of children and Mr. Savu, after which it was agreed that the old man would tell, instead of a story with *moroi* (ghosts), one with *pricolici* (werewolves). *Pricolici* was another new word for me. Such stories, I was to realize later when I became an anthropologist, was quite widespread in the rural Southern Romania world, reflecting the social order of the countryside, and its deepest fears and superstitions. In short, the story of Mr. Savu started with a couple of peasants returning with their horse wagon from the field on a fall evening. At one point, the woman asks the man to stop the wagon to relieve herself in the bushes next to the road. The man stops and his wife disappears into the bushes at the edge of the road. The man waits for more than half an hour and, seeing that his wife does not return, finally decides to look for her. This was the moment when the moon had risen in the sky and the sun had set. That moment, a big black wolf comes from the bushes on the roadside and jumps to the man's chest. After a few seconds of scramble, the wolf finally flees into the forest nearby. The peasant had been lucky with his thick red woolen flannel protecting his chest from the bite of the terrible creature. Terrified, he goes back to his wagon. However, he cannot bear the thought of abandoning his wife in that dangerous place. After a few minutes, she appears, coming out of the forest edge. Horrified by the incident with the wolf, the man tells her the story. But the woman begins to laugh, apparently not believing a word of what had happened. And while she is laughing in the moonlight, the man notices that between the woman's teeth, there is an unmistakably red woolen piece of thread coming from his own flannel. The story ends abruptly with this sentence, leaving the listener to imagine every-thing about the relation between the two and what might happen next.

This was the world of the village, seen through the child's eyes. It was a universe not fully understood, and maybe that is why perceived as full of ambiguities and oddities. Similarly, the human who had made it possible—the peasant—seemed to have been born out of a multitude of paradoxes intertwined in the very core of his being. Over several years, I discovered, one by one, the paradoxes of the peasant's nature. Some of the most visible ones I noticed were the stark difference between the peasant's unabashed habit for physical labor and his almost reckless indulgence for play and fun during religious holidays and rituals of all kinds that populated the rural world. Already from childhood I discovered how every soul in the village took part in the rituals as if their whole life depended on them. And during these events, any kind of work on the field ceased and the whole community focused exclusively on organizing the ritual. Among the most important customs that I witnessed and remembered years after, were the days of wor-ship in the local parishes. Not only Easter, Christmas, and the New Year, but also the Whitsuntide, or other rituals such as *Paparudele*.[5] These traditions seemed back then, for me as a child, outwardly absurd, and in total opposition to the rigid rules of the rural world. Since then, I was drawn to find the deeper meaning behind this paradox that I felt needed further explanation.

A STORY OF PEASANTS

I returned to these thoughts in 2008, shortly after leaving Romania and starting my doctoral studies in Anthropology in the United States. It was between Christmas and New Year and I was watching a documentary broadcasted by the Romanian Television about Second World War veterans who had survived the horrors of this world conflagration and narrated their experiences in front of the cameras. Most of these former combatants were peasants and all of them returned to their home villages at the end of the war, and went on with their life from where they had left it when they went to the front. Such stories, some of which were terrifying, narrated in most cases with extraordinary lucidity, emanated an incredible force. In my view, they all spoke about the psychological robustness of the peasant as human type.

I would become much more aware of the psychological robustness of peasants in 2012, after starting my anthropological field research in eastern Romania, while interviewing the veterans in the village of Heleşteni about their experiences during World War II. All of them were between 80 and 90 years old. Many related, in voices overwhelmed by emotion, about the deaths of their platoon colleagues, and some could not control their tears. Clearly, they continued to bear a strong emotional load even six decades later. Yet each had returned to his village, set up a family and lived a normal life, without the help of any psychologists or doctors.

This new experience produced in the context of my new research on peasants' plays made me wonder: does the peasant's psychological robustness relate to his almost addictive propensity to play and story? Did rural plays, rituals and stories serve as a relief valve for the very rigid, potentially soul-crushing, rules of his world?

Indeed, these questions had two major ramifications regarding both peasant life itself and the intentions and ideological and intellectual views of those who have studied it. On the one hand, I am considering the psychological robustness and social persistence of a long-enduring human cultural type. On the other, I am talking about a social class that underwent incredible transformation in the 20th century. Thus, we find peasants among the proletarians on whose shoulders the industrial revolution developed, among the soldiers who fought in the major conflicts of the last century, among the protesters of the great revolutions that shook political regimes, among the great political figures of the 20th century, and among the immigrants who left their native places to live and work in other regions, countries, and continents. Peasants have adapted to all these new realities of the last century, and they have managed to cope with all these challenges.

In this book I will often use the term peasants to refer to the communities and individuals I have studied during my field research for over a decade in North-Eastern Romania. I do this because the subjects I studied frequently identify themselves as peasants. Even though I used this term frequently, I was always aware of its conceptual limits. The peasantry is a reality that extends to all continents and includes even today, at the beginning of the 21st century, an enormous number of people belonging to different countries, cultures, religions, political and economic systems. Thus, many statements about peasants could be in certain contexts perceived as generalizations. This aspect was also well understood since beginning by Peasant Studies, a field that has managed to provide valuable research on the peasantry despite the limits of this concept to fully characterize the whole social reality to which it refers. Aware of all these methodological and conceptual difficulties, I will highlight in the next section other currents and trends that I identified when I studied this complex reality called peasantry.

A STORY OF PEASANT STUDIES AND RURAL PLAYS

This complex and sometimes elusive landscape may have led the intellectuals who analyze it to talk rather about workers, soldiers, revolutionaries, politicians and immigrants, consciously or unconsciously ignoring the reality underlying these other important representations of 20th century life—a human cultural type with origins in rural culture (Frevert and Haupt 2002). Perhaps more than any other human cultural type of the last century, the peasant was analyzed through rigid ideological filters: as a member of a subordinate social class—an underdog (Shanin 1971), a humble worker of the earth, or, conversely, as a "noble" national representative and reservoir of its traditions.

These perspectives have concealed a wider understanding of the peasant from the point of view of his plays and the stories that have populated his universe for centuries. Mikhail Bakhtin was one of the few authors who come with a different perspective on peasantry. He observed that peasant society contains a burlesque vein and a carnivalesque component that should not be ignored (Bakhtin 1984). However, even Bakhtin does not have the peasant as his main subject; he was examining the linguistic and cultural universe of François Rabelais that happens to speak about the rural world. Unlike other studies, I seek to understand the individual of rural culture through the prism of his plays. This approach is innovative and somewhat risky. It is innovative, because it analyzes from a completely different angle a cultural type that has been the subject of ideological dispute among intellectuals and politicians since the end of the 19th century, with the launch of Karl Kautsky's famous agrarian question. And, it is risky because, from the perspective of the capitalist market-oriented view of human beings, the study of play must focuses on children, rather than adults (Brown 2009).

Therefore, one direction of this study is to help flesh out an incomplete vision in the social sciences that analyzed peasants during time. It reveals the playful nature of individuals living in rural societies. From this perspective, it is the peasant who, despite his daily life problems, or perhaps because of them, knew how to make fun of his own troubles. As I mentioned earlier, I am not the first to observe this, but I have had the privilege of experiences that make me clearly see the relations between peasant world and the realm of play. In fact, the peasants themself were the authors who described their society in the most varied and complex hypostases. It is enough to analyze rural plays and peasants' stories to get a complex portrait which remains full of paradoxes in the meantime. Thus, the peasants may appear not only under the image of the humans urged by the exploiting classes, but also under the appearance of Păcală[6] (The Trickster), an irretrievable naïve at first glance who could be perceived in various situations as being stupid or thick-headed. However, in the end, this character comes out victorious from all attempts precisely because he possesses a popular wisdom that allows him to transcend the vicissitudes and troubles of the world, and to successfully deal with them through a waggish nature and positive energy.[7]

The second direction of this book is to oppose a trend embedded in the market economy of global capitalism—the idea that play mainly belongs to children or professionals, and that it has little to do with adults, except as consumers of professional competitive play (White 2000). This view undermines spontaneity and the true spirit of play, as Johan Huizinga observed (Huizinga 1968). Thus, this book is a pointed critique of capitalist culture and its view on play, since even humans in rural societies with very strict rules, have made room for fantasy, imagination and play, which are extremely important elements for the proper functioning of the human mind (Brown and Vaughan 2010). Moreover, based on a case study that allows me to scrutinize the transformation of peasantry over several decades, the work reveals the mechanisms of the consumer society through which play has been confiscated and metamorphosed into merchandise and turned in something other than it had been before.

At the beginning of the 21st century, when time and global economy are no longer favorable to the perpetuation of peasant culture, this work fills in an important gap in our understanding of peasantry. The ambition has pitfalls. One is to replace the old ideological tendencies with one in which the peasant appears as a jester. This is not my intention. To avoid this trap, I explore peasant plays in all their complexity, from waggish, lively plays to solemn ones, full of seriousness; from violent and brutal plays to ones that bring peace and joy to the community; from dances to pantomime; from deceiving plays to plays charged with erotic energy. All this will reveal a hidden face of peasants less known to the public and will complete Peasant Studies with a new dimension. At the same time, it will contribute to Play Studies, whose interest in peasant plays is totally missing today.

However, the present work is not a comprehensive work of the richly diverse universe of rural plays. Given their diversity, such an approach would be impossible to achieve. That is why, among peasant plays, I have focused on mummers' plays[8] that encompass an extremely complex range of manifestations, including the many elements listed above. Such plays have been analyzed for decades by the Folkloristics of England, Sweden, Norway, Russia, Romania, and the Newfoundland Islands of Canada (Chambers 1969 [1933]; Gunnell 2007b; Halpert and Story 1969). A systematic review of these works it was also necessary. My book seeks to overcome what I see as a limited perspective that has dominated mummers' plays studies from the end of the 19th century until recently, namely, that they have been conducted through a nationalist filter and have viewed these plays as quaint relics of a lost time, rather than trying to explore their meanings for those communities that produced them. It should be mentioned that the thinking framework underlying these writings has become obsolete.

As can be seen, the complexity and extent of this subject is extraordinary, and it needs a new vision and methodology. Thus, in this research I aimed to analyze rural plays through a new methodology and an innovative theoretical framework. I must mention from the beginning that this study operates with several theoretical and conceptual frameworks that were necessary mainly due to the complexity of my topic. I considered that the transformation of rural plays under the influence of globalization cannot be sufficiently comprehended unless the peasants' system of values together with its decline due to a set of economic, social, political, and cultural factors, is well understood. Or, understanding peasants' system of values without an in-depth inquiry from the perspective of Cultural Anthropology is almost impossible. This field approached peasants from their relationship with the goods, persons, actions, and ideas they valorize, and explains why they are important for peasants. Another field that complements this analysis is Peasants Studies. The lens of this field is necessary because it explains the various trends that marked the view of peasantry over time and how it built a series of long-lasting representations that influenced the consciousness of scholars and intellectuals regarding peasants in various historical periods, sometimes impeding the creation of competing views regarding the way peasants might be conceived.

Play Studies is another discipline whose theoretical frameworks were used in my book. Analyzing peasant plays from the perspective of Play Studies is fruitful as it gives a holistic perspective on a set of rural plays and settings that were not investigated yet with the means of this discipline. The last chapters of the study propose a deeper theoretical vision talking about cognitive abilities that make possible human relationship with the play/game. Although folklore scholars are tempted to talk about the disappearance of rural plays, I have shown that it is rather only a profound transformation of them under the influence of modernity so that they became unrecognizable. But it underlies the same human propensity to play, which has existed since time immemorial and continues to exist today, although the plays have changed over time in relation to the transformations of the social, economic, and political universe of humans. I analyzed these transformations using a theoretical framework from the philosophy of language, cognitive science, and sociology.

Finally, I have advanced an analysis from the perspective of heritage studies. This book is based on field research conducted in the early 21st century when rural communities were caught up in a visible dissolution process. Thus, I describe peasants' attempts to safeguard and promote their intangible cultural heritage in a global society that is rapidly eroding the traditions of rural communities. In particular, the last chapter of my study is devoted almost entirely to the dynamics of power relations resulting from the attempts of the peasants to promote their cultural heritage. In this context, the present book is an ethnographic investigation of how rural plays are transformed in a postsocialist landscape dominated by globalization processes and forces. It examines various cultural forms from the perspective of peasant values caught themselves in the process of dissolution due to globalization. It also demonstrates how global capitalism has affected the dynamics of rural communities' intangible heritage that, just like peasants, migrates from their communities of origin to urban areas with a higher concentration of capital. My analysis exemplifies the Bourdieusian concept of symbolic violence by depicting labor migration and other processes that accompany globalization as eroding rural cultural heritage. It describes peasants' struggle to maintain their binary identity as workers in Western countries and as custodians of customs that embody their national and (more recently) their transnational cultural heritage.

I am aware that all this theoretical baggage may seem disconcerting to the reader. At the same time, it can be turned into a source of new approaches and interpretations for researchers in several fields like: anthropology, folklore, rural studies, play studies, philosophy, and heritage studies.

THE STRUCTURE OF THE BOOK

The book is divided into six chapters preceded by an introduction and followed by an afterword. The first two chapters represent complex ethnographies of rural plays in two neighboring villages from North-Eastern Romania, Heleşteni and Ruginoasa, both practicing and promoting different folk plays. The plays of the two communities are described based on historical archival studies that give an account of their continuity in those villages for centuries. At the same time the study traces the recent transformation of several folk plays such as the *Play of the Deer*, the *Play of the Goat*, and the *Pantomimic Mummers* in Heleşteni village and the *Traditional Battle with Sticks*, *Malanca* and *Târâitul* in Ruginoasa village. It presents the way rural inhabitants of these villages, from an early age, organize, communicate, and connect with each other through the means of rural plays.

Through the detailed analysis, and extended interviews, the local oral histories, and the data coming from participant observation, the first two chapters of the study contains the ingredients of a historically informed ethnography, guided by a twofold question: How did the global influences of the last decades transform the relationship between peasants and their community plays, and reshape the way they think, interact, and behave like humans? and How can rural plays be used as lens to look at the global transformations that affected rural communities in the last decades?

The study begins from a fundamental observation that the play has been an indispensable ingredient of rural communities throughout their history. It has been a catalyst, giving social cohesion to countryside communities, decisively contributing to shaping peasant values and their cultural profile. But with the influences of modernity in the rural world, such as the media, the market economy, and digital culture, we are witnessing the transformation of the peasantry and its culture into something other than it was ever before. In Romania, a country with a strong peasant culture (Chirot 1989), these influences come relatively late in the rural world, in some areas only with the fall of communism, and allowed the perpetuation of older forms of culture such as folk plays until the beginning of the 21st century.

In the introduction, I build an argument based on my own experience with the rural world from childhood to the present. My experience with rural culture reveals the strong presence of peasantry in Romania until the late 1980s. Thus, even someone like me, born in the second half of the 20th century and raised in the city, was able to experience a peasant culture that had long since disappeared in the West. The main point is to describe the paradox of peasant life, which is inexorably bound to the physical work of the land, yet strongly connected to community rituals and plays that demand the cessation of work for everyone. I briefly present the main arguments of the book and its structure and describe each chapter and the relationship among them. I emphasize the contribution of the book to the existing literature and how it connects some fields of research that have not previously been brought together.

Chapter one depicts the village community of Heleșteni in North-Eastern Romania, a locality where peasants still practice some of their winter rural plays, such as the *Play of the Goat*, the *Play of the Deer*, and the *Pantomimic Mummers*. The location of Heleșteni in the hilly area between Târgu-Frumos and Pașcani city, favorable to agriculture and relatively far from national roads, has contributed to the perpetuation of a genuine rural culture that maintained a set of traditions that have long disappeared in other regions. I do archival research to connect older data with current local oral histories. The morphology and symbols related to Heleșteni's winter plays demonstrate how they function as lens through which the history of a community can be deciphered. The chapter presents the history of a small village through winter plays that show its transformation over decades. I use folk plays as lens to understand current phenomena of the postsocialist society like labor migration, demographic decline, poverty, and social inequalities. The cultural history model proposed in this chapter can be used to demonstrate the heuristic value of peasant communities' plays more generally. It also reveals differences between realities discovered in the field and the idealized perspectives of city dwellers regarding peasant traditions.

Following the same microhistory model (Ginzburg 1993) like the previous chapter, Chapter two examines the evolution of a violent winter game in recent decades. Turned into breaking news in the early 2000s, the end of the year rural ritual *The Mummers Battle with Sticks* has polarized Romanian society into camps of supporters and opponents. This physical confrontation between two groups of villagers triggered a second battle, waged on social media platforms and news websites, regarding the right interpretation of this violent rural game. I argue that this symbolic confrontation has deep significance for Romanian society because it is a struggle for conflicting representations about the ideas of rural traditions, authenticity, masculinity, and national identity in a country formed under the aegis of nationalist rhetoric influenced by Romantic Folkloristics. However, such debates reveal the volatility of a postsocialist society in transition, without stable frames of reference, in which a rural game can become the subject of sensational national broadcast news. Thus, folk plays became once again lens for viewing the history of a community over many years and tools for deciphering mainstream societal views regarding core topics such as authenticity, community, playfulness, bravery, and manhood. The extreme violence of *The Mummers Battle with Sticks* hindered its heritagisation through folklore festivals, and other safeguarding means. A cultural history analysis shows that *The Mummers Battle with Sticks* was once part of a cultural micro-ecosystem in which it had a precise role in shaping relationships between members of a rural community. It should not be analyzed separately (as mass media has done), but in the context of other two plays, such as *Malanca* and *Târâitul*, that altogether create the landscape of manhood rituals in Ruginoasa, a locality with a long history of violence.

If the first two chapters of the study are more descriptive, the next four chapters are more analytical, guided by the question: how could we explain the enormous success of rural plays in agricultural societies for centuries, followed by their mass extinction with the emergence of the Industrial Revolution?

Chapter three analyzes, based on the theories of values coined by the anthropologist Clyde Kluckhohn and the philosopher Robert Hartman, the relationship between the peasant system of values and rural plays. It presents mummers' plays, some of the most widespread rural plays, in relationship to rural communities' system of values. I adopt a critical stance against the view that described mummers' plays as a reversal of the rural social order. Based on my participant observation and "looking over people's shoulders," I show how peasants' winter plays are tributary to some rigorous rules that are strictly enforced. My argument is that rural plays are an essential component of the peasant system of values in rural customary communities. Before the industrial revolution overtook rural Europe, rural plays in general and mumming was a means of responding to the inevitable problems of peasant life; through satire, they could help people transcend their burdensome rural life's realities. This approach reveals a new narrative on folk plays and a different vision of their peasant performers than in most peasant studies narratives. Thus, this chapter restates the idea that rural plays be regarded as lenses through which the history of rural communities in Europe (and elsewhere) can be understood. It can help to more accurately understand humans who have lived in agrarian societies for centuries.

The fourth chapter is more complex and presents a dialogue between the present study and two intellectual traditions that have analyzed the rural universe over time. The first is represented by Marxist-influenced studies that have described the peasantry from a class and political-economy perspective. The second is represented by folklore studies from various European countries and Canada, which analyzed mummers plays mostly from a folklore nationalist-romantic perspective. Both currents are placed in the category of grand narrative and are criticized from the perspective of Jean-François Lyotard's postmodern theory. The basic idea of this chapter is that grand narratives that have tried to give a holistic explanation of peasants are risky and can be exposed to overgeneralization. The proposed approach is a simpler one, that of looking rather at the rural plays formed between the borders of small rural communities, which focuses the researcher's attention on the so-called petits récits (little narratives), approaches with a smaller coverage area and rather analyzing local histories instead of universal truths.

In the fifth chapter I am analyzing on a philosophical basis, the way in which rural plays have been transformed with the industrial revolution, becoming events with large audiences such as football or rugby. The investigation of these transformations does not stop at the advent of mass sports but comes more recently, at the beginning of the 21st century, when the unprecedented success of digital culture, represented in this case by video games and social media, led to the disintegration of rural plays in the cohesive village communities that still held them. Based on the analytic philosophy of Ludwig Wittgenstein, the philosophy of religion of Ioan Petru Culianu, the cognitive critique of Manfred Spitzer and sociological investigations of Sherry Turkle, this chapter analyzes how globalization and its consequences changed the way peasants interact, socialize, and identify themselves. Rural plays have been formed in close connection with rural values, responding to human needs of communication and socialization, while video games and social networks via the Internet can lead to the fragmentation of the connection between the real social world and the person, ultimately leading to atomization and alienation of individuals from society. My fieldwork from 2009 to 2020 provided a good opportunity to observe the sharp decline of the rural plays and their replacement with other more spectacular forms of socialization such as sports games, video games, and social media. The explanation for this situation, proposed by this study, is that the competition between rural plays and modern sports, video games, and social media is for the same "patch of land," to use a metaphor. It is about that part of the human consciousness by which humans as social beings are inextricably linked to play/*jocus*, in all its forms and expressions, from theater to dance, from pantomime to competition, and from tricks to logical games.

The last chapter describes the final stage of my field research conducted in Chernivtsi County, Ukraine. Following a team of players from Heleşteni village who I studied for years, I crossed the Romanian border to see this team participate in *The International Festival of Cultural Traditions—Bucovina's Malanca* in Chernivtsi city. I observed how many local customs from Romania and Ukraine were exoticized as extravagant cultural forms for consumption, in a kind of Rio festival of Eastern Europe, in the frameworks of cultural entertainment industry (Horkheimer and Adorno 2002). Thus, the profound relationship between rural communities and their social environment is replaced by capitalist models of consumption. Nevertheless, local political leaders and peasant artists choose to take part in these competitions to spotlight their village's rituals on the stage. My argument is that peasant cultural forms, like peasants themselves who migrate from their villages in search of a better life, leave their village communities of origin and become transnational intangible cultural heritage forms. In my view, this embodies Bourdieu's process of symbolic violence, a subtle form of aggression different from other types of violence in that the social agents who are the victims of it contribute to its emergence (Bourdieu and Wacquant 2004). This is because cultural rural forms lose their local significance for their local communities, becoming only objects of consumption for tourists.

The book concludes with an afterword in which the last stage of my fieldwork, conducted at the end of 2020, is presented, providing an account of the relationship between the coronavirus pandemic and the rural plays. The afterword contains my meditations on human freedom, based on a comparison between the masks wore during different kinds of folk plays and the obligation to wear a face mask during the pandemic. It concludes with a critical stance against one of the most influential studies of human games, Roger Caillois's *Man, Play and Games*. The afterword mainly criticizes the typology built by the French sociologist to categorize the game universe. The argument against this approach is that the games cannot be subscribed to certain categories due to their extraordinary diversity. This diversity ultimately coincides with the multiplicity of cultures and experiences acquired by humans throughout their social life in their communities, by interacting in multifarious ways, besides other means, through plays.

NOTES

1. I do not use the word "play" (a translation of Romanian word *joc*) in the narrow sense of its usual English meaning. In the Romanian language *joc* encompasses an extremely wide range of activities, including dance, joking, sports games language games, word play, theater, pantomime, trick, farce, eroticism, and even dangerous activities. When I use the term play, I am referring rather to this broader connotation.

2. In his book *The Age of Extremes*, Eric Hobsbawm made a shocking statement that describe "the death of peasantry" by the end of the 20th century. He is mainly talking about the disappearance of rural culture perpetuated by peasants. However he admits that by the 1980s "the ancient strongholds of peasant agriculture (Romania, Poland, Yugoslavia, Greece)" in Europe, still had about one third of their labour force involved in farming (Hobsbawm 1994:291).

3. Jiu Valley—the largest coal mine exploitation area in Romania. At the end of the 1970s, the president of the Romanian Communist Party, Nicolae Ceauşescu, launched a massive program to increase Romania's industrial production. To this end, in the late 1970s and early 1980s, 30,000 people were brought to the Jiu Valley, especially from the rural area of eastern Romania (Rus 2003).

4. In the Romanian language, *country* and *countryside* are called by the same word *ţară*.

5. Paparudele—a ritual magic consisting of a dance in a costume made of shoots and green leaves to invoke the rain during drought.

6. Păcală (The Trickster)—a character from Romanian folklore, has been an inspiration for Romanian writers such as Ion Creangă, Ioan Slavici, and Petre Dulfu who turned him into a comic character in various novels. Stories in the Păcală series have as a hero a common peasant bearing this name and who seems stupid or extremely naïve, but who has hidden wisdom, and eventually manages to overcome all difficulties, and to finish victorious in confrontations with various negative characters.

7. One of the most famous stories about Păcală is called "Păcală—the Servant of the Priest." The story is about a stingy priest who used to make onerous bargains with the villagers to pay them miserable wages for hard work. The priest tried to make such an agreement with Păcală, signing together a document in which both parts agrees that they will not be upset with each other regardless of their behavior towards each other, otherwise the one who is upset will have his nose cut. The harassment immediately begins with the stingy priest who gives Păcală hard tasks on the field, offering him a bread and a round cheese as a meal, but Păcală must bring back the goods in "the same shape that they are right now." Păcală ate the bread and cheese kernels and brought them "in the same shape they were before." The next day the priest did not bring Păcală any food at all, although he had promised him a rich meal at noon. On the other side, Păcală had to harvest an entire rye field. Towards evening, when Păcală returns with the rye bags, the priest tells him that he forgot to bring him the meal and hopes that he was not upset on him. Păcală replies that he realized the priest forgot and ate well at a nearby neighbor, for which he gave her a sack of rye from the priest's harvest. After multiple such attempts in which Păcală always wins, the priest declares that he is upset, and Păcală ends up cutting priest's nose.

8. Throughout this study I used several terms to describe the peasants plays: most often I used the term rural play, seen as an umbrella concept that includes a wide range of cultural events in the countryside. At the same time, I used the terms folk plays and mummers' plays to refer more specifically to certain ritualized customs of the peasants, often involving masked characters, and taking place especially between Christmas and New Year.

Chapter One

Heleșteni Community
and Its Plays

HELEȘTENI—A MOLDAVIAN COMUNĂ[1]

Heleșteni is the place where I spent most of my research, and where I lived during my successive stages of research in the region of Moldova from December 2009 to January 2021. Many readers of these lines might wonder what makes Heleșteni a favourite target for anthropological research. The answer is not very simple. If someone would travel today by accident through Heleșteni it is very likely that nothing should draw his or her attention. The two gigantic pyramids of earth of late Hallstattian origin from the area of the village Movileni would resemble to a stranger as two awkward relief forms. Today's Heleșteni does not look like anything special compared to any other village from the hilly area which follows the stretching from the Eastern part of Oriental Carpathians. Yet, more than a century ago the well-known literary critic, sociologist, and philosopher of Armenian origin Garabet Ibrăileanu wrote memorable pages in which he depicts Heleșteni as it was seen through his teenager eyes: "How beautiful it was there! A house like a palace, surrounded by flower gardens—with a huge pond in the middle of the gardens, with a beautiful bridge across the pond, with benches and kiosks through the gardens. A bell called us to supper. Sometimes at table there were 40 guests. Even today I seem to remember things from another world. I have never seen such a rich life with no cares in the world, beautiful and abundant (Ibraileanu 1966:256)." Since then, Heleșteni went through two world wars. Particularly the Second World War replaced the old palace of the family of Armenian boyars Goilav with a lot of rubble and a line of fortifications with casemates (destroyed at the end of the war by the Russian army) which can be noticed even now, but which can be easily mistaken for an irrigation ditch for

19

agricultural lands, ditch which dried up and became unfunctional. The palace seems to exist only in the memories of older villagers who speak of "the giant stuffed crocodile at the entrance to the large hall" and "peacocks which walked at leisure through the park with artesian well and with lake." In the meantime the village went through Communism and the family of Armenian boyars, identified as kulaks, so part of the exploiting class, disappeared from the village just like the palace which could have reminded someone of their presence on this land. Only a few photographs taken by George Goilav, a passionate of photographic art and son of the landowner Ariton Goilav remained as testimony. But these photographs remain hidden in the pages of a less known magazine and exposed only in the small library from behind the cultural house, library which could never draw the attention of a stranger who might travel through this locality.[2]

However, the traces of the Second World War could be memorable for a tourist who would adventure through this village relatively far from the main county and national roads. This is because, unlike other Romanian villages, Heleșteni was completely destroyed by the Romanian army at the end of the war "in order to offer visibility to the Romanian artillery grouped behind the fortified line which crossed the village." The story of evacuation of the whole population in the village Băcești from Vaslui county, 70 kilometres away, of the destruction of the village and then its reconstruction during the period that followed the Second World War, there are things whose marks can be seen, much more than in the constructions of the village, their form and architecture, in the hearts of the older inhabitants. Even at present they are ready to speak for hours and hours about the "troubled ages of dislocation" and "the return a year later to a village where weeds had grown higher than a house, but the houses were nowhere to be seen." Only one old building survived from the old village Heleșteni: the church built by the noble Mihail Sturdza in 1870 (Lahovari, Brătianu, and Tocilescu 1899). This building is the only one which the Romanian army did not destroy "for fear of God's punishment" as the elders of the village say these days. Its bent cross on the dome remained testimony of the artillery fights between the Romanian army and the Russian army in the tumultuous summer of 1944.

Today in Heleșteni there are few visible testimonies which could remind a traveller of the centuries of history which marked this area: a Medieval tombstone recently brought from the village Movileni, where it lay half buried on an agricultural field, in the yard of the mayor's office and a few Neolithic archaeological sites of Cucuteni type, all marked only on the maps of archaeologists and not promoted for commercial purposes. All these could easily go unnoticed by a tourist who would accidentally pass today through the commune Heleșteni.

But there is something fascinating in Heleşteni, something which although does not immediately catch the eyes of a stranger to Heleşteni, would still remain memorable for anyone who would visit the village, especially if he or she had the occasion to pass here more than a few days. This something is the intangible cultural heritage—a phenomenon promoted through the entire community and visible especially during the winter holidays. In those days of December, a stranger to the village would be surprised to see tens of masked people on the streets of the village, characters dressed in stags, goats, ostriches, bears, little horses, but also Halloween ugly masks. Most of the participants wear bells around their waist, bells which make a lot of noise, being meant to draw attention from far away. This is so much more as the masked people dance all the time and the bells stir all the time in the jerky movements of the dancers. The pageants go from house to house and announce the coming of the New Year and the householders receive them in their yards with wine, cakes, and money. All this would not be possible if in Heleşteni the community was not still cohesive and attached to its own values as we seldom see in many other Romanian villages.

These rituals not only can be seen on the streets of the commune at the end of the year but are also an integral part of the identity of the inhabitants who are convinced about their archaic nature and their transmission from generation to generation in an unaltered form from immemorial times until present. All these statements made me curious about these rituals' relationship with the locality past, and how they were transformed over time in relations with social, political, and economic realities.

HELEŞTENI—ITS PAST . . . AND ITS FOLK PLAY'S PAST

The analysis of the archives about Heleşteni and its neighborhood shows that the origin of villages in today's territory of Heleşteni *comună* dates back to the beginning of the 17th century. Beyond this time, the population of these localities was extremely sparse, just a few hamlets, and the documentary references regarding these are very rare.[3] The 17th century is also the context where I discovered the first mentions of rural plays in the area. Such a document, published by historian Nicolae Iorga, tells us a story happening on December 28, 1656, during Gheorghe Ştefan's reign (July 1653–March 1658), Vasile Lupu's successor to throne. The document is a letter by a Swedish ambassador called Welling on a diplomatic mission in Iaşi, the capital of the Moldavian Kingdom, together with his secretary Hildebrandt. He describes the ruler Gheorghe Ştefan as "Christian, kind, and worried about the menacing dangers approaching the country." The letter itself reveals the dangers of traveling to Iaşi city mostly for a Christian emissary from

Northern Europe. The Swedish ambassador and his team are welcomed by a boyar sent by the ruler to warn the travelers that Iaşi should only be entered at night; one of the Turkish clerks sent there by the Ottoman Court could spot them in daylight, and the visit of a Christian diplomat at the Moldavian Court should rather remain secret.

Arriving in the evening in the town of Iaşi, Welling describes its numerous churches and oak tree pavements, with Christmas markets full of game and especially quails. He describes the holiday atmosphere, the *hore* (round group dances) performed even by soldiers, and also a particular folk play the author witnessed. The custom the Swedish diplomat describes is definitely *Jocul Caprei/Play of the Goat* that he presents as "a dance envisaging a goat covering a man, and performed by a man. At the end of the play, a boy used to shoot an arrow at the goat, thus ending the sketch, with the boy getting a tip. Thus, a sort of primitive hunting scene was performed" (Iorga 1928).[4]

Only 14 years after the event that the Swedish ambassador describes, there is another mention of the same winter play, this time in an ecclesiastical text written by Dimitrie Barilă, Moldova's metropolitan. Known under the name Dosoftei, he is considered one of the first Romanian scholars and first national Romanian poet, especially because of the translation of the versified *Book of Psalms*. In one of the verses in the *Book of Psalms*, Dosoftei enumerates a series of pagan rituals that the people used to perform and the church condemned[5]: "We also have black magic charms for God's evil eye/That transform the inner self of any man/Together with farces, goat dances, cuckoos[6] and monster-puppets,[7]/And magic spells from maids that bathe down the valley[8] and many other pagan customs" (Dosoftei 1974 [1673]).

The fact that Dosoftei, author of the versified *Book of Pslams*, lived in Iaşi when writing the work, is relevant for my analysis, since this city is only 62 km away from Ruginoasa and 68 km away from Heleşteni. Obviously, the ritual of *Ţurca* or *Jocul Caprei/Play of the Goat,* mentioned by Moldova's metropolitan at that time, was part of the cultural area including Heleşteni, too.

Less than 50 years after the publication of Dosoftei's *Book of Psalms*, one of the most appreciated old literature works about Moldova was published. This was *Descrierea Moldovei/The Description of Moldova*, written by Moldova's ruler himself, Dimitrie Cantemir (reigning in March–April 1693 and 1710–1711). Cantemir was also one of the most prestigious scholars of his time, the first to realize a written synthesis of the religious and pagan beliefs of the people living in Moldova. Within the third part of *Descriptio Moldaviae* (1714), discussing the Moldavians' pagan beliefs, Cantemir also mentions a custom called *Ţurca*—a name still used today, especially in Transylvania, to name the *Play of the Goat.* The way the Moldavian ruler describes it, *Ţurca* resembles closely, more contemporary the *Play of the Deer*, as folklorists observed a few decades ago (Adăscăliţei 1968).

Dimitrie Cantemir describes *Ţurca* as

> a dance imagined in times long ago because of the hate against the Turks. At Christmas, someone puts on a deer head with big antlers to which a mask made out of colored textile strings is added, long enough to cover the legs of the one wearing it. Another one stays on his shoulders, depicting an old hunchback, and this is how they walk the narrow streets, going from door to door, dancing and singing with a lot of people following them. (Cantemir [1714]2016:91)

Thus, Dimitrie Cantemir describes the *Play of the Goat* or the *Play of the Deer*, as some other authors claimed, as a mocking ritual, directed at that time against the Turkish occupation and oppression, rather than a magic rite related to the fertility of the crops or the arrival of the New Year, as it was interpreted by more recent folklore studies (Rosetti, Pop, and Pervain 1964:70).

This historical analysis allows us to see that folk plays have been mentioned since the first consistent documents about Moldova's population and history were available. These practices go far back in time, but even the analysis of the first documents mentioning them shows us custom variations that makes it difficult to gather them all under the same umbrella, in a single category, or to regard them from a unique interpretation. From the ritual killing of an animal described by the Swedish ambassador Welling in 1656—to Cantemir's dance of the masked couple bantering about Ottoman domination—one can envisage a diversity of goals and symbols folk plays could represent.

In this context, it becomes more difficult to accept the assertion that rural plays have been transmitted with little changes for generations, and that what we witness today represents surviving elements of extinct cultures, ideas supported by Romanian (Haja 2003; Oişteanu 2012 [1980]:85) and also British old fashion Folkloristics (Ordish 1891). Instead, I argue that it is more fruitful to study the dynamics of these rural plays in parallel with the historical, social, political and economic transformations of the small rural communities that have performed them over time.

THE *PLAY OF THE GOAT*—HISTORY AND COVERAGE AREA

The *Play of the Goat*, *Christmas Goat*, *New Year Goat* or simply *The Goat* is one of the most widespread folk plays in Europe and in the world. Recent comparative research (Gunnell 2007a), next to a few archiving efforts conducted during the last century (Cawte, Helm, and Peacock 1967), revealed the fact that this ritual had been incredibly widespread until a few decades ago, covering all Europe from North to South and on large areas of Russia, too

(Warner 1977). Known as *julebukk* in Norway, *julbock* in Sweden, *julebuk* in Denmark, *joulupouki* in Finland, *naarisokk* in Estonia and *hobbyhorse* in England,[9] *capra* in Romania, коза in Ukraine, козел in Russia, the play appears under different names over a gigantic geographic area. A simple overview of this immense material shows us that this folk play—considered simple or even primitive—might be in fact one of the most largely performed and the most successful theatrical performance of humans, viewed more times and by more viewers than any play by Shakespeare, Ibsen, or Sophocles. The reason is that, even within a single village, at the end of December, three or four such folk play teams would be formed. Then, they would perform at least 100 times during the few days of the winter holidays this ritual in the yards and houses of the householders. If we were to gather all the villages where the ritual had been performed and to count all the representations of the *Play of the Goat*, the immediate conclusion is that this simple performance was extremely successful for people who lived in agricultural societies for centuries. The common element in all the diversity of the *Play of the Goat* is precisely the ritual mask consisting of a wooden head with a moveable jaw, tied with a string that allows manipulation by the person wearing the mask so that the jaws clatter rhythmically or even grab objects like a living creature.

THE GOAT'S OFFICERS AND THE RECENT HISTORY OF THE LOCALITY

In Heleşteni *comună*, this ritual is named *Capra/The Goat*; nevertheless, I am going to call it the *Play of the Goat*,[10] following a long tradition of the Romanian Folkloristics that cemented this term in specialized texts (Rosetti, Pop, and Pervain 1964:67). The *Play of the Goat* is still present in this *comună* today, being performed each winter in three of its four villages: Oboroceni, Hărmăneasa and Heleşteni.[11] In these three villages, the *Play of the Goat* looks more like a dance then like a theater play, and most of the team members wear military uniforms. That is why a better name for Heleşteni Goat teams would be the *Dance of the Goat*.

I was surprised to see that the current version of the *Play of the Goat* in Heleşteni does not include the traditional goat mask with the nicely adorned blanket covering the man maneuvering the clattering lower jaw of the goat mask, mimicking a goat that bites people from the crowd, as I saw it in other villages during my previous two decades research in Romanian villages.

While the moving mandible and the wooden goat head are still preserved in the mask's structure, the blanket that once prevented onlookers from seeing who was manipulating the goat, making it behave like a funny, troublesome animal, it is absent now from the traditional paraphernalia. Today, in Heleșteni, the goat head is a small simple mask hanging on a stick, called, in folklore studies, *mascoidă*[12] (Vulcănescu 1970:208). It is embellished with beads, tinsel and small goat or deer antlers. An unmasked man holds the mask in his hand, simply making its wooden jaw clatter, while hopping around on the sounds of pipe and drum music performed by two other unmasked men. None of the members of the goat play team wears a mask. Besides the abovementioned companions of the goat, the band also includes five or six teenagers, with three or four of them wearing Romanian military uniforms, and two of them dressed in traditional homespun festive clothes called "Irod" clothes, which explains why these latter performers are known by the name of "Irozi." One of the six lads is the so-called "*comoraș*" (the leader), who is actually the lead performer and the one establishing the team's structure.

Since the beginning of the research I was surprised by the presence of the military officers' suits in Heleșteni's Goat ritual. Why does Heleșteni's Play of the Goat teams include 3–4 officers while the bands of the neighboring localities include a Turk, a Greek, the so-called Irozi in their traditional clothes but not the officers? Can all these elements find their explanation in the history of these localities?, I was wondering. My intuition was that an answer to these questions could provide the key to a question at the beginning of this chapter and show how a series of political, economic, and social transformations led to important changes in the symbolism and morphology of these plays.

A simple investigation of the team members' outfits sent me immediately to the recent history of the locality and at the tumultuous events of World War II. One of the oldest persons I spoke to, Catinca Horneț stated: "Young people started wearing military clothes while accompanying the *Goat* especially after World War II. Before, they used to wear homemade Irod clothes. But after the war, they started to dress like officers, probably under the impact of the officers' costumes they had seen, but also because women began sewing less clothes at home" (Catinca Horneț, 94 years old, Heleșteni village, June 29, 2012, Interview). Other villagers in Heleșteni brought additional, sometimes even more fascinating information about this aspect: "In fact, the *Goat*'s uniforms were first worn to mock the Soviet Army regarded as the military occupant following World War II. So, it was rather a way to ridicule the Soviet officers' uniforms, since Romanians perceived them as enemy after World War II. This kind of irony is traceable in all New Year customs and, above all, in folk plays; in mummers' performances they are even more frequent than with the *Goat*" (Aurel Crișu, 63 years old, Heleșteni village, June 29, 2012, Interview).

The fact that in Heleșteni the symbols from the military universe are more important than in the folk plays of other localities can find a good explanation

Figure 1.1. The goat team from Heleșteni village in the yard of a householder—January 1, 2015.
Photo credit: Alin Rus

through the analysis of the village's recent history. The Second World War has affected Heleșteni much more than other localities around. During the Second World War this *comună* was crossed by a line of casemates built by the Romanian army to defend against the Soviet troops attacking from the east of the country. Thus, unlike in other villages, Heleșteni's buildings were demolished by the Romanian army at the end of the war to offer visibility to its artillery grouped behind the fortified line which crossed the village. The story of evacuation of the whole civilian population in the village Băcești from Vaslui county, 70 kilometres away, of the destruction of the village and then its reconstruction during the period that followed the Second World War, are troublesome events of the recent past. Even at present the elders are ready to speak for hours and hours about the "troubled ages of dislocation" and "the painful return to an empty village." But the nightmare of the inhabitants of this area did not end immediately after the war. Due to the front line that crossed the locality and the heavy fighting that took place in these places at the end of World War II, the whole area was filled with mines who took their oblation in human lives even more than a decade after the war ended. Thus, the image of the officers in uniform, especially the sappers, was a marker that lengthened there more than a whole decade after the Second World War. All these events speak of the powerful presence of military uniforms in the collective memory of the inhabitants of Heleşteni.

THE *PLAY OF THE GOAT*—A
LIMINAL RITE OF PASSAGE

Another important piece of information regarding the military symbols of Heleşteni's Goat teams I learned during my participant observation I conducted among locals throughout my entire research. Many of the villagers I talked to mentioned that "the *Play of the Goat* ritual is performed by young men of the village one or two years before, as well as one or two years after their military service."

For many young Romanian peasants, attending military service was perceived as a test of manhood, involving two stages. Firstly, during military service the young recruit had to overcome the barriers and obstacles designed to prove his strong character, his physical strength, his ambition and determination, that is, in one word, all the skills and abilities that define manhood in the view of many peasants. Secondly, for young peasants, especially a few decades ago, the conscription represented most of the time their first long-term contact with the outside world and with types of social relationships other than the typical social network of their own village.

When military service used to be compulsory in Romania, before 2005, the *Play of the Goat* in Heleşteni was undoubtedly linked to the two important events in the life of every young man: the conscription and the discharging from the army (*lăsare la vatră*). Military service and its rigors were seen as a necessary step towards adulthood and as a way for the young man to be prepared for his life as a future husband, father, and head of household.

The common belief of the local peasants was that the military service was not only an obligation regulated by a set of laws and rigors, but also the chance to learn how to handle a weapon, an ability regarded as an act of bravery meant to turn a young lad into a man. Moreover, leaving for the military camp meant the young conscript was to be separated from his village—the familiar and friendly environment governed by well-known rules—to enter a new environment ruled by the principles of a more complex and larger world. For many young peasants, this new world would represent their first longer contact with the town and required them to adapt to the principles governing a totally strange and unfamiliar universe. This assertion is clearly proven by the rural folklore surrounding the moment, including the multitude of recruit songs that may be heard in any region of Romania. These songs deal with several major themes: the pain caused by the separation of the lad from his familiar village community, the homesickness felt during military service, the longing for the family and for the sweetheart back home, and the hardships of the military service. These recruit songs are typically sad and melancholic, expressing the deep feelings of the young peasant who is forced to leave behind his familiar environment to join the tough and sometimes brutal world of the military service.[13]

All these demonstrate that before the extensive industrialization of Romania in the communist era, most peasants lived within the narrow borders of their village world, which was in fact also the case of other rural communities in many other parts of the planet at different moments in time after Industrial Revolution (Wolf 1966:13). Borrowing a metaphor from the philosopher Alexander Koyre, Pierre Bourdieu emphasizes a series of conditions that contributed to the openness of the relatively closed peasant communities, guiding them "from the closed world to the infinite universe" (Bourdieu 2008:174). Among those conditions, obligatory military service could be added as a factor maintaining a permanent relation between "the closed world of the peasants" and "the infinite universe of the urban world."

When coming back from the army, the recruit would recount that experience for his fellows in the form of the so-called *demobee's story*.[14] This kind of stories played an important role in the life of the mature man, too, because they proved that his knowledge about the world went beyond the narrow boundaries of his village. At the same time, for the conscript and his sweetheart, military service was regarded as a chance to test their patience and loyalty to each other, to prove the depth or, on the contrary, the frailty of their feelings. The young man resumed his old way of life in the familiar world of the village and, if fortunate enough, he found his girl desperately waiting for him. Of course, "hardened" by the rigors of military life, the young man joined the *Play of the Goat* team once again, this time as a bridegroom-to-be. Now, the ritual would be meant to prove the whole village community that the young man had passed important tests that made him stronger and demonstrated his qualities as a future head of family. This happened because marriage was not just an ordinary event but a crucial one in the lives of the peasants.

As such, we are dealing with a complete Gennepian cyclical scheme, with the stages of separation from one's usual environment, the stages of aggregation to a different environment, and the stages of reintegration into the familiar environment, this time under a new identity that speaks about the internal changes undergone by the person who had managed to pass successfully through all the stages of the aforementioned rites of passage. All these facts show that the *Play of the Goat* in the village of Heleşteni fits perfectly into the Geneppian description of the rites of passage (Gennep 1909). The *Goat Play* works in this case as a rite of separation of the rural world and, later on, upon return from the army, it serves as a rite of reintegration into the familiar world, facilitating the transition to another significant moment in the young peasant's life: marriage. Therefore, the *Play of the Goat* in the villages of Heleşteni *comună* comprises a series of stages designed to prepare the young lad to enter a new phase in his life: manhood, as well as the passage from bachelorhood to the status of married man. In all these stages, the young man should prove that he is capable of striding for two days and nights almost continuously, resisting the bad weather and the fatigue, and demonstrating his future wife and her kin that he is also a strong and reliable man.

This explains why, besides the preliminary stages of putting up a team and choosing the *comoraş* (the leader), which happen in an informal environment among friends, some other more formal phases take place at the end of the year, when the *Play of the Goat* teams and their leaders have to appear before the whole village community, in the public space of the village. In order to understand the entire cycle of events regarding this complex ritual I proceed to describe step by step the most important stages of it, which prove the rigorousness of its organization.

THE *PLAY OF THE GOAT*—LOGISTICS AND ORGANIZATION

The first stage in organizing a Goat team begins with a deal between the young men. To form a *Goat team*, at least four or five lads are needed, plus the *comoraş* leading the group. This initial team is settled after December 1 or a bit later. In the case of *Goat teams*, organization is easier because these young people are major, aged between 18 and 21, and they may decide for themselves. The participants' age has to do with a pragmatic reason: villagers say that boys could not dance with girls if they were too young or especially if they were too short.

After gathering together and deciding how to form the team, the teenagers immediately envisage what options they have for choosing a pipe player—a very important character in the performance because he is not that easy to find and because the *Play of the Goat* would not be possible without him. Pipe players became more difficult to find at least since late Communist era, when many adults went to the city, while the young ones started attending various primary and secondary schools in the city. The new situation distanced the young from certain activities typical of village life such as that of playing the pipe. Yet, a complete *Goat* team needs to have six or at least five members, plus the pipe and the drum players, and the man wearing the *mascoidă* representing *the Goat*. Unlike the pipe player, the drummer is easier to find in the village, whereas the one wearing the *mascoidă* could be any of the young men in the band.

Thus, usually starting from December 1, the *Goat team* organizer, the *comoraş*, goes searching for the pipe player. Once he finds a possible player, the *comoraş* first asks: "Are you engaged?" If the answer is "Yes," it means that pipe player has already made a deal with another team. In case the player is available, negotiations start right away, and the price for which the pipe player agrees to accompany the team is settled. These negotiations are called *tocmeală/haggling,* and the one accepting the money offer made by the *comoraş* is said to have been *haggled.* Though a mere verbal agreement between the *comoraş* and the musicians, the haggling is in most cases strictly enforced. Money is paid to the musicians a few days before the winter holidays or at least one day before the team goes traveling through the village, dancing and singing from one household to another. I was told that the fee paid to each musician ranges between 500 to 600 lei ($135–$150) for a pipe player, a bit less for a drummer and even less for the Goat mask handler. The price includes the rehearsals taking place between 5–10 p.m., from December 15 to December 27.

The three members of the team—the drummer, the pipe player and the *Goat* mask handler—may be older, sometimes even over 60 years old. They are not considered to be true members of the team, as my interviewees told me repeatedly. The current team members are in fact the lads dressed in military uniforms and in traditional outfits. This happens because the three older men are paid by *comoraş* to do their part in the show, thus having a different motivation to participate in the play then the young boys. The leader of the *Goat team*, the *comoraş*, and the other team members usually compensate the expenses for hiring the drummer and the pipe player from the money they earn during the caroling period. Usually, when the caroling period is over and the costs are recovered, each lad in the *Goat team* remains with a net gain of 600–800 lei ($150–$200).

After the start of the communist period, the sums the *Goat team* would get increased considerably. From the interviews with people in the *comună*, I found out that the peasants becoming part of the proletariat during Communism would give larger amounts of money than others when they came back to the village for holidays. The same phenomenon is observable in postsocialism. The largest sums—much over the average money other locals pay—are offered by migrants from Western Europe who come back home for holidays or by those who did successful business after 1989. Unlike the last decades of Communism and postsocialism, the sums offered to a *Goat team* in the distant past, in the interwar period, were much smaller. "We would get a few coins, that's all," some of the ex-Goat team members now in their old age, declared. Nevertheless, back then the population was larger and more households welcomed the Goat teams, whereas today the number of houses opening their doors to the band is about 50% lower. I managed to get this information by joining the *Goat team* around the village, as well as from interviews with various team members. However, for the *Goat teams* in the villages of Heleşteni *comună*, money is not the only attraction. The *Play of the Goat* has (or, at least, used to have as we will soon see) a stake higher than the financial reward itself; that is why the *Goat Play* involves a large part of the rural community, in other words is a big social event in the *comună*.

The first public appearance of the *Goat teams* takes place on December 27 each year, late in the evening (after 10 p.m.), when the young people gather at the Cultural Community Center, a building with a large hall and a stage, housing many other cultural events in the village throughout the year. In 2011, the cultural center was rented by the city hall to a club (MMM Club) that would turn the center into a discotheque every weekend. However, even today the location serves as meeting place for the *Play of the Goat* teams. Once, the music used to be provided by the young people themselves or by the town hall. In recent years, the music is provided by the MMM Club that rented the cultural center from the town hall and requires an entry fee from customers. The club has a bar selling alcoholic and soft drinks, chips, peanuts and crackers. As we can see, there is a combination of the old elements of the ritual with new ones, such as the principles of the market economy expressed in the desire of some local businesses to make a profit during important social events for the local community.

Usually, the discotheque opens before the *Goat teams* reach the club. The young people gather together at the club and dance to disco music and to the most popular folk songs. Around 10:30–11:00 p.m., one can hear the drum beat and the pipe playing. It is a sign that the Goat teams are approaching. Many of the people in the club go out to watch the teams arriving. Usually, the bands show up one by one, with no prior understanding or consensus in this regard because an approximate time of the beginning of the ritual is known to all the villagers. Once in front of the cultural center, each *Goat team* starts dancing a *hora* (round dance) at a devilish speed, by the music of the drum and the pipes, while the others in the club are watching. There are a total of three to five *Goat bands*, representing the three villages of the comună that held this custom. Once all the teams are in front of the cultural center, they gather into a huge round dance symbolizing their brotherhood. It is the first time in the ritual that the village community has the opportunity to see the members of the *Goat bands*, though well in advance rumors go around the villages about who the leaders and the band members are, and about the number of teams performing. However, the official "grand opening" of the event is regarded as a moment of great importance by both teams and village community.

After about half an hour of vivid dance, all the bands enter the club. It is time for the festive and formal presentation of the teams in front of the public. The drummer and the piper in each team start playing their instruments while the lads follow them into the club hall. There they dance again and, at the end, the leaders of the teams (*comoraşii*) are thrown up in the air several times by the members of their teams and their friends. As in the case of other rituals that mark important moments in the life of a young man, there is a test of endurance to violence and pain that the lad is expected to pass. While the young man is tossed up in the air several times, his companions slap him hard on his back. Sometimes, the slapping can get very rough indeed, and I have often seen the protagonists with their faces contorted with pain after this phase of the ritual. The tossing and the slapping continue until all the leaders of the *Goat teams* go through the ordeal. Only two decades ago, as I was told by several of my interlocutors this ritual used to be even more violent, sometimes ending up with the *comoraş* taken out of the building, thrown into the snow, taken the coat and shirt off, dragged through the snow and literally washed with it by the team members and the young people, friends, neighbors and relatives around him. Yet, after 2005, when the military service was not compulsory anymore, the event we are talking about has become less rough. It is obvious that compulsory military service functioned as a catalyst for certain moments of this village ritual. This stage of going through a pain test can be interpreted as preparation for the difficult moments that will follow in the recruit's life once he joins the army. But with the abolition of compulsory military service, these stages of the ritual lost their functional value in the ritual as well.

After this harsh moment, the lads in the *Goat teams* go dancing on folk music with their girlfriends on the dance floor inside the disco. Usually, the other disco dancers gather around in a circle, while the leaders of the *Goat teams* and their girlfriends dance inside the circle before the eyes of the village community. While in the beginning the ones dancing are mostly young bachelors, later on married people—the so-called *gospodari* (householders[15])—and even village officials such as the mayor and the deputy mayor might join in, a thing that does not happen on any other day of the year. At this point, the parents of the *comoraşi* and the *comoraşi* themselves are expected to pay a round of drinks for all the people in the disco. I interpreted this moment as a family acknowledgement of the fact that the young teenager is close to becoming a mature man and that the event should be celebrated together with the entire village community. The first to be offered a drink are the local dignitaries like the mayor and deputy mayor, followed by close relatives, friends of the *comoraş* and, finally, the other villagers around. This moment is simultaneously a kind of community acceptance and validation of the teams in front of the whole rural community. Once this event is over, villagers do no longer see the Goat teams again until December 31 in the afternoon.

Following this show, the members in the *Goat team* meet once again between Christmas and New Year in order to settle down the logistics necessary for the two days of ritual, to fix the itinerary, and to do the costumes' final touch. The meeting usually takes place on December 30 (sometimes on December 29), always in the *comoraș'* house. All the team members are obliged to join in. There is a lot of discussion about the route and the houses that are going to be visited, the places where they would stop to eat and to rest of the itinerary. The team usually rests and eats in one of the *Goat team* members' houses, most of the times at the *comoraș*. The food is offered by the owner of the household that had previously promised to offer a meal to the team members.

The next meeting takes place on December 31 at noon in the house of the *comoraș*. Most *Goat team* members also join another separate ritual, that of the pantomimic mummers starting at 5 or 6 a.m. on December 31. One of the reasons for joining the mummers' ritual is to convince some of the youngsters in the mummers' teams to participate, with their masks on, in that part of the ritual where they accompany the *comoraș* to the *comună* hall. The main reason for that is that the leader of each *Goat team* is seated on several hardwood stakes carried on the shoulders by four masked men or sometimes by his own team members when the team come to the front of the township hall. Once in front of the building, where the officials of the institution and the villagers stand waiting, the leader is put down and the ensemble starts dancing passionately in a circle, accompanied by the pipe, the drum, and the clatter of the *Goat mask*. At the end of the performance, the mayor thanks the dancers, and the next team begins its performance.

Before a theatrical scenery was erected in the *comună* hall courtyard, in 2010, the dancing used to happen in the middle of the people, whereas nowadays it happens onstage. Meanwhile, the *comună* hall issues a certificate guaranteeing the team's right to perform throughout the village. To obtain these authorizations, invented during Communism, the *Goat team* used to pay a tax, but around 2004–2005, the mayor decided not to collect that money anymore in order not to discourage these vanishing customs.

After getting the certificate, the teams dance a few more times in the *comună* hall courtyard, while the *Goat team* members invite especially young girls to dance. Unlike the *Pantomimic Mummers*, the *Goat team* members do not rush girls or women; on the contrary, they behave like gentlemen. The whole meeting event in the yard of *comună* hall ends around 5 p.m.; the gathering there also means that householders saw them, and they might welcome them in their homes. It is also the moment when elder people with no money may see *the Goat*, since the lack of financial resources or the little money given for the performance do not encourage the team's visit of these elders' households.

During the event in front of the *comună* hall local dignitaries are subject to mild mockery, women—especially young ones—are fondled publicly, and even elders and grown-up men are slapped with a belt on the bottom, while they desperately try to escape the gang of two or three mummers chasing them away. In the middle of this effervescent mob, *the Goat teams* behave very decently, contrasting with the classic theatrical *Play of the Goat* from other villages where the main character engages in troublesome scenes, bites the onlookers or pushes the girls from the crowd with the horns. None of these funny tricks are to be found in the *Play of the Goat* ritual of Heleșteni.

While for the event of December 27, the *Goat team* members are dressed in regular clothes, for the event in front of the town hall, the lads in the teams wear either nice military uniforms or *Irod* outfits. One or two of them puts on a folk costume made out of women clothes. This disguise has a programmatic reason: in case there is a household where there are no daughters or young women who could dance to the *Goat team*, the members would dance together. Only the drummer, the piper and the Goat mask handler wear ordinary winter clothes. In fact, this makes the difference between them and the other members of the group, each of the two categories having different goals in their relationship with the ritual.

Usually, the event in front of *comună* hall lasts two to three hours. This is the only time when the theatrical groups perform in public without being paid for that. Immediately after, the team begins its walk through the village from one household to another where villagers pay to watch the performance. The first stop is at the priest's house. Once there, the priest blesses the young men. Winter holidays are the time for party and cheerfulness. But sometimes villagers, and in particular youngsters, drink too much, a fact causing scandals and even accidents. This is one more reason for the *Goat team* to ask the priest to bless them and say a prayer for the team members, so that they may "be protected against the evils of the devil." The priest pays the young men a sum of money for their dance in his courtyard. During the communist era, when the *goat bands* had to pay a tax to the village town hall to be allowed to roam through the village and perform their play, the priest would usually pay the dancers roughly the equivalent of the tax charged to them by the local council.

Each team of *Goat Play* performers goes to the priest's house in their village, meaning that the teams from Obroceni go to the priest in Obroceni, while the teams from Hărmăneasa and Heleșteni go to the priest in Heleșteni village, because these two villages share a common parish. Interestingly, the priests in these localities have nothing against the *Play of the Goat* custom. Although the Orthodox Church has fought for hundreds of years to get rid of what it was considered to be a pagan tradition, nowadays village priests support these rituals and regard them as an intrinsic part of the rural traditions (information from discussions with the priest Dorel Crăcană, 50 years old, Oboroceni village, April 20, 2012, field notes).

After the visit to the parish house, the *Play of the Goat* performers travels through three of the four villages of Heleşteni comună, namely: Oboroceni, Hărmăneasa, Heleşteni. Movileni village is not on the *Goat teams'* itinerary because that village does not have a team of its own that could, in turn, carol around the other villages in the comună; therefore, the other teams do not visit the households in Movileni, either. The route is established by the *comoraş*, in agreement with the other lads in the team. The drummer, the piper and the mask handler have nothing to do with establishing the route, as they are somehow considered to be hired team members and are therefore expected to follow the team leader's orders.

As leader of the band, the *comoraş* is also the one responsible for collecting the money from the villagers they visit during the journey. Starting with this stage of the ritual, all performances given by the band take place solely for money and on the householders' premises. However, as I mentioned before, money is not the only reason behind the *Play of the Goat*. The only members of the team who participate in the show mainly for money are the musicians, though even in their case the exclusive financial motivation is sometimes questionable. During my interviews with them, many of them told me that the money they received do not pay for their efforts to sing and walk for two days and nights altogether, and that if they did not love the old traditions of their place, nothing could persuade them to join the ritual. The stopovers along the route established by the *comoraş* include primarily the households with "marriageable girls" who are, once again, an important motivator for the lads to join the *Goat team*. In fact, as it unfolds, the *Play of the Goat* ritual in Heleşteni *comună* would not be any fun without the courtship element.

Once in front of a house in the village, the *comoraş* or one of the band members asks out loud: "May the Goat come in"? If the householder's answer is "Yes," then the whole band enters the courtyard. If the answer is "No," the entire procession moves on to the next household. If the householder invites the *Play of the Goat* team in, then he and the women in his family have to come out of the house. In case no woman comes out to welcome the *Goat team*, the situation is considered a sign of disrespect. As soon as the host appears on the porch or on the doorway (in the case of a small house), the musicians start playing and the lads start dancing in circle. Some of the lads carry referee whistles with them and blow them to the rhythm of the drumbeat, accompanying the piper and the clattering of the Goat mask. During this moment, the other lads shout out loud *Asta-i Caaa-pra căprelor, Caaa-praaa Oborocenilor* (Heleştenilor or Hărmănenilor)/*Here's the Goat of all the*

Goats, the Gooooaaaat of the Oboroceni inhabitants (or of the Heleşteni's
or of the Hărmăneni's, depending on team's village of origin). After a short
round dance to the music of the piper and the drummer, the lads invite the
girls and the women of the house to dance. Women are expected to dance at
least once with the lads in the Goat team, but, if they are asked to dance again,
they may dance two or three times.

A special moment is when the *Goat band* goes to the house of their leader's
girlfriend. There, the girl dances the first dance with the *comoraş*. Then, if
invited, she dances with other team members as well. The evening before the
day the *Goat dancers* start their ritual, the leader's sweetheart has to bake a
big *colac*/braided bread roll and offer it as a gift to her boyfriend right after
their dance together. The baking of the bread roll is supposed to prove she is
a skillful cook because cooking is considered to be an essential skill of any
peasant wife-to-be. Even if they are not team leaders, the other lads in the
team are generally welcomed in the houses of their sweethearts, where the
band normally stays a while longer so that the "lovebirds" can spend about
half an hour together. In some cases, however, the entire team is invited into
the house for a longer chit-chat which may last up to one hour. Sometimes,
above all in the houses of the girlfriends of the team members, the householder may offer the team a snack, especially when the team has traveled a
long distance.

But even if the team is invited into the courtyard instead of the house, the
team members are usually offered fruit juice, wine, plum brandy, and cakes.
During my research work at Oboroceni village, I had the chance to watch
all the stages of the ritual described above, except for the offering of the big
bread roll to the *comoraş* by his girlfriend. It seems that this part of the ritual
was very important in the past, judging by the fact that it was specifically
mentioned as a special moment of the ritual by most of my interviewees.
Today, however, it seems to have completely vanished. It looks like the bread
roll moment disappeared during the 1950s or 1960s. People born around
the years 1935–1940, who had organized *Goat teams* during their youth,
confessed that they had witnessed the bread roll offering or that they had
been *comoraşi* themselves and, as such, had received this bread. During my
fieldwork, from 2009 to 2017, I for one have never managed to capture this
moment but, interestingly enough, I found it mentioned in all the interviews
with villagers older than 45. The disappearance of this ritual element denotes
a series of changes in the village world in recent decades, including changes
related to the representation of gender roles, the position of women in relation
to men and the weakening of the local paternalistic system.

After performing the ritual dance with the girls and women in the household that welcomed them, the *Goat team* members engage in conversations

with the householder and his family for about 10 or 15 minutes. Sometimes, the conversation is an opportunity to exchange news about other villagers or to talk politics. If the householder is a political leader in the village, such as mayor or deputy mayor, the team members take the opportunity to ask the officials various questions of interest to the community. For example, when the team finished its performance at the mayor's household, the piper of a team of *Goat Play* I followed during its travel through the village, asked the mayor whether he knew anything about the government's intention to increase pensions. That piece of information seemed to be of vital importance for the piper who was over 70 years old and lived on a small pension as a former cooperative farmer during the communist regime.

Once the conversation is over and right before the Goat team prepares to leave, the householder gives the team leader a sum of money. Usually, the master of the house asks rhetorically the whole team out loud "Who is the *comoraș*?" and the leader answers "I am!" The householder takes the money out of his pocket and gives it to the leader of the band, saying: "Thanks for dropping by guys! Come again next year!" This is the end of the ritual conducted at that household, and then the band moves on to the next one, repeating the *Play of the Goat* over and over again. *Goat teams* travel through the villages of Heleșteni comună for two days and one night without cease, usually until the evening of January 1. The performances are quite tiresome and involve a great deal of effort from the team members, mainly because they walk long distances. The distance from one village to another is four or five kilometers and the weather is often bad, with heavy snowfalls, low temperatures and harsh winds. In spite of all the hardship, the teams perform the ritual for two days and one night, beginning on December 31, starting in front of the township hall, and going on day and night until 4:00 or 5:00 in the morning. Then, the teams finally go to the house of *comoraș* and sleep for three or four hours, until around 9:00 a.m. when they start roaming again until 7:00 or 8:00 p.m. the next day, January 1.

The two days' *Goat ritual* is a real strength and endurance test. That is why it sometimes happens that older members of the band, such as the pipe or drum players, give up or get so drunk that they are no longer able to wake up the next morning and join the team. When that happens, the strongest and most motivated team members continue their journey throughout the *comună* until the next day which, according to tradition, is the last day villagers may receive the *Goat dancers*, usually January 1 from early morning until evening.

ALTERATION OF THE PLAY OF THE GOAT
IN POSTSOCIALISM: FROM A RITE OF
PASSAGE TO A COMMODIFIED PLAY

The issues discussed in the previous section, dealing with the *Play of the Goat* refer specifically to the ritual with its main stages. In this section I will focus my analysis on the changes that occurred in this rural play during postsocialism. This period was marked by profound political, economic, and social transformations that were reflected in the morphology and the dynamics of the goat ritual in the villages of Heleșteni *comună*.

The elimination of the mandatory military service in 2005 in Romania turned the *Play of the Goat* into a simple parade in search of money and fun, devoid of its original profound significance in relation with marital market. Of course, the habit has continued by inertia of tradition. Lads in the *Goat team* still wear military uniforms. However, the elimination of the mandatory military service has destroyed the whole scaffolding of the rite of passage. With it, the system of peasant values woven around this custom—according to which the military service was considered a milestone in the passage of the young man towards adulthood—disintegrated. From that point onwards, the lad was no longer expected to leave for the military camp and his sweetheart was spared the sorrow of being separated from him for a whole year.

In fact, the cancellation of the mandatory military service was the last of the waves that began to erode the *Play of the Goat* custom as rite of passage long time ago. The first big wave that altered not only the *Play of the Goat* as rite of passage, but also the entire set of values of the rural world, hit right at the start of the modernization of the agriculture and of the villages in Romania, back in communist times. This ample process occurred not only in Romania, but across the globe, with a greater or lesser intensity, depending on the continent, country, and level of industrial development. As Teodor Shanin well stated: [t]he process of industrialization has also been a process of depeasantification" (Shanin 1990:143).

Pierre Bourdieu examine the way peasant society has moved from "the closed world" to the "infinite universe" represented by urbanity, and the complexity of the social relations they involve (Bourdieu 2008:178). The French sociologist shows how those who are less privileged by the paternalistic rules of the rural world, especially women and young people with low-income, become "the Trojan horse" of the urban world whose rules and values are subtly penetrating the very heart of the rural world, attracting those peasants' sons and daughters who are less attached to rural culture (Idem 178). We are not dealing with a fair and peaceful process, but with an invisible form of symbolic violence that, according to Bourdieu, "is exercised upon a social agent with his or her complicity" (Bourdieu and Wacquant, 1992:272), where social agents are aware even when they are subjected to determinisms, and "contribute to producing the efficacy of that which determines them insofar as they structure what determines them" (Idem 272).

This form of symbolic violence that began to erode the Romanian rural culture in the early decades of the communist era took a more striking form in the postcommunist period. After 1989 and especially after 2000, the massive emergence of media industry, and in particular of cable television, has opened the gates of the rural world forever, turning it into a sort of obsolete appendix of the urban world and its principles. And those who stubbornly clang to the paternalistic rules of the rural universe were regarded as losers of a social lottery, having drawn the empty lottery ticket from the urn of social prestige and hierarchy. In his work *The Bachelors' Ball*, based on the field research Bourdieu conducted in the 1960s in southern France, the author shows how rural matrimonial market, governed by the paternalistic rules of the old rural order, was destabilized immediately after the market economy had succeeded in penetrating even the most conservative areas of peasant culture. In all those rural areas that had stubbornly stuck to traditional marital rules, the young men who were condemned to bachelorhood were precisely those who had been the most privileged by the old rural order: the eldest siblings in the family who were expected to get the largest share of the family possessions and land. However, it soon became obvious that, in spite of their rich dowry, they could not possibly compete with the men from the city, who had better incomes, better dancing skills and conversational abilities. As a result, these village men became the victims of a system that would otherwise be supposed to protect them and to help them acquire a higher status compared to the other young men in the community. Somehow, the system that was normally expected to protect and promote them to the forefront of the rural communities was, in fact, condemning them to bachelorhood.

A similar state of affairs is common for the Moldavian villages where I conducted my field research. The communist industrialization forced young people from the villages to migrate to urban centers and to get a job as factory workers. The new status of city dwellers allowed them some degree of independence from their parents and grandparents. The phenomenon continued and even intensified in postsocialist times, with many young people starting to migrate to western European countries, seeking for a job. Those who were successful abroad also managed to acquire a better social status than what they would have gained, had they remained at home within their village world. Upon returning to the rural community, they enjoyed a higher degree of appreciation from the local community as compared to their fellows who chose to stay home and work as farmers for a few bucks. The local matrimonial market was deeply affected by these changes, as Constantin Curecheru, a villager from Sticlăria village, a locality close to Heleșteni, clearly stated: "When I was young, girls got married depending on the number of sheep and cattle their family possessed. I mean, if a girl, even an ugly one, had many sheep and cattle, she could marry quite easily. Now, things have changed. Girls look for guys with fat credit cards, while dowry isn't that important anymore" (Constantin Curecheru, 68 years old, Sticlăria village, January 3, 2015, Interview). Naturally, this change in the matrimonial market is also reflected in the way the *Play of the Goat* is practiced today in Heleșteni. Before the year 2005, village lads knew for certain that they would have to leave to attend their military duty. Nowadays, lads think about leaving for countries such as Italy or Spain to earn good money. Labor migration to Western Europe has somehow replaced the compulsory military service.[16] However, this rule is not a universal one and does not apply equally to all young people.

In addition, the money rush specific to the capitalist society has also started to be reflected in the way the *Play of the Goat* takes place these days. In this respect, a revealing fact is that many of the old people (mostly former workers in state collectivized farms) I managed to discuss with during my field research confessed they were disappointed that Goat dancers were no longer caroling them during winter holidays. For example, a 65-year-old woman, former schoolteacher who lives with her mother, told me: "The Goat band has not dropped by our house for several years. As a matter of fact, I can understand them: why would a bunch of young guys want to carol us, two old women! They prefer to visit households where there are young girls to marry" (Cornelia Voicu, 63 years old, April 5, 2012, Oboroceni village, Interview).

Wanting to check this piece of information from alternative sources, I asked a leader of the *Play of the Goat* performers why they avoided visiting households in the schoolteacher's neighborhood. The teenager answered quickly:

Yeah, I know exactly the area of the village you are talking about and that neighborhood, too. Indeed, we haven't been there for a long time. But my brother's team was there a few years ago and only one family from all the people living on that hill opened their door to them. The people living there are poor, so it is pointless to visit them, it's a waste of time to climb the difficult road up there only to carol one household or even none, when we could instead carol at least four or five wealthier families down here and earn good money. (Marius, 18 years old, May 15, 2012, Heleșteni village, field notes)

In other words, profitability has become a main component of the *Play of the Goat*. This element is also taken into account when it comes to baking the bread roll for the *comoraș*. I managed to find out from several informants why bagels and cakes are no longer offered to the *Goat band* or even to young children who come caroling. They all told me that "today, all those who come caroling us, including small children, want us to give them money. If you give them cakes, pretzels or fruits, you will find them thrown in the street around the corner." Consequently, the offering of the bread roll to the band leader by his girlfriend, once a deeply significant symbolic gesture and an intrinsic part of the ritual, seems to have become outdated.

As in the case described by Bourdieu, the rural matrimonial market in Moldovian villages has changed drastically. Most young people in the village go to study at high schools in cities such as Paşcani, Târgul-Frumos, or Iaşi. Those who are better off go to college and enroll in master programs too, usually in Iaşi, capital city of the county. During their studies, young people usually live in campuses and spend most of their time in the city instead of their village. Besides the fact that the urban environment leaves its mark on young people's way of thinking and on their educational background, most of them end up finding their partner in the city, and not in their village of origin as before. On top of that, many of them become IT literate during their studies or while living in the city. The computer and the Internet are the gateways to a world even wider than that of the city. Online matrimonial market cannot compete with the scarce marriage offer of the village. The virtual reality bringing together millions of people from different corners of the country—and the world as well—has the advantage of facilitating quick contact, devoid of the barriers of traditional rural culture, a situation that obviously stirs the resentment of older generations.

Under the current circumstances, we should not be surprised that the *Play of the Goat* as form of networking within the village community has become obsolete. Many young people who get used to the entertaining city life prefer spending the New Year's Eve in the city, partying in clubs or restaurants in Iaşi, Paşcani or other cities. Those who are still attracted to old rural traditions continue them in their own way. However, I have learned from several villagers in Heleşteni that the *Play of the Goat* tends to lose its fervor and, at times, it even contradicts its old status as a memorable moment in a young man's life.

For example, in the winter of 2014, I was surprised to see in Heleşteni a *Goat team* whose leader and members were teenagers ages 12 or 13 who, despite being very young, were also very short. The villagers, too, seemed very surprised, and I heard some of them complaining angrily: "What the heck, what kind of a *Goat team* is that?!? What is the matter with these little boys? When I was young and member of the *Goat band*, I was a real lad ready for marriage!" A few days later, I had the opportunity to have lunch with the mayor, the deputy-mayor and a few other villagers. They all complained about what they called "those *Goat team* babies," at which point I asked the village official a very straightforward question "But you, as community leaders, you can ask them to stick to the old tradition, can't you?" The mayor felt himself obliged to answer my question and said to me in a meek voice "How am I supposed to do that? Don't you see that traditions disappear day by day? If I stopped these little *Goat dancers*, there would be no more trace of the custom. . . . " In any case, despite the criticism, the band of teenagers continued their journey through the village, with their team, and, in the end, every one of them succeeded in gaining a little over $100.

More, 2016 brought another important change in the morphology of the ritual for the first time in the village history. One *Goat team* of the five caroling throughout Heleșteni comună replaced the pipe player with a hired music band. The band consisted of an accordion, a trumpet and a drum player, with all the musicians brought from other localities; in fact, they were all *lăutari* (professional traditional musicians) usually performing at weddings.

All in all, for me as a researcher, analyzing the *Play of the Goat* became a good opportunity to understand the great transformations of the rural world during the socialist period and especially during postsocialism. It is again, to became fully aware how a play can be an excellent filter to comprehend the great transformations that affect a community, and with that the entire society that comprise that community.

THE *PLAY OF THE DEER*—MORPHOLOGY, SIGNIFICANCE AND SYMBOLS

In the previous sections of this chapter, I examined the *Play of the Goat* as a rite of passage for young lads and how the social-economic transformations of the last decades challenged the way this ritual was performed in Heleșteni. In this section I will focus my attention on a folk play which contain as a central event the death and resurrection of the main character. Usually these types of folk plays are more spectacular and are loaded with a heavier theatrical content. This moment of resurrection, present in many European folk plays, represents one of the topics that raised interest and aroused the imagination of researchers in the field of mummers' plays for a long time; it also led to many theories, as well as haphazard hypotheses (see, e.g., Beatty 1906[17]). These often contradictory ideas emerged especially in British folkloristics (Baskerville 1924; Chambers 1969 [1933]; Gailey 1969), but were to be found also in folkloristics of countries like Russia (Warner 1977:9) and Romania (Oișteanu 2012:86).

Throughout my present analysis I keep in mind the findings of this rich literature but, like in the previous sections of my study, I mainly examine the discussions I had with the people whom I interviewed and who practiced themselves the *Play of the Dear*. I learned from these people that in Heleșteni, the *Play of the Deer* is performed by teenagers aged 10 to 15, whereas the

Play of the Goat is performed by young men aged 16 to 20. These discussions also made me aware of the fact that the *Play of the Deer* is actually a sort of preparation for a more significant ritual which is the *Play of the Goat.*

At the beginning of this analysis, it is important to mention that of all the rural plays studied in Iaşi County, this one is rapidly declining as a folk practice. This is probably the reason why the *Play of the Deer* has been intensely patrimonialized in recent years at the initiative of political and local leaders. I will discuss further these processes in the last chapter of the study. For now, I describe and analyze the morphology, the significance and the symbols characterizing the *Play of the Deer*, also known as *The Deer,* as it appears today in the *comună* of Heleşteni.

In all of the four villages of Heleşteni comună, right after the Christmas fast starts—on the day known as *Lăsata Secului*, on November 14—the first preparations for the ritual begin. First, the drums are made, and the teenagers wishing to participate in the ritual go to the center of Heleşteni *comună*. Some of them carry drums to prove their willingness to become members of a *Deer* team. To do this, on November 15, they meet a few steps away from the town hall, at the crossroads of two important streets in the comună. Usually, the number of teenagers gathered there ranges around 20 or 30. That moment, the teams are not yet formed. Thus, the negotiations for creating the teams start right there. From the perspective of the organizational skills of the teenagers involved and of the way they build their social networks, this moment is interesting. The young man who wants to become *comoraş* usually lets his friends know about his intention. But he needs to have the prior consent of the parents to do that. The parents' approval is necessary because the ritual involves from the start some expenses (covered by the family because teenagers, still minor, do not possess financial resources).

The meeting on November 15 starts with the *comoraşi* announcing their intention to form the *Deer* teams. That is when other youngsters who do not want or cannot be *comoraşi* due to financial or other reasons, but want to participate in the ritual anyway, begin discussing about joining the teams. The *comoraşi* select their team mates according to the drumming skills they have, but also as a result of family and friendship relationships. These discussions can last for hours. However, a few hours later, the teams are formed and it is knows exactly how many *Deer* teams are going to walk around the *comună*, as well as their members.

Once the team is established, the teenager who will be the *comoraş* goes to his father and tells him the news. That moment, father and son plan to look for a pipe player in the village, one that would accept to join the team. Once the pipe player is found and the offer accepted, the teenager's father pays a handsel (approximately one quarter of the final sum) to make the deal. This agreement also involves a series of obligations for the pipe player. One of these is that of rehearsing with the team of the *comoraș* every evening, starting at least three weeks before December 31. Sometimes, these rehearsals take place even one and a half month before. In recent years, one more mature person is needed next to the pipe player—the one playing the Deer mask. If in the 1960s both the pipe player and the deer mask performer were usually teenagers, too, lately they became more difficult to find. Thus, adult people with past experience playing these roles started to be recruited, and they are usually older than 40.

With its logistics, the *Play of the Deer* was not only the preliminary stage of a more important ritual—that of the *Play of the Goat*—but also a preparation for life, for its problems and difficulties. This was possible by means of socialization and teamwork. Teenagers joining the event would rehearse in the center of the village, and the rehearsals would end in long conversations on various topics, including school and lessons for different school subjects. Nowadays, according to my own observations and to what locals confessed, the rigors and the seriousness of the rehearsals are much lower than it used to be. Many of the *Deer team* today would rather watch TV than rehearse for the *Deer*.

A few evenings before the proper ritual, from December 27 to the evening of December 30, the *comoraș* and his team members had to prepare the *Deer*'s fur and the masks for the final rehearsal. The fur either came from somebody who has had it for years or was made that year by a furrier. The same was true for the *Deer*'s head. Those *comorași* who did not possess these artifacts had to find solutions for acquiring them. The preparations usually included sewing the fur on a strong fabric that would be easy to wear by the *Deer* mask performer; then the fur was being decorated with multicolored ribbons and, sometimes, even with a ribbon with the colors of the Romanian flag; the trousers, scarves, helmets, etc., of the members were then ironed. All team members would attend these preliminary activities before the proper ritual took place; finally, the preparation of artifacts also included the last rehearsals with the fur and the *Deer* head put on by the designated performer, and with the pipe player ready as if the proper ritual were happening.

On December 31, team members meet in the house of the *comoraș* around noon. Relatives also gather there since, in its way to the town hall, the team had been accompanied by the friends and relatives of the *comoraș* and other members of the team. Once at the gates of the *comună* hall, a play is being performed in the middle of the street, then another one in front of the mayor's office employees. Sometimes, youngsters perform a play while local authorities issue the authorization for caroling around the village. Just as in the case of the *Play of the Goat*, the *Deer team* first visits the priest. The priest offers money to the Deer team and, according to what locals say, there has never been a priest who would not welcome the *Deer*.

Just like the *Play of the Goat,* the *Play of the Deer* usually occurs between December 31 at 4:00–5:00 p.m. and January 1 at 8:00–9:00 p.m. During these two days, the *Deer teams* wander ceaselessly through the entire *comună*, day and night, with just a short break on January 1 from 5:00 a.m. to 8:00 a.m. The ritual presents itself under the theatrical form of sketch, with multiple characters playing various pre-established roles, each conducting a dialogue about the *Deer*'s fate. The theatre team usually consists of 8–12 members and may include 5–8 *bear-leaders*, one *dragoman*, one *shepherd*, one *officer*, a pair of *gypsies* (man and woman), a *merchant* (Jewish or Greek), an *old man*, a pipe player and the *Deer* dancer. I saw such a large team with diverse characters in Cucuteni comună. In Heleşteni, the team usually consists of five-six *bear-leaders* (*ursari*), one *dragoman* (*interpretor*), one *shepherd*, one *Gypsy*, a *Jew* or a *Greek*, the *Deer dancer* and the *pipe player*. The characters' names show that we are dealing with an ancient play about social realities long vanished from the Romanian countryside. Most readers may find it offensive to encounter characters in this play that are called the *Jew*, *The Gypsy*, or the *Greek*, especially since these characters enact negative stereotypes extant in the villages where I conducted my field research. However, to this day, these are the recognized names of these stock characters.

A detail that fascinated and perplexed the scholars studying this ritual was the name of the most numerous characters in the play: *ursari*/bear-leaders (Adăscăliţei 1968). The name surprises because there are no bears in the sketch. It is even harder to grasp an understanding of this title as most of the actors involved in the play, including elder ones, know nothing of its significance in spite of upholding the tradition and currently using the term. Vasile Adăscăliţei, the researcher who studied this ritual more thoroughly in the 1960s, came out with an interesting hypothesis: "At a first glance, this name seems to be senseless. But the deep analysis of the (local n.a.) traditions shows us that (in the past n.a.) all wild animal trainers were called bear-leaders." (Idem 1968:424)

Another striking character of the play is the *dragoman*. Nowadays considered an archaism, the word is little used in the Romanian language. It names a translator who usually worked in the service of the Moldavian kings or royal governors during Middle Ages (Oprişan 1981). The character seems to be introduced in the play as an irony, since it had no role other than to play and dance with the rest of the bear-leaders. But he is the only one who could translate for the outsiders the seemingly absurd disenchantment whispered by a bear-leader in the ear of the *Deer*. Last, but not least, *the Jew* (sometimes replaced by the *Greek*) is a member of an ethnic group almost totally vanished in Eastern Romania. The connection between Jews and the rural community's

Figure 1.2. The deer team from Heleşteni village playing their sketch in the front of township hall in Heleşteni village—December 31, 2014.
Photo credit: Alin Rus

past is obvious, as they were the main traders in Iaşi city area during the inter-war period and before. Tragically, during World War II, this ethnic group was the object of *Iaşi Pogrom*, along with massive deportations to Nazi extermination camps that took place in the Romanian region of Moldova. After these events, most Romanian Jews who survived the genocide immigrated to other European countries, to the United States or to Israel (Ioanid 2008). Despite this unfortunate history, I was able to observe that *the Jew* still appears as a character in this local ritual as a merchant trying to make a deal with the master of the Deer to buy it.

The presence of another character—the *Gypsy*—in this theatrical performance is less surprising since, after Romanians, Romani people represent the second largest ethnic group in Iaşi County. Again, some readers may find it offensive to see this term in a scientific text. However, throughout my one-decade research in these villages I have never meet performers who were referring to their stock characters with the name Roma or Romani, a more accepted concept from a political correctness perspective. During my field research in 2012, I met a group of traveling Romani who stopped for a month in Heleşteni and made commerce with the local population, selling and repairing pots and other metal objects in the household. So, I can confirm that they are still an active presence in the villages of Iaşi County.

The last important character is *the shepherd* (sometimes replaced by the *Old Man* or *Bulibaşa—the Gypsy-king*), considered the master of the *Deer* in some versions of the play. The economic activity of the shepherd is widespread and economically profitable in the villages of Heleşteni *comună*, and also in the localities around (like Strunga *comună* and Vascani village from Ruginoasa *comună*) where the *Deer* ritual is still performed.

The *Deer Play* follows a simple logical line expressed in a few sequences: one of the bear-leaders or the shepherd first goes to the gate of a village house and asks the householder if he wants to let the team perform its sketch. The bear-leader, the shepherd or the *bulibaşa/the Gypsy-king* usually approaches the householder with one simple question: "Do you receive the deer?" If the answer is "Yes," he opens the gate so that the entire group can enter.

The main character playing the *Deer*, wearing a deer head-shaped wooden mask and a fur covering all over his body, performs an exuberant dance full of vitality, clattering rhythmically the mobile wooden jaw of the mask (quite cleverly triggered with a rope hidden under the fur). Very soon after, the *Deer* falls down because he is sick. Immediately, there is a short dialogue between the shepherd or a bear-leader and the merchant (the Greek or the Jew) who wants to buy the *Deer* from its master at a low price. Meanwhile, the Gypsy shows up and try to steal the *Deer*. That moment, one of the characters accompanying the *Deer*, usually the *bulibaşa* or a bear-leader, utters an incantation or a spell into the *Deer*'s ear which has fallen ill because of the evil eye, as we may deduce from the incantation (information collected from the *Deer* team members in the villages Cucuteni, Heleşteni, Sticlăria, Strunga, Vascani, field notes).

This play is valuable as we can see in it the paradox of stereotypical peasant representations about various ethnic groups. The Gypsy is the one who steals the deer when his master is not careful. At the same time, *the Bulibaşa/ the Gypsy-king* is the one who manages to bring the deer back to life through a magical enchantment. Likewise, the Jew or the Greek merchand tries to buy the deer at a lower price. However, the presence of the merchant is necessary in the village because he is the person who can buy even a sick animal that no longer has too much value for a peasant's household.

In this respect, I agree with some other researchers who concluded that this incantation is the most beautiful and original part of the entire ritual (Adăscăliței 1968:429). It is fascinating mainly for those who comprehend its meaning and are able to connect it to the social and economic realities of peasant communities. The bear-leader begins his disenchantment by telling his own story: how he, the king of the Gypsies (the so-called *bulibaşa* or *old man* in some other versions), found the *Deer* in a deep forest entangled in blackberry brambles, thus recalling a fairytale landscape: "I was walking down a path/Trodden by nobody,/On which no one set foot yet,/Beaten by little ants only/And charmed by an ol' judy/I saw snakes with nine iron fangs,/With nine of steel,/With nine rovers,/With nine hoofers,/With nine soothsayers."[18] Furthermore, the bear-leader presents a series of seemingly disconnected scenes that may be disconcerting especially to the outsider who does not understand the deeper implications of the play.

Peasants who understood the play in depth explained to me that the *Play of the Deer* ritual, like many other winter rituals in Moldova, mocks the social evils of village life: "old maids" who became too old for marriage; marital infidelity, especially that of women cheating on their husbands with younger men; decrepitude; rural poverty; and the Greeks or the Jews traveling merchants trying to profit from peasants' ignorance of the grain market. All this data agrees with the information provided by Dimitrie Cantemir who described the *Deer Dance* in 1714, regarding it as a satire (Cantemir 1714:91).

Unfortunately, although quite widespread in Europe in the past, this ritual was little understood and widely suppressed by Church authorities who perceived it as a senseless and irrational devilish folk custom (Clark 2014:211–213; du Cange 1678)[19]. In spite of this Church opposition and of the prevalent misunderstanding, variations of the custom are still performed under different forms and names in various parts of Europe, as is the case with *The Ritual Horse* (Warner 1977: 8–9) or *Brezaia* (Beza 1928:11). Nevertheless, the meaning and the development of the play are quite similar in all these occurrences.

In the case studies I observed, including the Heleșteni ritual, the innovative elements, as well as the old ones, came together into an original folk creation expressing the creativeness of peasants. Thus, the *Play of the Deer* can be regarded as a social snapshot of Moldova's past rural world. Not so long ago, Gypsy bear-trainers would walk through villages with trained bears dancing on pipe music; and, one of the most common remedies for various diseases was bloodletting from the tongue or the ear of the sick person or animal. During those times, village girls faced social pressure and a severe local marriage market that pushed them to get married when still teenagers to escape the contempt of other villagers. In this narrow world, peasants distrusted the travelling Greek and Jewish merchants who bought maize and wheat directly from villagers to get the best price. The peasants were also suspicious of the Gypsies, whose shows they still enjoyed and whose wares were in great demand as they could not be produced in the peasant household. All of these social realities, which can sometimes be very burdensome, are embodied in the folk play the *Play of the Deer,* and are presented to the audience in the *Disenchantment of the Deer*, in a humorous and waggish way.

The ritual comes to an end when the disenchantment stops, and the *Deer* miraculously recovers and stands up. That moment, the shepherd expresses his incommensurable joy by performing a short exuberant dance. Right afterwards, the *Deer* begins dancing again and this time it is unstoppable. The bear-leaders accompanying it, wearing drums and colored crests, dance around it in a rhythmic manner, beating their small drums frantically— expressing the joy brought by the *Deer*'s incredible revival.

The supernatural recovery of the sick animal is not new at all at the country-side, and it also appears in other winter and spring plays throughout Europe:

> Around both the Ritual Horse and the Goat, there evolved an extraordinary dra-matic game, a close parallel to many spring and summer rites, in which the death and subsequent resurrection of the animal were performed with much bucolic humor and boisterous play. Here, for instance, is a comic scene from Smolensk's *uezd*, revolving round the supposed illness of a peasant's horse and its miracu-lous recovery through the agency of an old wise woman. (Warner 1977:9)

Another important aspect of the ritual is when the *Deer team* goes through the village and offer performances to any household where peasants are willing to welcome them. This is done by the householder paying a sum of money for the performance of the dramatic game. The sum of money varies widely: the heads of the village (mayor, vice-mayor, priest or doctor) are expected to pay approximately 100 lei ($25), the better-off peasants usually pay 50 lei ($13) and the poor peasants—a mere sum of 20 lei ($6). It is obvious that the community's social network works as a vessel and a medium for the promo-tion and practice of the ritual. In the absence of a community that promotes the custom and encourages its transmission to the next generation, chances are that the ritual, already severely threatened, vanishes quickly. Today, more than ever before, rural customary communities face major threats endanger-ing their values, principles, and rituals.

CURRENT PRESSURES ON PLAY OF THE DEER: DEMOGRAPHIC DECLINE, LABOR MIGRATION, AND POVERTY

Since I began fieldwork in Iaşi County, I have repeatedly heard from my informants statements such as: "The *Play of the Deer* is not performed any-more like in the past." The deeper analysis of my interviews with villagers revealed two more interesting details. They believe that the repertoire of the ritual is less rich and less beautiful than in the past, and they claim the teams are much smaller and invest less effort in performance. I attempted to corroborate the information from multiple informants by comparing it with data from archives, books, and other sources. What I found contradicted my beliefs and assumptions. For instance, upon hearing such statements, one of my assumptions was that many of my informants, especially elder ones, tried to give me a nostalgic picture of their youth as a time when the community was more cohesive, people were kinder, life—more beautiful and community rituals—richer and more diverse. Yet, this was not the case, as I discovered by comparing the different types of data I collected.

First, I got similar statements, from both my oldest informants (65–95 years old), and younger interviewees 26–64 years old). I was surprised to find that even much younger informants gave me similar statements regarding the richness of the village rituals in the past compared to a much poorer picture in the present. I found that in certain villages around the area where I have recorded the *Deer* ritual since 2009, the custom has completely disappeared in the following years of my research. According to some of those villagers' statements, this process happened mainly within the last two decades after the collapse of Communism, and became even more accelerated after 2007, when Romania joined the European Union.

Second, the *Deer* incantations collected in the 1960s and 1970s (Adăscăliței 1968; Ciubotaru 2010) are richer than the incantations I collected since 2009, in different villages of Iași County. The comparison of the *Deer* incantations I collected in the village of Oboroceni in 2012 with the ones collected in the 1970s by the folklorist Ciubotaru in the same village, revealed many interesting pieces of information (Ciubotaru 2010). The recent incantation is significantly shorter. Although many verses coincide, others are missing from the incantation I collected in 2012. The missing parts of the incantation are significant in terms of the changes produced in the rural world over the last four decades. These stanzas talk about magic (the description of a fairy-tale landscape where the deer had been found and the magic relationship between the *Gypsy-king* and the deer), poverty (the description of the house and the belongings of the deer's owner), interethnic relations in the village (more interethnic characters in the older version; for example, the presence of the Greek) and romantic love. The owner of the deer in the older incantation version is a *Gypsy-king* (*bulibașa*), while in the new version he is replaced with the *bourgeois*, obviously a more recent presence in the rural world, probably a reminiscence of communist times when the class of the capitalist *bourgeois* were persecuted by communists in the name of social equality. Significantly, the stanza about romantic love has been replaced in the newer version with a scene about domestic violence; in the meantime, smoking and alcohol addiction is included. Apart from this, in the newer version there is one more stanza warning about the possible negative effects of too much alcohol consumption during winter holidays.

Third, in villages like Heleșteni and Oboroceni, for example, during the last three winters, I saw caroling only one anemic *Deer team* made out of four–five children no older than 13, three-four bear-leaders, the shepherd, one *Deer* dancer and one pipe player. In one of the instances, even the pipe player was missing, and the explanation was that he had gotten drunk. The more acute problem was the fact that the team could not replace him on the spur of the moment because pipe players in the village could be counted on the fingers of one hand, and had all committed to some other team months before. In most of the sketches presented by these weaker teams, the introductory part of the play was missing together with the characters that usually perform it. Thus, the whole dramatic game had reverted to the scene of the *Deer*'s dance, an abbreviated form of the incantation and the final recovery of the *Deer*, followed by the dance of the shepherd. It was hard not to agree with my informants that these sketches were indeed quite frail when compared to other more coherent representations such as the performance I witnessed during the winter of 2009 in the village of Cucuteni. In that case, the team was composed of fourteen young men, none of them younger than 16, and none (except the *Deer* dancer and the pipe player who would usually keep their roles for many years) older than 26. They presented a very well-organized play with a lot of characters including a gypsy couple, an old man, an old woman, a Jew, a shepherd, six bear-leaders, the *Deer* dancer, and the pipe player. Unfortunately, during my research, most of the plays I saw were closer to the feeble versions performed in the villages of Heleșteni and Oboroceni than to the cohesive representations done in Cucuteni village in 2009.

Given this situation, I began asking my interviewees their opinion about the transformation of this custom during the last decades. I usually opened my interview or discussion with a simple question, "What do you think about the *Deer team* from your village?" The answers I usually got fit into a rage-filled reaction rather than into a rational statement. The speaker would often exclaim, "Is this a *Deer*!?!" or, more categorically, "This is not a *Deer* anymore!" After such an exclamation, the discussion veered toward the right track and the interviewee would then relate his/her story about how much better the *Deer team* used to be when the speaker was younger.

One particular day during my field work, I was lucky enough to assist to a discussion between two men, both of them locals of Hărmăneasa village. The younger one was Florin Chiperi, a 26-year-old sport teacher, who became one of my best friend and valuable collaborator in Heleșteni. Florin had been a *comoraș* for three years consecutively when he was 12–14 years old, in the 1990s. His interlocutor was Gheorghe Aghiorghiesei, the 67-year-old pipe player of the *Deer* team in Heleșteni village.

> G.A.—There were much more customs (other types of folk theater)
> and *Deer teams* when I was a child in the fourth grade. . . . This
> was in 1955–1957. In those days, people gave us much less money
> than now, but we played the *Deer* more energetically. Now, as I am

the pipe player of the *Deer* team, I tell them about all these things
and about the powerful way we played it in the past, but they don't
really care and only want to rest after going to perform in just a
couple of houses.

F.C.—Even when I was a child, bear-leaders played their drums
only in the position of a deep squat. . . . This had a meaning. The
bear-leaders had to prevent the *Deer* from running. So, if you did
not squat all around the *Deer*, he kept running away like a wild
animal. This was part of the play. Today's *Deer* teams don't do this
anymore.

G.A.—Yes, that is right. Back then, no bear-leaders beat their drum
standing up, but only in the deep squat position.

F.C.—Plus, they don't disenchant the *Deer* so long as when I was a
child.

Alin Rus—So, the *Deer* doesn't run away anymore today?

G.A.—Yes, that is right!

A.R.—Could we say that the *Deer* has been tamed in recent years?

F.C. (laughing)—Yes, we could say that!

G.A.—Year by year, these customs keep disappearing. These young
teenagers don't want to learn those things we try to teach them
(March 25, 2012, Heleșteni village, field notes).

The same remark about the richness of rural plays in the past was reported
by many other peasants in different villages throughout Iași County. All of
these remarks motivated me to look for deeper explanations. This is how I
began asking my informants how they explained the ritual decline. One common explanation I received was that there is a ritual downturn—the *Play of
the Deer* included in it—and that it is strongly connected to the demographic
decline of the villages after 1989. This came out clearly in an interview with
the mayor of Heleșteni comună:

Truth is that these customs are fewer and fewer each year. But my generation
had a lot of children because of the Ceaușescu's decree that forbade abortions
[for references regarding this topic see (Kligman 1998) n.a.]. For this reason,
there were so many mummers and folk play teams in the village, as well as
a strong competition between these teams during winter holidays. Back then,
Heleșteni *comună* had around 3,500 people. Today, the population of the
comună is around 2,500 people. (Constantin Hâra, 46 years old, Oboroceni village, March 4, 2012, Interview)

As I had heard similar statements from multiple interviewees, I decided to
check the validity of the data from alternative sources. I went to the Iași
City Bureau of Statistics and collected the censuses from 1900 to 2011 for
Heleșteni *comună*. The picture given by the analysis of the data proved that

the remarks of my informants about the villages' demographic decline were accurate. The population of this *comună* increased gradually from 1900 to 1977. That year marked the maximum population boom for this locality, followed by a gradual decrease until 1989, when the decrease became very sharp. Thus, the 2011 census, the last for which there was available information, recorded a village population similar to that of 1945 (Iași City Bureau of Statistics and the Archive of Heleșteni comună). It is obvious that the population boom of the 1960s and 1970s must have had a major influence on community rural plays (see Appendix III).

In the discourse of my interviewees, this reason was connected with other arguments that might explain the weakening in the peasants' traditions. Following the population decline, the second most frequent explanation evoked in the villagers' discourses was the labor migration to western European countries. The phenomenon was perceived by peasants as having a negative impact on community rituals mainly for two reasons: it drained human resources from the villages, and it changed the mentality of those who left, estranging them from village culture. If the first reason seemed rather natural when perceived by the villagers—as a kind of inevitability or something taken for granted—the second one was delivered with inflamed comments such as this:

This decline of community rituals started mainly after 1989 Revolution. As the country borders were opened after 1989, many young people leave their villages to work in some other countries where they can make more money. The problem is that they forget too easily their village and its traditions. They became too self-conceited and many of them don't care anymore about our traditions. (Petrică Horneț, 52 years old, Heleșteni village, June 29, 2012, Interview)

A younger man and a labor migrant himself explained the same situation from a different perspective:

When they come back home during winter holidays, most migrants are too tired to wander days and nights through the village as folk players do. Instead, they prefer to stay with their families and to receive those teams who come to their doors. Moreover, they now have enough money, and they are not interested anymore in making, let's say, $100 during New Year Eve. They make much more money anyway while working in constructions in Spain and Italy. (Alin Zaharia, 20 years old, Oboroceni village, December 27, 2011, Interview)

Whatever the best explanation may be, it is more than obvious that labor migration pays a costly contribution to the winter rituals' decline. To validate this statement scientifically, I tried to find out the percentage of labor migrants from the total local population. Unfortunately, the data about migration is very hard to get and even state institutions are struggling to determine a fair estimation; the reason for this situation is that people are oftentimes engaged in circular migration, making it difficult to classify them according to rigid categories such as "migrant" or "non-migrant." Aware of that, I used a totally different method to get more accurate data. During a few hours, I interviewed one person from each village of Heleşteni comună which worked either in administration or in a local school, and practically knew the entire village population by name. With the census data that contained all the households and family members in the village in front of us, I asked questions about the migration status of each family member. This way, the cohesive village network, doubled by village gossip, provided useful information.

Those outstanding members of the four villages whom I interviewed were able to deliver a plethora of data about how many people migrated to foreign countries, to which countries, for how many months or years, and in what field they were working. In the period between April 24 and May 3, 2012, I was able to apply this method to all four villages of Heleşteni *comună*: Oboroceni, Hărmăneasa, Movileni and Heleşteni. Thus, I was able to find out that 12–15% of the population was or still is engaged in international labor migration, either circular migration or long-term migration. Furthermore, this represented one of the most active parts of the village population, usually comprising people between 18–35 years old. This is exactly the population sample responsible for transmitting the rural customs and knowledge related to winter rituals, or actively involved in the performance of these rituals.

This conclusion was reinforced in my field observations in the evening of December 27 2011 in the village of Heleşteni; I was filming the preparation for the *Deer* ritual, including the sewing of the *Deer* fur, the decoration of the *Deer* mask and the rehearsal for the roles in the play. These events happened in a small house in the village. Inside that house, there were two elders who, besides doing all those activities, taught the four young teenagers present there these skills. I learned from these elders that the parents of the children had all left to Spain as labor migrants and could not return home during winter holidays. As a result, the elders had to get involved to ensure the cultural transmission of knowledge and skills related to ritual practices. This was what I saw and learned while witnessing and filming the manufacturing process of the *Deer* costume. During this event, an old man who was the soul of this entire activity, told me:

> The parents of the children you see here are working in Spain. My son-in-law works in construction, and my daughter in a restaurant. And these children, including the *comoraş*, are my grandchildren, and I take care of them while their parents are there. There is no other way for me to help them because my pension is very low. I grow a pig all year long and then I sell it for almost nothing just

before Christmas. I get 400 lei ($100) for it, nothing more. But at least I know I still do something for my children. . . . This year, my son-in-law wanted to come home for the holidays, but his boss could not let him go. So that's why I'm here, teaching my grandchildren do the *Deer*. I even bought a Deer head from a craftsman in Costeşti village. I paid 800 lei ($200) for it, but we'll be using it for at least a few years. Together with the pipe player, we sew the Deer's fur and we teach these children how to do it for the time when we'll no longer be able to. (Ion Scripcaru, 76 years old, Heleşteni village, December 27, 2011, Interview)

The third reason often mentioned in relation to the weakening of winter rituals was poverty. The common explanation of my informants was that villagers have no more money to offer to the ritual practitioners when they came to perform in the householders' courtyards. Despite this explanation, it seems quite plain at a first glance that poverty was actually one of the more complex and complicated aspects of village life that were sometimes very difficult to analyze. Initially, I received too many contradictory statements about poverty in the past versus poverty in the present. It was mainly the young villagers who emphasized some aspects of village poverty after the collapse of Communism, while the elders presented remote and fragmentary images of their excruciating experiences of famine and poverty during, after and even before World War II. I heard fewer statements about the poverty during Communism. During Communism, the majority of my interviewees agreed, "People in the village were pretty equal. There were nor very rich people in the village, and neither very poor." The analysis of all this information brought me to the conclusion that poverty today was not deeper than in the past, when villagers were more committed to open the doors to folk actors and to pay them some money.

To unravel the complicated "mystery" around the issue of poverty in the villages, I had to put together a lot of information from many interviews, discussions, and participant observations that I collected during my several trips to Heleşteni. To get a clearer picture of how rural play actors are paid, I once tried to challenge the mayor of Heleşteni *comună*—a villager whom I was better acquainted with as he was hosting me.

> Alin Rus—I saw you giving 100 lei ($25) to these teams. It seems to me a bit too much. Why don't you give them less?
> C.H.—I have to give them at least this amount because, you see, there are many members in a band like the *Deer team*.
> A.R.—What would happen if you would give them 20 ($5) or 10 lei, let's say?
> C.H.—I cannot do that!
> A.R.—Why not?

C.H. (laughing)—The next day, the entire village would gossip about me.
(Constantin Hâra, 46 years old, Oboroceni village, January 2, 2011, field notes)

But, just as there are some people able to pay 100 lei for a team that entertains them, others are not well-off since they still make a living by working their small plots of land. Today, this work is usually unprofitable mainly because giant agricultural producers from the European Union and America such as BASF and Monsanto can sell the same agriculture goods at much lower prices. Thus, the poorest peasants are ashamed to receive the carolers during winter holidays as they are not able to afford paying a decent amount of money to folk play teams. This perspective was clarified in an interview with the head of the *Deer* team in the village of Sticlăria, close to Heleșteni, taken on January 2015.

Alin Rus—Are there many people who don't open the doors for you when you want to perform your sketch for them?
Constantin Curecheru—Yes. There are some people who don't receive us because they have no money. They want to receive us but they have no money at all to give us.
A young man from Mr. Curecheru's team—If the householder is ashamed to get out and to tell us he has no money, he would rather keep his door locked.
C. C.—Or they send a child to tell us, "We cannot receive the carolers because we have no money . . . " However, many people are very happy and receive us with wine, cakes and beverages and they also give us money.
A.R.—How much money do you get from them?C.C.—Some people give us 100 lei ($25) or 50 lei, more rarely we get 200 lei ($50) and there are, of course, people who give us 10 lei ($2.5). But actually, we don't have high pretentions. We say *Boda Proste* ["Thanks God!" in an old Bulgarian dialect[20]].
A.R.—But, for example, I know in the village there are elders with small pensions, ex-workers at the communist state farms. How much do they give you?
C.C.—Indeed, there are people like these. But, most of them have children who work in foreign countries and they send them money. For example, I have eight children and all of them live and work in Italy.
(Constantin Curecheru, 68 years old, Sticlăria village, January 03, 2015, Interview)

During my field research I had the chance to meet people who could not afford paying the prices mentioned above to watch the teams of folk artists performing in their courtyards. One interview with Mr. Petru Scripcaru, an 84-year-old man suffering from multiple diseases and having just a 600 lei ($150) pension per month, was very conclusive in this respect.

> Alin Rus—Did the teams come to carol you during the previous winter holiday?
> Petru Scripcaru—Yes, the *Goat team* came and performed here in my courtyard.
> A.R.—How much did you pay them?
> P. S.—I paid them 10 lei . . . (after a long pause and a kind of embarrassed grimace on his face, he continued) Maybe some other people paid more, but unfortunately, I cannot afford more.
> A.R.—What about the *Deer team*? Did they come to your door? I am asking this because I know there was a *Deer team* that walked through your village.
> P.S.—No, they did not come. Only one *Goat team* came because the son of my brother was the head of this team and I asked him in advance not to forget about me, as I wanted to see his team performing.
> (Petru Scripcaru, 84 years old, Heleșteni village, June 26, 2012, Interview)

This interview became relevant especially when corroborated with other information I had collected on the field, above all the statements made by the heads of the play teams during my discussions with them. It became clear that these teams had little motivation to perform for families of poor elders such as Mr. Scripcaru's. I learned that there are two primary motivators that push young guys performing these rituals in the villagers' homes: money and girls. If there is a wealthy family that gives good tips to the carolers, the team is very eager to go perform their ritual in their households. If the tips are small, but the householder has beautiful young daughters, especially unengaged, who would dance or talk to the young men performing the rituals, they would also be very happy to go there. Nevertheless, there is little motivation for them to go to some of the elders' houses where they get little money and don't have as much fun. Of course, there exist some other lesser motivations that can entice teams to perform for elders, too. One such example is family obligation and reciprocity regarding certain relatives; such an instance could be observed in the interview with Mr. Scripcaru.

The previously stated perspective about the peasants' explanations that "poverty led to the rural ritual's decline" was a bit more distinct and, at the same time, more nuanced and complex. As a conclusion to my analysis of the *Play of the Deer,* I suggest that the reason rituals are declining is not poverty itself, but rather a combination of poverty and social inequality. Social inequality grew deeper after the collapse of Communism and mainly after Romania joined the European Union; as a result, more villagers were able to migrate easily and get jobs in western European countries. As some peasants became richer after 1989, they were also expected to pay more for the teams of folk plays who caroled them. Additionally, I was told stories by labor migrants who showed off by offering big sums of money to the performers of winter rituals. These things raised the price for the winter rural plays performances and divided the rural communities into people who receive the play teams because they can afford to pay them, and people who cannot afford it. Finally, all these factors lead to a deeper atomization of the community—a process that has been negatively reflected in the practice of rural plays.

PANTOMIMIC MUMMERS—MUMMERS' PARADES AND MUMMERS' HOUSE-VISIT

This section describes the ritual performed by *Pantomimic Mummers*. Even if this name is not used by the inhabitants of the Heleșteni *comună,* I use it in this chapter precisely to distinguish this ritual from the more obviously theatrical plays such as the *Play of the Goat* and the *Play of the Deer.* But locals prefer the simpler version—that of *Mascați/The Mummers*—to describe this local custom. Because characters from other winter rituals are also masked and could be called *mascați/mummers,* I use "*Pantomimic Mummers*" to refer to the bands of masked actors employing a less formal style of winter rural plays.

Pantomimic Mummers are part of a very complex ritual that could be divided into several distinct moments: the morning parade on the village streets, the meeting in front of the *comună* hall, and the house-visit, accompanied by its permanent expressions: *speech disguise* and *guessing-game.* The ritual finishes with the general meeting in Oboroceni village, at the crossroads, on January 2, at 2 p.m.

Romanian folkloristics has largely debated the mummers' phenomenon (Vulcănescu 1970) and created consistent studies on this topic (Retegan 1957), but none of them described thoroughly a ritual resembling the one I analyzed in Heleșteni comună. Folklore studies on masks and masking in Romania were rather concerned with the elements common to all mummers' rituals, and divided those masks and their corresponding rituals in typologies, without offering a step by step presentation of some case studies; thus, they merged local differences altogether by reducing them to a general model.

Romulus Vulcănescu's substantial work *Măştile Populare /Folk Masks* (1970), uncover such an approach; other studies of smaller dimensions that follow the same approach are Retegan's study on *Dracii din Valea Ţibleşului/The Devils in Ţibleş Valley* (Retegan 1957), Lorinţ and Eretescu's article about masks in familiar life habits (Eretescu and Lorinţ 1967) and Constantin Eretescu's article on the origin and functioning of the *watch-eye masks/măşti de privegi*[21] (Eretescu 1968). But the process of dissolving the individual case and imposing generalizing typologies is not only related to Romanian Folkloristics. Examples as such are to be found in other works in the Folkloristics, in many countries, all of them trying to find typical marks and models rather than to explain and analyze the meanings practitioners give to these customs (Lommel 1972). Such approaches contributed to the exclusion of a whole series of important elements of particular rituals, as well as of the voices of the participating subjects that could have offered precious details about their hidden differences. Interestingly, the same observation was also made by other researchers studying this type of cultural forms in other geographical regions in Europe:

> The practice of mumming is mentioned in these written records [Swedish folklore archives n.a.], but seldom described in any detail. Personal stories and experiences are not mentioned at all. By and large, those who represented the social and cultural hegemonies were the ones who created the sources. They tell us that masking and disguising occurred, but do not give any insights into their cultural significance. They give us a glimpse into the phenomena without giving any detailed descriptions. (Knuts 2007:111)

However, the research into old archives showed that the study of mummers in Europe brings in front of us a complex phenomenon rooted deeply in the history of rural culture on the continent, and little understood by the first religious figures observing and describing these practices centuries ago, as we deduced from the texts systematized by a philologist such as du Cange. What we are dealing with a rich customary complex, with many variations and also with striking similarities between rituals situated in different moments in time and place (Gunnell 2007b; Halpert and Story 1969).

MUMMERS' PARADE ON VILLAGE STREETS

In the next pages I will provide a glimpse on my field research regarding the mumming phenomenon in Heleşteni *comună*. Unlike the *Goat* and *Deer teams* that required a detailed logistics, organizing *Pantomimic Mummers* is easier and involves fewer preliminary stages. In the meantime, one could observe that unlike the *Play of the Goat or* the *Play of the Deer, The Pantomimic Mummers* involve a higher diversity of the age and social status of the participants. Thus, *Pantomimic Mummers* can be performed by householders, married people, both men and women, sometimes even older than 50. Nevertheless, *The Pantomimic Mummers'* ritual does not exclude youngsters aged 14 to 18 or even children aged 9 to 13. All these aspects speak about the inclusiveness of the *Pantomimic Mummers'* ritual, accepting men and women, as well as people with very diverse ages, from 14 to 70. Despite all this, the most common age category is that between 21 and 35. This age interval is mainly valid for the first stage of the ritual (in the morning of December 31), whereas later in the same day and the following days, in the next stages of the ritual, the other ages mentioned above may well be present among mummers.

Just as in the case of the *Goat* and *Deer* dances, the pantomimic mummers' ritual comprises two kinds of performances. The first one is public and it is joined by the whole group of performers in the village or even in the entire *comună*. These performances, involving numerous participants, take place on the streets of Heleșteni, in front of the *comună* hall and, finally, at a crossroads in Oboroceni village. This kind of ritual expression is perfectly defined by the English term *pageantry* because of the public parade it includes. The second type is private and takes place in the courtyard and in the house of the householders, being performed by much smaller mummers' groups visit (usually 3–8 mummers). The folklorist Herbert Halpert called this ritual sequence *house-visit* (Halpert 1969), and I adopt the term for the rest of the present work.

The ritual starts with organizing three large mummers' teams, one in each village in the Heleșteni *comună* (namely Hărmăneasa, Oboroceni, and Heleșteni). The village of Movileni is an exception, as they don't have this ritual and the young lads in this small village are involved in organizing *Deer* plays. The participants in the ritual from each of the three villages mentioned above first meet in the evening of December 30, around 7–8 p.m., in the center of their own village. That is where they settle the place and the time for the meeting that is supposed to take place the second day. All those who want to join the pageant must design or buy their own mask and costume. These two elements are the necessary conditions to join the ritual. Nevertheless, it is worth mentioning that there are significant differences between the participants' mask and costumes. If some of them simply put on a cheap Halloween mask they bought in the supermarket or just cover their face with a piece of stocking, dressed in old fashioned clothes usually worn by the opposite sex, others make a giant effort, investing a lot of energy and money onto really artistic masks and outfits.

In recent years, labor migrants in Western Europe who come back home and join the ritual do not design their own masks and costumes anymore, but buy them instead from other locals. This phenomenon urged local craftsmen to design beautiful masks that could be sold before New Year. Migrants also bring materials—especially beads—from the countries where they work (Italy, Spain, Portugal, Greece) that could be used for manufacturing the masks. These artifacts make masks very different from those used only a few decades ago. Elders told me how their masks used to be done in the past, when the choice of available fabrics (ribbons, beads, mirrors, etc.) was not that impressive. Some of them still have such "ancient masks" and they serve as landmarks for memory. Besides these, by looking at these masks and the photos with them taken in the past, more than half a century ago, I observed that masks were much simpler, made out even of tree bark or colored cardboard. After Romania entered the European Union and the migration of the peasants around Iaşi County to the Western European countries increased, masks became transnational. Generally, the mask's helmet is made of sheep skin produced and manufactured in Heleşteni by local craftsmen; meanwhile, the beads and the ribbons are brought from supermarkets in Italy, Spain, Portugal and Greece, but are often made in China.

After the mummers' preliminary meeting on December 30, once the meeting place for the big group the day after is settled, participants separate and each of them goes home. They re-group the next morning, first in smaller teams of 4–8 persons. These small groups come together that morning in one of the participants' houses. They also bring the clothes, masks, and bells that they are going to wear. Usually, the meeting time for any of these groups is 4:30 a.m. on December 31. There is also a pragmatic dimension in the small group formation. Participants help each other in sewing and tying certain artifacts on the costumes and masks (such as bells, belts or *bârneţele*[22]). In most cases, these preparations take from half an hour to one hour. Afterwards, the groups of mummers—already wearing their costumes—arrive, one by one, at the place they decided. They often light a fire and, around it, they warm up and drink a shot of strong beverage before walking together through the village. On some occasions, temperature went as low as –20°C; that was the case at the end of 2014. In such conditions, fire and drink are necessary to cheer spirits up. The gathering around the fire lasts around half an hour, until around 5:30, when the mummers' group starts parading around the village. To the very noisy bells, mummers add rattles—wooden boxes with a handle that produce a deafening noise when the handle is rotated.

At that early morning hour, not too many locals are on the streets, and the mummers' noisy group is 'welcomed' only by dogs barking and poultry cackling. But they say that this noisy parade at around 6 a.m. lets the householders know the New Year is getting closer. Another idea I have heard about this

Figure. 1.3. A group of mummers on the streets of Heleșteni village—December 31, 2010.

Photo credit: Alin Rus

mummers' parade is that it is meant to send bad spirits away and to announce that the New Year is better than the one about to finish. After about an hour of walking on the village streets, mummers gather in front of the house of one of them where they are served *țuică*²³ and wine, cookies and cold meats: *cârnați* (sausages), *salam* (salami), *caltaboș*²⁴ and *maioș*²⁵. This reinvigorating moment gives mummers the energy to continue their pageantry around the village for the coming hours.

Only after 7:30 a.m., does the more exciting and in the meantime tensioned part of this ritual stage begin, when villagers start to show up outside their homes. Those seen by the mummers on the village streets are being chased by the entire large group. If they catch a villager, they hit the person with their stitched scarves, dolls, brooms, or old handbags that they possess. The sequence is repeated even in some courtyards where householders just go out to watch the noisy group in the street.

I once saw three persons in a courtyard, an old couple of about 75–80, and their son, aged around 40–45. Three of the masked men left their group and entered the courtyard. They "furiously" ran to hit the young man, one attacker armed with a broom and the other with a stitched scarf. The third mummer grabbed him from behind and tried to keep the victim's hands still. In a matter of seconds, other 6–7 mummers entered the courtyard. They seemed to prefer the same victim—the younger man. Another mummer started hitting him with an old wooden handbag, while the others just pushed him against the wall. The victim tried to defend himself by running and pushing his aggressors. But his opposition increased the other ones' furor, while the hits became stronger and quicker. Nevertheless, the man kept laughing and continued to fight his attackers.

This happened during the first minute of the confrontation. Immediately after, the old couple was also attacked, after having tried to stop several mummers from hitting their son that hard. The woman was hit with the scarf on her back and bottom. The man was pushed and harassed, but managed to confront the attackers quite well, hitting them back. Despite his age, he even grabbed the horns of one of the mummers who was wearing a male goat mask, hitting him to the ground. But other two mummers counteracted, surrounding the old man from behind and making him free his "victim." This household "attack" was one of the first ones I witnessed, and I was, for sure, very shocked by the whole episode. What confused me most was the final attack on the old couple. At the first glance, the whole scene of the "attack" seemed extremely violent and long to me. Later, I realized the feeling of time expansion was probably caused by the effect violence had on my own mind.

Luckily enough I filmed the whole scene from beginning to end. While re-watching it, I could observe some details that I had not noticed when recording. When the mummers hit the old women with the scarves, I saw a decrease of energy right before the hit; they would not hit with all their force so that what first seemed menacing finally turned out to be a series of relatively light strokes. The same stood for the hits the old man had received. The only one seriously hit was the young one. Yet, despite the aggressiveness of the attack, I saw him laughing at the end, quite satisfied with the way he had defended himself. The faces of the two elders were just as smiling and content. More than that, after a few successive views, I realized that the whole scene lasted exactly two and a half minutes. Watching the recording with my friend, Florin, I received pieces of information that helped clarifying the whole episode. One such information was that the two mummers attacking the old couple more strongly were, in fact, their grandchildren, whereas those attacking the young one were his friends or neighbors. One of the statements I have heard most often was "Mummers attack especially those whom they know better." So, in this respect, the situation we are talking about seemed obvious.

Another statement I heard was "Mummers always attack only those villagers who do not mask themselves and especially the men who could normally join the group, but decided not to." Even though this idea seemed to be one of the functioning principles of the mummers' group, it was later contradicted by one of the scenes I watched during the same morning. Around 9:00 am, I saw a group of about eight-ten masked children, aged 6 to 10, who approached the large mummers' group that I had been following since early morning. Before merging into the group, I asked Florin, what the masked children do among the adult mummers. Florin explained, to my surprise, that the children's group joins the older mummers later and only for a few hours, usually between 9:00 a.m. and 11:30 a.m.

The moment was followed by yet another surprise, meant to contradict the principle I did mention above. One of the masked children shouted something at one of the older mummer. That mummer grabbed the child's hand and hit him to the ground. Shocking enough but, I observed, amusing for the ones watching, the child—not more than 10 years old—jumped to hit the older mummer back. The mummer managed to avoid and hit the child to the ground violently. The child hardly abstained from uttering a cuss and was about to be hit once more. But that happened when more mummers in his team called Elvis (that was the mummer's name) insistently and urged him to stay away from the kid.

I managed to record that scene, too, and I was proud to present it later to my hosts as a sign of victory and as a counterexample for the idea that "mummers only attack un-masked people." While watching the scene, everybody in the house smiled indulgently and declared: "The problem with Elvis is that he cannot be regarded as the other mummers in the *comună*. He had an accident when he was a child and because of that he doesn't judge clearly. Had things have been different for him, he would not have hit another mummer and especially a child." This statement made me reflect, and afterwards I started to interpret the mummers' actions in a less rigid and inflexible way.

There is clearly a pattern in the mummers' group actions, and each mummer's behavior was mostly following this general pattern. Such an example is the "attack" I witnessed in the first household, later seen again in other places and with slight variations. Usually, the victims were younger men, not older than 50, whereas girls and women were rather groped, both brutally and erotically. But the assaults would not last more than 2 or 3 minutes in these cases either, and the girls would also hit back, slapping, pushing, and sending the mummers away. I have even seen women defending themselves with flexible hazelnut or willow twigs, and thus hitting the shameless mummers.

Anyway, the fact that puzzled me most was that I have not seen any villager under assault that would run inside the house or somewhere else out of the mummers' reach. Even in cases of more agile men who were attacked and managed to escape the mummers, they later came back to them willingly only to be chased again and to restart the initial play. The attack, the confrontation and the defense proved to be also some of the principles of this complex ritual-play. Apparently, the fact of going out in the street or out of your house into the courtyard is a signal indicating that you are willing to join the ritual, unmasked, and implicitly to be chased afterwards. I am stating this because I saw people who stayed indoors with the door shut even when mummers passed by their houses.

Nevertheless, I have also seen situations where innocent victims who had not expressed any wish to join the ritual fell into the mummers' hands out of the blue. Such was the case of a man around 35 years old who, together with his children—a nine-year-old girl and a five-year-old boy—was obviously going somewhere in the village to solve a personal business. Caught in the middle of the group, he was surrounded by around five mummers who snapped him right away with handbags, scarves and twigs. The man tried to defend himself and also to calm down his crying little boy. When the boy started crying, the mummers stopped and two of them came closer, taking their masks off; upon seeing his neighbors, friends or maybe relatives, the little boy started smiling. As a "reward" for having to unmask themselves, the two pinched the boy's nose and this caused another round of crying. Unlike the boy, the girl fought the mummers courageously, pushing and hitting. As a result, they did not harass her too much; in my opinion, this happened because they admired her courage and determination. After such an experience, I concluded that, for the locals of Heleşteni, mummers are, in a way, just like the events in one's own life. In order to overcome them, one has to face them bravely. Sometimes, running away or trying to avoid them only increases their aggressiveness. Therefore, even a little child should learn this, even though the life lesson is harsh.

Another similar event reinforced my conclusion. Usually, the day of December 31 was a real blessing for me as an anthropologist, with tens of events one after another; but it was also a marathon. Not only was I supposed to wake up at 4 a.m. and go to sleep the following day around 3:30–4:00, but I also had to ask my hosts and the friends I had made in the village to ease my contact with certain groups joining various rituals or to help me drive around faster, on my way from one event to the next. December 31, 2011, was just the same. From 4:00 to 6:00 a.m., I joined the mummers' parade in Heleşteni. At 6:00 a.m. Florin drove me to Ruginoasa *comună*. Then he came back to Heleşteni to join the *Pantomimic Mummers'* ritual, and I was left alone to film the ritual of the *Mummers' Battle with Sticks*. Since the event was over at around 8:30 a.m., the only solution left was to call my hosts and ask them to pick me up from Dumbrăviţa, a village part of Ruginoasa *comună*, eleven kilometers away from their house in Oboroceni village. My intention was to go back to Heleşteni to watch the mummers' ritual that was still going on in the streets. Since my hosts were busy with various home tasks, they sent their elder daughter, Evelina, to help me. Back then, Evelina was a student at Iaşi University, and she had come home to celebrate the New Year with her family.

Approximately half an hour after my phone call, Evelina got to Ruginoasa where I had already walked to Rediu village, at the border with Heleşteni. From there, we drove to Heleşteni village where the pantomimic mummers were still parading in the streets. I must admit, embarrassingly, that I had never anticipated what was about to happen. Once we got to Heleşteni with the mayor's car, close to where the mummers used to perform their shows, we were immediately surrounded by them. They knew me and let me get out the car. As a cameraman and photographer, I was treated well within their company, especially since they knew that they would get pictures from me at the end of the ritual interval. This meant I was not the one they were looking for. But a young and beautiful girl like Evelina, a student from Iaşi city, seemed to be a great target for the group of masked people.

Some mummers ran to the car, opened its doors and prepared the girl's expulsion from inside, making use of their twisted scarves, their manly force and large number. That moment I understood I could no longer prevent them from getting what they wanted, so I decided to record the whole scene that I felt I was responsible and guilty of. In the beginning, mummers took Evelina out of the car, and then drove the car about 100 meters away. I saw that Evelina—who, I later learned, even as a child had not been afraid of mummers—managed to defend herself well, pushing and slapping them fiercefully, and surprisingly quick. After a few moments of specific harassment and playful fighting, including messing her hair completely, the mummers around her unmasked themselves laughing. As I later found out, most of them were ex-primary school colleagues or close friends.

That same day, in the afternoon, when Evelina told her parents what had happened, they were curious to see the recording. They were not too happy to see their car "stolen" and abandoned 100 meters away, as I noticed. But they did not mention anything and just watched. While seeing them watch their daughter being "attacked" and their car drove away by drunken young men, I was left with the feeling they looked as two hard-working householders who watched through the window their garden being destroyed by hail. Just as in the case of a natural calamity, the mummers seemed to be a nature force set free that nobody could oppose and that only left space for contemplation. Experienced householders, my hosts understood that complaining about mummers' deeds or trying to avoid them would only reinforce their coming back.

Moving further in my journey with the mummers in Heleşteni, I had the chance to observe many other events that filled the missing pieces in the overall image of mummers and their relations with the village universe. Another memorable situation I witnessed involved a householder around 30 years old who was fixing a carriage wheel in front of his courtyard's gate. A group of mummers attacked him right away and the man started to fight them. Although the attack and the fight seemed very brutal to me, from the very beginning there was an element that contradicted my first impression. For fixing the wheel, the man had a hammer in his hand the moment he was attacked. And, strangely enough, he did not drop the hammer during the fight. Nevertheless, even during the most violent moments of the fight, he did not even show the intention of using the tool against his aggressors. On the contrary, even when attacked from all sides, he would rather move his elbows to protect himself than to make use of the hammer; to me, it seemed the hammer was rather an obstacle for him than a tool that could be useful for self-defense.

An hour later, I observed a similar situation. A man aged between 40 and 45 was attacked by mummers in front of his courtyard, close to the busiest street in the comună. Four of the mummers left their group and attacked him, hitting him with handbags and scarves. Well, it was just in the middle of this stampede that a car at a high speed was coming from the opposite direction. Despite the blows he was getting, he warned the mummers attacking him about the car approaching from behind. So, the whole group went aside, by the fence, and the car passed by at a high speed. All these things enforced my conviction that these confrontations did not involve hatred or rancor. It was rather a playful fight that seemed tough, but was actually more like a game.

But the game had risky sides, too. The danger increased because of the large alcohol consumption. The village bars were already open at 7 a.m., and mummers preferred them for resting in front of a glass of wine or beer. Besides all the short breaks mummers took in the pubs, many bottles were carried around, and then passed on from one to another while the parade advanced in the village. The moments mummers stopped cars in the streets were particularly dangerous. More than once, I saw mummers stopping cars, with the drivers forced to wait for 10–15 minutes until the attackers got bored and let them go. Sometimes, these games turned more aggressive, meant to threaten especially the drivers coming from somewhere else, unaware of what was going on. A woman from a neighboring town came to visit some friends in Heleșteni, and told me how her car had been blocked on the side of the road by some "giant masked men" that balanced the car from all sides. "I was so scared I thought I'd have a heart attack. I would have given them anything just to leave me alone. But I had no money with me because I was coming from the hairdresser. But I believe I would have given them even 100 lei, had I had that money with me" (45 years old woman, guest of my host, Oboroceni village, January 2, 2015, field notes).

Indeed, the frontier between play and harassment became very fragile during the ritual. The driver of a bakery's car from the neighborhood declared that, on December 31, the company he was working for decided not to deliver bread to the villages where mummers were performing. The reason was that, some years before, one of the company's cars had been stopped on the street for about 15 minutes, and meanwhile its back door had opened. Thus, the driver lost about 100 loaves of bread until he realized what had happened. Probably this kind of events led to the creation of a superstition deeply rooted among locals. It says that if one died with the mask on, he would go straight to hell without any judgment. As anthropologist, I recognized the functionalist dimension of this belief, and especially its tight bond with all the episodes I had witnessed or heard involving mummers.

The large group of mummers wanders on the streets of the *comună* from 5:00 a.m. until around 11:30 a.m. After midday, mummers split because some of them, such as those aged between 18 and 21, often join the *Play of the Goat*, too. Many of the morning mummers also join the large gathering at 2:00 p.m. in front of the mayor's office. Getting there, some of them join the *Goat teams*, and sometimes even the *comoraș* of the *Goat team* is brought by a group of mummers on wooden poles carried on their shoulders, until in front of the *comună* hall. In the *comună* hall's park, mummers go on harassing passers-by, unlike the more temperate *Deer* or *Goat teams*. This time, the category most likely to be harassed was that of the young girls. They were chased in the park and, if caught, pushed to the ground and sometimes hit with snow. The girls were frequently scared by the rough noise mummers uttered. But they often managed to convince mummers to take pictures together or even dance with some of the mummers to the pipe and drum music the *Goat teams* were playing.

Another attraction in this part of the public ceremony in front of the town hall is the presentation of the pantomimic sketches of the mummers' groups. Various characters such as politicians in power, television stars, football players or singers are embodied as caricatures, ironized by means of masks, costumes and pantomimic sketches performed by mummers. Throughout this parade, the irony and humor—sometimes black humor—are easily noticed. In 2011, for example, a couple of mummers were dressed up as follows: one in the orange garments of the government party, wearing a mask representing a death demon; the other one in policeman garments with a toy-gun in hand. The inscription on the garments said: "I've peppered you!!!" This was an allusion to the country's president after winning the elections. The president had said that addressing the opposition but, subsequently, after the economic crisis began in 2008, his statement was undertaken by different opposition newspapers, showing that, by means of austerity measures, the ones governing have peppered the Romanian people. Or, this is exactly what the mummers group, by their behavior and clothes, wanted to express: with its anti-crisis measures, the government had peppered the Romanian people.

Some other time I saw a mummer who wore clothes typical to the electing campaign of the Democratic Party, thus expressing political membership.

Figure 1.4. Two mummers mocking the president of the country and the prime minister—December 31, 2010.
Photo credit: Alin Rus

His mask represented a clown's face. But the mouth was full of blood, as if the clown had just suck someone's blood. In all of these cases, meanings and interpretations are multiple, but the critique of government is very obvious, being represented as a vampire for the Romanian people. I also saw mummers which had their clothes printed with the name of a character in the government panoply—for example, the name of the prime minister or of the president—while their mask represented a werewolf or Frankenstein, probably trying to unveil the real essence of these two characters. In other cases, criticism towards the political power was subtler. For example, a mummer dressed up as a bride, but wore a pillow under his dress, over the belly, suggesting pregnancy. At the same time, the character simulated sickness. Being asked if (s)he wanted to go outside—informally, that refers to going to the toilet -, (s)he would answer: "Yes, yes, I really want outside, I really want to go outside (*only to add after a long break*) . . . but outside the country!" In this case, the critique was also subtle, suggesting that life in Romania is so unbearable that one must leave the country to live abroad.

After this public performance that usually takes about two hours, the large group of mummers splits and, from this moment on, they are supposed to walk around the village in groups of 5–8 members, each visiting householders separately. This sequence in the ritual shall be private from now on, with all sketches taking part in the householders' houses and courtyards. The division of the large group of mummers is based on two pragmatic criteria: first, a family could not welcome more than 8–10 people simultaneously in their house; second, mummers' groups do not go caroling to each house, but only to the places they prefer. So, every group of mummers usually visits only their own relatives, friends and neighbors, without stopping in every house that could actually welcome them, as the *Goat* and *Deer teams* do.

HOUSE-VISIT, SPEECH DISGUISE AND GUESSING-GAME

Whereas the *Goat* or *Deer team* goes immediately to the households in the village to carol village householders, mummers act differently. *Pantomimic mummers* generally start their visits in the village only when evening comes and, especially, when night falls. Therefore, their image is associated to gloominess and night darkness. The symbolic parallel between mummers' behavior and the dark of the night is more than obvious.

Another visible distinction between *Pantomimic Mummers'* teams and those of the *Goat* and the *Deer* is the duration of each visit. *Deer* and *Goat teams* are very quick when visiting and do not spend more than 6–20 minutes at each house, but pantomimic mummers stay in a household sometimes more than half an hour. Of all the teams caroling in the Heleșteni comună during winter holidays, mummers are the only ones that do not take any money from people. They are happy with the householders' hospitality and generosity in terms of food, sweets, and drinks. When it comes to *Deer* and *Goat* rituals, eating and drinking is exactly the stage that can be absent. These teams are rather interested in getting money than in spending too much time with the villagers—and especially in houses where there are no young girls and thus flirting and courting are not possible. Meanwhile, since *Pantomimic Mummers* do not take any money, it becomes clear that their motivation is different and has to do more with the mutual relations in the village than with the immediate financial benefit. Therefore, during one of my discussions with my hosts and their friends about "the most traditional ritual of all those performed for the New Year," many argued that is the *Pantomimic Mummers* precisely because householders do not pay money to mummers, and their relationship is an exchange of goods. Mummers wish the householders wealth and abundance; meanwhile, householders offer food and drinks back.

Generally, the script depicting the mummers' behavior in the household follows an already established pattern, usually with five or six stages. In an amazing coincidence, these stages of the mummers' actions in all the three villages of Heleșteni comună (Oboroceni, Hărmăneasa and Heleșteni) resembles perfectly what the American folklorist Herbert Halpert called *informal visits* or *house-visist* upon describing the mummers' actions in the Canadian island of Newfoundland.

Below I present the behavioral pattern described by Halpert and I indicate only the slight differences between the actions of the mummers in Newfoundland and those of the mummers in Heleșteni.

The salient features of the house-visit are as follows:

a. "The visitors are an informal group of varying composition [This feature coincides completely with the mummers in Heleșteni who, unlike the *Deer* and *Goat* ritual, also include women and older people, sometimes even older than 50 n.a.].

b. Members of the group attempt complete disguise. This involves (1) disguise of face and body with varying degrees of elaboration, and with sex-reversal (the man-woman figures) as a frequent pattern; (2) disguise of gestures and body movement; (3) disguise of voice, especially, though not invariably, the use of ingressive speech [All these elements are present in the case of the Heleșteni mummers, with just few outfit differences. While in Newfoundland the dominating mask is that of a fisherman, in Heleșteni we have the so-called beautiful mummers, with multicolored costumes and masks decorated with a lot of beads. People disguised in the opposite sex are just as frequent as in Newfoundland n.a.].

b1) [One or more people in the mummers' group utter an *urătură*[26] before the householder opens the door. This stage only appears in the case of the Heleșteni mummers and I have not found it mentioned in any of the studies on the Newfoundland mummers n.a.].

c. The behavior of the disguised visitors tends to be uninhibited and the reverse of normal. On request, however, they may entertain by singing, playing musical instruments, and dancing [The uninhibited behavior of the mummers in Heleșteni is just as notorious as that of their Newfoundland homologues, and it consists especially of hitting the household's head—the man—with handbags, twisted scarves and plastic cables, and hugging by force, fondling and harassing women and girls. The difference between them and the Newfoundland mummers is that in Heleșteni mummers do not have musical instruments. I have only once seen an accordion, but this is a rare occurrence among mummers in the locality n.a.].

d. The hosts attempt to penetrate the disguises by a form of guessing-game, sometimes accompanied by roughness; unmasking by the visitors usually, though not invariably, follows successful identification [This stage is identical to the one I saw at the Heleșteni mummers. The act of pushing the hosts around by hitting, poking and brutally hugging, with a background of rough sounds and short statements produced by the mummers, and with short pantomimes performed simultaneously, made me call these teams *Pantomimic Mummers* n.a.].

e. The unmasked figures return to their normal social roles and are usually offered, and accept, food and drink. Unlike the pattern of many of the English *collectors*[27], however, no part of this offering is taken away [This stage also coincides perfectly with the behavior mummers adopt in the end in the households they visit in Heleșteni n.a.] (Halpert 1969:37–38)."

The poignant thing is that, after describing the typology, the American folklorist moves on to generalizing and stating the Newfoundland mummers' singularity: "It might, theoretically, be posited that the house-visit is a peculiar Newfoundland development, originating perhaps in special local conditions and spreading internally through the movement of population or through contact in the seal hunt, the Labrador fishery, or logging" (Halpert 1969:38). Nevertheless, his research experience and his knowledgeable folklorist intuition save him in the last moment from a hasty generalization; therefore, he adds: "But against such an assumption is the fact that many parts of the Island, and Labrador, were settled at different times and by different groups who often came directly from Great Britain and Ireland. . . . An origin in the British Isles is therefore to be assumed despite the lack of detailed reports from England itself" (Halpert 1969:38).

According to the pre-established ritual of Heleșteni's mummers, their house-visits start on the late evening of December 31, and last until 5 a.m. the next morning. The same program is respected for January 1 and 2. Generally, there is a clear distinction between the mummers' public and private manifestations. This separation is defined by a series of clear-cut time sequences, but especially by the place where a particular ritual sequence occurs: either on the public space of the communal streets or in the private realm of a village household.

On January 2, the last public appearance of the mummers takes place within a festive gathering similar to the one happening in front of the *comună* hall on December 31. This meeting is in Oboroceni village, at the intersection of the 208G county road and the 99 communal road coming from Hărmăneasa village. This is the spot where the routes coming from all the four villages of Heleșteni converge, being a real crossroad. Only a few tens of meters away, a bar was opened, and this event made the area more appealing to mummers. From 2 p.m. to 4 p.m., the large mummers' group reaches the place to present their sketches.

Figure 1.5. A group of pantomimic mummers in their house-visit stage—January 1, 2011.

Photo credit: Alin Rus

Just as in front of the town hall, mummers mock various aspects of society, from greed and vanity to TV addiction, excessive bashfulness, etc. Stock characters in such contexts—like the prostitute, the transvestite—are present, next to monstrous figures like demons, Frankenstein, and hangmen. Characters popular in national or international politics are also present. In the photos I had collected from villagers or taken by me throughout the years, I have managed to identify mummers impersonating dictators such as Saddam Hussein and Ceaușescu, terrorists like Osama bin Laden, but also important figures of the December 1989 Revolution like the priest László Tőkés. This time, mummers wearing beautiful masks decorated with beads are present, too. Most often, they perform sketches in groups of two or three, or even on their own. For instance, I once saw two mummers dragging a TV wherever they went, and showing to the locals watching that it was impossible to separate from the device. Another year, I even saw a mummer performing a fragment of a folk tale. The character was playing *Păcală* and carried a door on his back. This scene—with *Păcală* carrying the door—had been included in a screen adaptation of a novel having as a main character *Păcală*. The comedy's success went well beyond the 1974, when the movie was produced, and it led to the movie being broadcasted more times by national television channels even in recent years.

Sometimes, this meeting also includes larger sketches. The most complex sketch I observed took place on January 2, 2014. It was complex because it "staged" and, in fact, satirized an entire funeral. But the priest was an ugly and ulcerous demon, stepping in front of the cortege, rhythmically moving his censer. He was accompanied by a cantor wearing a skull mask on his head— a popular death depiction—strongly contrasting with his bright red hat. The cross bearer came after, wearing a demon mask, too, and a white petticoat. The cross was made out of two twisted branches and the icon usually fixed in its middle had been replaced by a photo of a couple engaged in an intercourse. Behind came wailing old women (*bocitoare*) wearing black skirts, who were actually men in disguise, their face covered with demon masks, too. The funeral cortege produced an unbearable noise, mimicking the wailing and crying of the dead man's relatives. Inside the coffin, improvised out of fir planks, the dead lied dressed in his best suit. But, according to the mask on his head, it was Dracula himself. On the "Eternal remembrance" slogan written on the coffin, pornographic photos had been stuck. The "funerary" cortege moved until reaching the crossroad where they met other masked persons, next to a mainly unmasked group of villager-viewers. There, the funerary cortege started dancing lively and, at this point, according to his own nature, Dracula went out of the coffin and became the most important dancer, while villagers took photos with him. This structure somehow reminds us of classic Ion Creangă's short story *Ivan Turbincă*, a story begotten on Moldavian land, too. In this satire about death and its consequences, Creangă invents Ivan, a character who takes advantage of the power God had given him, mocks Death—making it eat nothing but trees—and, in the end, locks Death inside the coffin by inversing their roles (Creangă [1880] 2010).

Attacks on the villagers watching the performance happen here, too. Mummers harass especially unmasked youngsters, either male or female. In the meantime, taking advantage of the geostrategic location—a road with cars passing by—mummers stop cars in the street and bother the drivers, showing them obscene signs through the windows and coming with their grinning masks closer to the car's windows. All these actions are even more intense in case young girls are inside the car, and mummers welcome them with throaty sounds meant to scare them. Some mummers even ask for money from the drivers and, in some cases, they are given 1–2 lei (50 cents). However, the play's main purpose is not the money, but the desire to have fun by mocking certain aspects of the global and national society, as well as of the local village community.

It should be mentioned that the masquerade in Oboroceni ends the proper cycle of the mummers' public performances in the comună of Heleșteni. The *Goat* and *Deer teams* stop caroling at the villagers' houses after January 1. The only teams that still walk around the villages of the comună that evening are the smaller *Pantomimic Mummers'* groups in their private visits at various householders. But they are also going to end their wander around 3 or 4 a.m. on January 3.

PANTOMIMIC MUMMERS: HYPOTHESES, THEORIES, AND INTERPRETATIONS—MUMMERS VIOLENCE

All the events described throughout this chapter lay out an extremely complex picture of the expressions that mummers' plays embody. This landscape can be examined from several perspectives. Of these, the ones that seemed most obvious to me were violence, sexuality, and play. In the following pages I will analyze each of them in turn.

One of the most striking aspects of the mummers' actions in Heleșteni, which is also very conspicuous, is physical violence. It created a very complex entanglement of situations and cultural expressions whose analysis is sometimes difficult to cope with. Physical violence generally afflicts the bodies, the psychics and the socio-cultural order, Rubben and Suarez tell us in an article dealing with the topic of violence (Robben and Suarez-Orozco 2000). When I had the opportunity to analyze closely the traces mummers' violence leaves on individuals and on their culture, I saw the embodiment of the principle quoted above. More than once, bringing the mummers' wandering in the comună to discussion, my interviewees showed me bruises on their arms and legs, all caused during the confrontation with the mummers. One of the images that stayed in my mind was that of a young woman called Roxana who showed me about three bruises the size of a chicken egg on both her arms. Other people I talked to showed me serious signs on their thighs and back. All these were still present in the people's psyche even years after. A teenager recalled how, a few years before, when caroling with a team of *Small Horses (Căiuții)*, he and all his team colleagues had been chased by a group of drunken mummers, and managed to save themselves due to an older local who took all of the children inside his house. Other locals told me stories that had happened years before, when drunken mummers pushed around people in the village so hard that they broke the victims' arms and ribs. The stories must have had a traumatic effect on the interviewees' psyche, since even 20 years later they could still give detailed accounts about those events.

Nevertheless, the most visible effect these acts of violence had on the socio-cultural order was noticeable when I heard people's talks during the holidays, around a family table abundantly covered with food, where relatives, friends and neighbors had gathered. Having the chance to join these discussions a few times, I always tried to check one of my initial hypotheses.

One of these hypotheses was that the mummers' increased violence could have been caused by the economic and political transformations of the capitalist society, the harsh economic competition and perhaps even the political tensions in the country and in the region following the fall of Communism. My initial questions were seeking information for a comparison between the intensity of mummers' violent acts now and in the past (during communist times or even before). In trying this, I got the most ambiguous and confusing data, and in the end, I had no clue on the rise or decline of violence intensity in postsocialist times.

A relevant example for the ambiguous state of my initial hypotheses was provided during an interview taken on January 3, 2015, inside the house of one of my most important collaborators in Oboroceni. Mitică and Roxana, a young couple around age 30 started complaining about mummers' violence and the bruises they got during the holidays. The next moment, Mitică decreed, and Roxana supported his statement, that these very brutal acts of violence started only in recent years. But, in order to confirm his idea, I asked his brother's opinion, since that one was eight years older. The brother, who had remained silent until that moment, contradicted his sibling passionately, stating that when he had been younger, violence was even fiercer.

I recorded the same polemical discussion on January 2, 2015, in my hosts' house in Oboroceni. This time, eight people sat around the table and each tried to express his or her opinion on the topic. Yet, the discussions did not seem to bring any decisive argument in favor of any of the hypotheses regarding the increase of violence in recent years. However, suddenly, the mayor himself brought about a case study and a remark that everybody agreed with. "This trend of tough violence was brought to us by Lică Bordea, our neighbor here, down the valley." "Yeah, and ever since then he does not dare to go outside his house during holidays because he's afraid of mummers, for all this has turned against him," a guest of the mayor confirmed. "Yeah, that's true!," agreed Mrs. Doina, the mayor's wife, too.

The remark made during the discussion switch the focus of my attention not only on the mummers' group in general, but also on certain individuals, their behavior and gestures. With this aim in mind, I started analyzing more conscientiously the videos I had taken since the beginning of my research, and, identifying the mummers with the help of my friend Florin, I discovered that tougher acts of violence were committed by impulsive people in real life too, who were inclined to find brutal solutions even to daily life issues. The same people were the ones wearing the most extravagant clothes, with phalluses attached and sometimes with prostitutes' or transvestites' daring outfits. The entire carnivalesque atmosphere of the closing year looked like an embodiment of Milan Kundera's maxim in his *The Book of Laughter and*

Forgetting: "life among his kind is nothing other than a battle to seize the ear [and the eyes I would add] of others" (Kundera 1999).

But not all mummers used the same methods to mesmerize the eyes and ears of the others. While some used mostly violence and sexual representations, many others used their intelligence to create humorous sketches that brought fun and cheerfulness on people's faces. In fact, these were the acts the householders appreciated most, and the authors were always welcomed with smiles and satisfaction. Despite this, it seems nobody actually tried to prevent brutal acts like the ones already described; as a result, some of the community members used the extra freedom the community granted them during holidays to express their moral and psychological traits, marked by impulsiveness and basic instincts that involved brutal solutions to any potential conflict.

MUMMERS AND SEXUALITY

The violence accompanying all these forms and manifestations of the mummers' plays has almost always been doubled by sexuality. During my field research, from 2009 to 2017, I have had the chance to observe many expressions of sexuality in the pantomimic mummers' plays. Either involving the image of the transvestite, the homosexual or the prostitute, the phalluses hidden underneath the clothes, porn magazines pages stuck ostentatiously on clothes, various other artifacts (such as clubs, crosses) or simple slogans with sexual content usually painted on garments, these representations were ever-present in the mummers' group on December 31—January 2. The immediate tendency is to link these representations to concepts such as masculinity, homoeroticism or homophobia, and to parallel them to postsocialist transformations like unemployment, labor migration and the emancipation following the fall of Communism (Creed 2011:70–104). But, despite this strong temptation, the careful observation of mummers and of the context of their disguise, and especially the comparative study of more sources relating to mummers, convinced me that the theme of sexual transgression shows continuity with past ritual practice not a break from it.

I reached this conclusion especially after examining ancient sources about mummers. du Cange, for instance, in his *Glossarium mediae et infimae latinitatis*, when analyzing medieval sources, mentions transvestites during some peasant holidays centuries ago: "Pirminius in Excerptis de sacris Scripturis: Cervulos et vehiculas (leg. vetulas, aut veticulas[28]) in quadragesima vel aliud tempus nolite ambulare. Viri vestes femineas, feminæ vestes viriles in ipsis Kalendis, vel in alia lusa[29] quamplurima nolite vestire (see Appendix I)."[30]

In this case, not even the modern concepts of transsexual and transvestite, already charged by modern society with very different connotations, would prove useful regarding the actual events in these rural societies that possess a rich history of the carnivalesque and the transvestite. Bakhtin observed all these and developed a theory regarding the apparently bizarre behavior of peasants during various holidays, and especially during winter carnivalesque gatherings. He noticed that sexuality, many times accompanied by obscenity, mocking and deriding are constituent parts of the carnivalesque humor that, in turn, is an integral part of folk humor (Bakhtin 1984).

I reached similar conclusions when I analyzed the context of the mummers' dressing. While some of them care a lot about their garments and masks, designing them passionately long before, others decide to join the mummers' parades only one or two days (sometimes even a few hours) before the event begins. Usually, they are the ones adopting transvestite or prostitute's outfits, since its creation would be much more accessible and easier. In 2012, I accepted a group of friends' invitation to such an event in Heleșteni, and I had taken the decision just a few hours prior to the ritual. Our group had five men and three young women. While girls wore beautiful costumes and masks decorated with beads, three of the young men dressed as transvestites, putting on only some old-fashioned female garments and nylons found among the old clothes of their opposite-sex relatives. Without any such clothes, I took an old blanket I had found abandoned among my host's old stuff, covered myself with it, and added a Halloween mask. This type of disguise, as well as cross-dressing that the other men in our group adopted, seemed extremely natural in the carnivalesque atmosphere of the winter holidays.

I reached this conclusion not only by analyzing the way the young men in my group behaved, but also by paying attention to the photos taken during Communism (a period characterized by much more bashfulness than postsocialism) or even before, when figures such as the transvestite, the prostitute and the homosexual were almost always there inside the mummers' groups. Therefore, the most convincing conclusion I reached was that sexual representations in end of year carnivalesque expressions in Heleșteni embodied a challenge to the rigid and less tolerant norms of a peasant community that did not allow many digressions throughout the year.

Despite this preliminary conclusion, I could not help thinking about the mummers' physical violence and about the visual aggression staged by means of the explicit sexual representations: what was the meaning in hurting or offending somebody who was about to become your host and to welcome you to their home? My assumption was that, apart from the negative side involved by all the physical and visual violence, there had to be something positive in all this. Otherwise, the community would have eliminated these acts during the carnivalesque manifestations when a lot of freedom was allowed, but not all types of acts were acceptable. The positive aspect is that all these mani-festations are part of a play designed to temporarily relax the rigid rules of the rural community.

MUMMERS AND PLAY

The big question I asked regarding all the plethora of mummers' manifesta-tions was: what is the positive element that makes all these manifestations possible? What is the engine behind this whole gear of cultural forms and expressions? I found just one answer: the play. Beyond the violence of the mummers and beyond their sexualized manifestations, beyond the exuber-ance and even madness, there is something that connects them all and at the same time makes them possible. This is the play and the story that follows, the story about those plays. This story is always an interesting one, even if not necessarily positive. But it is an experience that can be remembered, and which remains as an anchor in the mind of the individual, an anchor that can be linked later to other events of the year and which can be a landmark on the individual and collective memory's map.

In one of his recent books about play, Stuart Brown asks a deep question, strongly related to my research findings: "what the world would be like without play?" He comes with a straightforward answer: "It's not just an absence of games or sports. Life without play is a life without books, without movies, art, music, jokes, dramatic stories. Imagine a world with no flirting, no day-dreaming, no comedy, no irony. Such a world would be a pretty grim place to live. In a broad sense, play is what lifts people out of the mundane" (Brown and Vaughan 2010:6).

Thus, for a small and relatively isolated community, the mummers' ritual offered the chance to mark dates in the calendar that would otherwise have passed unnoticed, just as any other day, with the monotony of the agricultural labor rhythms, dictated by seasons and their specific activities. Mummers opened a window to a world that was normally censured by the strict rules of peasant society in day-to-day life. Because of this particular reason, mummers represented a sort of anchor for the ontological security (Giddens 1991) of individuals and a good remedy for fighting existential anxiety in agricultural societies where the events in the individual's social life followed a sometimes dreary regularity. Within this picture, one did not need something that would reinforce daily routines, but rather a series of memorable landmarks where routine would melt away together with the depression and the anxieties of a life that is too formal. As Anthony Giddens—the sociologist who coined the term "ontological security"—said: "In premodern contexts, tradition has a key role in articulating action and ontological frameworks; tradition offers an

organizing medium of social life specifically geared to ontological precepts"
(Idem 1991:48). Here, we are talking about a tradition where the play and the
story are central elements.

Somehow, just as in fairy tales where monsters and demons often show
up, mummers and their world are the foundation of the process preparing
the inhabitants of these small societies based on agrarian rhythms for the
confrontation with the challenges, tensions, and dangers of life. If in the
case of mummers, this fact has not yet been theorized, for fairy tales this
approaches exist and one of these theories belongs to Bruno Bettelheim,
an author from psychoanalytical school, who thought the world in fairy
tales prepared children for life much better than cartoons or modern cinema
(Heisig 1977).[31] Moreover, Karl Groos, one of the early theorists of play
argue that play is a useful tool that help humans, and especially children, as
they are a preparation for real life (Groos and Baldwin [1899] 2012). More
recently Stuart Brown stated: "Of all animal species, humans are the biggest
players of all. We are built to play and built through play. When we play, we
are engaged in the purest expression of our humanity, the truest expression
of our individuality. Is it any wonder that often the times we feel most alive,
those that make up our best memories, are moments of play?" (Brown and
Vaughan 2010:6)

On the one hand *Pantomimic Mummers* express simultaneously humans'
ugly face, violence, callousness, brutality, shamelessness, uncontrolled lust,
on the other hand they embody humans' peaceful side, their tendency to dialogue, humor, communication, empathy, exchange of ideas and mutualness.
All of these elements are elements of play and they are present especially in
the mummers' escapades inside the households, during the ritual sequence
knows as *house-visit*, when they are violent, brutal and shameless, only to
become peaceful, communicative and friendly afterwards. Therefore, mummers present both sides of human society—the negative and the positive—
and these two are staged during a play that offers the premises for preparing
individuals to face real events during the whole year. And, maybe not accidentally, children were always allowed to see the mummers' house-visits,
though sometimes they were utterly terrified by what they saw.

My supposition that mummers are directly connected to the individuals'
ontological security and mental stability was reinforced by an interview I
conducted on June 12, 2012, outside the winter holiday season. The family I
visited had three members—the grandparents and a grandson. At first, I had
been interested in the grandson's own experience as seasonal migrant to Italy.
Alin was a 20-year-old man who, just like many other people of his age, had
left his native village and went to try his luck in a country where construction workers are paid better. Health issues made him come back to the village
sooner than he had expected. Right after revealing this piece of information,

Alin started telling me about his work in the village, in agriculture, making his grandparents interrupt and reorient the discussion towards family and family issues. Thus, I found out that the son of the two elders had passed away 18 years ago, on December 1994, killed by a sudden severe illness right before winter holidays. Shortly after, given the difficult financial situation, Alin's mother decided to leave her four-year-old son in the grandparents' care. She emigrated to Italy and settled there.

After this sad story, the grandparents and their grandson talked to me about the pain and their immense *dor*[32] after the untimely death of their son. In this context, they told me about their son's passion for the mummers' rituals and for designing the masks. Thus, I was able to find out that, only two weeks before his death, Alin's father managed to finish his last mask—the one he would no longer be able to wear that year. After this startling disclosure, their faces lit up instantly and, as in front of a miracle, they took a carefully packed mask out of a plastic bag, where it had been preserved in a corner of the room. "This mask is what reminds me best of my father," Alin stated. Then he put the mask on the bed next to him and left it there until the end of our talk. Before leaving this family's house, I offered to take some photos of them. That moment, Alin naturally embraced the mask his father had made, as

Figure 1.6. Alin and his grandparents together with the mask made by his father—June 12, 2012.

Photo credit: Alin Rus

if it were a symbolic representation of his untimely gone father. This way, my photo had brought all the family members together, next to the precious mask.

I collected a similar story from Mihăiță, a young migrant. He described to me passionately his bitter experience as seasonal worker in constructions, in a town close to Craiova, in Southern Romania. For more than three months, he had been working there to build a road. Workers were accommodated in horrible conditions, in unhealthy barracks, being paid back only two meals each day, with the money promised to be given "the following month." After three months of hard work, Mihăiță knew that the payment promise was just a story meant to deceive the workers. So, despite all the effort, he decided to go back home to Heleșteni penniless. "While traveling to Iași by train, all I had in mind were images of mummers and holidays in the village," Mihăiță confessed to me. "But do you enjoy walking with mummers?," I asked him. "Oh, I'm crazy about them!," he replied. If during the entire interview I could notice the grimace on his face, according to the insults he threw at his "bosses who took advantage of the workers," upon hearing my question his face was illuminated suddenly and a large smile expressed his deep joy, as well as his profound relation with the ritual.

These both examples embody perfectly another observation made by Stuart Brown: "I don't think it is too much to say that play can save your life. It certainly has salvaged mine. Life without play is a grinding, mechanical existence organized around doing the things necessary for survival. Play is the stick that stirs the drink. It is the basis of all art, games, books, sports, movies, fashion, fun, and wonder—in short, the basis of what we think of as civilization. Play is the vital essence of life. It is what makes life lively" (Brown and Vaughan 2010:11)

In both cases presented above, mummers offered my interviewees a sense of continuity and stability, inside an increasingly stressful postsocialist universe where greed, deceit, betrayal, and untimely death were more and more frequent.

CONCLUSION

In his introduction to *Christmas Mumming in Newfoundland*, Herbert Halpert and G.M. Story made the following observation: "[I]n many ways we know less about the small fishing settlements of Newfoundland than about portions of East and West Africa, which have for many years been subjected to intensive sociological and anthropological study" (Halpert and Story 1969:4). Almost five decades after this statement was expressed, we could say the same thing about the mummers from Romania whose complex rituals have been ignored for decades by Western anthropology, and little studied by local

Folkloristics. In addition, the studies that aimed to understand the social life of peasants, the economy and history of their community through the lenses of rural plays are totally absent.

With this chapter, I tried to fill this gap in the anthropological literature and, in the meantime, to research the mummers in relation with its most passionate performers—the peasants. I conceived my study on rural plays relating it to the new transformations of peasant society under the influence of industrialization and under the influence of global capitalism. Paradoxically, "[o]ver the past two decades, peasants have been slipping from the political and academic gaze" (Bryceson 2000b), despite that an incredible opportunity has just shown up—the study of the disintegration of this peasant mode of production (Berdichewsky 1979), influenced by the modernization of national states and the globalization of world economy. In one of his studies the sociologist Pierre Bourdieu talked about the conditions that contributed to the openness of relatively close peasant communities, and used an expressive metaphor to characterize their communities transition "from the closed world to the infinite universe" (Bourdieu 2008:174). That was precisely the opportunity I tried to respond to, by unfolding a brief history of north-eastern Romanian rural plays, from when they were just community rituals to the first decade of the 21st century when they became part of the globalized world.

Following the history of folk plays in Heleşteni over a few decades, I have tried to capture the tension between the values and principles of the rural world and those of the modern (globalized, globalizing, capitalist) society. This tension expresses the disintegration of a way of living, together with the values and principles that used to form the tissue of a fascinating culture. I am talking about cultural micro-ecosystems—the village communities, where all the dramas, tensions, anguishes, and joys of humans usually happened. And folk plays belonged to these cultural micro-ecosystems where local rules and traditions mattered more for the individual's life than the big narratives and events of European history's that many historians considered crucial for the continent's fate. This is the reason why, as I have shown throughout this chapter, winter mummers were not only ways of entertainment, but also means of responding to inevitable problems in the local rural community, with the use of play and based on the rules of local rural traditions.

One of the main ideas of this chapter was that in rural communities such as Heleşteni, which, due to its isolation, has been less affected by the path of changes produced by modernity, we can see as through a window to a past of peasant communities. There we can discover another human relationship with the community, a relationship in which play is a major component that involves strong links between values, beliefs, morals and rules. Or, after analyzing the material in this chapter, I understood some of the main functions of the play: to create connections between individuals and their inner world, between individuals and members of the community in which he/she lives, between groups within the community, between the values of a community and the narratives that make them possible, between the rules of the community and the moments of possible transgression of them, between principles, values and cultural behaviors, between violence, sexuality, friendship and camaraderie. Thus, I try to open a new path of research: by understanding the plays of a rural community to shed light on the history of that community.

Unfortunately, anthropology and folklore studies have almost completely ignored the profound relation between peasants and their plays as well as between their plays and the historical geography of their own locality. Folklore especially was focused mainly on classifying peasant rituals and customs than analyzing their role for rural communities' social, economic, and aesthetic life in the local context. A demonstration similar in many respects to my approach was done by the historian Graham Robb in the case of the French peasants whose sense of identity was strongly connected to their own settlement and geographic space; this is also the origin of the incredible cultural diversity of rural France, next to the feelings of local patriotism that are identifiable in almost all rural localities:

> Local identity consisted, ultimately, not in ethnic origins, but in the fact that a community happened to be where it was rather than somewhere else (Robb 2008:49) . . . Away from the noisy, carnage-strewn main roads of French history, the picture is unexpectedly calm. It suggests compromise and tolerance rather than hatred and fear: priests led pilgrimages to Gallo-Roman shrines, parishioners performed pagan rites under the eyes of the village priest. (Robb 2008:136)

The statements about Robb's French peasants are valid for Romanian peasants too. For a long time, Romanian peasants had been living in close relationship with the geography of their own place, rather in a natural economy than strongly connected to the important events in national and European history. In these monadic worlds (Leibniz 1999[1714]), mumming represented ways of articulating human problems—from entertainment production to matchmaking and love relationships, from irony towards certain aspects of society to the ritual regularization of conflicts and animosities within the community. Once these small rural communities were integrated into the "infinite universe" of the global world, rural plays stopped being what they used to be, and their ability to respond to certain problems within the rural community slowly disintegrated, being undertaken by state institutions. The state institutions have not only taken the roles of the dying folk plays, but have also provided the premises for safeguarding them in a world where they were increasingly rare. But, I am going to develop this idea in the last chapter of the book.

NOTES

1. Comună/Comune [plural]—An administrative-territorial unit on the territory of Romania, usually comprising 3–6 villages under the jurisdiction of the same mayoralty. Heleşteni comună comprises four villages: Hărmăneasa, Heleşteni, Oboroceni, and Movileni.

2. Revista de Literatură Universală Secolul 20, No. 200/1989.

3. This does not mean that the study of the rural plays could not go further in time, especially in other localities much older than Heleşteni, and especially by using other methods. Such an attempt was made by historian John Clark in his 2015 study *"Playing the Stag" in Medieval Middlesex? A perforated antler from South Mimms Castle - parallels and possibilities*. In this article, Clark highlights, in addition to the documents attesting the *Deer's Dance* in England, certain archaeological findings of ancient artifacts, for example, few perforated deer horns that could have been part of a deer mask used during deer-like rituals (Clark 2015). However, in the context of the research and methodology chosen in the present research, the first historical evidence to discuss the mummers' plays in the county of Iaşi are certain historical documents that do not go beyond the first decades of the 17th century.

4. This ritual is more complex than the short version described by Welling and, at least in its variants investigated after the end of the 19th century, it also comprised the goat's hunting, its ritual killing and the following weep, ending with the ritual burial of the mask—in this case the goat's head. The custom of killing, weeping and burying the goat is nowadays gone in the region of Moldova, but it can still be found in Transylvania where a variant very close to the one the Swedish ambassador described was even documented and filmed in the early 2000s by the ethnologist Bogdan Neagota in the villages of Romos, Romoşel and Vaidei, close to Orăştie town, in Hunedoara county.

5. "Avem şi pentru farmeci la Dumnezău ură/Şi ce omul să schimbă dintr-a sa făptură,/Cu ghiduşuri, cu ţurcă, cuci şi cu geamale,/Tras în vale ş-alte din păgâni tocmeale" (Dosoftei 1974 [1673]).

6. Cuckoo's Day is a traditional rural custom commonly practiced in Romanian villages close to the Danube before Passover, during the Shrove Tuesday. During the ritual, young men and women dressed as male and female cuckoos, wearing huge, absolutely impressive masks, are tapped by villagers on the shoulder in order to "chase the evil away" or "to be healthy throughout the year." The play is described by various old church documents as a "devilish inquisitiveness" perhaps because of the huge and ugly masks and the carnival-like show of the masked characters walking round and round the village. For references, see Mircea Vulcănescu (1970: 173–176). Today the custom is almost extinct, being practiced only in few villages in Southern Romania, most notably in Brăneşti, Ilfov County.

7. "*Geamalele*" (monster-puppets) are huge two-headed monstrous puppets, carried on the shoulders by the performers of the play. In time, these puppets have been described in various literary works, a brief presentation being made in an article.

8. *Trasul în Vale* (bathing into a creek down the valley) is a traditional custom that is most frequently encountered in Moldova. It was first mentioned in documents

dating back to the 17th century. During the night of the Resurrection, right before dawn, girls used to go and bathe into a creek in their village, while reciting an incantation that was supposed to lure the village lads into falling in love with them, and to assure them a lucky love life.

9. In England, the play where the ritual mask named *hobby-horse* appears is very different morphologically from those of all the other countries mentioned in the list. Still, the ritual mask bears an incredible resemblance to those in the countries mentioned above.

10. A better translation of this term would be *The Dance of the Goat*. However, the theatrical component of this custom made me adopt the name of the *Play of the Goat* for this rural ritual.

11. In the village of Movileni—the smallest village of Heleșteni comună, the *Play of the Goat*, quite different from the one in the neighboring villages, became extinct around the 1950–1960s.

12. *Mascoidă*—a small mask kept in hand and maneuvered by the person holding it in front of the viewers.

13. *"Da io mă duc mandra mă duc, în cătane nu la plug"/"Io mă duc mândra-n cătane, tu rămâi și spală haine"/"Ca io de aici mă duc cu dor, cum mere luna prin nor"/"Io de aici mă duc cu jele, cum mere luna prin stele."* "Yes, I'm going, honey, I'm going, not to the plow but to the army"/"I'm going to the army, honey, while you stay and wash our clothes"/"I'm leaving here with longing, like the moon through the cloud"/"I'm leaving here with longing, like the moon going through the stars."

14. Demobee is a term used in the jargon of countries that have a compulsory military service for all male citizens. The demobee soldier was the one who had finished his obligatory military stage, being also called from then on reservist.

15. Householders are men who got married and started a family. Because of their status as married couple they are allowed less freedom than the teenagers in a village community as it is considered that they have family obligations to fulfill. Going to disco would be one of these freedoms that the married men could only take. Nevertheless, there are a few special occasions during the year when a householder can go to the disco. One of these events is the *Play of the Goat*'s team presentation in the building where the disco is held.

16. This is because 12–15% of the active population of Heleșteni comună works permanently or temporarily in various countries in Western Europe. I reached this figure by corroborating the data from the 2011 National Census for Heleșteni comună with those from my interviews on local migration phenomenon. I will discuss the collection of this data by the end of this chapter.

17. In his 1906 study *The St. George or Mummers' Plays: a Study in the Protology of Drama*, Arthur Beatty draw the conclusion that all mummers' plays that include in their structure the element of a wild animal ressurection are based on ancestral magical thinking that have as a main purpose the humans' desire to influence the nature through a magic ritual.

18. *The Dance of the Deer* disenchantment, village of Oboroceni, collected by Ion Ciubotaru at the end of 1970s, translation by Mirona Palas.

19. du Cange opens a window on this world where Church and administrative authorities tried to suppress the ritual, considering it primitive, pagan and a devilish expression. http://ducange.enc.sorbonne.fr/CERVULA. Du Cange's texts referring to *Deer* can be find in the Appendix I.

20. This expression is also present in some Romanian villages that preserve an old traditional culture.

21. *Măştile de priveghi* are worn by practitioners of a rural ritual in which the watch of the dead body before burial was accompanied by a series of pantomimic representations made to stir up humor.

22. Bârneaţă—a very resistent hemp girdle decorated with small beads. It is worn around the waist or across the chest during the ritual.

23. Ţuică—a strong alcoolic beverage made out of fermented plums.

24. Caltaboş—pork sausage made with rice, onion, pepper and pork intestins.

25. Maioş—pork sausage made with pork liver, pork fat, pepper and onion.

26. *Urătura* (pl. *urături*) is a text structured as a poem or as a song that the carolers recite when they visit a household belonging to their village community. In peasant communities, the text included messages about that particular family and household benefitting from wealth of the harvest and a rich agricultural year. Along with the transition of agricultural societies to a different mode of production—such as the industrial one—the texts of the *urături* acquired carnivalesque traits and were rather meant to entertain and to make fun than to transmit a magical message about the fertility of the crops.

27. "*Collectors* is the term conventionally used by English folklorists to refer to the figures (usually performers) who on various calendar occasions collect food or coins in return for their visit and occasional performances. Not all *collectors* wear disguises" (Halpert 1969: 38).

28. Noun not to be found in dictionaries.

29. Noun *lusa* <vb. *ludo, -ēre* (?).

30. "Do not wear/walk with the Deers [Cervulos] and with carriages [vehiculas] (to be read = old women) in the fourteenth day or on any other. Man should not wear women's clothes, nor should women wear men's clothes during the calends of January or during many other plays."

31. I owe this quote to my friend and collaborator, Bogdan Neagota, who has done a more in-depth and yet unfinished research on the relationship between the individual's exposure to fairy tales and his/her subsequent ability to adapt to certain challenging situations in the adult life.

32. Dor—specific concept in Romanian language evoking at the same time feelings of nostalgia, melancholy, profound wish towards something or someone far from you, doubled by a sense of loss.

Chapter Two

Ruginoasa Community
and Its Plays

RUGINOASA—THE RESIDENCE OF
ALEXANDRU IOAN CUZA RULER

A few years year before starting my research in Moldova region, some nationwide TV channels such as ProTV and Antena 1 had broadcasted a rural game[1] held in Ruginoasa *comună*,[2] Iași county. The ritual was presented as: "the traditional battle of the mummers" or "the traditional battle with sticks."[3] I had the chance to watch the short reports broadcasted by ProTV channel, and I saw two groups of young peasants disguised with heavy masks made of sheep fur, armed with long and hard wooden clubs, hitting each other in a kind of chaotic brawl where sometimes some were hospitalized with wounded heads or broken limbs. The fight did not last more than five minutes on the morning of December 31, but its spectacular character caught the attention of many viewers, including some of my friends and relatives whom I heard remarking: "Have you seen the battle of the mummers in Ruginoasa? That's a ritual really like back then in ancient times!" Most probably, such comments were not only the result of watching the barbaric nature of the game and the ugly masks of the fighters, but also of the way television reports were wrapping the fight as "a millenary tradition of the Romanian people."

Ruginoasa was the first locality I visited when I started my fieldwork. Driving to that region on December 30, 2009, was not easy as the roads were narrow and in bad shape. I had never driven before in that part of the country. Thus, I have to say I knew little about Ruginoasa when I started my research there. Moreover, it seemed I had been misled by TV programs that broadcasted the battle and wrapped it in a package where "barbaric ancestry" and "the real peasant—holders of ancient traditions" blended in creating a

representation of an oasis of timeless tradition. For this reason, I had somehow expected a small village isolated on a hill, a remote *comună* far away
from the main car roads or something similar. I had this representation in
mind despite I knew this locality had been the residency of Alexandru Ioan
Cuza, ruler of Moldavia whose name was linked to the union of Moldavia
and Walachia in 1859.

I was even more surprised to find out that the battle ritual would take
place not far away from the main road that crossed the locality and connected
two important cities in Iași county: Târgu Frumos and Pașcani. Actually,
Ruginoasa's downtown was very close to that road. Right there was a large
square. Two pubs were on the parallel sides of the square, and on the other
side stood the building of the railway station. The carriageway paralleled
the railway and bordered the square on the other side of the station, while
just behind the road one could see Cuza's impressive palace surrounded by
a solid brick wall. These village pubs are usually centers of social interaction between peasants, and the place where gossip emerges. As I could see,
Ruginoasa was no exception. When I got there, it was already dark outside
and a small lamp in the square shed a dim light that allowed me to see some
human shadows inside both pubs. I had the chance to spot three villagers outside of the pubs that looked a little drunk, but I was lucky enough I could ask
them a few questions before they disappeared into the night. This was how
I learned that the battle took place less than one kilometer away, on a road
going along the walls of Cuza's residency, connecting the lower part of the
comună's village—called *the valley* to the upper part—called *the hill*. After
this short talk with the three men, there was no one else on the streets. I was
hoping for somebody to arrive so that I could ask them more things about the
next day's main event: *the Mummers Battle with Sticks.*

After having waited for about fifteen minutes in the dark, I was lucky
enough to see two young men getting out of the fog on the village streets.
This was an opportunity I could not miss. Cautiously, I approached the two
young men and asked them about the next day's battle. They looked at me,
saw my camera bags and identified me immediately as TV cameramen. One
of the young men who introduced himself as an organizer of the next day's
confrontation gave me some very accurate details that matched well with
what I had learned from the drunken men I had previously talked to. These
villagers whom I could never identify later, gave me the first information
about the battle. They described it as a confrontation between two groups of
young men: one from a village situated in the lower part of the locality, informally called *the valley*, and the other one from the upper part of it, called *the
hill*. It sounded to me like a rite of passage, something resembling a transition
to adulthood. I could not wait to see the battle so that I could consolidate my
first hypothesis and add more information to what I had just found. While

having that conversation with the two young men, a villager around 50 and quite drunk, joined our group and started talking to us in a hoarse voice: "You will see tomorrow! There will be a big battle! You must film it! Which television do you belong to? Pro TV? I like Pro TV! They always present the battle very well." These were my firsts impressions and memories when I started my field research in Ruginoasa.

In this chapter I focus my attention on Ruginoasa's rural plays. This is a locality where one of the most mediatized rural customs of the postsocialist period in Romania takes place. Adopting the same methodology and vision as in the previous chapter, I look at this confrontation from the point of view of locals—those who know best the history of the locality and the role of the confrontation in shaping the relations between the inhabitants of the *comună*. At the same time, I analyze the mummers' confrontation from a wider perspective, that of a whole ritual complex including two other traditions in the series of mummers' plays: *Malanca* and *Târâitul*. Using the anthropological theories of violence—such as Galtung's *cultural violence*, and Whitehead's view of violence as *cultural performance*—I try to understand the role of this end-of-the-year aggressive game for the local community, but also the meanings that villagers and even combatants give it. Besides, I observe how the presence of journalists, through their sometimes-hindering intrusions and on-the-spot reports, enhanced the violence of the confrontation during the last decade.

Finally, just as in the previous chapter, I approach an entire ritual complex comprising the *Mummers' Battle with Sticks*, *Malanca*, and *Târâitul* in Ruginoasa, through the lens of microhistory (Ginzburg 1993). Through these lens I look at the economic, social, and political transformations that have affected the locality for the last half century.

METHODOLOGICAL INCONVENIENCES WHILE ANALYZING RUGINOASA'S BATTLE WITH STICKS

Unlike the *Play of the Goat* and the *Play of the Deer*—which have attracted folklorists' attention since the very 19th century and about which we possess even much older evidence—the *Battle with Sticks* in Ruginoasa has not been the topic of any scientific study. This state of facts left many questions and blank spaces regarding the unfolding of this rural ritual in relation to political, historical, economic, and social changes in the region where Ruginoasa is located. All these gaps in the history of the *Ruginoasa Battle with Sticks* are explainable and will be analyzed in the following pages. In the meantime, the lack of any scientific written records about this violent confrontation caused me, as researcher, major methodological and theoretical difficulties. In this context, the answers to my questions about the game's development and its causes came as a result of a detailed analytical exercise based almost entirely on participant observations and interviews with locals. I also included in my approach the scrutiny of the local history and the corroboration of data from my interviews and discussions with elements from this history, so that only the stories with the highest degree of internal coherence and narrated by multiple persons could be validated.

Another source of information that I used in my analysis was provided by the multitude of data produced by journalists in their reportages on *Mummers Battle with Sticks* in Ruginoasa. Starting with 2004 the tradition became the most mediatized on television, internet, radio, and YouTube, acquiring the status of the most popular and, in the meantime, the most controversial winter rural custom at national scale. Some of the most famous national television channels (such as ProTV, Realitatea TV, Antena 3, TVR1), but also local televisions (like BitTV Pașcani and Iași TvLife) broadcasted every year, and especially after 2004, news and reports about the mummers' confrontation in Ruginoasa.

The show *Românii au talent* (*Romania's Got Talent*) also contributed not only to the notoriety but also to the confusion about this tradition at national level. On March 1, 2013, a group of fighters from Ruginoasa participated in the pre-selection for the highly popular television show *Romania's Got Talent* broadcasted by the national television channel ProTV, where viewers were presented this *Traditional Battle with Sticks*. These were the reasons why the mummers' confrontation in Dumbrăvița village, Ruginoasa *comună*, became known nationwide, and one of the most sensational topics for every year's last day. Worth adding that, in Romania, December 31 is the day with a much higher television audience than in any other day of the year. This national notoriety of the battle of Ruginoasa complicates the analysis of the holistic picture of a local tradition about which until very recently there were very few reliable data.

VIOLENCE AND MASS-MEDIA IN RUGINOASA BATTLE WITH STICKS

Many of the data about *Ruginoasa's Traditional Fight* were published on the web pages of the media that broadcasted materials recorded in the day of the battle. Thus, right now there are dozens of internet websites that present details about the *Battle with Sticks* ritual in Ruginoasa. All this data is available online for potential readers interested in the topic. However, unlike other topics largely dealt with on television and newspapers' websites, in this case getting information from all these sources might probably contribute to the most distorted and incorrect representations of an extremely complex local social phenomenon that has a rich history behind. Therefore, I could state without doubt that *The Battle of the Mummers* in Ruginoasa is probably one of the most erroneously covered topics in the postsocialist Romanian media. Thus, it had contributed to sensationalizing a local tradition that, until around 2000, had little to do with the principles and values of the mainstream culture.

The construction of the distorted representation of the confrontation is based on multiple causes. One of these was the postsocialist media chasing the sensational. During the wild capitalism of the postsocialist period (Harper 2006), sensational news became a well sold commodity where the number of viewers was proportional with the profit. Another case that complicated the understanding and the analysis of the battle was the physical (and sometimes extreme) violence of the participants, many times inflated by the television cameras presence nearby. They teleported a tradition embedded with local values to the viewers' homes, most of which lived in urban settings that had little things in common with the values of the rural world that created the confrontation. This rural violence was superposed on the idyllic image of village traditions that the nationalist folkloristics of Romantic inspiration had imposed; these two vectors resulted in a disjunctive relation that, in its turn, contributed to the general confusion about the subject. Last but not least, the general confusion was also reinforced by the statements of the villagers, fragmented and recombined hastily by field reporters who did not have the time, patience and adequate background to deeply analyze this material.

Because of these reasons, I am going to shed light on some of the most common confusions and errors the press has done when referring to the *Battle of the Mummers* in Ruginoasa. One of the most amazing and unreasonable ideas that mass media popularized regarded the battle's origins. Many television and radio channels spread the information that the mummers' traditional battle is a few thousand years old. "From a ritual that dates back to a few millennia ago, the meeting between the villagers uphill (*din Deal*/eng. *from the Hill*) who call themselves *Delenii*, and the rival team downhill (*din Vale*/eng. *from the Valley*), it has turned into an ugly drubbing" (*Stirileprotv.ro*), ProTV channel once transmitted. It is obvious that the production of such information has to do with the autochthonism thesis begotten by the Romanian folkloristics where rural traditions had millennia of history behind, and thus represent a proof of the Romanian people's continuation on a certain geographic area (Neagota 2000).

However, the case of Ruginoasa's battle goes against the grain when it comes to this thesis. The oldest mentions of Ruginoasa and its neighboring comună—such as Strunga—do not go further than 1400 AD, when these settlements were simple hamlets inhabited by a few dozen individuals (Cihodaru, Caproşu, and Ciocan 1980). More, as underlined in the following lines, the confrontation of two rival groups of mummers turned into a *Battle with Sticks* only in the late 1970s, about three decades ago.

Another wrong information the press transmitted was that the *Traditional Mummers' Battle* in Ruginoasa is called *Malanca*. "The tradition is known under the folk name *Malanca*, as the ethnographic data demonstrate," readers could learn on the website of the newspaper *Bună Ziua Iași* (www.bzi.ro). On *Viața Liberă*'s website—another local newspaper—the information is added complementary data, just as far from the truth as the previous one, but worth mentioning in the analysis. "The custom of caroling with masks and whips is known by locals as *Malanca* and, according to tradition, the winners celebrate the victory by hitting the ground with their clubs (www.viata-libera.ro)." In an article published by Ștefan Bacu at *Radio România Internațional*, he says that in fact the two rival groups are called *malănci* and that, in the past, they were symbolic representations of the *New Year* and the *Old Year*. By tradition, the *Old Year* should lose the fight so that the new one can be rich and prosperous.

All these reports mix truth and fiction, factual observation and de-contextualized statements made by villagers, so that the resulting overall representation can only cause perplexity and confusion. In fact, the name of this tradition is not *Malanca*, but *Confruntarea Tradițională cu Bâte*/ eng. *Traditional Battle with Sticks*. But locals use other alternative terms when referring to the ritual. The most frequent terms are: *Traditional Fight, Mummers' Fight, Mummers' Battle, Battle with Sticks, Mummers' Traditional Battle with Sticks* and *Mummers' Morning Battle*. On the other hand, it is true that the *Mummers' Battle* is in fact part of a manifold ritual complex that includes *Malanca* and another ritual called *Târâitul*. These two traditions are included in the category of ritual *urături/caroling* performed by peasants on the last day of December and the first two days of January. However, the name of *Malanca* is never used by villagers to name the *Traditional Battle with Sticks*, which is not a caroling tradition.

Finally, the assumption that there is ethnographic data attesting to the antiquity of this tradition is also false. Ethnographic sources regarding the ritual are completely absent, and the press materials calling the battle "an ancient tradition of Romanians" are distorted presentations of reality, too. Other media reports provide information about the past of the confrontation gathered from the local elders, presenting them as truthful facts for the confrontation that took place today. "Villagers are not allowed to interfere in favor of any of the teams. . . . The ones acknowledged as winners have the privilege to choose the most beautiful girls for the upcoming balls (www .novaappolonia.ro)." Other websites—including the prestigious national publication *Adevărul*—adds similar statements: "According to tradition, each year the winners have the privilege to organize balls where they invite the girls they want. . . . Winners take precedence in asking the girls to marry and in organizing balls (www.adevarul.ro)." The main two statements mentioned above are in huge contrast with the current observations on the battle, and the recent marriage rituals in Ruginoasa area.

The press reports are also unclear because many journalists have taken without a critical examination some assertions of the locals. An anthropological skepticism like the one promoted by Margaret Mead in her statement "What people say, what people do, and what they say they do are entirely different things," (Mead 1975)[4] would be necessary in this context. Even if some locals have repeatedly said that the traditional battle follows certain rules well supported by the comună's tradition, the image of the battle I got after field observations during many consecutive years is quite different. *The Mummers' Confruntation* it is rather a chaotic and brutal fight, with just few rules, where tens of unmasked peasants interfere actively in favor of their mummers' group and contribute decisively to the outcome of the battle. Meanwhile, the information about the winners' privilege for organizing balls in the comună and the organized character of the battle according to the rules of the traditions are both blatantly contradicted by the factual realities gathered from the field. Out of context, this data undermines any trace of deontology both for field reporters and article writers. In fact, there are no more balls in Ruginoasa ever since the 1960s and the latest editions of the confrontation have clearly proved the lack of any clear rules and regulations regarding the conduct of the fighters.

Finally, a series of confusions the press did concerning the place of the battle complete the general picture of the outsiders' misunderstandings of the ritual and the confronting groups. Although most televisions and newspapers name the *Mummers' Fight* "the battle in Ruginoasa," only few know that the event happens in the village of Dumbrăviţa, belonging to Ruginoasa *comună*. Even fewer outsiders know that this comună comprises four villages one of which is called Ruginoasa—just like the comună itself—and that the mummers' battle, filmed each year by televisions, does not take place in this village. Furthermore, there are journalists who believe that *Deleni* and *Văleni* are in fact the names of two distinct villages in Ruginoasa comună. Actually, *deleni* and *văleni* are just two symbolic names that the two mummers' groups in Dumbrăviţa village take in order to define their identity as fighters. The reason is that one of the two confronting groups lives in the hilly part of the village—*deal*, whereas the other lives in the southern part, symbolically known as *vale* (eng. *valley*).

The striking fact is that even experienced folklorists that were familiar with the ritual showed a hostile attitude towards it, describing it as "a silly tradition that is not representative for the people in Ruginoasa" because "they have other beautiful traditions that they should perform and promote during the New Year" (Adrian Ardelean, folklorist, 60 years old, Iași City, July 15, 2015, Interview). This kind of vision, coming from certain professional folklorists, increased the doubts and confusions surrounding the *Mummers' Battle.*

All these hesitations, confusions, misunderstandings, and phantasmagoria on the *Mummers' Battle* in Dumbrăvița village, Ruginoasa *comună*, transformed a simple rural game with local symbolic significance, into a national event in correlation with the postsocialist unrest where the moral and social crisis was expressed through a chase of the authentic and the sensational. Quite often in postsocialist times, the authentic and the sensational became the sides of the same coin, offering a fulcrum or at least a temporary consolation to many people in a world fallen into economic, social, and moral unrest. Surprisingly, the battle in Ruginoasa could embody both the authentic and the sensational. For some Romanians, the primitive aspect of the young mummers wearing hideous masks made of sheep skin and fighting with acacia clubs two meters high, spoke about an archaic world where manhood and dignity were won in fair fight, clubs in hand, not with tricks and guile like in the wild post-1989 capitalism. Meanwhile, the image of mummers— a symbol of maleness and virility—was perceived as authentic because it embodied an ancient manhood model, recalling medieval and ancient battles where people—especially men—were brave, unlike the doubtful, depressed, and anguished individuals of modern times.

On the other hand, there were also Romanians who asked insistently for the ritual to be banned, labelling it as barbarian and inadequate to the contemporary world where conflicts are being mediated by the police or in court. The strongest voices on this side launched long and relentless speeches against the battle, calling it "a shitty tradition" and "a typical idiocy"; the performers were described as "idiots," "insane," and "brainless," and Ruginoasa comună as "village of stupid people." Nevertheless, within the two sides of the battle, the admirers of the confrontation and its opponents proved to be just as active on blogs, commenting at every video recording of the battle published on YouTube or on newspaper or television websites, blogs or other electronic resources mentioning the *Battle in Ruginoasa.*

These polemic discussions and the impossibility of an agreement regarding the battle of Ruginoasa is representative for the tensions and discrepancies in the Romanian society after the fall of Communism where, faced with an unusual yet traditional custom, the serious effort to analyze and understand it was replaced by either exaltation or complete rejection through slander and insults. All these elements produced a social phenomenon that has long surpassed Ruginoasa and even Iași county's borders, turning into a subject of national dispute between the two opposite sides. The case could also be called *The Battle of Ruginoasa*, although many of the disputes go much beyond the geographic and cultural borders of the rural settlement Ruginoasa in Eastern Romania. Faced with the complex social phenomenon symbolically called *The Battle of Ruginoasa*, post-1989 mass media could not remain an unbiased arbitrator that would help understanding it with a lucid and analytical mind; instead, it managed to inflate spirits, transforming a local custom into a sensational news, making it more ambiguous and harder to decipher even for experienced researchers.

As the anthropologist Neal Whitehead well observed, when researching several forms of violence around the world, mass media always play a decisive (but not always positive) role when it comes to analyzing and debating forms of violence:

> [A]ll these specific forms of violence are not produced by the febrile excess of savage or pathological minds but are cultural performances whose poetics derive from the history and sociocultural relationships of the locale. However, representations of such intimate violence are also globalized through the media so that the intimacy of local violence is paraded on a global stage. (Whitehead 2004:74)

Precisely because of this, I decided to analyze deeply this ritual in the following pages, and, according to my information, this enterprise is the first ethnographic description of the *Battle in Ruginoasa*.

THE GEOGRAPHY AND HISTORY OF RUGINOASA

More than in other rural rituals I had had the chance to study, the geography and history of Ruginoasa *comună* are extremely relevant for understanding the *Mummers Battle*. I reached this conclusion after long talks with various villagers on the topic. One of the most competent connoisseurs of the local geography and history proved to be Mihai Lupu, primary school teacher born in Ruginoasa in 1940, who managed to acquire a well-articulated representation of the ritual over a lifetime spent within the locality. Despite his life experience within the comună and the very well thought discourse of this remarkable intellectual, it took me several hours of interviewing and more discussions to understand thoroughly where, when and how the events connected to the history of Ruginoasa and the mummers' battle had taken place.

The complexity of certain events in the history of the *comună*, the details about the unfolding of the traditional battle and especially its displacement from one village to another over a few decades resulted in a puzzle whose solution I discovered with great difficulty and after a relatively long period of time. In the following lines, I will try to retrace this landscape so that any reader of these pages could get an overall picture of the ritual's evolution during an entire century. I start this story by presenting Mihai Lupu's point of view, a synthesis of the few hours of discussions and interviews that he was kind and patient enough to offer me. This shall play the important part of introduction to the geography and history of the traditional battle.

The comună of Ruginoasa comprises four villages: Dumbrăvița, Rediu, Vascani and Ruginoasa. In the past, the village of Ruginoasa was also called Bugioaia, and even today locals use this name when talking to one another about the village. Vascani is slightly different because it became part of the Ruginoasa comună only in 1968 when a series of administrative and territorial changes happened in Romania. Until then, Vascani had belonged to Hărmănești *comună*. Because of this reason, Vascani is the only village among the four that does not have and has never had the tradition of the *Mummers' Battle*; however, it has the *Play of the Deer*, a custom extinct today in the other villages of the *comună*.

Back in the 1950s, when I was a child, there used to be a battle between the mummers in Bugioaia (now called Ruginoasa) and the ones in Rediu. This traditional battle was mostly since the young men in Rediu used to visit the girls in Bugioaia and, similarly, the lads in Bugioaia used to visit the girls in Rediu. In case a man from Rediu, for instance, seduced a girl from Bugioaia, the young men in her village would be ashamed, and the expression they would use for the situation was: *He stole our fox!* Thus, the battle was a sort of reaction against these incursions. But the confrontation took the shape of a ritual and always happened on the morning of December 31.

The young men who would take part in the ritual were usually with the military service done or a short while before it. They used to wear multicolored clothes like those nomad gypsies (*căldărari*) wore when they roamed the villages to sell objects to our villagers. Among the things they sold, there were also pots (usually known as *căldări*) and this explains the name given to the gypsies doing this kind of commerce—*căldărari*. They would also sell a very interesting type of brushes for whitewashing, called *badanale*; these were not like the ones we have nowadays (with a short handle), but had a one-meter-long handle and were made out of horsehair. So, the young men joining the battle were armed with these *badanale*[5] that imitated the brushes that the *căldărari* gypsies used to sell back then. But these tools were not used to fight; they were rather meant to impress the opponents. They were held with the brush upwards and resembled flags such as *Dracon*—the fabulous animal with a wolf head and snake body carried by Dacians on top of clubs during battles. This meant they functioned as a kind of scarecrows. But nowadays a whole country gets scared when seeing the youngsters in Ruginoasa rising their clubs. But these weapons are not as dangerous as people believe. This is because the risen clubs are rather meant to intimidate. Besides these brushes, the men involved in the fight used to wear the so-called *șuhoaie* around their waist. The *șuhoaie* were large bronze bells with smaller bells inside, and they sounded terrific when the fighters ran, jumped, or even just moved. Finally, the young men also had whips that were actually the main weapon in the battle back then.

In the 1950s, the battle rather meant pushing and whipping. If the *Bugioieni* (the inhabitants of Bugioaia village) crossed the stone bridge—also called *bolta de la Heleșteni*—and managed to go halfway up the hill to Rediu, this meant the *Rădenii* (inhabitants of Rediu) were beaten. If, on the contrary, the Rădeni crossed the stone bridge and reached the mill near the train station, it meant the Bugioieni were beaten. That moment, the battle would stop, and they would go to have a glass of wine together. This meant that the confrontation was not motivated by hatred. So, in the beginning, the battle only took place between two villages: Bugioaia and Rediu—the southernmost village in the Ruginoasa comună and the closest to Heleșteni, the neighboring *comună*. The *Dumbrăvițeni* (inhabitants of Dumbrăvița) had not joined the battle at first because they had Ukrainian origins and would not interfere with the Romanians. Likewise, for a long time, until around the 1950s and a little bit after, Romanians would not interfere with them either. Back then, villages were more isolated because the population was smaller than today when nobody really knows exactly where a village ends and another one begins because of the large number of houses. Back then, all that was between the villages was an empty field. So, later on, around 1970, the Dumbrăvițeni entered the battle, too. And the history of the comună explains this fact quite well.

The Rădeni have always been hardworking people who encouraged their children to learn. And their children got to be among the first in college, too. Thus, they gradually distanced themselves of the traditional battle and, around the early 1970s, quit it completely. Slowly, simultaneous to this tendency and to the disappearance of the "enemies" in Rediu, the Dumbrăvițeni started to create their own tradition of the battle. By the late 1970s, clubs were introduced into the battle—a new invention of the Dumbrăvițeni, I would say. In Dumbrăvița, the battle was between *deal* (the hill) and *vale* (the valley); in other words, between the inhabitants of the same village, divided into the ones living in the hilly side of the village, and the ones downhill, in *vale*, close to the castle of Cuza (the Romanian ruler during 19th century) situated at the border with the village of Ruginoasa. This is in fact the battle that the televisions started to record and that came to public attention in recent years. Once this tradition was founded in Dumbrăvița, the people in Ruginoasa village followed the example and started to fight, too, since their village had a hill—*deal* and a valley—*vale*, too (smaller than the other village, though). The *Deal* in Ruginoasa goes north from the railway until the driveway to Pașcani city; the *Vale* is to the south, towards the area called Dealul Drăghici, next to the archaeological center of the comună, to the south of Heleșteni *comun*ă. But the battles here happen at a smaller scale than in Dumbrăvița.

The battle also has a symbolic dimension, meaning that the participants pay for all their deeds throughout the year; for instance, if some of them went to the other village to see the girls or things like that. Therefore, they say that after the battle one can enter the *New Year* with a clean soul. There are also other symbols in their outfits for example. The *Old Year* is represented by ugly and rough masks made of sheep skin and fur, worn by the fighters in the morning. But in the afternoon, things change. The ones that join the ritual called *Malanca*, which is very different that the morning battle, show up dressed in beautiful and expensive clothes, prepared in detail, and their masks are decorated with colorful beads and ribbons. In fact, all these represent the *New Year*—beautiful, young, just beginning. (Mihai Lupu, 76 years old, Dumbrăvița village, series of interviews taken between July 17, 2015, and May 4, 2017)

Mihai Lupu's panoramic vision of the battle in Ruginoasa *comună* prepares the field for a deeper analysis and eliminates a series of misunderstandings regarding the location of the fight and the way it has transformed during the last six decades. However, Mihai Lupu was rather inclined to present the violence during the battle through the lenses provided by symbolism and an archaic cosmogony about the birth of the New Year, but also by emphasizing the strict rules of tradition that are meant to prevent very violent and brutal behaviors.

I have noticed this kind of attitude with most of my interviewees in Ruginoasa, and I explain it best using the *cultural violence* concept, coined by sociologist Johan Galtung. He defines cultural violence as "those aspects of culture, the symbolic sphere of our existence—exemplified by religion and ideology, language and art, empirical science and formal science (logic, mathematics)—that can be used to justify or legitimize direct or structural violence" (Galtung 1990:291). It seems that the *comună*'s inhabitants have created a specific ideology that makes the violence of the *Battle with Sticks* become invisible or at least justifiable.

I observed this vision in persons of both genders, very different ages— from 18 to 90. Gica Lupu, a 57-year-old teacher in the village of Rediu, declared the following:

> I agree with this battle. I have liked all our winter traditions and I believe that this ten-second spark, this brief impact, has to happen. And I believe this way because my dad had taken me to see this battle ever since I was a three year old little girl, and he showed me their costumes and explained their behavior to me. He would tell me: *Look, these ones are coming from up the hill, and these ones from down the valley, and then they are going to clash.* This was somewhere around 1960–65, for I was born in 1955. In 1965 they would still fight with whips. (Gica Lupu, 57 years old, Rediu village, July 6, 2012, Interview)

A mask maker in whose house I had the privilege to see the last stage in the process of mask making, on December 30, 2011, made a similar statement:

There is no definite purpose of the battle. It is a tradition coming from our ancestors. It's always been like that. There's a sort of pride in winning it. But the hatred does not make it to the next year. Nobody has ever died during the battle. Maybe someone broke an arm, hurt a finger, etc. *For you cannot stay in the rain without getting wet* [Romanian proverb n.a], that's not possible. Those that fight better and remain standing stiffer win, while the rest lose and ran to their side of the village. Sometimes they throw stones at each other, but usually this doesn't happen. Sometimes civilians[6] also get into the battle. (Ion, mask maker, 48 years old, Dumbrăvița village, December 30, 2011, Interview)

A township-hall councilor from the village of Dumbrăvița, also present there in the evening of December 30, 2011, brought a traditional-symbolic vision of the battle, too:

The ugly masks worn by the fighters represent the *Old Year* and with the morning battle we chase the *Old Year* away, together with all the evil in the village. And for the *Malancă* we bring our beautiful masks representing in fact the *New Year* with its new, beautiful face and with hope. Therefore, it is not about hatred. Later on, we meet to drink some wine, to laugh of one another. That's how it should actually be. (Vasile, township-hall councilor in Ruginoasa *comună*, 52 years old, December 30, 2011, Interview)

All the statements made by my interviewees correspond with the conceptual framework designed by Galtung when analyzing cultural violence.

Cultural violence makes direct and structural violence look, even feel, right—or at least not wrong. . . . One way, cultural violence works by changing the moral color of an act from red/wrong to green/right or at least to yellow/acceptable; an example being "murder on behalf of the country as right, on behalf of oneself wrong." Another way is by making reality opaque, so that we do not see the violent act or fact, or at least not as violent. (Idem 1990:292)

Obviously, the talks with the villagers in Ruginoasa *comună* had a significant impact on the journalists reporting on the battle. Almost all the field coverage included—in a distorted and misinforming manner—fragments about the relation between the violence of the battle and the village traditions. Although the reporters' initial idea was to have a sensational news, the outcome was, in most cases, the lack of transparency about the violent acts, creating a total discrepancy between the facts presented and their "deeper" meaning in the *comună*'s set of traditions. But, for me, as an anthropologist, the superficial analyses of the journalists (all outsiders of Ruginoasa) regarding local violence made me dig deeper into the history of this rural settlement in order to discover data that would clarify this aggressiveness and its causes. My initial assumption was that there had to be a long history of violence that gave locals the time to get used to its effects and, later, to justify it by means of an ideology anchored in local traditions.

A HISTORY OF VENDETTA AND CULTURAL VIOLENCE IN RUGINOASA BATTLE WITH STICKS

When studying documents about Ruginoasa's past, there is plenty of information about acts of physical violence, aside with testimonials about the bravery of the *comună*'s inhabitants. One of the classics of Romanian literature, Ion Creangă mentions Ruginoasa briefly in his monumental work *Childhood Memories* published in 1892 where he narrated events happening around the mid-19th century. In the fourth part of this autobiography, Creangă describes his passage through Ruginoasa *comună*, together with some fellows, and includes it in the larger description of the journey from his native village, Humuleşti, to Iaşi—Moldova's capital—where he began his studying to become a priest:

> And as soon as we were out on the high-road by good fortune we came upon some men with cartloads of shingles driving to Iaşi. We travelled with them for fear of the gypsies of Ruginoasa and we made splendid progress till, at daybreak, there we were at Târgu-Frumos where we forthwith split a few water-melons to quench our thirst and still our hunger. (Creangă 1978 [1892])

The rough reputation of the people from Ruginoasa is mentioned also by Boris Crăciun, a historian and author of the monograph dedicated to the *comună*. The locals' fighting spirit is described by the author when speaking about *The 1907 Romanian Peasants' Revolt*. The spark that created the riot, Crăciun tells us, appeared in Northern Moldova and from there it spread to Suceava county of which Ruginoasa was part at that time.

> It was the spring of 1907. On Thursdays, people used to go to Târgu-Frumos where a fair was held. Here, in February, they found out about the outbreak of the riot in Flămânzi, Frumuşica, Stroieşti and other localities in Northern Moldova. The news came exactly when the peasants felt the knife had reached bone in the village. From the counties of Botoşani, Dorohoi and Iaşi, the riot spread to Suceava, and the signal was given by the peasants in Ruginoasa. (Crăciun 1969)

Further on, Crăciun gives an account of the events in Ruginoasa where peasants destroyed the landlords' registers that kept the cumbersome debts the locals had to pay to landholders. One of the extensively discussed events, later promoted by the Romanian communist ideology, took place on March

3, 1907. That day, the peasants in Ruginoasa allied with the railway workers from the Paşcani city railway station and tried to liberate 15 peasants from Ruginoasa considered to be the heads of the Ruginoasa riot. The ones arrested were about to be sent to the town of Fălticeni where they would be judged. The soldiers appointed to keep the train safe were forced to open fire and wounded severely a railway worker. The event was later included in history textbooks during the Communist Era and provided an example of the brotherhood between peasants and workers in the fight against the common enemy, namely the capitalist exploiter (Idem 1969:63–64).

These writings depict the peasants of Ruginoasa as rough and courageous, and, more than that, as people used to perceive violence as a legitimate solution to either personal or social problems. The oral history of Ruginoasa also mentions other events that have to do with the violence in the locality's past, including the origin of the *Mummers' Battle*. One of the most interesting accounts in this respect goes back in time, presenting events from the early 20th century, involving the local landlords and the peasants in Ruginoasa. This account was collected from Michi Balcan, inhabitant of Dumbrăviţa village, who claims the story was transmitted to him via his paternal grandfather. I heard the same account, with slight variations, in other two sources, both in Dumbrăviţa village—a proof that the story is quite popular among locals.

Around 1900–1910, there were two landlords, Teodorescu and Sturdza, owning several hundred hectares of agricultural lands. These fields had to be protected of the thieves who would sometimes run into the crops during harvesting. So, these boyars had appointed guards in the fields. And the chosen guards were the handiest and strongest young men, especially those without family obligations, that could thus spend more nights guarding without having to explain this to their wives and family. Thus, youngsters like these were usually recruited as guardsmen. Well, the guardsmen appointed by the two boyars would also go to the local bars to warm up next to a glass of hot wine. And the guards of the two teams used to meet there. At the bar, people would sometimes talk about which team is better, which men are stronger. This is how many fights began, such as wrestling to see who is the strongest and, consequently, the best guardsman. Others would also do arm wrestling. Sometimes, these meetings resulted in more serious fights that were later transformed in collective battles between the lads uphill and the ones downhill. The explanation is that one of the boyars had land uphill to the north of Dumbrăviţa, while the other one's land was located more downhill, to the south. So, the boyar in the north appointed rather lads from the hill—*deal*, while the one in the south appointed young people from the valley—*vale*. This is how the rivalry between *deal* and *vale* began in the village of Dumbrăviţa. (Michi Balcan, 50 years old, Dumbrăviţa village, January 3, 2012, Interview)

Michi Balcan, local of Dumbrăviţa, aged 50, was one of the active fighters of the team in the *vale* when he was young. Over time, he managed to get a good understanding on the fighting mummers' ritual. His stories have valuable information about the battle's history and especially about its transition from wrestling to whips and from whips to clubs.

> My grandfather joined this wrestling type of competitions that also used whips back then. My granddad put on his mask, so did my dad and so did I for nine years, from 1979 until about 1987. I experienced the time between the whips and the clubs. But in the beginning the clubs were shorter, thinner, more decent. They were not longer than the whip's handle. It's fascinating to know how they got from whips to clubs (*măciuci*). When I was a small child, around the year 1965–70, a clever young man made a longer handle to his whip. And that year he beat everyone. The ones who had lost the battle designed longer handles for their whips the following year. And they continued like this each year, until they reached a moment when these tools could no longer be of use as handles for whips. Then the fighters started using them as clubs. Personally, I lived times when I had a club on my left hand and a whip on the right hand. (Michi Balcan, 50 years old, Dumbrăviţa village, January 3, 2012, Interview)

The transition from whips to clubs is explained by other locals through a local vendetta between two large families in the village, which transformed the traditional fair-play confrontation into a rough fight thirsty of revenge.

> In the past, the fight was not carried with clubs, but with whips, and mummers also wore bells on them. Until 1975–1976, it was still with whips. That was also when the murder of a villager named Maghercă took place. Two families, which had been in conflict for many years, have met. Being drunk, on the evening of January 1, when the *Malănci teams* were walking around the village, they started arguing and the members of the Cernăuţeanu family hit Maghercă in the head with a club, so hard that his eye was plucked and, if I remember well, the man eventually died. The aggressor spent about 20 years in prison. But, if I remember well, from that moment on these families became thirstier of revenge year by year. Around the following year, clubs appeared; it must've been around 1976. So, it's possible that the *Battle with Sticks* started in 1977. From this grudge between the two families, the battle amplified each year. Maghercă and Cernăuţeanu were two larger families in the Ruginoasa *comună*. Being so large, they got more people involved into the end of year fight. Thus, people started to join in more and more, and since the village of Dumbrăviţa was split in two— *dealul* and *valea*—the two teams started to fight. (Dumitru Lupu, 57 years old, Rediu village, July 6, 2012, Interview)

The communist period generally represented an important stage in the development of the *Mummers' Battle*. Despite the strong policed state Romania was (Deletant 1999), the *Battle of Ruginoasa* was allowed to go on by communist authorities. Older locals who lived those times explain the situation.

During communist times, the battle between *deal* and *vale* was allowed to happen. People also wore bells—called *şuhoaie*—around their waists and these produced a noise that reached far. This way, the militia always knew where the fighters were. But mummers were allowed to meet. Usually, the militia just watched the whole fight that ended up without any victims. Communist authorities were just interested in preventing something against their power and domination. Therefore, they issued a law in the 1950s stating that any public manifestation where more than three people gathered in one place had to notify the town hall before it happened, and the institution would issue a certificate explaining the meeting. This was how they tried to control village traditions, not only *The Battle*, but also the other winter traditions such as *Malanca, The Goat, The Deer, The Bears,* etc. (Mihai Lupu, 76 years old, Dumbrăviţa village, May 4, 2017, Interview)

However, communist times also brought harsh measures against the fighters of the two teams—the *deal* and the *vale*. The ones involved in the confrontation remember the details of these events:

During Communism, you did not know what to expect from the police. If the chief of the police in Paşcani wanted to see the battle because he was fond of it, their measures were kinder. If not, he was tough with us. Yet, back then people were afraid of the law, afraid of the police. The police was very strong and could arrest whoever they wanted. If somebody was rude to them before or after the morning battle, they would take that person to their van right away. Sometimes they would even keep him for the entire New Year night under arrest only to let him go out one or two days later. The whole village suffered for that guy, even his opponents. Because we were always thinking: *See, I'm having fun, drinking, eating, and poor him is arrested.* There were a few such arrests during those times. (Michi Balcan, 50 years old, Dumbrăviţa village, January 3, 2012, Interview)

Furthermore, communist authorities knew how to exploit the violent acts during the battle to their own politic benefit, as Costică Nechifor, a 65 year old living in Dumbrăviţa, explains in an interview. All this political manipulation of the violent persons involved in the *Mummers' Battle* resulted in an inflammation of the battle's level of violence in the following years.

Forty years ago, when I was young, the custom of fighting with clubs did not exist. The opponents only had whips and whipped one another. When I was a child, the locals of Rediu met the ones of Bugioaia, and they would fight with whips. I recall quite well an episode where the *bugioieni* chased the *rădeni* uphill to Rediu. The whips could only cause bruises, but would never break limbs or skulls like wooden clubs can do now. I can only remember one battle as violent as the one we had a few days ago. It happened right before the collectivization and it was dreadful, with poles and clubs. In other words, it was very similar to the one nowadays. A young man in Ruginoasa, member of the Bârloi family, was hit with the club close to his ear; the ear was broken and he was left deaf afterwards. Others were taken to the hospital, too, so it was pretty bad. The *collectivization* of agriculture [(Iordachi and Dobrincu 2009) n.a.] was done here in 1962, so this was a bit before, perhaps even the winter before, in 1961. I remember that the mayor of Ruginoasa was a man called Toarbă Vasile. The policemen that were sent on the spot were also insulted by the mummers in the village. Some of them were taken their pistols and had the guns thrown into a well, others were harassed and pushed around. Afterwards, the authors of the violent acts were caught and the police, together with the legal authorities in the comună, made an agreement with the fighters: *We don't send you to prison, but you are going to be responsible for the collectivization of the comună!* In a way, they made them do it because they had the means and knew how. These roughnecks were sent to the locals that had to be convinced to enter the *Colectiv* (kolhoz n.a.). If you did not want to enter the *Colectiv*, these guys beat you so hard that you lost your senses and finally accepted.[7] So, my belief is that from that moment on, the morning battle on December 31 became increasingly violent. (Costică Nechifor, 65 years old, Dumbrăvița village, January 3, 2012, Interview)

All these events tell a story of violence in Ruginoasa *comună*, a place known for its hot-spirited inhabitants ever since Ion Creangă's times. In other words, over time, the villagers of Ruginoasa have become famous as fierce people that use violence for managing conflicts with other people. During my field research, I had the opportunity to check this assumption many times. The weekly market, for instance, held every Wednesday at the Heleșteni village's margin, was the place where the inhabitants of Ruginoasa also used to come to sell their agricultural products. More than once, the friends from Heleșteni accompanying me drew my attention to the potentially aggressive behavior of the people from Ruginoasa: "Take care and don't stand in front of this guy's carriage for he has a registration plate from Ruginoasa, and he may hit you." Another time, while visiting a family in Heleșteni I observed the frisky behavior of their four-year-old niece. One of the family members tried to make an excuse mumbling that: "There's nothing one can do about this girl. She's like this all the time. It's obvious that her mom comes from Ruginoasa. For that's how those guys are—a bit crazy!"

Nevertheless, the violent acts during the 2011 battle caused perplexity even among Ruginoasa's inhabitants, going much beyond the ordinary villagers' power of understanding. On the days following this battle, but also in the months to come, I managed to take a series of interviews of many locals.

Figure 2.1. A fighter from the Valley area preparing his mask before the battle—December 31, 2009.
Photo credit: Alin Rus

The violence of that battle between the two groups had left deep marks in the memory of the villagers witnessing the events:

> I was the one who wiped the blood pouring from the nose, ears and mouth of a guy who was severely beaten in the battle. I washed him with water next to a well, I wiped him afterwards. . . . I still have the t-shirt I was wearing back then. It's still full of blood. . . . From that turmoil he came directly to me. In the moment I saw him in that state, I moved him aside and took him somewhere else, and then I washed him until he came back to his senses. He had fallen and all the other ones coming from uphill hit him repeatedly with their clubs. Eventually, a woman from the village stopped those hitting him and that's how he managed to escape. In the end, after I washed him, the ambulance from Paşcani city arrived and took him to the hospital. . . . Usually, it's people with little education that get involved in this battle. If there were a decent mayor, the battle would only happen between mummers. I believe that right now this battle should only happen when the police and the gendarmes are here. (Gabi Nechifor, 35 years old, Dumbrăviţa village, January 3, 2012, Interview)

I got a similar and very lucid prediction of *Ruginoasa's Battle* fate from Mr. Michi Balcan during a long two-hour interview. Here is his declaration just three days after the 2011 battle:

After everything that has happened this time, I say it's the last year the battle takes place. I believe the Prefecture of the Iași County will issue a special law that forbids this battle forever. Or they shall bring here every year huge troops of gendarmes that would prevent the battle from happening. For I have never seen what I could witness this year: civilians and mummers hitting anyone, even the ones fallen to the ground. And if the *deleni* had won this year, they should have gone to the *comună* hall afterwards and carol the mayor, wait for the music and the *Malănci teams* and celebrate their victory in a beautiful way. Instead, they went to a neighboring street and made even more victims. Then they continued somewhere else in the village and beat some young men there, too. Even I, though local counselor, and representative of the *comună* hall, feared them and ran away. They did not care that I was over fifty and father of children their age. They would have hit me, too, to chill down. And I saw how, at a given moment, heading towards the *comună* hall, they took their masks off, showing everybody they were the winners and the toughest. Meanwhile, had they caught even civilians from the *vale* they would have beat those, too . . . I had been a mummer for years in the past, and I can say that I'm no fearful guy. I even did wrestling in the past and I can say that I'm quite fit even now when I'm fifty. But this year one of my brothers joined the battle and I was terrified that he might get caught in a hustle and crippled, and I would not be able to do anything for him. Since certain civilians tried to save the mummers fallen to the ground wounded, they were hit, too. Well, I could say this year was the first time I was afraid. And I think you, as a witness there of all the events, you know well why. My eyes have never seen something like what happened this year. There were more civilians than mummers armed with clubs, and they were all as involved in the battle as the mummers. So, both civilians and mummers were fighting, and nobody could have told who the civilian and the mummer were, and who was fighting whom. This is not a fair-play match anymore. It's just human evil and stupid thirst for revenge. This time eight people went to the hospital—mummers and civilians together. That's not a thing to do anymore. (Michi Balcan, 50 years old, Dumbrăvița village, January 3, 2012, Interview)

Intriguingly enough, many locals of both genders reached similar conclusions, without being nonetheless capable of offering a valid explanation for the radicalization of the battle.

Now I find this battle rougher, sillier and more meaningless and especially more shameless than ever before. For now, they no longer care where and whom they hit. As a fighter, you have to think that there is a human being behind the mask. No matter how many sorrows and quarrels you've had throughout the year with somebody, you still have to behave humanly in those moments. You should not only think about the revenge. Because I have the impression that now this battle is just a kind of revenge. It seems that in the past the battle used to be more connected to manhood and supremacy, not with revenge. But look how two years ago many were taken by ambulances, and the same thing happened last year on December 31. So, this is how things are. Besides rumor went that here in Ruginoasa we are barbarian and so on. I believe it's not normal for a young man like the one beaten last year to be left with marks for the rest of his life. As I said before, I would not like this tradition to vanish, but I would not like it to stay like it is right now. This New Year tradition opens in fact all the New Year rituals and that's why it is important for us. (Gica Lupu, 57 years old, Rediu village, July 6, 2012, Interview)

Not only did the battle on December 31, 2011, produce bewilderment among locals, but it also led to understanding lucidly that this tradition could not go on in its current form. The fact also became obvious for local and county authorities who decided after December 2011 that they should issue a law forbidding this type of battle. The people of Ruginoasa felt regretful and nostalgic about that, since they had been used to the ritual their entire life. As many of my interviewees mentioned, the morning battle was part of a ritual complex that comprised two other rituals with a theatrical dimension more obvious than in the case of the mummers' battle. These two rituals were *Malanca* and *Târâitul*.

Figure 2.2. Two fighters from the Valley area right before the morning battle—December 31, 2010.

Photo credit: Alin Rus

THE MUMMERS' BATTLE, MALANCA AND TÂRÂITUL—THE MANIFOLD RITUAL COMPLEX RELATED TO MANHOOD IN RUGINOASA COMUNĂ

Despite the violence it involves, the *Mummers' Battle* is considered a winter tradition or a traditional game by the inhabitants of Ruginoasa. During the talks and interviews I had with villagers, many drew my attention that this custom should be nothing more than a test of manhood and bravery, dominated by fair play because it belongs to a manifold ritual complex that includes two more rituals, the *Malanca* and the *Târâitul*. The first time I heard such an assumption was in the evening of December 30, 2011, when I had the chance to witness the last stage in the process of mask making for the fighters in the *vale*. One of the fighters that planned to mask himself on the following morning declared:

> Despite these acts of violence, fighters make up when the battle is over. Because they meet afterwards for the *Malancă* and maybe even join the same team for this ritual. Yet, they can even be relatives and still fight against one another in the morning. In the afternoon they meet in the center, they have a beer or a glass of wine, and the relations between them must remain decent. (Mihai, fighter for the team in *the valley*, December 30, 2011, field notes)

Following the line of logical continuity between the two rituals, I observed similar statements during my formal interviews, too:

> *Malanca* could be considered a sort of reconciliation because the ones who mask themselves in the morning and join the battle, later join the *Malanca*, so they get to visit the houses of the one they had fought with in the morning. And then you ask yourself: what do they do if they get to the house of the one they had beaten in the morning? Do they expect for his relatives to hit them back? Well, there might be exceptions too, maybe the ones with *Malanca* won't visit the house of a hardly beaten young man like the one whose skull had been fractured in 2011. As for the rest, they go, nobody stops them and they are welcomed almost everywhere. (Cosmin Ungureanu, 23 years old, Dumbrăvița village, April 4, 2017, Interview)

Another interviewee argued in the same direction: "Despite the violence during the mummers' battle, the main idea is that, even if you fight in the morning, in the afternoon, with the *Malanca*, you have to make up" (Dumitru Lupu, 57 years old, Rediu village, July 6, 2012, Interview).

But the most appealing observation about the relation between *Malanca* and *The Mummers's Battle* comes from my talk with Mr. Michi Balcan who participated in both rituals many times. As a well-situated local in the social world of Dumbrăvița village, he welcomed the *Malanca* teams for many consecutive years to his own courtyard. "*Malanca* is exactly the opposite of the morning battle. If I, for instance, organize a *Malanca*, even if I am from the *valley*, I can have five–six young men from the hill in my *Malanca team*. That's not a problem. Once the *Malanca* begins, all the evil is forgotten and stepped on. This is the real beauty of these rituals!" Mr. Michi Balcan declared with a triumphant smile on his face, and then took his idea further.

> With the *Malanca*, the war hatchet is buried and all the people on the other side of the village, from the *hill*, come to me singing and smiling. And I welcome everybody because there is no more problems between us. That's how *Malanca* has to be. Because if I, for instance, organize *Malanca*, everybody knows I make huge efforts. On this occasion, I have to slaughter a 100–150 kilograms pig, to pay a band of six–seven musicians, to offer five–six meals for all of them. Therefore, nobody is allowed to quarrel within my *Malanca team*, no matter where he comes from, either the *hill* or the *valley*. Because this would offend me after spending so much and making an effort so that this ritual can take place. (Michi Balcan, 50 years old, Dumbrăvița village, January 3, 2012, Interview)

But what is actually *Malanca*? One of the few folklorists having researched the ritual of *Malanca* for decades, Horea Barbu Oprișan gives a very expressive depiction of it:

> The *Malanca* parade impresses everyone. It looks as if the entire village started to party, cheering up all the ones who stayed at home. *Malanca* is a spectacular manifestation extant in Bukovina. In time, it spread towards the Moldavian areas, until Roman, but not under the forms it has in Bukovina. . . . In the beginning, Malanca was a carol and it used to be expressed simply; maybe that is how it arrived or was brought from the North, from the Slavic world. With the time passing, *Malanca* developed its forms, evolving to a parade that looked like a performance with multiple numbers; nothing is fix. Everything depends on the actors, but especially on the participants. (Oprișan 1981:176)

Many of the observations Oprișan made stand for the *Malanca* in the villages of Ruginoasa too. In Ruginoasa, the *Malanca* teams are big parades with fifteen to twenty-five members, sometimes even thirty. Such a team had two to four *arnăuți*[8] (usually two *in buttons*—dressed in military uniform, and two *in flowers*—dressed in folk costumes), ten–twenty *căldărari* and the music band with four–five musicians usually, including two trumpetists, one or two trombone players (also called *baritons* in local language), one clarinetist and one drummer. The most important team member is the organizing *arnăut* also known as *arnăut-șef*. He is responsible for organizing the whole group and for planning the ritual from A to Z. Therefore, that *Malanca* is named after the family name of that young man. I heard the locals from Ruginoasa saying "Here's Lupu's Malanca!" or "Cernăuțeanu's Malanca is coming!"

The *arnăutul-șef*, necessarily dressed in buttoned-up *arnăut* clothes, usually takes a close and trustworthy friend to help him, and this one is also dressed in a similar costume. They have to control the ten–fifteen *căldărari* who sometimes tend to be too cheerful and disorganized when the fanfare is singing, and the dance begins. Apart from the fact that they are also dancing, the other two *arnăuți*, also called *arnăuți in flowers*, have to knock at people's gates and ask if they want to welcome the *Malanca team*. *Căldărarii* are dressed in multicolored costumes, have metal bells around their waists and brushes and rattles in hand. The name of all these characters is strictly linked to the *comună*'s history. We know that the ruler Alexandru Ioan Cuza had appointed at his court around the palace in Ruginoasa mercenaries of Albanian origin, dressed in specific uniforms, with buttons sewn diagonally on their chest and back. So, the *arnăuți in buttons* within the *Malanca* wear exactly this type of military outfit, imitating the uniforms the Albanian mercenaries hired by Cuza Vodă used to wear. The *arnăuți in flowers* wear folk costumes like the ones most of the peasants in Ruginoasa used to wear before World War II. The *căldărari* in the *Malanca* wear, as their name suggests, the clothes of the nomad gypsies who in the past used to sell various products (like pots, metal and wooden objects, brushes and even rattles—a kind of wooden box with a handle that produces a deafening noise whenever the handle is turned) to peasants.

Apart from the music band paid before the ritual by the *arnăut-șef* and composed of older persons, the other team members are youngsters that had reached the age of marriage. This is how the participants describe the *Malanca* and its stages:

> In November at *Lăsata Secului*, on November 14, the *arnăut-șef* already know whether he wants to organize a *Malanca*. As soon as a firm decision was taken he first calls for music bands—the so-called *fanfares*—in neighboring towns such as Roman, Sirețel, Pașcani and even Iași. Such a fanfare costs between 7500–8000 lei ($1800–2000). The *arnăut* organizing the *Malanca* pays the mummers that join him according to a sum they decide before, and from the money he receives, a part goes to his band's members, and the rest is his. He is also the one deciding how much each mummer is to be paid. Thus, some mummers could get more if they are good dancers and especially if they are serious (do not get drunk, do not do stupid things like leaving the team out of the blue, etc.). Most of the times, *arnăuții-șefi* (the leaders of Malanca's teams) get their money back and even get a profit. I have rarely heard of *arnăuți* that lose the money invested. If they walk around the entire comună, the *arnăut-șef* gets all his money back and even some extra. But most often his profit ranges about 1000–2000 lei ($250–500) for him alone. So, the *arnăut-șef* is a sort of manager

who has to share the resources available very well so that in the end some profit is possible. To do that, he has to choose very well the young men for the team. He must get those who are resistant, go from house to house, do not lose time chatting uselessly, and do not run the risk of getting drunk, etc. Well, each such team member can even get 100 lei extra from the *arnăut*. (Cosmin Ungureanu, 23 years old, Dumbrăvița village, April 4, 2017, Interview)

Malanca is the most complex ritual in the series of winter holiday customs taking place in Ruginoasa *comună*.

The *Malanca* starts on December 31 around 5–6 p.m., and finishes on January 2, at 2 p.m. During this time, there are some moments of break when the team members rest and eat. The most important break is on the night of December 31, from 4 a.m. until 8 p.m. when the people in the band go to sleep. Usually, they all sleep in the same house, previously chosen by the *arnăut-șef*. In most cases, it is his parents' house, but it could well be the house of an uncle or a relative if this person agrees, and if the house occupies a strategic place in the comună (a place from where the band can start a route that would bring a larger profit to the *Malanca* led by that *arnăut*. (Mihai Lupu, 76 years old, Dumbrăvița village, May 4, 2017, Interview)

The most important moments in the *Malanca* ritual are the ones when the group enters the family's courtyard.

In my courtyard, for instance, after I allow them to get in, the band starts singing and the guys start dancing right away, involving my daughters in their dance. Because I have three young daughters my household is in high demand during the *Malanca*. It's mostly the *arnăuți in buttons* who invite the girls to dance. That's how it always happens. In my courtyard, they usually sing three or four songs. But I also reward them with at least 50 lei ($13). We should all know that a fanfare is very expensive, and its organizer has to get back the money he had invested in the music. Then, there is the food the *arnăut* pays for all the meals offered to the team members, at least four–five times during the entire ritual. You need to slaughter at least one pig to prepare all food for the occasion. But most money go to the musicians that come from neighboring towns and cities. I have even had bands from Zece Prăjini and from Belcești, Iași, Valea Mare. The organizers of the *Malanca* have to bring the best bands available in the area; otherwise, people don't welcome them, and the teams cannot cope with the competition either (Michi Balcan, 50 years old, Dumbrăvița village, January 3, 2012, Interview).

Just like with the *Play of the Deer* in Heleșteni comună, the *Malanca* team in the villages of Ruginoasa is interested a lot in the money collected from the householders.

Usually, they stay for about 5–10 minutes at each house, and the householder pays about 50–100 lei ($13–26). The least amount one could give is 30 lei ($8). But only a few people give that little. More, if the householder is well-off, he may ask for a *badana*[9] dance. This is an individual rhythmic dance performed by a *căldărar* or an *arnăut* on his knees, around his *badana* that lies down on the ground. For this dance, the *căldărar* or *arnăut* receives some extra 10–15 lei ($2.5–$3.5). All in all, a householder might pay even 1000 lei ($260) for all the teams that visit him during the holidays. There are about three to five *Malănci* organized in the entire comună. (Cosmin Ungureanu, 23 years old, Dumbrăvița village, April 4, 2017, Interview)

Extending the comparison with the Heleșteni rituals, one can notice that the *Malanca* in Ruginoasa has things in common with the courtship elements in the *Play of the Goat* from the neighboring locality; it thus stands for the same trends and values within a peasant world strictly and rigorously regulated. Maybe this is precisely the reason why some people in Ruginoasa also call the *Malanca* by the name of *Goat*. And, just as with the *Play of the Deer* in Heleșteni, I have experienced the ritual towards its final stage, when the strict rules of the peasant family started to be replaced by new ones, only to be able to keep alive a disintegrating custom. The statements the people of Ruginoasa have made lead to this conclusion.

Being an *arnăut-șef* was a great honor especially in the past. The reason was that organizing a *Malanca* and managing everything well during the ritual was a difficult task. First of all, it involved expenses that not anybody could afford. All the youngsters joining the ritual had their military service accomplished and were interested in getting married. And *Malanca* was like a sort of chance to build a reputation in front of the girls. So, the ritual was strongly connected to the idea of marriage and founding a family. In recent times, younger children and even girls acting as *arnăuți* started to organize a *Malancă*. But this happened only after the 1989 Revolution. Before, the young people organizing the *Malanca* would not have allowed this to happen. But now the ritual could disappear if these children would not create teams, too. (Mihai Lupu, 76 years old, Dumbrăvița village, May 4, 2017, Interview)

The slow decline of the *Malanca* goes hand in hand with the tendency to accumulate more profit from performing it, a fact that has become obvious even in the case of the *Play of the Goat* and the *Deer* in Heleșteni.

For the last couple of years, there's been a competition between the *arnăuți-șefi* for attracting the most skilled dancers that they pay better, too. This is something recent. There was no such thing before. And this happens because an increasing number of young people don't preserve the tradition and don't want to join these customs anymore. That is why it is increasingly difficult to make a team. Let's take my example: I am among those who care about village traditions; even if I won less, I would not want to go work abroad. I want to spend winter holidays every year here in Ruginoasa. I am happy with the salary I have here in the village as a teacher. (Cosmin Ungureanu, 23 years old, Dumbrăvița village, April 4, 2017, Interview)

Meanwhile, a kind of atomization of the community is observable, given the fact that some richer householders offer more money to the *Malanca* teams whereas others who cannot compete with these prices, stopped opening their doors when caroling teams approached. Besides, the increasing violence of the morning confrontation shed a negative light on the whole village world, and this was also reflected in the way *Malanca* was performed.

This *Mummers' Battle* should go on, even if the two teams stop fighting, and just walk around the village in ugly outfits. Now the battle has kind of changed. People have kind of lost their mind. In the past, the New Year used to last three days. I remember that in the past the *Malanca* used to come here in Rediu—a rather isolated village in the *comună*—only on January 3. And people would welcome everybody. When I was a teenager, householders would always open their doors and ask: *Whose are you?* And we would reply: *We are the Malanca of Lupu from Rediu.* Now there are many who stopped welcoming the *Malanca*. But the ones welcoming the ritual offer more money than they used to in the past. In the past, more people opened, but less money was given. But in the past one could trust the mummers. Because, after the morning battle, they would stop fooling around. So, even if they quarreled in the morning, then they would walk together with *Malanca* and other rituals in all the villages. It was like an unwritten law. After the morning battle, everyone stopped fighting. But now one cannot trust them anymore. People are much nastier. Youngsters are more shameless. (Dumitru Lupu, 57 years old, Rediu village, July 6, 2012, Interview)

Indeed, the socio-economic changes in recent years had an increasing impact on the performance of these rural plays, gradually leading to their detachment from each other. In the past, however, the relation between the *Mummers Battle* and other village rituals was much stronger. All these were well observed by the inhabitants of Ruginoasa themselves.

I say that *Malanca* was born at the same time with the morning confrontation. I'm saying this because they are somehow connected. After the battle, there had to be a party, too. For, if we were to regard the morning confrontation as a sort of sports game, it's normal that, after winning, the winner has to be acclaimed, and the victory has to be celebrated with play and music. *Malanca* takes all sorrows out of us. It washes our worries away and breaks burdens into pieces. When I hear the *Malanca* fanfare playing and I see the men dancing, I find myself with tears of happiness in my eyes. I enjoy the moment, I like it. But, after the tough fight on December 31 a few days ago, it looks as if a complete silence covered Ruginoasa, and everyone shut up, too. Even the masks used for the fight were dropped and nobody used them for the ritual called *Târâitul.* (Michi Balcan, 50 years old, Dumbrăviţa village, January 3, 2012, Interview)

Târâitul is a ritual that resembles a lot the *Pantomimic Mummers* in Heleşteni. But, unlike the mummers in Heleşteni who visit their friends' households, youngsters in Ruginoasa who join the *Târâit* only visit the houses of the girls they consider fancy or for which team members nourish even more profound feelings. Generally, *Târâitul* is a ritual with a simple morphology. One of the participants described it very clearly in a few sentences:

> *Târâitul* takes place on the evening of January 1, but also on January 2, from evening to morning or depending on each one's tether. The aim of this ritual is that men old enough to get married visit the young ladies' houses. Four–five lads, usually very best friends, form a group and visit the households where marriageable girls live; they all put on ugly masks like those wear during the *Morning Battle with Sticks*. So, they don't use those beautiful helmets that *căldărari* wear for the *Malanca.* In the case of the *Târâit*, the organization is much less complex that in the *Malanca* and many times the decision is taken on the spot. The same happens for choosing the houses where they go. But they only pay attention to houses where young unmarried girls live. First of all, the group makes noise in front of the window, and then utters a caroling (*urare*). Then, when the girl gets out, the mummers put lipstick or flour on her face. They push her around a little and she tries to guess who is behind the mask. If he is nearby, the householder shares the same fate, being teased and hit with knitted scarves, old handbags or rubber hoses. With *Târâitul*, one only visits the girls he knows. As a result, the team does not usually visit more than four–five houses. Wishing (making an *urare*) is necessary because one cannot visit a house only to tease. One also has to make an *urare (caroling)*, and the householder is then obliged to ask the men to join the dinner, or at least to offer some wine and cook-ies. No money is given to the *Târâit*, and the main idea is not that of performing it for the money; therefore, a team may well remain even for half an hour at somebody's house, whereas with the *Malanca* the main idea is that of getting the money and moving quickly to the next house, so such a thing as with the *Târâit* would not happen. (Cosmin Ungureanu, 23 years old, Dumbrăviţa village, April 4, 2017, Interview)

From the interviews I have taken to elder people in the village, the logical sequence of the rituals was supposed to be as follows: *Mummers' Battle, Malanca* and *Târâit.* While *Malanca* displayed youngsters as good organizers which, in the meantime, had sufficient resources to organize such a complex ritual, *Târâitul* presented the strong-spirited young men in the village as true, courageous men who were not afraid of a tough confrontation. Precisely because of this reason, until a few years ago, *Târâitul* had been strongly linked to the *Morning Mummers' Battle*. This was especially because the ones who joined the ritual use the same ugly masks that fighters use in the battle between the two groups. Wearing these masks in front of their sweethearts, the young men proved their maleness. Young lads presented themselves in front of their lovers as real knights who had joined a real battle, and their ugly masks proved the experience. At least that is how things looked like until a few years ago when the fight between mummers became increasingly violent.

Once the *Morning Battle* became a national news subject, it started to look rather like a fight for victory, despite the risks and the costs, thus detaching itself of all the other traditions performed in the comună. This tendency has also been marked by the gradual disappearance of any rules imposed by tradition, also including here its firm connection to the *Malanca* and the *Târâit*. Thus, if in 2009 I was a witness myself of the way elder men from the *valley* trained the youngsters and accompanied them to the place of the fight where they would make sure civilians stayed out of the battle and fallen mummers are not being hit, in 2011 this was not possible any longer. During that confrontation, all older men who tried to interfere were beaten and sometimes had their heads injured by flying stones.

In 2009, few minutes after the battle was over, I had the opportunity to talk to a fighter from the *valley* who, despite having lost the battle, stated: "It was beautiful! This year was the most beautiful one!" The following day, watching the recordings of the battle, I saw that fighter from the *valley* was one of the last ones to run of his opponents. Before, although he had had the chance to hit harshly a fighter from the *deal*, he only hit him once with the club, right in the middle of his head—the spot best protected by the mask, where no serious injury can happen. Afterwards, he threw his club and ran down the *valley*. Well, all these elements disappeared in 2011, and the battle turned into a bloody slaughter with clubs, stones, bricks, fists, and feet hitting without mercy; the luckiest ones managed to escape, and the most unfortunate got to the hospital. Mr. Michi Balcan was able to offer me a very expressive conclusion on the effects of the 2011 battle by comparing it with the way most battles used to be when he was young:

> Well, when I was young, there was no event like the one that happened a few days ago [December 31, 2011]. Back then, mummers from the *hill* ran back to their area, we would stay in ours, jumping with joy and excitement and then we would go to the center in small groups. And let me give you an example. When I was young, uphill there lived a very strong and brave man, an exceptional fighter called Claidei. Right before the battle, he came alone among our people and said: *I know that my people have no team this year but, if you agree, I dare to fight with any of your men one by one. Or, if you want, I put my mask*

on next to your team and fight against my people to show them they were not capable of forming a decent team this year. Well, nobody had anything against this young man. Nobody touched him and they all admired his courage. This is what fair play used to be. And fair play also meant nobody would hit the fallen opponents. If I saw anybody from the rival team fallen to the ground, I would not touch him. I would fight with the ones still standing. The one who had fallen was already a victim.

The present events and the consequences of the recent fights are usually presented in contrast to the fair-play that exists between combatants in the past, by my interviewees.

But it's revealing to see what happened after the victims had been sent to the hospital this year. Today I have found out an information: there are eight people from Ruginoasa at the neurosurgery department of the hospital in Iași. Four are from the *deal* and four are from the *valley*. They all cry on each other's shoulders and they are sorry for what happened. Their medical condition is quite serious: one had a brain surgery and could not hear anything afterwards, so he had to go through an ear surgery. Another one is in a coma and his condition is critical. Another one, civilian, had a bone in his arm broken so bad that they had to add an implant to fix it. Even one of my brothers, also civilian, ran away, but was caught and they broke his head, fractured his arm bone, and made his hip black and blue with their clubs. They caught him on a side street when he was heading back home, and they crushed him on the spot. His luck was a man called Chiriac (from the *deal*) who interfered between the attackers and my brother. That's how he managed to escape because otherwise they might have killed him. And these are not all the victims; some with head injuries and less serious wounds were hospitalized in Pașcani city, and later the same day they were sent home after basic medical care.

As inhabitant of Ruginoasa, I would not want this ritual to vanish. Because without it we are only half of what we really are. But we will definitely have to ask for support from the security forces so that this custom is done in a civilized way, and especially without the civilians' intervention; they have nothing to do with this battle. Authorities have to help us so that mummers could fight decently and not with civilians. (Michi Balcan, 50 years old, Dumbrăvița village, January 3, 2012, Interview)

The battle of 2011 proved that the rules of the rural traditions—already in a process of slow disintegration since communist times—are almost extinct, and that a fight that used to be part of a manifold ritual complex related to manhood became just a sensational news topic resembling a *Reality TV* where violence and brutality met no other opposition. This fact was excellently underlined by one of my interviewees who made the following remark:

The young lads from the *deal* who fool around also during the year—also men-acing the politicians in the opposition, for example—are called *pirates* or *huns*. Generally, these people have little or no education at all. A few decades ago, villages would fight each other. Now, people from within the same village fight with each other. If you had discovered these *pirates* from the *deal* behind their masks, you would have seen they don't belong to any other band like *Malanca* and *Târâitul* except for the *Morning Battle*. They don't organize anything as such. Additionally, more than half of them are married people who would normally have nothing to do in there. They should be taken by the police right away. Normally, the first ones who should put their masks on are those organiz-ing the *Malănci* and walking with the *Târâitul*. (Costică Nechifor, 65 years old, Dumbrăvița village, January 3, 2012, Interview)

Mr. Nechifor's observations are eloquent for the situation presented. The slow disintegration of peasant values and principles in Ruginoasa *comună* finally led to isolating all the rituals within Ruginoasa' villages. While the *Malanca*—just as the *Play of the Goat* in Helești—became a com-modity and an increasingly profitable business, the confrontation between *deleni* and *văleni* in the village of Dumbrăvița became a *Reality TV* type of sensational news, where the battle's winners were happy to see their faces for a few minutes on local and national television screens. Yet, despite this preliminary conclusion, there were still a few doubts regarding the participa-tion of the so-called *civilians* and of the mature men into the fight in recent years. Teacher Mihai Lupu provided an explanation based on a compara-tive approach:

A short while ago, I participated in a conference in Iași dealing with tradition, and I raised a question: *Why would the fight with tomatoes in Buñol in Eastern Spain or the crowd's battle with the running bulls in Pamplona in Northern Spain be more legitimate than the battle of the mummers in Ruginoasa? Why Ruginoasa battle is always sanctioned by the police and the gendarmes while these customs in Spain turned into huge tourist attractions?* Maybe it's our own fault, too, since, as teachers in the *comună*, we have not get involved enough to explain to all locals the aim and the symbolism of this battle. On the other hand, I understand that the interference of civilians in the battle turned it into a very violent fight. I believe *civilians* are those who generate the most violent acts during the battle. But I know from my own experience that these *civilians'* pres-ence in the battle is a recent phenomenon, appeared after the 1989 Revolution. But I simply cannot explain myself the mutation provoked in the mind of the *civilian* locals who began to join the battle more actively and more violently. I still believe it's a mutation produced over time, during many years, and linked to certain social and maybe economic processes affecting the community. (Mihai Lupu, 76 years old, Dumbrăvița village, May 4, 2017, Interview)

The deep observations made by the teacher Mihai Lupu—who has well understood the relation between the economic, political, and social changes, and the winter rituals of the people in Ruginoasa—represent the starting point for the analysis in the last section of this chapter.

LABOR MIGRATION, SOCIAL INEQUALITIES, AND THEIR RELATIONSHIP WITH RUGINOASA'S BATTLE WITH STICKS

Mihai Lupu's observations led me to striking revelations regarding the relationship between the battle with sticks, social inequalities and labor migration in Ruginoasa comună. In 1969, in the chapter *From Local Folklore/Din folclorul local* of his monography about Ruginoasa, the historian Boris Crăciun was already remarking the big social and economic transformations of the locality during the first two decades of Communism. Crăciun linked these social changes to the privileged geographic location of the *comună*, between two important towns in the region—Paşcani and Târgul-Frumos—and close to communication routes such as the car roads and the railways. All these elements enhanced the migration to urban areas and commuting to jobs in nearby towns. In its turn, labor migration produced important changes in the locals' mentality. Many of them gave up their furniture, their traditional house decorations, and their old activities such as sunflower and hemp oil pressing with the primitive tools extant within the peasant household (Crăciun 1969:84–85).

The people I interviewed in Ruginoasa also mentioned the socio-economic changes the settlement went through during Communism and Postsocialism. Mr. Mihai Lupu even explained the disappearance of the battle between the mummers' teams in the villages Rediu and Bugioaia through the migration of youngsters from Rediu towards larger urban centers like Iaşi where they subsequently attended university studies and, later on, many of them settled down. Under these circumstances, those who were left to continue this sort of violent confrontation were "a rather poor peasant category that had less contact with the city world and more with agriculture, field work and village world (Mihai Lupu, 76 years old, Dumbrăviţa village, May 4, 2017, Interview)."

Mr. Michi Balcan, in his youth nine times a participant in the mummers' battle, also observed this tendency:

Usually, if the men who masked themselves for the battle had a neighbor or friend who was their age and would study and be passionate about books, they would not urge him to join the battle. On the contrary, they would say: *Leave this one alone for he is delicate, he goes to the university, he's got nothing to do with us here!* (Michi Balcan, 50 years old, Dumbrăviţa village, January 3, 2012, Interview)

These observations were confirmed when I had the chance to talk to a 21-year-old student in the Veterinary Medicine University in Iaşi, from Rediu village. Asked whether or not he would like to join the morning battle of the mummers, he replied to me on a very annoyed and convincing tone: "You think I'm a fool to join the battle?!? I have got exams to pass, a lot to study. If a club hits my head, I would no longer be capable of anything. Why would I do that?" (Dănuţ Lupu, 21 years old, Rediu village, July 6, 2012, Interview).

Other young people with university studies from Ruginoasa, such as the sports teacher Cosmin Ungureanu, aged 23, denied even the idea that the battle's winners would nowadays be of more importance for the girls in the comună: "I don't think the young mummers who win the battle are more prestigious for the girls, as some televisions reported many times. This is stupid! A decent girl shall look for a normal young man, not a crazy one like this!" (Cosmin Ungureanu, 23 years old, Dumbrăviţa village, April 4, 2017, Interview). On the other hand, the young men currently involved in the battle state different opinions: "Men who don't like to fight cannot be considered real men. This is a knight's tradition! It's a test of courage" (young participant in the battle, the evening before the battle on December 31, 2011).

It was not only differences in education and social status that had an increasingly important role in selecting those who join the battle and those who do not. The evening before the violent battle of 2011, while chatting with Mr. Michi Balcan in a village bar, I saw a young man entering with his mummer clothes on and the club in his hand. He sat down at a table close to ours, next to some people of his age, and ordered a vodka shot. Watching him with admiration, Mr. Balcan said: "I like this young man. He's a brave fighter and he fights really well. He's a bit poor, though. In fact, the poorer men fight better and get involved more into the battle." Asked why it is rather the poor ones that join the battle and not the ones positioned on a higher social level, Mr. Mihai Lupu provided a concise answer:

The poor always had to fight to get something in life, to be someone. I know this from my own experience because I had a very difficult life. Therefore, I had to work enormously to become a teacher and to get to where I am now. Whereas someone from a richer family got all these and even more than that much easier. (Mihai Lupu, 76 years old, Dumbrăviţa village, May 4, 2017, Interview)

Differences in social status became very visible especially after the battle of 2011, when the people of Ruginoasa found out who were the victims and the ones most seriously wounded in the battle:

> Three days ago, the most seriously injured was a 17-year-old youngster. He's from the Coţovanu family, a large family with a dad who's a tractor driver. I even feel pity for these people because they are poor, and they don't even have a medical insurance. I'm thinking of what's going to happen to this poor guy, injured like that and with no medical cover. Oh dear! (Costică Nechifor, 65 years old, Dumbrăviţa village, January 3, 2012, Interview)

The urbanization tendency in Ruginoasa and the loss of traditional customs became very visible in the communist period, but continued in postsocialist times, along with the beginning of the massive labor migration wave to western European countries. Among the big changes brought by capitalism, after the fall of the communist block in 1989, social polarization became more obvious, based on class and social status differences. In this context, a significant segment of the active and more qualified population tried its luck and chances by emigrating to more developed European countries. But, as many of my interviewees noticed, most of those migrating even temporarily for work to western European countries, stopped joining the morning battle:

> The young men coming from foreign countries usually don't join the battle anymore. They say the risks are too high and find it meaningless. Usually most of them have a well-paid job in Italy, Belgium, or England, and do not want to risk losing their contract for a few crazy moments. They got used to another way of thinking, with respect for work discipline, health and so on. Joining the morning battle would involve the risk of breaking a hand or leg and then losing everything they have there. But I saw many of them coming to record. They bought professional cameras and would rather film the battle than getting involved as participants. (Dumitru Lupu, 57 years old, Rediu village, July 6, 2012, Interview)

During my field research, I have tried to better understand the relation between migrant workers and their participation in the morning battle. Indeed, I managed to find only a single fighter who has also migrated abroad. He is Ionel, Mr. Michi Balcan's younger brother, and he came back from Italy specially to see the New Year's rituals. His story is fascinating from the perspective of the motivation that made him join the battle, but also for his idealist traditional vision that made him travel 2000 km only to join the fight:

> Every year I come from Italy for this tradition. But not everybody is like me. Many who are westernized while working abroad don't come back to fight.

However, I'm still sure that 80% of the migrants come to spend their holidays at home. Because in Italy, for instance, you don't find this kind of New Year customs. I work in construction in a town 60 km away from Rome. I arrived yesterday evening. I drove 2000 km without stopping the car's engine and without any rest at all. I'm going to join the morning battle and then I'm walking with the *Malanca* and *Târâitul.* That's me, I can't be otherwise. . . . This battle is more like a bullfight. But the bull tears you into pieces. But here, even somebody from the opposite team may lend you a hand. But it's somehow close to the bullfight in Spain—a tough yet legal game. The *Mummers' Battle* is a tradition that only the people in the area feel, despite the fact that everybody watching provides all sorts of philosophical explanations. Even the policemen that belong here know what it is all about and let it be. But outsiders regard it as an act of barbarianism. You should know that there are even women who wouldn't eat a *sarma*[10] in the morning unless they saw the morning battle on December 31. (Ionel Balcan, 32 years old, Dumbrăvița village, December 30, 2011, Interview)

Ionel brief interview is relevant for the way an individual with a transnational identity regards the world and life, with he being at the same time a successful migrant to Italy and a peasant grown in a rural culture, within a family strongly attached to the rural traditions. Talking about this type of transnational identity, Michael Kearney compared it to that of global corporations' identity that is hard to understand from the perspective of the binary logic or the *We-The Others* dualist model adopted in the construction of national identities (Kearney 1996:146). This type of identity is not only more complex, but also more difficult to define and analyze because it is more volatile than the ancient peasant identity connected to the village world and agricultural life in a small rural household based on the work done by family members. Analyzing the new global living and production conditions that the individual in agrarian societies experiences, Van der Ploeg also speaks about a *new peasantry* (Ploeg 2009) while Kearney uses the term *polybians* to describe the multitude of situations, expressions, and circumstances where peasants show up in global society (Kearney 1996:147). From this perspective, the discourse of Ionel Balcan, is revealing. It also brings valuable information about the sequences of the ritual of *Mummers' Battle* in Ruginoasa.

Tonight we organize our team just like a trainer organizes his team before the football match and tells them: you are the striker, you are the midfielder, you are the defender, you do this, you do that. So, this evening is even more important than tomorrow morning's battle because tomorrow's result depends on it. We are 25 now in the team. The opposite team had 20–30 members, too. The most important players are those in the first row. Because the ones in the back might not get to fight if the ones ahead fought well or badly.

Maybe I shouldn't have come home, but I'm too attracted to these rituals. First of all, I left my work aside. I'll lose two weeks of work, as well as the salary I would have got had I stayed there. Besides, there's also all the expenses here that reached almost 3000 Euro. In addition, there were some issues at work and I should've stayed there until they are solved. But I told my boss that I have to go. I told him straight: *You may fire me or shoot me, but for the New Year I go back to my village.* I have my traditions, my parents, and my brothers here in the village, and nobody can stop me from seeing them. My birthday is on December 19, so I wanted to be home for my birthday. And my father who is 80 now is the one dressing me in the morning when I go to the battle. I cannot live without this battle. This is my blood; I have to respect the tradition. When I left Italy my heart was as big as a fist, now it's like a watermelon because I'm happy to be back home and to be able to join all these traditions. (Ionel Balcan, 32 years old, Dumbrăvița village, December 30, 2011, Interview)

Despite my interviewees' repeated reassurance that both the *Traditional Morning Battle* and the *Malanca* (or other traditions in the locality) have preserved their symbolism and structure unchanged, my impression was totally different. The migrants' attendance—either as passive viewers or as active participants in the winter rituals of the comună—has had a decisive influence on the relationships and social networks involved in the designing of these customs. Another element added was the globalization of all these traditions, and especially of the *Mummers' Battle*, by press mediatization and by the dozens of video recordings of the ritual published on YouTube and on newspaper and television websites. In their own turn, all these aspects began to influence the way the traditions were organized, their aim, as well as the way locals approached them.

Under these circumstances, the participants' selection for the *Mummers' Battle* became more serious. Those more educated or coming from the richest families in the *comună* or from the migrants' category join the tradition less or do not join it at all. On the contrary, those who still live in the *comună* and work in agriculture, unskilled or low-skilled labor, in Ruginoasa or nearby, join the battle more and more, despite their age or their relationship with other rituals in the comună (such as *Malanca* or *Târâitul*). These tendencies led to the increase in violence during the battle and, simultaneously, to a more sophisticated strategy for the battle. In the middle of such a violent battle, the presence of the *civilians*, so harshly criticized by my interviewees who were attached to the old morphology and symbolism of the battle, has now become necessary. Without mask and costume, but with clubs in their hands, the *civilians* benefit from greater mobility and visibility than mummers and have the task of covering the sides of the mummers' groups that cannot see the opponents' attempts to surround and to infiltrate from the laterals. The *civilians* also have to push the mummers' group forward, in a sort of rugby scrum where what matters most is not the individuals' skillfulness, strengths and fighting talent, but the size of the group itself and thus its push force.

The talks I had with the fighters themselves reinforced this conclusion. On the evening of December 30, 2011, I had the chance to witness the final moment when the masks were sewn, as well as the discussions the evening before the fight. That night, many of the fighters involved in the battle the following day criticized the active participation of civilians in the battle. Nevertheless, the following day, while watching the recordings I had done on the spot, I was surprised to see that exactly those who were critical about the civilians' interference in the battle were actually on the position of civilians defending the sides of the mummers' groups with their long and strong acacia clubs. Put together, these details made me understand that the desire of winning the battle had become stronger than the fighting norms and principles of the peasant tradition. The dissipation of these traditional norms has been a slow process that started in the communist period when the authorities tried to use politically the violence during the battle, and the most violent individuals remarked during it were used to complete the *comună*'s collectivization by responding harshly to any voice that would state a different opinion. Once the young people in the village started migrating to university centers in the region and, following the December 1989 Revolution, migrating to foreign countries, these tendencies accelerated along with the social discrepancies between villagers.

My interview with Ionel Balcan—who emigrated to Italy—is relevant in this respect. According to traditional norms, he should not have joined the battle anymore. His age—over 32—and the fact that he had already been married for many years when the battle took place, were conditions that would have normally disqualified him as active presence within the fighting group. But the nostalgia about his village traditions turned hyperbolical inside his migrant soul, and gave him a transnational identity, always caught between two or more worlds, condemned to travel ceaselessly between them, and left without the possibility to find himself fully without this permanent move. These facts are representative for most of the migrants from Ruginoasa whom I had the opportunity to talk to. Many of them do not join actively their village traditions, but are incapable of spending holidays in the country they migrated to. A short fragment from my interview with Cosmin Ungureanu is relevant in this respect:

> There are men who do not find jobs around here, and they leave. They go especially to England, Italy, and Belgium. These are mostly the countries they want to get to. I have a friend who went to England and could not come back home for holidays. So, I had FaceTime phone conversation with him, so that he could watch live the *Malanca* and all the other rituals, and he was just staying

there and crying. (Cosmin Ungureanu, 23 years old, Dumbrăvița village, April 4, 2017, Interview)

Another fragment from my interview with Dumitru Lupu, social aid office chief in the Ruginoasa *comună* hall, also reinforces the conclusions above. This is his comprehensive outlook on the comună's winter rituals:

> If the most active young men in the *comună* went to foreign countries, and the most intelligent went to university, the ones who are still in the village are the ones least prepared intellectually. And these ones knew nothing else except for the *Morning Battle* and maybe the *Malanca*. Because for these two customs, you don't have to learn any lines, whereas with the *Play of the Goat* or the *Play of the Deer* you have to prepare many consecutive days to perform your part. In the past parents used to get involved into this. They would teach their children the lines. Nowadays they no longer do that because they have less spare time than in the past, and all children would rather be *căldărari* at the *Malanca* because all they have to do there is dance, and this does not involve days of rehearsal. (Dumitru Lupu, 57 years old, Rediu village, July 6, 2012, Interview)

THE IMPOSSIBLE PATRIMONIALIZATION OF RUGINOASA'S BATTLE WITH STICKS

Another aspect of the *Ruginoasa Mummers' Battle with Sticks* that has not been yet examined is patrimonialization. While most of the winter plays analyzed in both Heleșteni and Ruginoasa—such as the *Play of the Goat,* the *Play of the Deer* and *Malanca*—have undergone patrimonialization attempts by being exported to folklore festivals in various cities in Iași County, nothing similar has ever happened with the *Mummers' Battle.* The leaders and members of institutions who promote traditional culture in Iași County have rejected *The Battle* firmly and sometimes even aggressively, by excluding it from the list of customs that had to be promoted and safeguarded.

This is completely explainable. "Modern images of the peasant have historically been constructed as part of the nation-states with which they have been identified (Kearney 1996:42)," Michael Kearney stated. So, influenced by—nationalism, Folkloristics promoted only the positive aspect in the mummers' tradition—for example the peaceful carols and the wishes (*urare*) for a wealthy New Year. Other traditions involving negative elements such as violence have been excluded from this list. This is explicable, as the peasant had been perceived by folklorists in Rousseauian manner, as the *noble savage.* In the anthropology practiced by western countries with a colonial history, the focus on "peasant" had been successful for a few decades in replacing the representation of the exotic "primitive" of the tribal worlds, as Kearney well demonstrated: "With the disappearance of 'the primitive,' 'the peasant' increasingly came to typify the generalized Other, but an Other seen not as primitive, nor primordial, but as 'underdeveloped'" (Kearney 1996:35).

From this perspective the peasant had to be a peaceful *Other* embodying hospitality, amiability, diligence, and other such values. Elements like opportunism, aggressiveness, tensions in the rural world, the fragile marital market inextricably linked to the peasant's attachment to the land, had been taken out of the picture. Therefore, the *Battle of Ruginoasa* has so far been an offence for all the representations the Romanian folkloristics tradition had established. This state was amplified especially because of its wide broadcasting at national level during the last decade. Consequently, a tradition that could have still been ignored by autochthonous Folkloristics and even by anthropology, became a sensational national news subject, and the debate surrounding it could not be avoided any longer. Furthermore, the *Mummers' Battle in Ruginoasa* has opened the discussion about the peasants' aggressiveness, and shed light on other such rituals in the rural world. For it should be emphasized that the *Mummers' Battle in Ruginoasa* is not unique in rural Romania. It could be encompassed in the larger sphere of the battles between groups of young men in the countryside. In my two decades of field research in the rural areas, I have discovered many such ritual manifestations that express local tensions, being in the meantime a type of passage rites—maturity tests for countryside lads. One such ritual is *Țic*, performed by groups of *momârlani* in the west of the Jiu Valley area; during winter holidays, youngsters dressed in thick sheep fur overcoats hit each other's shoulders violently until one of the two opponents falls to the ground.

One of the few anthropological works dealing with violence in the world of the Romanian countryside was written by Ruth Benedict, and fulfills the American Army's demand during World War II. In the section called *Opportunism and Aggression* in Chapter 5 (*Some Romanian Characteristics*), the author dedicates no less than seven pages to describing the Romanian peasant's attitude when faced with violence and aggressiveness, but also the constant use of these two—considered legitimate and regulated through rural proverbs and bywords—in the children's education and in the relation between spouses (Benedict 1943). Although Romanian folklorists were hesitant in describing these facts, the realities were incredibly well captured by many writers who knew the village world in detail and described it with incredible honesty. Among them, Ion Creangă, Ioan Slavici, Liviu Rebreanu, and Marin Preda—classics of Romanian literature—wrote unforgettable pages about the rural universe, with all its aspects, including violence, tensions, hatred, and aggressiveness.

Regardless of the evidence, the fact that Folkloristics perceived the peasant in an idyllic way made Romanian folklorists ignore the ritual aggressiveness present in the Romanian rural world and even exclude the *Battle of Ruginoasa* from the panoply of acceptable traditional customs. For this reason, within the patrimonialization attempts decided at county level, decision makers rejected efforts to present the custom onstage in county folklore festivals. Notwithstanding, the teams of *Malanca* from Ruginoasa *comună* that joined these festivals have almost always comprised several fighting mummers with ugly masks and acacia clubs. With the intense mediatization the battle ritual had witnessed, these mummers were always incredibly popular among city dwellers who would repeatedly ask for group photos whenever they saw them during the festival. My assumption is that all these elements have increased the general confusion regarding the customs in Ruginoasa and led to confusing the *Mummers' Battle with Sticks* and the *Malanca*. This "furtive" patrimonialization of the battle was probably reflected on recent media accounts of the phenomenon; one of the consequences was the fact that serious confusions have been transmitted this way, distorting the image of a phenomenon deeply rooted in the settlement's history. However, the anthropological analysis I have conducted regarding this ritual, and the social, economic, and political relations the actual ritual involves prove its complexity and, above all, its indissoluble connection to the rural universe of the locality.

The basic idea of this section is that the disintegration of the ritualic rules and of the rural set of values is precisely what caused the burst of unprecedented violence in the *Battle of Ruginoasa*, later amplified by the presence of the local and national television cameras. These tendencies have been doubled by the folklorists' ignorance of the ritual, and the rejection of any attempt of patrimonializing it because of ideological reasons that have to do with the way Folkloristics was defined as science in the 19th century Romania. In this heterogeneous and increasingly anomic landscape, the Romanian state had to interfere through its institutions when the rules and values of the rural community in Ruginoasa were no longer functioning or were no longer efficient, while the traditional battle turned into a brutal vendetta that made many victims. Under the influence of global capitalism and the rush to self-achievement it is built upon, the lower-class people in the village of Dumbrăvița, less educated and poorer, transformed the traditional battle into a fight for victory at all costs, in a context where the battle's arena has been de-localized and globalized. Harshly criticized by defenders of village traditions and values, the presence of *civilians* is also an indicator that the mummers' battle has been de-ritualized and has become an aggressive game rather than a rural custom anchored in the village world and connected to a manifold and coherent ritual complex.

After 2011, when the fighting and the mere possession of acacia clubs during the New Year days was forbidden by a local law, locals experienced strong resentments because they had been used to join or watch the ritual every year. As a sign of protest against the authorities' decision, since 2014 the young men who had fought with clubs in previous years started going out wearing the same costumes and masks, but with corn stalks in their hands instead of clubs. Right under the anthropologist's eyes, the custom transformed from a violent fight into a ritual contesting state authority, and into an ironic protest against those who interfered for eliminating a custom that everybody in Ruginoasa considered to be part of the village community traditions. With this transformation, the *Mummers' Battle* in Ruginoasa *comună* has not only refused to disappear, but proved that it is still alive, transmitted under a distinct cultural form, specific in its turn to the European mummers' tradition—that of contesting and ridiculing those authorities that try to control the village world and peasants, together with their principles and values.

Therefore, studying the manifold ritual complex of the mummers in Ruginoasa—including the *Traditional Mummers' Battle*, too—was an extraordinary opportunity for a field anthropologist, one that may not exist a few years from now. But for the time being, the ritual is still alive, and it proves that the *mummers' plays* represent ways of responding to social, economic and aesthetic problems within the village community. This does not always involve peaceful feelings, hospitality, and harmony; instead, it can engender disagreements, conflicts, and animosities. Thus, its gnoseological value for Anthropology is extraordinary.

CONCLUSION

Throughout this chapter my interviewees were frequently referring to the *Mummers Battle* in Ruginoasa through the concept of play/game. They were building legitimate parallels between the *Mummers Battle with Sticks* and the crowd's battle with the running bulls in Pamplona, the fight with tomatoes in Buñol in eastern Spain, and the modern soccer. These comparisons are very relevant, and the history of some very popular sports today, such as soccer and rugby, show that they have developed from violent peasant practices. "If you love football, you've probably only been aware of its history from recent times. But football has a long, gruesomely violent, and hugely interesting past. And so begins the tale of how a violent peasant pastime became a multimillion pound industry," historian Ariel Hessayon tells us in a recent article (Hessayon 2018). Another sport known as *The Atherstone Ball Game*, recognized as one of the most brutal sports on Earth, also emerged from a peasant tradition that began in England in 1199 (Reid 2017). While some of these sports have evolved into successful modern competitions, others have managed to maintain their rural and somewhat primitive form until the beginning of the 21st century. An example of this would be a brutal ball game—Lelo Burti, played among the peasants of Shukhuti, in western Georgia, once a year, on Orthodox Easter (Keh 2019). Another example in this respect is a harsh game called Buzkashi (goat-grabbing). It is considered a national sport in Afghanistan today and involved two teams of male riders who struggle to grab the carcass of a dead goat and place it into a circle located at the edge of a 400 meters field (Rachel Martin and Sean Carberry 2014).

Nevertheless, my goal here is not to make a list of all violent games with origins in peasant culture, but to meditate on the relationship between plays, culture and the humans who practices them. In most articles from the field of Play Studies the positive aspect of the plays on the human mind is often emphasized. Indeed, this aspect can hardly be challenged. Still, most of these studies rarely highlight the risks and costs involved by participating in these competitions, sometimes very aggressive.

What is the most relevant for my argumentation here are mainly two aspects. The first is to understand the portrait of the human who lived in peasant culture, beyond the Romantic ideologies and the idealizations of the nationalist Folkloristics. The second is to understand the landscape left behind by the dissipation of the peasant culture and its replacement with the principles of modern society. The *Mummers Battle with Sticks* in Ruginoasa provides the anthropologist this almost unique chance to capture a rural play during its clash with the values of modern society. It is also important to be able to look at the *Mummers Battle* in Ruginoasa in its relation to modernity but especially to the expansion of global capitalism and its incredible power to commodify everything that can be turn into consumption goods and to eliminate everything that cannot fit in the principles of market economy. In one of his recent works on global capitalism, William I. Robinson paralleled its expansion with the ongoing crisis of humanity. According to Robinson, the global crisis embodies a series of features specific to all major political and economic crises. Among these, several are unique to the current state of global capitalism. One of them refers specifically to the de-ruralization process of the early 21st century.

> Capitalism is reaching apparent limits to its extensive expansion. There are no longer any new territories of significance that can be integrated into world capitalism, de-ruralization is now well-advanced, and the commodification of the countryside and of pre- and noncapitalist spaces has intensified. (Robinson 2014)

But this expansion, doubled by de-ruralization the American sociologist talks about, should not be seen as a merely political-economic or geographic phenomenon. It also affects the culture and values of those regions where global capitalism expands its dominance. At the same time, global capitalism should not only be perceived as the hegemony of corporate power and monetary policy on all corners of the planet. Commodification may also mean a transformation of local cultural elements into media consumption objects and into a topic of sterile dispute on the Internet's virtual space, under the influence of television reports; in this case, television, too, is based on consumption, high audience, and economic efficiency.

In this regard, *Ruginoasa's Mummers' Battle* may be approached as a compelling case study of how certain economic, social and political transformations have affected the locality during previous decades. Grafted on a local history of violence, this confrontation may be, together with the rural plays of Heleşteni, regarded as a lens through which one could see the great transformations brought along by Romania's modernization that started in the interwar period and continued during the communist and postsocialist times.

The very beginning of the confrontation at the beginning of the 20th century intertwines with the dawn of capitalist emergence, along with the development of capitalist relations in the rural area, and the emergence of great economic and social inequalities. Subsequently, in the communist period, besides the positive aspects related for instance to the spread of school education, including in the rural area, the modernization of Romania involved huge projects of social engineering such as the communist plan of the cooperativization of agriculture, and the transfer of the peasants' private agricultural patrimony into the state's ownership. The communist state authorities did not hesitate to use coercion and intimidation to achieve goals deemed desirable for state policy. A careful look at the accentuation of the repressive policy in the Romanian dictatorial state of the Ceauşescu period may find itself a pendant in the escalating violence of mummers' confrontations in the late 1970s, and in the beginning of the use of acacia clubs during a ritual whose degree of physical violence was milder before.

However, the harshest acts of violence during this confrontation occurred after the fall of communism, and especially after the early 2000s, when certain local and national televisions began broadcasting reports related to this rural ritual. The desire to win at all costs and to get to the spotlight—two of the tendencies encouraged by the capitalist society, a system based on competition and success—were to be seen in *Mummers' Traditional Battle*. In these new conditions, the confrontation—part of the rituals demonstrating manhood, actually existing in other localities and rural areas, too—has become a fierce battle for victory at any cost. The fair play and strict rules of the past have begun to be increasingly replaced by the aggressiveness of the combatants and the involvement of civilians and men beyond their early youth in a ritual initially intended only for young people and only for those dressed in costumes and protected by the thick mummers' masks.

Two of the best-known theories of violence helped me analyze and outline the traditional confrontation of the mummers. Galtung's *cultural violence* theory has been a useful tool in understanding a local history where violence has always been used to articulate relations between locals in a rural settlement with a history of conflict and physical violence. At the same time, Whitehead's theory of *violence seen as cultural performance* has guided me understand the violence of the *Mummers' Traditional Battle with Sticks* as part of the local cultural landscape where the influences of mainstream society have played an important role in recent decades. Ruginoasa, a *comună* located on the major road and railways of the Iași County, was more exposed to these external influences than Heleşteni. During the last decade, the transformation of the *Mummers' Battle* relates to Robinson's idea of a crisis that is not only economic and politic, but also humanitarian, specific to what humankind has gone through in recent decades. This crisis is also very evident in the traditional societies whose values and principles have been replaced by those of global capitalism. Ruginoasa is a good case study in this regard too.

Due to these external influences and its aggressive stance, the ritual has become impossible to patrimonialize in official ways through state institutions. Violence during the confrontation flagrantly contradicted the Rousseauist image of the peaceful and hospitable peasant imposed by Romanian Folkloristics when trying to construct an archetypal human type from which the Romanian people would have presumably emerged. However, the ideological disputes over the traditional confrontation of the Ruginoasa masks, consumed in the virtual space of the Internet, on blogs or in comments on YouTube posts, clearly denote the ambivalent image of the peasant in the minds of the Romanians. Thus, if some of the Romanians turned into fervent defenders of the confrontation, it was because they perceived *the peasant* as incarnating a series of features such as bravery, fearlessness, and manhood. On the contrary, the most vocal contestants of this custom were in fact those who considered the Romanian *peasant* in the light of the Rousseauist model, incarnating features such as hospitality, humanity, and goodwill.

The complexity of the Ruginoasa's *Traditional Battle with Sticks* demonstrates precisely that the image of the peasant is much more elaborate than the stereotypical representations promoted by the Romanian media or Folkloristics. The entire manhood ritual complex consisting of the *Mummers' Battle with Sticks*, *Malanca* and *Târâitul* in Ruginoasa demonstrates the antithetic features of the human spirit, from brutality and cruelty to innocence, empathy, and care. The same ritualistic complex shows that the problems of the peasant community in Ruginoasa are not much different from those of the Heleşteni community. In this case, it is also a cultural response in front of the same great problems of humans in agricultural societies—their social, economic, and existential dilemmas.

Just as in the case of the rural plays in Heleşteni, in Ruginoasa's case, too, it is obvious that the ritualistic complex analyzed is an expression of a cultural micro-ecosystem, but one that has been strongly affected by the influences of mainstream society since decades ago. The Romanian society tried to understand the *Traditional Battle with Sticks* in terms of its own rules, principles, and values, and it failed, trapped in an ethnocentrism. The sterile disputes on blogs, YouTube and newspaper platforms are an expression of this failure but also of the obvious ethnocentrism of the Romanian society incapable of understanding a rural game from the perspective of the values and rules of the rural world from which it emerged.

NOTES

1. I decided to use the term *game* instead of *play* to refer to this custom. As I mentioned at the beginning of this study, the concept of *joc* in Romanian language, which covers a wide range of events, is more suitable to characterize this confrontation.

2. Comună/Comune [plural]—An administrative-territorial unit on the territory of Romania, usually comprising 3–6 villages under the jurisdiction of the same mayoralty.

3. Throughout this book I call this game "the traditional battle with sticks." Nevertheless, a more suitable name would be "the traditional battle with clubs." The participants in this ritual use two meters long, and taught acacia clubs to fight with each other. But, the homonymy between the words *club* (wooden weapon) and *club* (an association or organization dedicated to a particular interest or activity) in the English language can create misunderstandings. For this reason I opted for the term *stick* in spite of its imperfect characterization of the weapons used by the actants in this game.

4. This quote is often attributed to the famous anthropologist Margaret Mead. However, it seems that the passage is rather a condensation of Mead's vision regarding field research, as it is stated in the work "Architecture and Field/Work," edited by Suzanne Ewing, Jeremie Michael McGowan, Chris Speed, and Victoria Clare Bernie (Ewing et al. 2011:80).

5. *Badana/Badanale* (plural)—A one-meter long stick with horse hair at one end, which is hold together with a metal ring. Used in the past as a painting instrument, it is now only present on festive occasions such as the winter rituals of the Moldavian region.

6. Civilians—the locals of Ruginoasa always make a crucial distinction, using terms from the military jargon, between masked fighters—those who should be active combatants—and civilians. The civilians are the villagers who, according to tradition, should only watch the battle and not participate in it. The involvement of civilians in this confrontation was severely criticized by many villagers during the interviews and discussions I had with them. Still, their presence among fighters is constant in the last years.

7. For more information about collectivization in Romania see Verdery and Kligman's book *Peasants under Siege: The Collectivization of Romanian Agriculture, 1949–1962*.

8. Arnăut (pl. arnăuți)—mercenaries of Albanian origin present in the Romanian court and army in the 19th century and before.

9. Badana—a decorated stick with horsehair stuck at one end.

10. *Sarma/Sarmale* [plural]—specific meal for the Mediterranean and Balkan areas. A *sarma* is made up of a cabbage leaf filled with a mixture of rice, pork meat, pork fat, onion, carrots, pepper, and dill.

Chapter Three

Rural Customary Communities[1] and Their System of Values[2]

RURAL VALUES AND THEIR ANALYSIS

In the previous two chapters I analyzed a few rural plays in the Heleșteni and Ruginoasa *comune*, placing the locals' voices ahead, next to their way of understanding and approaching these cultural forms. In this chapter, I am following a path opened by anthropologists who warned of the limits in understanding a culture just by listening to the natives' voice. These anthropologists believed that one must "read over the shoulders" of those people whose culture one studies and who are the active producers of this culture (Geertz 1972:29). This happens because "what people say, what people do, and what they say they do are entirely different things" (Mead 1975). Such an approach is suitable for this chapter's purpose mainly because I am analyzing the peasant system of values and I struggle to understand rural plays in relation to these values. To examine this complex picture, I explore the theories of two social scientists who had a highly articulated vision in the field of values: Clyde Kluckhohn and Robert Hartman.

My starting point for this chapter is the idea that the peasantry's system of values was formed under a set of influences. Henri Mendras, a French sociologist, designed a well-articulated model on peasantry already in 1976 (Mendras 1976; Mendras 2002). According to him there are five basic characteristics of a peasant society: "relative autonomy of the local group in relation to the encompassing society that both dominates it and respects its originality; domestic group structuring economic and social life, leaving almost no role to broader kinship structures; economic autarky oriented toward family consumption, with no distinction made between consumption and production; surplus skimmed off by the encompassing society and sold on the market, with family labor not accounted for in any register; interconnaissance (everyone knowing everyone else within the group and able to identify all aspects of the others' personalities and social positions); mediating role of 'important persons' [notables] understood to be in charge of all political, economic, cultural, and religious relations with the encompassing society" (Idem 2002:168). For the convenience of my argument throughout this chapter, I grouped these five elaborate features in three more concise characteristics: 1. subordinate position in relation to other social classes that have always skimmed off the surplus of the peasants and, at the same time devalued peasants through their ideology; 2. interconnaissance - domestic group structure the economic and social life and establish the rules that govern the lives of individuals; 3. economic autarky based on family production and consumption, from which results a subsistence ethic and a relative autonomy of the peasants in relation to the encompassing society. All these specific features created for peasants a world vision strongly connected with a certain system of values. Having this model in mind, I engage in the analysis of peasants' system of values in relation to peasants' plays.

There are two questions at the background of my investigation: what is the role of rural plays within the peasants' system of values? How did these plays contribute to the shaping the peasants' profile in time? Before answering these questions, I offer a theoretical basis to my approach. This theoretical framework comes from the work of two pioneers in the field of value: Clyde Kluckhohn[3] and his theory of "value and value-orientation in the theory of action" (Kluckhohn 1951) and Robert S. Hartman's formal axiology concerning "the structure of value" (Hartman 1969).

CLYDE KLUCKHOHN AND ROBERT HARTMAN'S THEORIES ON VALUES[4] AND THEIR APPLICATION WHEN STUDYING PEASANT SYSTEM OF VALUES

In building his theory on values, the anthropologist Clyde Kluckhohn often provided examples taken from the peasants' rural universe mostly because he considered peasant culture "heavily laden with values." On the other hand, the philosopher Robert Hartman was the first creator of a formal axiology system, apprehending in the meantime that this framework could be later applied to more disciplines, including sociology, political science, psychology and anthropology (Hartman 1969).

Both Kluckhohn and Hartman observed that the values of the individual and of society are closely linked to one another in a complex system of connections. The way people valorize and express their values by means of assertions, actions, and behaviors is not the same with the values they possess. However, these values may be deciphered and understood by analyzing people's judgments and assertions. This exercise was developed mainly by Hartman when he created the so-called *Hartman Value Profile*, an axiological portrayal of individuals that has proved its applicability to psychology, counseling, psychotherapy, employer–employee relations, ethics, and religion.

Robert S. Hartman is the thinker who coined the field of *Formal and Applied Axiology*, thus laying the foundation of a systematic theory of value. He developed a general framework for the study of values and created a definition of *good*—the origin of any theory and discussion about morals and values, based on formal logic and away from the relativity of individuals' statements and the cultural expressions it may take. Thus, Hartman objectively defined *good* as a concept fulfilling all its properties for being good. In his words, "a thing is good if it fulfills the intension of its concept" (Hartman 1969:103). Hartman further unpacked his axiom: the valuation involved in a sentence like "this car is good" and "the value predicate good, thus, is a property of concepts rather than of objects." So, if somebody makes a statement like: "My car is good," what he would like to say is that his car is in perfect mechanical condition and doesn't have any missing parts that would prevent it from running. The same thing can be said about a good chair; for example, a good chair can well fulfill its function when being used for sitting, which implies that the chair doesn't have a missing leg or a broken part that would make it unsuitable for its intended purpose. And what one applies to material things may also apply to human relationships and behaviors in certain situations; these, in their turn, may be evaluated by the same criteria, according to a definition of good found in the subjects' own system of valuation.

The definitions given by people to exemplary moral behaviors, to correct attitudes in certain social contexts, to humanity and hospitality, to give just a few examples, differ radically from one culture to another. However, all these definitions are based on the idea of *good*. Thus, no matter what culture they belong to, people define humanity, hospitality, fairness based on characteristics considered relevant for defining these moral stances. From the perspective of formal logics, according to Robert Hartman, all these characteristics are always part of the intension of the concepts of humanity, hospitality, fairness. Hence the universal basis of Hartman's axiology. Whenever we act in a moral or axiological sense, we perform this set of actions by referring to a series of pre-established definitions that we have in our minds. These definitions are very similar or even identical for individuals belonging to cohesive cultures like those of peasant communities, and can be very different from one individual to another when we talk about complex societies where people have very diverse experiences and levels of education. Even though these definitions are the product of our interactions within a social and cultural environment—thus tributary to the context where they emerged and, accordingly, depending on a relative horizon—these definitions are always connected to the intension of specific concepts. Thus, as defined by Hartman, *the good* lies precisely in this intensional sphere of concepts. This holds true for any rational being who makes moral assertions in a certain social environment.

What makes Hartman's theory reliable is the fact that it draws attention to something quite simple: everybody makes assertions about what is good and what is bad, and these are strictly related to definitions they have in mind. Particularly within communities where peer pressure on individual behavior is strong, people guide their actions mostly around such definitions. These definitions might never or almost never be evident in discourse at the level of formal assertions, but they exist behind it and might later be discovered through the analysis of people's actions and behaviors inside the community. With this Hartmanian model in mind, one might pay more attention to the cultural-political-economic interstices where people's assertions are formed, and to the way they produce these judgments depending on the definitions they have in mind.

In his turn, Kluckhohn emphasized that there is an intrinsic relation between values/morals on one side and human action on the other side. "Morals—and all group values—are the products of social interaction as embodied in culture" (Kluckhohn 1951:338). From a very general perspective, all value judgments are nothing else than "selective and discriminate ways of responding" (Kluckhohn, 1951:390). Nevertheless, "[a] value is not just a preference, but is a preference which is felt and/or considered to be justified morally," states Kluckhohn at the beginning of his study (Kluckhohn 1951:396). He soon leaves this general framework and begins to set up a more concise circumscription of value. Thus, "value implies a code or a standard which has some persistence through time and organizes a system of action . . . and places things, acts, ways of behaving, goals of action on the approval-disapproval continuum" (Kluckhohn 1951:397). Thus, Kluckhohn stated that there is a connection between people's thought, their moral preferences, their actions, and behaviors.

Therefore, Kluckhohn and Hartman make us aware that people's value judgments are always connected inside a system of values where the individual ego is always linked to a system of community networks, to things, to actions, to statements and to relations and realities that are born as a result of these interactions. From these interactions, result "realities" like personhood, work ethics, family relations, community relations including reciprocity and so on. But these are connected to a logical horizon—that of the intension of the concepts (all the terms included in the definition of a concept). This horizon remains unchanged irrespective of the more or less relative value of the definitions that make it up. In other words, it doesn't matter what culture an individual lives in. He/she will always make a series of assessments based on the clearer or less clear definitions he/she has in mind. He/she will always valorize things and actions based on a set of principles which he has built over time and which are all intertwined in the intention of concepts that exist in his/her mind. That is why, looking at people's system of values and especially at its daily reproduction is not an easy task. First of all, these values are not always made clear by people; however, their behaviors and actions are shaped by these values. That is why most of the time it is impossible to find them in well-articulated statements. It is more useful to do what Geertz recommended when he said that anthropologists should "read over the shoulders" of the people they study and who are the active producers of a culture (Geertz 1972:29). Thereby, speaking about the peasants' system of values in particular and, above all, analyzing their particular values by scrutinizing the way a culture promotes value, I struggled to apply the Hartmanian model to a culture understood in an anthropological sense, and to relate Kluckhohn's theoretical frameworks to a peasant community's actions in their relation to the community's system of values.

THE EXPLOITATION AND DEVALUATION OF PEASANTS

In this section I analyze the first feature of the peasant society based on Mendras's model and I show how this led to the formation of a certain type of values in this society. In the end, I relate it to peasant plays. This first feature emphasized the subordinate position of peasants in relation to other social classes that have always skimmed off the surplus of their communities and, at the same time, devalued peasants through their ideology.

In his book *Debt*, David Graeber analyzes the concept of debt, from the origins of human civilization to the present day. The peasants occupy an important place in his demonstration, being always given as an example of an exploited class, starting from the first Mesopotamian kingdoms until the 20th century. In fact, Graeber's entire book can be read as a bitter story of man's exploitation of man through various methods, from violence and persuasion to creating debtors by treacherous or aggressive means. Throughout his study, the reader can notice the empathy of the author for peasants who were always described as being at the bottom of the hierarchy of social classes. Peasants were those who worked hard to produce food for the whole society in exchange for protection from their landlords. Despite this seemingly equitable social exchange, Graeber tell us, the supraordinate classes were rather committed to extort as much resources as they could from peasants, leaving them too often in miserable living conditions (Graeber 2011).

There is evidence from different historical epochs showing that we are dealing with a double proceeding, and the exploitation of the peasants has always gone hand in hand with a process of devaluing them as a social class. Alex Drace-Francis speaks about the stereotypes and social representations that had marked the evolution of perceptions regarding peasants. Far from being recent in history, negative stereotypes about rural inhabitants go back to ancient times where peasants were regarded as "barbarian," "uncivilized," "brutal," and "unmannerly" (2013:11–62).

It looks like this scenario happened over and over again throughout history, although we have more accurate descriptions about such relations from times more recent than those described by Graeber and Drace-Francis in their works. Talking about medieval times, George Dalton, an economic anthropologist, emphasizes that "Peasants were legal, political, social, and economic inferiors in medieval Europe. The structured subordination of peasants to non-peasants was expressed in many ways, *de jure* and *de facto*, from restraints on their physical movement to sumptuary restrictions on what kinds of weapons, clothing and adornments they could wear and use, and foods they could legally consume" (Dalton 1972).

Even Marx's view of the peasants seems to be affected by these representations and the author of *Capital* embraces an ambivalent attitude about this class. On the one hand, he deplores peasants' miserable state; on the other hand, he blames them for their lack of revolutionary spirit in overthrowing the existing social hierarchy. A well-known passage on peasants comes from his work *The Eighteenth Brumaire of Louis Bonaparte*, and it is revealing in this respect:

> The small-holding peasants form a vast mass, the members of which live in similar conditions but without entering into manifold relations with one another. Their mode of production isolates them from one another instead of bringing them into mutual intercourse. The isolation is increased by France's bad means of communication and by the poverty of the peasants. Their field of production, the small holding admits of no division of labor in its cultivation, no application of science and, therefore, no diversity of development, no variety of talent, and no wealth of social relationships. Each individual peasant family is almost self-sufficient; it itself directly produces the major part of its consumption, and thus acquires its means of life more through exchange with nature than in intercourse with society. A small holding, a peasant and his family; alongside them another small holding, another peasant and another family. A few score of these make up a village, and a few score of villages make up a Department. In this way, the great mass of the French nation is formed by simple addition of homologous magnitudes, much as potatoes in a sack form a sack of potatoes.

Insofar as millions of families live under economic conditions of existence that separate their mode of life, their interests, and their culture from those of other classes and put them in hostile opposition to the latter, they form a class. Insofar as there is merely a local interconnection among these small-holding peasants and the identity of their interests begets no community, no national bond, and no political organization among them, they do not form a class. They are consequently incapable of enforcing their class interest in their own name, whether through a parliament or through a convention. (Marx 1994 [1852]:62)

Despite this ambivalent position towards peasants, Marx is, however, the author who has influenced a whole generation of writers and sociologists who have written about this class. Most Marxist authors have taken from the work of the German sociologist only the idea of exploitation, and some of them have built their whole career, especially with the advent of nationalism in 19th century Europe, writing many books about the bitter destiny of this exploited class. The emergence of communism in the 20th century, in particular, created an entire literature in which the communist ideology began to deal with peasants viewed exclusively from the lens of exploitation. This cohabitation between Marxism and Nationalism produced a series of works whose propagandistic nature became easily recognizable, while the truth about peasants was increasingly difficult to distinguish from the ideological "soup" of all of these writings.

As a citizen of Romania, a country located on the eastern side of the Iron Curtain, where the ideology of the Communist Party had been felt in all aspects of public life, I have been exposed since primary school to such works about peasants. Most of the stories in the textbooks were based on eloquent parables about people's work and life in a socialist society. In addition to these, textbooks contained novels critical of the bourgeois society that had been overthrown with the coming of Communism to power. One of these short stories stayed in my mind for a long time. At one point, when I started my research on peasants' plays, I tried to find the textbook containing that story. To my luck, I found a website with scanned versions of communist textbooks, and I managed to identify the novel inside a 4th grade reading textbook of the 1980s.

The story had a simple narrative thread. A row of peasants' carts came filled with corn collected from the field. The last car belonged to a poor peasant and was drawn by two small oxen that advanced slowly because of the rain and the mud accumulated on the road. At a certain point, the cart sinks into the mud, the oxen can no longer pull it despite the peasant's whips, and they finally collapse on their knees. The peasant understands that the oxen are too weak to pull the cart out of the mud and, in a moment of tenderness, he hugs his oxen and begs them to forgive him for sometimes hitting them with the whip. The story ends with the memorable image of the peasant feeding the oxen a little of the corn he had harvested, and saying: "Tears and poverty unite us. Eat! You plowed the land, you fell on the field for this corn, just like now! Let's share it! And when we finish it, we will die together!" (Vissarion 1987)

The moral of such a story is simple. The peasants exploited by the boyars are brought to the stage of animality. Thus, death is seen as a solution to end the suffering in the life of a common peasant. Although the short story written by I.C. Vissarion impressed me deeply at the age of ten, from my parents and friends, but especially from the *Voice of America* radio broadcast that my parents used to listen to frequently, I knew that the official discourse contained a high dose of propaganda and that we should regard these texts more like inventions of communist ideology than as true stories. Later, as doctoral student having studied such themes in detail, I would find out that this kind of peasant stories could be true. The mentioned story, in particular, had been written by Ion C. Vissarion, an active participant in *The 1907 Romanian Peasants' Revolt.* He was at the same time an author with deep roots in the rural world, who wrote true frescos about Costeștii din Vale, the village where he was born and spent most of his life.

I realized later that the problem with this type of Marxist-inspired texts was not necessarily their falsity, but their incompleteness. As a researcher of the rural world, I have always felt that there is something wrong with this kind of gray landscape in which life unfolds, slowly and uniformly, without radical changes, and without any trace of joy. I would find the answer to my dilemma not by reading more Marxist literature, but in the Play Studies:

> Imagine a world with no flirting, no day-dreaming, no comedy, no irony. Such a world would be a pretty grim place to live. In a broad sense, play is what lifts people out of the mundane. I sometimes compare play to oxygen—it's all around us, yet goes mostly unnoticed or unappreciated until it is missing. (Brown and Vaughan 2010:6)

In this short paragraph I found the key to my dilemma. It seems that a plethora of great thinkers have been enthralled by the landscape of peasant exploitation by the upper hierarchical classes, omitting to observe a relatively simple fact. Even an exploited and impoverished class like peasants must have had at least occasionally access to play, irony, joke, theater, flirtation, dreaming, and comedy. I was to find all these in their rural plays. In fact, the history of folk plays goes hand in hand with the history of peasant communities. It is actually an expression of the peasants' system of values. Like an old fresco, the history of folk plays tells us about the peasants' devaluation by superordinate classes, about their relations to outsiders, their perception of the world and life, but also about the way their everyday problems and difficulties could be overcome by play, dance, irony, and guising.

All these expressions of human freedom are embodied by the peasant communities in their rural plays. This could be the reason mummers' plays encountered a harsh ecclesiastical opposition (Chambers 1969 [1933]), and Christian church authorities tried to suppress them during the entire Middle Ages. As a proof we have a bunch of documents issued by the church for eliminating mummers' plays:

> For what wise man could think that there are people with a sound mind who would want to change [their face/their appearance] to wild beasts/animals, celebrating the Deer? Some put cattle skins on, others wear animal heads, feasting and bouncing so that, should they turn into such wild animals, they would not seem to be human anymore. (du Cange 1678)[5]

Inasmuch as the folk plays represent a world of irony, bantering, dance, theater, and play, with different rules than those of daily life, I also discovered it from the oldest documents about mummers found on Romanian territory. I already mentioned the memorable visit of the Swedish ambassador Welling to Iași, the capital of the Moldavian Kingdom, in 1656, when he describes the *Play of the Goat* as a theater in which a hunting scene is embodied. In 1673, the Metropolitan of Moldova, Dosoftei, also speaks about the animal skins' costumes that the characters of this play wore, together with the waggish nature of the main character—the goat. But the most relevant description of this play belongs to the king Dimitrie Cantemir who, in 1714, offers the most detailed portrayal of a *Goat Play* together with the costume worn by the players, and the purpose of the play. This is one of the first testimonies that present the Play of the Goat as a sarcastic irony directed against the Turkish occupation. Besides, one of the actors is depicted as wearing the nicely decorated costume specific to this ritual, completely hiding the Goat performer's face and body. Moreover, Cantemir also talks about the extraordinary success of this play, as a proof that a lot of people follow the players throughout the village.

These representations have been perpetuated over time and some of them could be identified even today. During my research in 2009–2020, in the *Play of the Goat* from Blăgești village—a locality near the commune Ruginoasa, I discovered the character called the Turk, wearing Turkish clothes and clearly representing a testimony of the Ottoman domination over the territory of Moldova from the 15th century until 1877. In the *Play of the Deer* there are also characters such as the Jew, the Greek, and the Gypsy. Such figures did not belong to the village world and its system of values, they only interfered with it for commercial purposes. However, business relationships are often strained. That is why folk artists have regarded these ethnic groups with critical eyes and have highlighted their negative traits, especially through sarcasm and satire.

In the previous chapter, I also mentioned the character called *arnăut*, present in the Malanca folk play. Arnăuții were mercenaries of Albanian origin, dressed in specific uniforms, with buttons sewn diagonally on their chest and back, appointed by the ruler Alexandru Ioan Cuza at his court at the palace of Ruginoasa. From the beginning, I noticed a semantic similarity between the embodiment of this character in the Malanca from Ruginoasa and the Cargo Cult. In the Cargo Cult, several members of the tribal societies of Melanesia and New Guinea practiced a kind of ritual imitation of behaviors of the members of the more technologically developed colonial societies. These rituals were practiced to convince the supernatural entities they believed in to bring the welfare of the imitated persons to the members of the tribe. We will probably never know the initial meaning of the creation of the Albanian Arnăuți's uniforms in the folk play of Malanca. However, it could be assumed that wearing the uniforms of mercenaries with a high social status during the Malanca ritual gave the peasant actors a sense of pride and superiority, and could even inspire their belief that they would once succeed in accessing that status. This assumption is based on the fact that the Arnăut has the most important role in the Ruginoasa Malanca. The Arnăut is also Malanca's commander, so the character with the highest status within this play.

But the place where I found the most eloquent expression of the tense relations between the peasants and the superordinate classes, including here the small traders, were the verses of the old variants of the *Play of the Deer* collected from the villages of the Helești comună in the 1970s (Appendix II). Of extraordinary complexity, these verses speak not only about the relationships between the peasants and other social classes, but also about the poverty of the peasants. Finally, these verses talk about the possibility of transcending the limits of this narrow world through persuasion and irony. For instance, the realities exposed in the *Play of the Deer*, including sickness, decrepitude, poverty, marriage market difficulties, tense ethnic relations and the pressure of the external economic market against the rural domestic mode of production, were problems faced regularly by peasants (see Wolf 1966). Satirizing all these realities at the end of the year was a way of transcending them and at the same time dealing with the conflicts and problems with superordinate classes beyond the control of the fragile peasant world. Even the whispering of all these into the ear of an animal was a parody, as peasants' problems were never listened to by political leaders or landlords. This interpretation is reinforced by passages from the *deer master*'s disenchantment talking about the deep poverty of the villages in a mocking way: "I hung the knapsack on the hook/Flour in it there is nary/I put the pot on the fire/Firewood there is not any (see Appendix II)."

Thus, the *Play of the Deer* in Heleșteni embodies the whole complexity of the peasants' world, a world dominated not only by economic realities and pressures, but also by magic, tales, superstitions, a sense of play and playfulness. These dimensions belong to the peasants' world and, together, they are part of the system of values around which this world revolves. This includes economic and moral values as well as aesthetic and ludic ones.

The idea of transcending the social norms and all the problems of the mundane world appears not only in the *Play of the Deer* and in the incantation whispered by the bear leader in the wild animal's ear, but also in the *Pantomimic Mummers'* ritual. The groups of mummers go to the households and, instead of behaving according to the ethic rural norms, they grab the householder by the head, hitting him with crochet scarves, puppets,or thin wooden sticks. At the same time, the household women are kissed and groped in front of the head of the family. Despite this, the mummers are offered cookies, food and drinks, and the families receive them happily. During the whole unfolding of these rituals, there are no class, status, social position, or ethnic differences. Moreover, people belonging to the lower rungs of the social hierarchy get into their community's spotlight due to their reputation as talented dancers in the *Deer dance* ritual, as flute players in the suite of the *Deer* and *Goat*, or due to their inspired sketches performed within the groups of mummers.

Anything that might be a problem during the year, including dissension, fear, or anxiety, is ridiculed, scoffed, and mocked on this occasion. Dreadful realities such as death, illness, decrepitude, poverty, and deprivation of all kinds, as well as inter-ethnic and social class relationships, along with the pride, the pomposity and the stupidity of politicians and TV stars are derided through these rituals.

Besides their multiple meanings revealed in chapter one, the mummers' plays from the area of Heleșteni-Ruginoasa may be interpreted as a cultural response of the peasant rural communities against the strict rules of society, the inequalities and social injustices of all sorts, the absurd and wrong policies, corrupt politicians, disease, poverty, decrepitude, and even death. In this response, can be revealed the adaptive power of the village community, based on a system of values that allows villagers to transcend the narrow limits of their own social rules and all the dreads that keep them under the burden of immediate causality. Thus, from the analysis of these rituals, can be observed various positions of the peasants in their relation to the superordinate classes. At the same time, can be seen a whole range of expressions their plays comprise: dance, irony, trick, satire, and guise. All these demonstrate that the world of the peasants is far from being a total grey landscape devoid of play, as it had often been described by Marxist authors. On the contrary, it contains all the multitude of experiences and feelings included in the very broad concept of play.

INTERCONNAISSANCE—DOMESTIC GROUP STRUCTURES, THE ECONOMIC AND SOCIAL LIFE OF INDIVIDUALS

In this section, I analyze the second feature of the peasant society based on Mendras's model: the interconnaissance—domestic group structures the economic and social life and establishes the rules that govern the lives of individuals (everyone knowing everyone else within the group and is able to identify all aspects of the others' personalities and social positions). For this purpose, I considered it most productive to analyze the works of the writers who knew peasant universe as insiders. The great writers of the late 19th century and the first decades of the 20th century wrote memorable pages about the peasants' world view, and about peasants' customs. More, some of these writers understood the importance of folk plays in the cultural, aesthetic, social, and economic life of the village.

The writers born in the village and who had spent their childhood in the countryside—and thus knew well the realities of the peasant world—wrote memorable pages about rural plays. One of them, a Nobel laureate for literature, the Polish writer Władysław Reymont, opens a window towards the complex world of the mummers and their strong connection with peasant customary communities, in his best-known and most substantial four volumes work, *The Peasants* (Reymont 1925):

Have they been here, with the 'bear?' Roch asked, to change the subject.
They are at the organist's now, and will be here at once.
Who are the performers?
Why, the sons of Gulbas and Filipka; who but they, the rogues!
Here they come! the lasses cried. In front of the cabin, a long-drawn roar resounded; then various animals' cries: cocks crowing, sheep bleating, horses whinnying: all this to the accompaniment of a fife. Finally, the door opened, and a young fellow came in, clad in a sheepskin coat, turned inside out, and a tall fur cap, with his face so blackened, he looked like a gipsy. He came pulling the 'bear' in question after him by a rope, covered all over with shaggy brown pea-straw, save for a head of fur with paper ears that he could shake at will, and a tongue that hung out for more than a foot. To his arms were fastened staves with pea-straw twisted round them, so that he seemed to go on all fours. After him went the other bear-leader, wielding a straw lash in one hand, and in the other a club that bristled all over with sharp pegs, to which bits of fat bacon, loaves

and bulky packets were stuck. In the rear walked Michael, the organist's boy, playing the fife, and a number of youngsters with sticks, tapping on the floor and shouting vociferously. (Reymont 1925:195)

The custom described by the Polish writer is called The Bear or the Play of the Bear.[6] Along with the Play of the Goat, this is one of the most widespread winter rituals in the mummers' plays category across the entire Europe. In the screening of Reymont's novel by film director Jan Rybkowski,[7] the scene of the Bear team's visit is one of the most exciting in the entire movie. It is even more spirited than the scene described by Reymont in his novel, the visit being presented as a tolerated indecency, accompanied by a shameless goosing of all women in the household by the members of the Bear team. All this happens in a rural universe marked by the strict rules of tradition regarding the issue of eroticism and intimate relationships. This episode demonstrates once again the freedom and permissiveness granted by the peasants to the mummers during the ritual period, but not allowed at other times of the year and under other circumstances. Thus, the scene of this ritual, in both novel and movie, is in line with the central story in the novel, that of Jagna, a young woman who loves erotic pleasures and romantic adventures, and gets harshly punished by a village community promoting a rigorous and very restrictive morality in this respect.

The bear-leader 'praised God,' crowed, bleated, neighed like a rampant stallion, and, lifting up his voice, spoke thus: *We, bear-leaders, come from a foreign clime, beyond the ocean and the endless forests, where men walk upside down, use sausages for palings, and fire to cool themselves; where pots are set to boil in the sun, and where the sky rains vodka: thence have we brought this savage bear! It has been told us that there are in this village wealthy husbandmen, good-natured housewives—and fair maidens too. And therefore from that foreign clime have we come, beyond the Danube, to obtain kind treatment, have our needs supplied, and something given us for our pains!—Amen.* (Idem 1925:196)

As Reymont shows, sometimes the Play of the Bear appears accompanied by a carol/urătură that differ from region to region. Most of the time, this carol includes elements that highlight the moral flaws and weaknesses of the visited households, with clear allusions to events that had happened in the village community throughout the year. Currently, the Play of the Bear disappeared in Heleşteni village. However, the ritual's attribute of revealing deeds and character traits considered immoral by the village community, appears in the carols/urături of Pantomimic Mummers, a Heleşteni's custom that contains the most numerous improvisations. Reymont's description of this custom in a 19th century Polish village supports the hypothesis that when the village communities were vivid and full of life, mummers' plays were also rich in improvisations, having a close connection to the social relationships within the village community and acting as a guide for human characters in the village world.

> *Show, then, what ye can do*, said Klemba; *peradventure there may be something for you in the larder.*
>   *Instantly.—Ho, play the fife there; and you, bear, dance!* the bear-leader cried. Then the fife poured forth one of its sweetest tunes, and the lads tapped the floor with their sticks, and shouted loudly in cadence, while the leader mimicked the voices of many a beast, and the 'bear' jumped about as on all fours, twitching his ears, putting his tongue out and in again, and running after the girls. The bear-leader seemed to be pulling him back, and struck with his lash at everyone within his reach, crying. (Ibidem 1925:196)

A common feature of the Bear play is the dance of the trained bear. It consists of a *strenuous* dance performed by the animal at the orders of his master, usually a character disguised as a gypsy. As we have seen in previous chapters, the gypsy character appears in the Play of the Deer and sometimes in the Play of the Goat, too. For the rural world, the gypsy is the animal trainer by excellence, and perhaps because of this skill, he is also a character surrounded by a magic halo. Perhaps because of that, even in the case of the Play of the Deer in Heleșteni, the most numerous characters in the team of the Deer and at the same time those appointed to guard the deer, bear the name of ursari/ bear-leaders. In late 19th century Europe, when Władysław Reymont wrote his novel, Gypsy artists still wandered through the village and town fairs with trained bears dancing to the sound of the pipe. There is a hypothesis that the Play of the Bear performed by peasants was inspired by those traveling artists.

> *Have found no husband yet, lass?—A rope's end you shall get, lass!*
>   The noise in the room, with the racket and scampering and squealing, waxed louder and louder; and the merriment grew to its height, when the bear began to frolic wildly, rolling on the floor, roaring, leaping for fun, and catching at the girls with his long wooden arms, making them dance to the tunes played on Michael's fife: the two bear-leaders, meanwhile, and the lads who accompanied them, making such an uproar that the old cabin might well have fallen to pieces with the horse-play and the din and fun of it. (Ibidem 1925:196)

Just like in many other mummers' plays, the theme of the marriage, and the allusions to girls who may remain unmarried is also highlighted in this fragment. From this point of view, the mummers' plays are a method of the village community to persuade young girls to start a family from the age of early youth, before getting twenty-four years old. In the incantations of the deer gathered from Heleșteni *comună* and the neighboring localities, the irony against the girls becoming too old for marriage, gets sarcastic accents. The same fact is highlighted with talent in the novel of the Polish writer.

Then, Klemba's wife having treated them very bountifully, they left the place; but far along the road came the sound of shouting men and barking dogs.
Who played the bear? Sohova asked, when they had quieted down.
Could ye not find out? Why, Yasyek Topsy-turvy.
How could I know him, with that shaggy head of fur?
My dear, Kobusova observed, *for such games as that, the doodle has quite enough sense.*
Yasyek is not such a fool as ye make him out to be! said Nastka, taking his part. No one contradicted her; but sly significant smiles flickered on many faces. They again sat down and began chattering merrily. (Ibidem 1925:197)

The discussions between householders on the mummers' performance and on the villagers who interpreted it are also an expression of village social life and rural values related to interconnaissance. In my field research, both in Heleşteni and in Ruginoasa, I witnessed discussions similar to those described by Reymont and I will analyze some of them by the end of this chapter.

For now, I am presenting some fragments from another novel that describes in detail the rural world and the relations between peasants. In his realistic novel—*The Morometes*, another writer famous for his work on peasantry, too, Marin Preda, describes the life of a peasant family living in the Wallachian Plain (Preda 1957). Inside the novel, he depicts an entire episode on *Căluşarii*, a rural play already well-known in the 19th and early 20th century by English folklorists with interest in folk plays (Chambers 1969 [1933]).

Tita, where are you? Come along, the căluşari are just passing!
In the quietude of the village the music of the gypsy band could be heard, even nearer. Birică, Nilă and Tita pricked their ears. Suddenly, the hoarse shout of 'the mute' was heard, followed by the shrill shrieks of the women and girls.
Abreaaaau! . . .
Tita got up, Nilă wanted to do the same, but looked at his friend:
Shall we go and have a look at the căluşarii?
To hell with them! We shall see them later on anyhow . . . Go and dress, and we shall look them up later! answered Birică.
Come on, Tita! Well, if you won't go just send Ilinca, said Nilă angrily.
Tita left, but Ilinca didn't turn up. The *căluşari* had stopped somewhere nearby, and the merry shrieks of terror of the women and girls never stopped. (Preda 1957)

Just like the *Pantomimic Mummers* in Heleşteni, the *Căluşari* sometimes harass those people who seem to be weaker and less prepared to defend themselves. Through such acts, the mummers work as a "vaccine" for those

who may have "low immunity" against possible unexpected life events. As
I have shown in the discussion at the end of chapter one, mummers may be
unpredictable, just like the events of human life in general. That is why they
could be considered an antidote to fears, uncertainties, hesitations, and to
other feelings that could turn humans into victims of the life's vicissitudes.

> *Come on, let's go up to the road, to see where they're dancing*! Nilă said
> impatiently.
>   They got up. Ilinca came running up to tell them that she couldn't call
> Polina, because the *călușari* had stopped in front of her house, and Polina was
> inside, dressing.
>   *Let's go there*! Birică decided.
>   Bălosu's whole yard was full of villagers. There was no more room, so they
> crowded on the porch and in the garden at the back of the Morometes's cottage.
> The children perched on top of the fences, stared at *the mute*, ready to shriek and
> run away. Bălosu had opened the gate leading to the road, and though the house
> and yard were crammed, a dense crowd of people was still outside in the road.
>   Birică and Nilă edged their way through the garden to get nearer to the show.
> Birică told Ilinca to sit up in the porch, and when Polina came out told her to
> come to the mulberry-tree at the back of the garden, after the dance. But he
> tried to get nearer to the *călușari* to see Polina when she came out. He was
> lucky, for the 'mute' rushed into the crowd howling lustily and hitting out with
> his red sword to make room for the *călușari*. He stood the ebb of the crowd,
> and elbowed his way forward, without minding the blows of the frantic 'mute.'
> (Idem 1957)

Marin Preda's description of the *Călușari* play, and its parallel to a love
story that does not conform to the rules and values of rural tradition, does not
seem to be random. Just like in the case of unconventional love stories, the
rural plays represent moments when the peasants perceive the limits of their
own world and the relativity of their own system of values, and struggle to
cope with these forces. That is why the unfolding of a love story episode that
tends to threaten the fragile social balance of a rural community, during a rural
play episode, acquires a special significance. Human feelings may sometimes
be just like the rural plays—an unstoppable torrent that does not seem to take
into account the strict morality and the firm rules of the rural world.

> The famous dance was just starting, and the *călușari* called one another
> together*: hupp*! *hupp*! *hupp*! They lined up in the middle of the yard, facing
> Bălosu's verandah and waited for the leader to give the signal. Tudor Bălosu
> with his wife and with Victor had come out onto the verandah. Victor stood there
> dressed in a grey suit with red-striped tie to his yellow silk shirt, bareheaded,
> his hair carefully plastered. He looked rather pale, but was smartly attired and
> carried himself erectly. Tudor Bălosu and his wife had also put on their Sunday

clothes. Tudor was wearing a black waistcoat over his wide-sleeved white shirt, and Aristiţa a blue velvet dress. They were both sitting on chairs, Victor standing between them. Not many of the villagers were wealthy enough to receive the căluş-dancers, and the way Victor was standing there stiffly, looking down at the crowd, showed that Bălosu's were people of mark. *Hallo there, you chief of the căluşari!* he shouted, and when the latter came up to Victor, he told him: *Dance the whole căluş-dance!* a thing that pleased all the assistance, because it was only in the courtyard of Aristide and of a small number of villagers that this rare dance could be fully performed. Aristiţa Bălosu looked a little more reserved and less haughty, and she kept glancing from time to time at the lobby whence Polina was due to come out. (Ibidem 1957)

Rural plays have an intricate relationship with the social inequalities in the rural universe. On the one hand, those with a higher social status in the village are not among those performing the plays; instead, they have the privilege of receiving the mummers' teams for a sum of money, thus demonstrating their status as good householders and owners of a surplus that could be given to the artists. Moreover, as we have seen in chapter two, in some cases the plays have their own methods of abolishing temporarily—at least during the practice of these rituals—the social inequalities in the village.

> *Hey 'mute'!* the chief of the *căluşari* called out to the mime. *I say Abreau, come right here!* Abreau, 'the mute' came nearer, pot in his hand, and stopped in front of the lined-up căluşari. He was neither dumb, nor was his name Abreau; he was Costică Guigudel, and his role of a dumb mute in the căluş-dance also entailed the task of theatrical producer or stage-manager. During the dance he was meant to strike fearful blows with his sword at the căluşari who were slack or danced badly, but the căluşari had taken an oath not to be angry and not to hit back, but only to stave off the blows with their finely carved staffs to which small bells were attached. The căluş-dance lasted for three whole days, at Whitsuntide, and utterly exhausted the căluşari's strength, because the more intense and vehement its rhythm, the more beautiful the dance.

> When he scared the women and children throwing rotten eggs at them, the 'mute' growled like a bear or bellowed like a bull: *Aabreau!* He wore a dirty, ragged skirt concealing a wooden phallus. His hands and his face were stained with red paint, and he was really a terrifying sight. (Ibidem 1957)

Just like the winter mummers' rituals, the display of erotic-sexual objects like phalluses is one of the characteristics of the many rural plays, including the *Căluşari*. Folklorists considered them to be symbols of nature's rebirth and cornucopia. However, they mostly act as elements used for intimidating young girls and, in general, all those members of the community who have a minimal or no sexual life. During my field research in Iaşi County, I noticed the display of such phalluses by both the *Pantomimic Mummers* of Heleşteni and the members of the *Deer* team in the village of Cucuteni.

> Abreau hastened to make the so-called counting-up, passing from one călușar to the other, muttering God knows what, when he came upon one whom he knew to be less efficient. He drew back and shouted at them in a commanding voice:
> *Hupp-shah!*
> *Hupp-shah!* answered the chief of the călușari who then turned away from the 'mute' and stepped out to the rhythm of the music, walking round in a circle, followed by the dancers. They all had long red robes on, with bells on their legs, staffs and fez, and red waist-bands. They were peasants from the village, but nobody could recognize them; so handsome did they look in that costume of theirs. Their dance delighted the villagers exceedingly; it was the only dance that rigorously conformed to the ancient rules: it could only be danced in a set formation, in motley-colored costumes, with a 'mute' and with that which was particularly difficult to find and keep: an untiring leader, a better dancer than all the other who should know the full ritual of the căluș, remembering the number and order of every dance-figure and steps. (Ibidem 1957)

In Marin Preda's view, for the villagers, the *Călușari* represent one of the few funny moments and opportunities of delight in their life, within a universe dominated by strenuous physical work, burdensome daily worries, and the difficulties that derive from a mode of production based on subsistence agriculture.

> With the fourth measure, the chief turned his face toward the dancers and called out: *hupp-shah!* and the others, in the following measure, answered in the same way.
> But the chief's call took on ever more a tone of entreaty, and at the same time of command, until he suddenly turned round facing the dancers, raised his staff above his head, and shouted harshly:
> *Hupp-shah!*
> *Hupp-shah!* answered the dancers who now began to dance the căluș in earnest, their chief dancing in front of them, stepping backwards and continually shouting—to the exciting rhythm of music—the same call.
> *Abreaaau!* yelled the 'mute' rushing with his sword at the crowd which at his sight shrunk back hastily with wild shouts of merriment and terror.
> 'The mute' took out the wooden phallus, and muttering beast-like sounds, chased round the circle formed by the călușari scattering milk and eggs upon it. (Ibidem 1957)

Just like the *Play of the Deer*, the *Play of the Goat* or the *Malanca*, the members of the *Călușari* team are subject to strict rules respected by all the participants in the rituals. Thus, the team itself becomes a kind of brotherhood where the *mute* in the case of *Călușari*, the *arnăut* in the case of *Malanca* and the *comoraș* in the case of the *Play of the Deer* watch carefully so that none of the team members behaves in a way that might lead to an event that could break up the entire group structure.

> Without looking at the verandah, Birică felt that Polina had come out of her room, and he turned his head in that direction, fighting against those who were crowding around him. He saw Ilinca approaching.
>
> Polina was standing behind her mother, with crossed arms. As soon as he saw her, Birică forgot everything for a moment, and his bitter feelings melted within him as if they had never existed.
>
> She was looking cheerful and quiet, and when Moromete's daughter Ilinca came close to her and whispered into her ear, Polina nodded that she had understood and continued to be cheerful, whilst watching the *călușari*. (Ibidem 1957)

Wolf, Shanin, Redfield, and other classical authors of peasant studies did never describe Romantic relationships in the rural universe. Peasants were depicted rather as economic agents interested in keeping the household at a level that allowed them to perpetuate their economic model, doubled by the tendency to obtain the *caloric minima* necessary for their survival (Wolf 1966:4). On the contrary, writer Marin Preda presents a much more complex peasant universe where people are eager to fight for their love, and sometimes confront the harsh principles of an intolerant community directed against all those who could possibly violate them.

Reymont and Preda described mummers not only in their relation to the village social life but also to peasant values. This is a vivid universe with tough rules where the life of the individual is strictly regulated by the principles and norms of village community. Within this universe, rural plays represented a kind of valve through which the pressure of a strict and vigilant community was temporarily released, and the villagers had the chance to watch and participate in a folk play where both actors and spectators were engaged in a dynamic and interactive play. With a great deal of talent, Reymont and Preda's descriptions of mummers highlight a set of attributes that theatrical performances hold: they include absurd elements and dialogues hard to understand by an outsider, but completely meaningful to villagers; they include at least a few masked characters; they intermediate the relations between youngsters within their strict peasant communities; they are an important part of the peasant universe of social relations and networks. Above all these, they are an eloquent expression of peasants' values, moral principles and rules, and can be used as lenses enhancing the understanding of social relations, networks and social inequalities in small village communities.

ECONOMIC AUTARKY. RURAL PLAYS AND
THE PEOPLE WITHOUT HISTORY

In this section I analyze the third feature of the peasant society build on Mendras's model: economic autarky based on family production and consumption, resulting in a subsistence ethic and a relative autonomy of the peasants in relation to the encompassing society. To exemplify this analysis, I present two experiences from my life and show how they relate to the third feature highlighted by Mendras as being defining for the peasant societies. I show how this characteristic is expressed by rural plays and the rural universe they embody.

A couple of times, my life has given me by accident the opportunity to understand how countryside people imagine their world, and how they define themselves and their rural universe in relation to the larger world. I had one of my first revelations when I was just twenty years old, serving in the army. Situated in Southern Romania, my unit was a huge one, comprising more than a thousand soldiers and numerous officers. Nevertheless, by the end of my stage, in the dorm of my company there were only six soldiers left, the rest of them having been transferred in the meantime to different other units throughout the country. One of those days, just two months before finishing our service, we were announced that in the coming days, the dorm of our company was required to receive more than fifty reservists for two weeks. For these men, aged between 30 and 50, known as "reservists" in the military jargon, that two-weeks training was an obligatory requirement of the Romanian Army.

Indeed, the unit soon became overcrowded with men we called "elders"; all of them were peasants from the County of Dolj where our unit was located. By talking to them, I soon realized that most of the people who lived in that backward region had a low educational background, with barely five or six primary school classes attended. After a few days, when we got to know each other better during the evenings when there was nothing else to do—as the room did not even have TV or radio –, we used to gather in front of a huge two square meters' physical map of Romania and to look at different areas on it. As most of these reservists had not traveled too much in their life, they started to ask me few questions about various areas and localities, and I would provide quite a lot of details as I had been fond of geography and history since childhood. Impressed by my geography knowledge, the reservists whom I discussed told their comrades that I knew where each locality on the Romanian map was located. The same evening, I got involved involuntarily in a kind of game where more and more reservists came in the front of the map to try their luck with me, hoping they would find a small locality that I would not be able to trace on the map. This guessing game was easy for me to win. Their literacy was so poor that they had to stare at the map for a minute before being able to read and pronounce the name of that locality. Thus, by usually scanning the area of the map the person was staring at, I could easily find that locality and present myself as a winner once again. Every time I won, the person who lost expressed loudly their astonishment with brief statements like "Oh Hell!" together with his fellow reservists. They were amazed at how good my geography knowledge was, and at the same time felt frustrated for losing each time.

After playing this game more than two dozen times, they all started to look at me as if I were a geography guru, a sort of living miracle. That moment, a man in his mid-40s who had seen my performance from beginning to end, said that he would also like to try his luck with me. Without even looking at the map, he told me the name of a locality. I realized I was about to lose the game, but I asked him to give me five minutes. During those five minutes, knowing that the reservists came only from the county of Dolj, I start scanning from north to south all the localities of the county, hoping that I could finally find that village. When I was sure I had read almost all the localities of Dolj County, I asked him to give me the name of a larger locality close to that one, so that I could find it easier. The rest of the reservists involved in the game were already jubilating for I was about to lose the game, and so the miracle behind my knowledge started to crumble. However, when the guy gave me the name of a bigger locality in the proximity of that village, I realized immediately how close it was to our military unit. So, I started screening again, more intensely, all the localities around that bigger locality he had given me as a clue, and I declared with strong conviction that the locality he had named was not on the map.

My statement created a lot of confusion among peasants-reservists: "How could a locality exist and still not be on the map, especially on such a large map?," they wondered. The result of the game, as well as whether I was losing or wining became secondary, and their main concern was to find out if that locality really existed or was maybe just an invention of their fellow reservist. I faced the same dilemma, too. Thus, I asked him to look with me at the map and give me more details about that locality and its neighborhood, in the hope that perhaps we could find it together. He accepted immediately, as he himself had also become curious to find the location of that village. Thus, together with him, I was able to identify exactly the place he was talking about, but we all observed that there was no name written down. "How do we know this place really exists?," a fellow reservist asked that moment. "Because I was born and I've been living there for thirty years!," the man declared with a strong conviction in his voice.

After that event, we became friends and he started telling me stories about his small village, actually just a hamlet. This was how I learned a lot of interesting and fascinating life stories that had happened in the small, insignificant locality that was not even mentioned on the map. Some of the most impressive stories he narrated with a lot of talent were about the folk play called *Călușarii*, their *dansuri îndrăcite/crazy dances* and *vindecări miraculoase/amazing healings* during the Whitsuntide day (see Neagota and Benga 2011). These stories surprised me a lot particularly because I had heard about *Călușarii* only from the official radio and TV channels, and from propaganda newspapers during communist times; so I had the impression they are nothing else then a strenuous masculine folk dance. Nevertheless, as a young man, the narratives about the miraculous powers of *Călușari*, together with their magic forces and esoteric rules, mesmerized me and impressed my imagination greatly.[8]

Another similar story in my life happened almost twenty years after that event. This time I had already been for a few years in the United States where I started my PhD in anthropology. Like many other graduate students, I needed some extra money to pay for all my expenses. This was how I began working in a restaurant. At the restaurant, I soon became a good friend of the chef, a Mexican guy called Chavo who had immigrated to the United States from a small locality close to Puebla City. Besides the fact that he enjoyed teasing me all the time, calling me "The Russian Spy," I knew that, in fact, he admired me a lot. I knew he was impressed that I had much more education than anybody in his circle of friends. Besides "The Russian Spy" he also called me "The Doctor," especially when he introduced me to his friends.

Actually, Chavo was a curious and intelligent guy who loved to hear me telling stories of my country. Sometimes, he would also tell me stories about his own childhood and his family, and I enjoyed that, too. I was mostly impressed by the adventurous story of his migration when his father, one of his sisters and Chavo had crossed the border when he was just eleven years old, and came to work in Massachusetts. For this reason, since the age of thirteen, Chavo had ceased going to school and instead had started working in a bakery and afterwards in a pizzeria.

During a dull afternoon when the restaurant where we worked was not busy, Chavo begin to talk about the Mexican Revolution. Soon after he started the story, I realized his knowledge on the topic was vague and imprecise, a combination of what he saw in movies and what he heard in street discussions. Knowing a few things about this topic, but much more than Chavo expected, I interrupted him many times to complete the narration with more details. At a certain point, pretending to be very annoyed, Chavo bursted: "What the heck Doctor? How do you know about Emiliano Zapata and about Pancho Villa?" Half astonished, half irritated, Chavo exclaimed:

"Doctor, you know what? I will tell you a name from the Mexican history that you have never heard about!" "Go ahead!" I said, being curious to play his game and to see what character from Mexican history he would reveal with his "gotcha question." Then he exclaimed triumphantly: "Miguel Camaney!" When I heard the name, I scratched my head a couple of times and I had to declare, much to Chavo's delight, that I had no clue about who that character was. I also told him I was curious to find who he was. That moment, satisfied with his victory, Chavo exclaimed: "This is the man who sells avocados on my street!" His statement could not astonish me more. I realized immediately that it did not matter how much history somebody tried to learn in school, that history would be tributary to certain grand narratives that would always leave many people and places aside. That moment I remembered instantly the story with the reservist that had happened almost twenty years before, back when I was in the army. At the same time, I connected that story with the nostalgic memories that Chavo had told to me during the previous weeks about the Mexican mummers and their carnivals at the beginning of March that take place every year in Puebla City and the neighboring localities.

However, the moral of both stories became more relevant for me in the light of my new research on peasant rural plays. Today, there are still people in the world—and there were probably much more in the past—for whom the grand narratives of the accepted version of world history, as well as the geographic borders of their countries had less importance than the events happening in their own village. This was because most of their life had been spent inside the narrow borders of the village. In the field research I conducted as rural anthropologist since 2000 in the countryside of Romania, Moldova Republic, and Ukraine, I still had the chance to find elders who had not traveled in their entire lifetime more than 40–50 kilometers away from their own village, only to the closest town or city in the neighborhood. Even there, they had the chance to travel just several times in their entire life. All these people were connected to their own locality with all the particles of their being. For all of them, local plays like mummers meant much more than the official version of world history or the grand narratives students learn at school. Now, most of these people are elders and represent a minority of the countryside population.

Today, the countryside is populated mainly by a new peasantry (Ploeg 2009), a peasantry emigrating and living for a long part of its life in foreign countries or big cities (Kearney 2006:15–21). These people found a new way of life in the cities, far from their own village, or in a foreign more developed country. But these are the people who, just a century ago, used to form the majority of the world population (Hobsbawm 1994:289). And these are the people whom I called, borrowing one of Wolf's concepts, *people without history*. This huge "mass of peasants" was among the people "to whom history has been denied," Eric Wolf lets us know in one of his most influential books (Wolf [1982]1990:23). Peasants were one of the subordinated classes in history for centuries, and they remained subordinate in the hierarchy created by capitalism through the development of market relations. "People without history" is indeed a comprehensive, and inspirational concept coined by Eric Wolf. His great accomplishment is that of explaining through anthropological lenses the greatest events of modern history, including intercontinental trade, slavery and the accumulation of wealth. (Wolf [1982] 1990)

Wolf challenges the idea that communities living outside Europe were static and isolated instances, disconnected from global processes, before the European expansion of the 15th century when industrial capitalism penetrated, subordinated, destroyed, or absorbed their modes of production. His book struggles to separate the macro processes related to capitalism development and the dynamic of micro-populations caught in a big torrent of challenges. In Wolf's view, the people without history are the non-westerners who were engaged in various modes of production different from the Europeans' colonizers. Thus, "both the people who claim history as their own and the people to whom history has been denied emerge as participants in the same historical trajectory" (Wolf 1982:23). Unlike Eric Wolf, I focus my attention on rural communities in the very heart of Europe, not outside it. These people's lives gravitated for a long time, sometimes even decades after the beginning of the 20th century, around the values and norms of their local communities instead of revolving around the principles of the global society whose influences were much weaker between the borders of communities than they are today. Analyzing the plays of rural communities, my study, just like microhistory approaches, try "to ask large questions in small places" following the effects of capitalism and communism's development on the rural micro-populations located now in some remote pockets of rural Europe. Just like Wolf, I describe both macro and micro dimensions that result from the depiction of rural populations caught in the process of big economic and social transformations wrought by globalization. However, I show how some rural communities of Europe were able to promote their own values, rules, and principles that became apparent in their rural plays despite the hegemonic narratives of capitalism and communism in 20th century Europe. The "people to whom history have been denied" are not outsiders of Europe but rural European populations who, in spite of their continuous contact with the big economic and social transformations of Europe, were more attached by local principles, and their identities were heavily shaped by the values of their local communities. Scrutinizing their plays, I aim to provide the reader with a glimpse of their life, seen through the lens of their rural plays that work as door openers into the cohesive rural communities of rural Europe and their rich culture.

Borrowing Wolf's metaphor, and talking about peasants' autarchic economy, I refer to peasants as "people without history" not because they were "the people to whom history has been denied," but because their lives in their village communities have been little known and studied by "people who claimed history as their own." Working their small plots of land, using "the pastures and meadows, the waste, the bogs and woodlands that existed for the use of all" (Handlin 1967:459; Stahl 2008) or being under the domination of landowners and other elites (Scott 1977), these people contributed with their work to all the macro-processes described by Wolf. Yet, their life gravitated mostly inside the narrow borders of their village and the firm rules imposed by their communities' network and family ties (Stirling 1965).

Especially decades ago, when they were illiterate, rural people would never have the chance to see either the whole picture of the empire, country, or continent they were part of, or that chunk of history inside which they were significant through their work and presence. It is true that they fought in certain imperial armies or, later, mainly after mid-19th century, in those of national states, they paid tribute to boyars, landlords and state authorities, and rebelled against those in power when they were too oppressed (Scott 1977). Nevertheless, most of them had been, for a long period of time, more connected with the small world of their village community than with the grand narratives of superordinate political entities. For all these people, their rural plays and their local rituals were more important than many important events of the universal history mentioned today in our most common textbooks, from primary school to college.

Unfortunately, even today, few studies try to deal with these micro-processes and to understand them through the lenses provided by the moral-value horizon of the village communities' members in parallel with globalizing processes. Those anthropologists who studied peasants in different corners of Europe through extensive participant observation ended up talking about the dense social networks inside the village, doubled by the peasants' tendency to demarcate themselves from their neighbors (Stirling 1965). Kazimierz Dobrowolski, who focused on Polish peasants, described their "institutionalized social gatherings" that were "very important means for the preservation of traditional culture" (Dobrowolski 1958:284). He observed that of special importance were "the neighbors' meetings, which gathered for certain ceremonial occasions like spinning or tearing feather, as well as for more informal events like regular evening gatherings, especially in the winter months. These gatherings, common in Southern Poland by the end of the nineteenth century and early twentieth century, were the forerunners of the modern book or newspaper" (Idem 1958:284). This social-economic environment was responsible for the peasant village's strong solidarity and eternal preoccupation for drawing social and cultural borders between "our village" and "their village" (Stirling 1965:29–35).

The two tendencies illustrated above, next to the outsiders' inclination towards devaluing peasants and peasant culture, are traceable in the folk plays as they are still extant in areas preserving a vivid and dynamic rural culture. In these areas, one may observe that there are sometimes big differences in the morphology, functions and symbols staged for example by mummers living in neighboring villages; however, one may also find striking similarities between the mummers' plays situated at extremely remote points in time and space. These are all expressions of the peasants' economic autarky before their communities were integrated in the industrial system of production, and are one of the topics and paradoxes that my study tries to explain.

VILLAGE COMMUNITIES AND
THEIR SYSTEM OF VALUES

If in the first part of this chapter I have opened a technical discussion about values from the perspective of Clyde Kluckhohn and Robert Hartman, in its last two sections I will provide a series of examples and case studies that demonstrate how these two theories can find their applicability through the analysis of the rural world and of rural plays. Throughout these last sections I perform an elusive task, that of "looking over people's shoulders" which means looking beyond what people say and explicitly do, towards a deeper horizon, guided by the peasants' understanding of their own village world through their values.

All these things became more apparent when I had the chance to hear peasants gossiping. Kluckhohn was an anthropologist who understood the role of the gossip for small communities. In his study about values, he stated: "Where the gossip is most current is where that culture is most heavily laden with values. The discussability of values is one of their most essential properties, though the discussion may be oblique or disguised—not labeled as a consideration of values" (Kluckhohn 1951:404). This simple observation made me move my perspective from the anthropological/philosophical theories on values to the way values are expressed by people's behaviors, attitudes, statements, and actions in the rural communities I analyzed.

Only after spending a few months in Heleșteni and Ruginoasa, have I started developing a sort of dexterity in detecting peasants' values in their actions, behaviors and in the analysis of the unspoken meanings present behind their statements. One of the first such significant moments happened in early June 2012, during a day unusually hot for late Spring. I was waiting for Florin close to his parents' agriculture field, a few kilometers far from the village. That hot day, they were hoeing a potato field. Florin promised me that, after finishing his work, he would help me get in touch with a villager for an interview that was supposed to happen that day. While I was waiting for him in the shade of his horse carriage, I looked around and saw people hoeing their lands in small groups of usually two or three. When the sun temperature peaked at midday, I saw these people hiding away of the heat, and taking a small break in the shade of a tree, or even going home for a brief rest. A lady who seemed about thirty-five years old, together with her 10–11-year-old boy, were returning from the field, carrying their hoes on their shoulders. I saluted them when they passed by the carriage. They saluted me too, and then the lady asked me: "What's happened to you? Have you lost your hoe?"

This seemed to be a mere question, but, knowing the area and its inhabitants, I managed to seize its subtlety right away. What this rhetoric question wanted to say in fact was a critique of a man who was just waiting at edge of the field without doing any work. More, it also contained that woman's perspective on men. Beyond the proper assertion, there lay another unspoken one, somehow implied by the multiple meanings of the question: "I am a woman and I have worked hard all day in the field together with my young son, while you are a man, but you waste time uselessly by the field. So, I deserve respect and appreciation, and you don't!" More than that, this simple sentence also included a valuation of the physical labor that could be synthesized as: "In agriculture, physical labor is good even if it involves physical effort, while inactivity and laziness are bad and morally degrading." It also hid one more final allusion. The woman I am talking about realized immediately that I was not from the village. Thus, another type of moralizing perspective could be summarized as: "We, the inhabitants of this village, work hard and thus we deserve appreciation; but the people in other areas are not like us, they try to stay away from hard physical labor."

During my stay in Heleșteni, it became obvious many times that physical labor in agriculture was valued. However, after this meeting, I accepted the critique and, whenever I went to the field with a villager, I tried to lend a hand to the ones I knew, since it was obvious that this behavior would be appreciated. On June 19, 2012, the *comună*'s mayor organized a *clacă*[9] for hoeing the agricultural land belonging to *Centrul de Zi pentru Copii Săraci/The Day Center for Poor Children* in Hărmăneasa village. This center was under the township hall's administration and it functioned by self-management. The food offered to needy children came mostly from the agricultural lands of the center. However, to have these plots cultivated and taken care of, many people were needed. Therefore, when hoeing had to be done, the mayor asked the township hall's employees to do that. However, that work meant spending a weekend day for all the ones involved; so, the mayor had to make use of the prestige he had among his employees in order to convince them to perform the activity. That year, without being aware of that from the start, I managed to make things easier for him.

That morning, I joined the mayor and his wife at the center's land, and worked side by side with the township hall's employees for hoeing the potato field. This perplexed all the employees, since they knew I work at a university in the United States. As a result, they kept joking about me during the entire job. "See, professor, what happened if you didn't like America?! Is it better to hoe here, in Heleșteni?" one of the township hall's employees asked me. Again, his statement hid more meanings than one might notice at a first sight. The basic idea the villager wanted to transmit was: "If you want to be just like us, here, in Heleșteni, you have to work a great deal. But this hard work gives you moral nobility. Even if life in other corners of the world is easier, the hard work in a village makes the ones performing it superior to others." This is also a value judgment regarding the agricultural labor and the standpoint of the ones performing it. This type of valuation made by the members of the agricultural community about the physical labor they did has been observed by other anthropologists, too, under similar circumstances:

> For Bulgarian villagers, the physical labor that characterizes their activities is a means of claiming moral superiority: rural inhabitants see themselves as hard working and not afraid of 'dirtying their hands.' This same grounding of moral virtue through hard work is also evident in urban Hungarians' desire to maintain their links to the land. (Kaneff and Leonard 2001:33)

Another aspect about my status as an anthropologist in a small and relatively isolated locality: my presence created confusion among the inhabitants. One day in early April 2012, I was walking towards the mayor's office of Heleșteni, since my car was broken. From my host's house to the mayor's office, there were around four kilometers. The people I met on the village street answered my greeting, though they looked at me puzzled since I did not belong to that place. Suddenly, an older man asked me a question when I said hello: "Tu al cui ești, mă?!"/ eng. "Hey you, whose are you?" Once again, the question seemed simple, but it had a whole universe of meanings and value judgments behind it. For such a question, the answer was supposed to be simple and quite standardized, such as: "I am the son of Ion Chirilă known as Parafiru." Inside the village, youngsters used to be identified by the elder ones through their family of origin, to which they sometimes added a nickname that helped community members identify the family easier, or at least the head of the family—the father. The family somebody came from would already say a lot about its social status in the village world and the respect it enjoyed or, on the contrary, the peasants' disdain of it, automatically reflected on their perception of the person they were talking to. The answer

I gave to the villager's question was totally unlike standard answers: "You cannot know me. I am not from here." "That's what I've thought, too," the man said, satisfied with his intuition.

I experienced the same dilemma when, on April 23, 2012, I went to conduct an interview with one of the villagers in Oboroceni. The meeting I had with Vasile Lupu, the householder, was utterly memorable. When entering his courtyard, his wife—who already knew me - wanted to introduce me to her husband, but he greeted me as if he had been knowing me for a long time. When asked by his wife if he knew me, he mentioned the name of a villager he thought I was. That moment, his wife told him I was not even from that village. As a result, the man asked: "Then whom are you visiting in the village?" Once again, the peasant was trying to identify me by relating me to a family that I might have been visiting in the village. "I'm not here to visit anybody. I'm a teacher." I replied. "And you teach where? In Oboroceni or in Heleşteni village?" the man asks me once again. "No, no, I don't teach here, I teach at the university." I answer. "Ah, at the university in Iaşi . . . And you've come here to some friend in the village . . . " This confusion was not accidental at all since it came from the fact that, for most villagers living in the Heleşteni *comună*, the geographic universe of the locality was inextricably linked to that of the community and families populating it. Therefore, any person inside the locality's physical frontiers was somehow supposed to be related to the social, cultural, and moral world of their community.

Family and community have often been emphasized as important elements within the rural universe during the discussions I had while conducting my field research. In one of these discussions, Constantin Hâra declared: "Especially in the past, some decades ago, family was one of the most important things in the village world. This happened because everything you represented as individual—esteem, prestige, economic situation—came from the family. More directly, without a family, you as individual meant nothing and could not even live your life in the village. Because back then everything was based on agriculture and the land used to be inherited from the family, too. This situation still stands nowadays, but yet there are also many changes that society went through, especially economic changes that diminished the role of the family and also of the community in the relationships between people" (May 2, 2012, Oboroceni, field notes).

For villagers, the family as social cell was closely connected to their work in agriculture. The two were attaching to and strengthening one another in an indissoluble relation, creating in turn the profile of personhood in the village world. Thus, a good householder was hardworking, and his effort was precisely meant to provide the necessary resources for his family's well-being. On the contrary, the head of the family (husband and father) drinking alcohol and spending more time in pubs was not well-seen by the villagers. This behavior was perceived as an excessive waste of an important part of the income that should belong to his family. In the locals' vision, alcohol consumption was synthesized in a parable I have heard from at least a dozen people:

> In the past, just about 30–40 years ago, only married men were allowed to drink in local pubs. For a married man, drinking in a pub was a sign of high status and prestige. If a young man dared to enter a local pub, he would be kicked out by the elders, and sent home immediately.

Once again, the story's lesson is deeper and transmits much more than one could perceive at a first glance. The underlining meaning was that a family man could afford to have a glass of wine every once in a while, with his comrades who were also heads of families. This activity proved that the householder in question had enough economic resources to support his family and enjoyed the privilege of being able to spend some of his work's extra income together with other locals that had the same social status. But a young man had to be preoccupied to save his resources to set up a family for which he first had to provide a shelter and a decent life. These benefits could only come from an assiduous work.

I have also observed the way peasants value agricultural labor from an unusual perspective: the way the community regarded the thieves in the village. Sitting once at the table with my host, Mrs. Doina Hâra, and hearing the church bell tolling, I asked her if anybody had passed away. I knew that the bell is usually tolled on such occasions. The answer I got was utterly amazing. "This time they toll the bell for thieves!" "How come?," I asked again. "Well, if somebody from the village steals something, especially from another villager's corn barn, or any other of the neighbors' agricultural products, let's say, the bell is tolled. And the thief knows the bell tolls for him. Therefore, if he still has some trace of belief in God and humanity in him, he brings the stolen good back during the night. For if he doesn't do that, many evils and troubles might come upon him, as a sort of divine punishment" (March 20, 2012, Oboroceni village, field notes).

In this case, too, the story's hidden meanings had to be found by relation to other values in the village world. In this case, the basic idea was that the thief had no respect for the work done by the householder's family and, as a result, the thief had to be punished by invoking divine justice. Besides this divine justice, can be observed the community's willingness to solve its conflicts alone, without making use of external authorities such as the court or the police. This type of communitarian autonomy also spoke about an old way of mediating village conflicts—an approach deeply rooted in the village communities' history.

However, I managed to find out that the bell was tolled only in extreme cases and that it was regarded as an ultimate method of correcting those community members who "had taken dishonest paths in life," according to a frequent expression I had heard from many inhabitants of Heleșteni. I found out this from Mitică, one of the villagers who had become my close friend during my field research in the *comună*. Despite our closeness, I have never managed to convince him to call me by my first name. "I cannot, Mr. Professor, you are too schooled," Mitică would often justify, going on calling me "Mr. Alin" or "Mr. Professor." He was the bell-ringer of the village, and his wife worked as a seller in one of the village shops that belonged to their wedding godfather, the mayor of Heleșteni. Although both had low salaries, Mitică declared many times that he would never leave the village. It was a world that matched him, he had told me, and he would not change it for anything else. Despite he had two brothers living in Portugal where they had been working in constructions for years, Mitică had never been tempted to leave Heleșteni. Maybe that is precisely why he had also developed a strong attachment to this world and its values.

One day in early July, another villager told me that Mitică had hit a 65-year-old woman. The fact seemed a mere invention to me since I had never perceived him as either violent or capable of hitting an aged woman. When meeting him in the village street, I tried to joke about the rumor I had just heard. The openness he proved, by immediately unveiling the whole story to me, left me defenseless and disoriented. "Yes, Mr. Professor, it's true I beat her. I kicked her twice in the rear and pulled her head twice. I did this because I had caught her with my chicken in hand. Do you know how hard it is to raise a chicken?! And so, how was I supposed to stay and do nothing when I saw her with my chicken in her hand?!" "But why haven't you tolled the bell?," I thought of asking since Mitică was also the bell-ringer of the village church. "I don't want to do such things because the bell is very dangerous, Mr. Professor. Accidents happened to certain people, they were left without a hand or a leg or, God forbid, even worse! So, I just gave her what I considered she deserved and that was it. . . . But the weird thing is she complained to my godfather only now, and that's how afterwards everybody knew. The event happened around April, before Easter, and she's only complained now. Since then, she has come to hoe on my land and worked in my garden, she came a few times in our house. In case my godfather asks me what and how, I tell him the truth just as I have told you. I am not embarrassed at all!"

Mitică's story had its lesson, too. The violent correction applied to another community member seemed to be justified in the villagers' perspective precisely because that person had broken one of the basic principles of village community life: respecting a family's work and effort invested into its household goods. Nevertheless, the punishment had to be fair when compared to the damage, and should not cause irreversible losses to the person in question who was, finally and despite her deed, just another community member.

This entire journey inside the world of small rural localities—and especially in Heleșteni where the village community was more cohesive—can demonstrate the way the community members express value judgments, even if not by stating them explicitly. Such behaviors and facts—described by means of examples—prove that, within rural communities, there is a sort of deeply rooted set of values that may be revealed by analyzing the culture regarded as a text prone to be deciphered, but especially as a text that may be read between the lines. In the meanwhile, this analysis revealed the systemic structure of rural values, with the inextricable links between the elements forming it—elements that are never isolated or autonomous, but indissolubly connected in a sometimes very complex interweave of relations and associations that form the social fundament of the rural world. However, these relations and values may be very well observed—perhaps better than anywhere else—when analyzing the mummers' plays.

READING OVER PEOPLE'S SHOULDERS
WHEN THEY PERFORM FOLK PLAYS

It has been stated that folk plays are a social order reverse (Kligman 1981:xi). Without contradicting this statement, I shall try to present rural plays from a more nuanced perspective and to show how these collective rituals are strictly connected to the village community norms and to the moral values and principles of these rural communities, even when they seem to contradict them.

During these plays, there are behaviors that can be interpreted as transgressions of community norms. Because of this, the first impression could be that folk plays might also be perceived as cultural forms by which social norms functioning throughout the whole year inside the community are temporarily abolished. Impressed by the richness of manifestations, symbols, and representations during winter holidays, even I concluded during my first trip to Heleșteni area, that rural plays challenge the community social order.

By the end of 2010, my first impression was about to be invalidated during my second fieldwork session for the winter holidays. One of the youngsters with a bad reputation in Heleșteni, known by villagers as being violent, dishonest, and difficult to cope with, surprised everybody when he announced that he had organized a *Goat team*. The news surprised the locals who did not know how to perceive it: was it a positive change of the young man or just another challenge he had launched against the community? Everybody knew that organizing a *Goat team* was a difficult task that involved a flawless planning, had to be prepared in advance and seriously. It did not only concern the recruitment of the team members, but also the realization of costumes and the preparation of the play that was about to be performed in front of the house-holders. But it was difficult to believe that a person with such a bad reputation would be able to coordinate the whole event.

Indeed, problems have not stopped showing up beginning with the first sequences that were supposed to take place for the organization of the *Goat team*. According to village tradition, on December 27, the Goat team lead-ers had to present their team in front of the villagers, in the cultural center where afterwards they had to offer wine or *țuică/brandy* to the viewers. This settled the team's organization and was in the meantime the equivalent of an announcement made in front of the village community about the band's composition. However, that youngster's team did not join this event. The fact caused rumor among the villagers who criticized it harshly: "Well yes, as usual, this boy just wants to get as much as he can from the villagers, with-out giving anything back." The truth was that the beverage the *Goat team* leader was supposed to offer to the villagers present for the presentation on December 27 required money or at least some work investment in case the wine came from the family's vineyard. But it seems that that *comoraș* was not willing to invest this money and thus follow the village tradition. The villag-ers' comments included another critique. Although not willing to invest any money and giving back something to his village community, later on by visit-ing the family houses with his *Goat team* according to tradition, his goat team was supposed to receive money, food and drinks from the villagers. In this situation, there was a transformation of the kind of generalized reciprocity accepted by the community and meant to benefit both parties, into a negative reciprocity (Sahlins 1974:194–196) that would allow the *Goat team* leader to be the only one earning something.

But this was only the first of the whole series of problems this team caused. Once in the villagers' houses, the performance of the *Goat* team made people comment that "the representation offered had been weak," while "the mem-bers' costumes had been made in a hurry." But the last rumor came after the two days of ceremonies. On January 2, 2011, some of my close friends had already found out that the young man had not shared fairly the money got-ten after the two caroling days, giving only a very small amount to the other team members, and keeping the rest for himself. The village tradition was that the *comoraș* would gather the money given by the householders after the performance. However, in the end the sum of money collected was approxi-mate by the members of the team, and resulted that the leader of the team did not share it fairly with the rest of the team. Following this happening, I heard rough comments in the village about that youngster: "For sure this was his first and last *Goat*!" Indeed, in the following years that young man did not organize any other *Goat team*, and none of the guy of his age would want to join him, while householders in Heleșteni would not have opened their doors for him, either. This way, the *Goat ritual* proved once again its efficiency in channeling the community's values and principles, emphasizing eloquently a person's negative traits and censuring this person's behavior in relation to the community.

Not only folk plays such as the *Goat* or the *Deer* are circumscribed by the limits and rules established by the community, but also the *Pantomimic Mummers'* groups, where the freedom of action and improvisation is higher than in other customs within the large category of mummers' plays. An event that reinforced my conviction happened on December 24, 2011, and I was exactly the one causing it. By the end of 2011, I arrived for the third time in Heleșteni *comună*. My hosts and their entire family already knew me well, so I had taken the freedom of playing a joke. Arriving in Oboroceni in the afternoon of December 24, before entering the house, I put on a Halloween mask that I bought it from America. After having entered the courtyard, I performed my mummer part seriously and knocked at the door, changing my voice to avoid recognition.

The one who opened the door was my host's niece, Andreea. She was at home only together with another cousin of hers who had come from the town of Suceava to visit her relatives in Heleșteni. Half surprised, half scared by the appearance of the "mummer," Andreea asked me "What do you want?" "I came to carol." I replied decisively. "But why now, is this the time to carol?," Andreea asked annoyed suddenly. "But when?!," I replied with a sense of wonder in my voice. "Well, on December 31 as everybody else!" "But I want to do it now!" "What the hell does this man want?," Andreea asked her younger cousin who was also surprised. "Come on December 31, too, and we shall welcome you," she gave a sort of solution for the unpredicted situation. "No, I want it now!," I insisted on a seemingly furious tone. "This one is either drunk or crazy!," Andreea told her cousin. "Tell me what I should do about him!," she asked the other girl once more, visibly in trouble and trying to find a way out of the complicated situation she found herself in. That moment, I took my mask off and Andreea gave a sigh of relief: "Oh God, Alin, it's you! You really scared me! I thought there might have been who knows what crazy man!"

Seeing Andreea's reaction, I decided to go on with my joke and play it on other family members. Finding out that Mrs. Doina, my host, was at the shop she had in her courtyard, I went there. I entered the shop through the back door which was usually used only by employees and owners. Inside the shop, I saw Mrs. Doina and Dana, her younger daughter, serving the customers. "Do you welcome the mummers?," I began my sketch. Mrs. Doina was known to be a fierce woman, able to face even the rudest mummers, but now she needed a few seconds to come back from her state of amazement.

Afterwards, re-becoming herself—the decided and organized host I used to know—she started: "But, Sir, is this the time for mummers? And in such a manner, through the back door?" "But when is the right time?," I replied acting as if I did not know that at all. "Well, for sure you know it well, I don't have to tell you that. Look, I'm going to open here, and you are going to go out nice and easy through the front door." "Don't you want to welcome the mummers?," I went on. Inside the shop, some clients were watching the scene with curiosity and a bit of confusion. "Yes, we do welcome them, we do, but not now. We welcome them when it's the time, not when anybody decides to." That moment, from behind the counter, Dana started laughing: "Mom, it's Alin, can't you see?" That moment, as any mummer who had been recognized, I respected the rule of the play and took the mask off my face. The situation made Mrs. Doina laugh, and she let a few words with a sense of embarrassment: "But, Sir, what are you doing? You come and scare us like that! And look what a beautiful mask you have!" "I've brought it from America!" I replied right away. The next moment, a local who had witnessed the whole scene seized the opportunity and asked me: "I've noticed it's a *real* mask. Would you sell it to me?" "How much do you offer for it?," I asked, pretending to be interested. "40 lei" he shouted, hoping he would get the American mask. The price he had offered was the double of what I had paid in a Walmart shop. "I cannot sell it because I still need it," I answered, to the local's disappointment.

The sequence I had created voluntarily made me understand that, despite the apparent disorder that the mummers generated with their actions and behaviors, they were still subjected to certain strict rules. All the ritual events at the end of the year were perfectly circumscribed by what the community had decided that could happen during the short holiday season when the behavior of the people inside the community was different, but kept respecting some pre-established rules that were clear for everybody. Surprisingly, just a few days afterwards, I was about to witness another episode that completed the one I have just described above.

December 31 is one of the most tiresome days for the families in the village and especially for the wealthier ones—such as my hosts—since they always received all the bands that knocked at their door. Two days before, the family's members were involved in preparing the sweets and the food for the holidays. For the few dozens of teams that were about to visit the household, a household needed a huge quantity of sweets and food, next to the drinks—juice, beer, and wine. All these meant an increased effort for the most hospitable hosts who would only get few hours of sleep the nights before the New Year. But New Year's night was particularly exhausting because of the physical effort and the lack of sleep.

In 2011, the evening before the New Year's Eve and the whole following night, until 5 a.m., at least 20 mummers' groups come in their house-visit to the mayor's household. Besides them are also coming small groups of 2–3 children caroling, two *Goat teams* and other two *Deer teams*—about 25 groups in all. Around 4:30 a.m., a state of tranquility began, and the family members started a discussion about the possible arrival of some mummers' groups. Around 5 a.m., as no other group had shown up meanwhile, the last family members—the mayor and his wife—went to rest a little. They were probably hoping that in case an early morning mummers' team passed by, they would be woken up by the noises guisers usually make when entering the courtyard.

However, it seemed that the fatigue of the days before had affected all the family members as well as their relatives visiting them—they were all sleeping in various corners of the house filled with people to the last inch. Even I lay down a little on a bed I was offered close to the window where mummers would pass by and the door where they would be welcomed into the house. Less than half an hour later, just the moment I had managed to doze a little, I heard the specific noise produced by a mummers' team. All my life I have been a very light sleeper, no matter how tired I was. So, I heard mummers, and I expected to see some moves in the house at any moment, thinking that one of the family members would wake up, too, to welcome the last team. But it seemed that the fatigue had been stronger this time, and none of them woke up. That moment, I was curious to see what would happen, and I focused on hearing what mummers might say to one another in such a situation. At a certain point, one of them knocked at the door stronger, and the entire group made a very loud noise with their rattles. But this time, once again, the family members had no reaction. I immediately heard the mummers talking, but I could only grasp a few fragments from what they were saying. The only clear statement I heard at the end, when the mummers decided to leave, was: "We came too late. Mr. Mayor has gone to sleep."

The next day, around 8 a.m., I was woken up once again by some noises. This time, they were produced by the people of the house, woken up just a short while ago. Since the house was full of guests and any corner would be useful, I woke up in a hurry and made my bed, although my strongest wish was to sleep at least a few hours more. Right after I woke up, the hosts laid the table and started to talk about the mummers' teams, the *Goat* and *Deer* plays and all the other ones expected, as each year at this time. I let them talk for a while and then uttered a statement that would become the breaking news of the day, as I would soon found out: "But you know that there was another group of mummers after you went to bed, right?" The silence and the looks of the people upon hearing this statement made me understand that something was not alright. The first one coming back to her senses was Mrs.

Doina who encouraged me to tell them everything I knew. So, I presented them what had happened. "Should I have woken you up?," I asked them in the end. "It would've been better." the mayor managed to articulate. "Weeell, I had seen you were so tired and thought it was not worth waking you up since the mummers would anyway show up again the next day." "You see, things are not really like that. If they came and we didn't open the door for them, they would not show up again." "How come?," I asked. "They have their own sense of dignity and, then, that's the rule: if you didn't open the door for them, they would not come to you anymore." "And what will happen now?," I asked again curiously. "They are going to spread rumors around the village that I did not welcome them." "But it's also their fault, why did they show up so late?," I tried to find an excuse. "No, no, it's rather our fault, we were supposed to stay awake or at least to sleep in turns so that there is always someone to welcome these early morning mummers."

During the next hours, I witnessed worried discussions between the mayor and his wife, with suppositions about the identity of that team's members. After a detective search and the elimination of several possibilities, the mayor reached the conclusion that there were only few groups that could have made that early morning visit. Taking his courage in both hands, the mayor started making phone calls asking the potential carolers if they had not been the mummers visiting him. After about three such phones, he gave up and said, in a completely desolate and slightly embarrassed voice: "I knew that would happen! Nobody wants to admit now. That's it. There is nothing else we can do. It's gone now. Maybe I'll be able to find out somehow from the village."

Later I found that, in many cases, when the householders do not want to open the door, and mummers figure this out by hearing voices inside the house or seeing the lights turned on, they plan a little act of revenge. Often this consists of pulling the courtyard's gate out of the gutters and moving it a few tens of meters further. This way, the householder and his family would have to spend more time and energy to repair the damage than they would have spent by welcoming the mummers. Mentioning a similar tradition in Romanian villages, the folklorist Petru Caraman speaks about a ritual called *descolindat* (eng. *de-caroling/un-caroling*). Instead of reciting a poem that wishes the family wealth and good crops, the groups of carolers who had not been received by the householders recite the sorrows and misfortunes that are about to affect that particular family (Caraman 1997).

All these discussions and events revealed to me that, far from being just a reversal of the social order, these customs actually had their strict internal order, established by an unanimously accepted set of norms, closely connected to the values of the village. Among these ones, an important one was the generalized reciprocity requiring that the service provided at a certain moment to some persons within the community be given back immediately or after a certain time. In this case, it became obvious that these forms of folk plays embodied a generalized reciprocity. The carolers gave the householders their wishes and good thoughts, or a theatre play into which they had invested a good deal of their spare time before the holidays, and received in exchange the householders' hospitality, represented by the drinks, food, and sweets in the case of *Pantomimic Mummers*, and money in the case of folk plays like the *Goat* and the *Deer*.

The presence of money throughout these traditional rituals has caused long discussions in the mummers' literature (Gailey 1969). Most of the authors dealing with this topic have tried to detect a moment long ago when instead of money there was another type of service, since that would have been closer to a domestic mode of production specific to "cultures lacking a political state, and it applies only insofar as economy and social relations have not been modified by the historic penetration of states" (Sahlins 1974:188). Nevertheless, as I will show in the next chapter, such an attempt is in vain. In the recent history of peasantry and rural communities, various social, political and economic events influenced in different ways the climate of the cultural micro-ecosystems. As the fieldwork in Heleşteni *comună* revealed, along with the analysis of winter rituals, both types of reciprocity - one based on an exchange unmediated by money, the other on an exchange mediated by money, were present.

However, even the type of balanced reciprocity (Idem 1972:194–195) mediated by money could not be regarded roughly as a sort of intrusion of the monetary economy into the natural economy of rural communities, causing irreversible effects and transformations on it (Sorokin, Zimmerman, and Galpin 1971). In fact, what I have found was a sort of combination where local economy and market economy based on money were both present in the community networks and their rules. I reached this conclusion by analyzing several discussions and interviews with the performers of these rituals. Perhaps the most relevant discussion in this respect took place on January 1, 2010, with the members of the *Goat team* in Cucuteni village, just few kilometers away from Heleşteni. That day, I had joined their team for a few hours walk in Cucuteni village, visiting the householders, and thus I had the opportunity to have more detailed talks with the team members. "Why do you go with the *Deer* around the village? Is it for money?" "No. We don't do it for money. For you have also seen that we perform it the same way both for those who gave us 50 lei and for an old woman who gave us 5 lei. If we performed for the money, probably we would not visit the pensioners anymore. But we visit all those who welcome us. We do it because we like it, because it's beautiful" (January 1, 2010, Cucuteni village, field notes).

It became obvious that a type of combination between balanced and generalized reciprocity was transmitted through these customs. For this reason, the human relations involved in these folk plays were sometimes mediated by money. Nevertheless, money was not the only impetus that motivated performers to play in the courtyards of the householders. This kind of complex interactions among people through the medium of folk plays and the dense symbols and networks created around them was less visible at a first sight. I only discovered this hidden landscape later, during my third visit to Heleșteni, due to my friendship with some of the villagers involved in these rituals. On the evening of December 28, 2011, for instance, I had the chance to witness the process of mask designing by Mitică, one of the most skilled craftsmen in Oboroceni village. Mask design is very exquisite and could sometimes last even for a whole week. I only witnessed a part of the process, and that already seemed extremely painstaking and greatly time-consuming. Mitică told me that such a mask costs between 300 and 330 Euros. And indeed, in previous years he had managed to sell several masks to some boys from the village who worked in Italy and only came home for the New Year. The immigrants from Italy did not have time anymore to do the mask themselves, but they had the money to buy it, so they approached Mitică and other craftsmen in the village for that service. Mitică told me that the mask he was working at this time was to be offered to his godfather's younger daughter—Dana. She wanted very much to join the mummers that year and that was the reason why she had been present during different stages of the process of mask design.

"Are you going to ask Dana money for the mask?," I asked Mitică, knowing that the relations between godparents and *fini* (eng. *godchildren*) in that area of Moldova were very strong, similar to blood relations.
"Wouldn't I be a pig if I asked her for the money?," Mitică replied decisively.
"Why do you say that?," I asked somehow puzzled by his aggressive answer.
"Well, how could I do such a thing when my godfather helps me whenever I need, my wife works in his store and, more, they often lend me money. In addition, I would want Dana to mention me when she wears the mask I gave her. That is to say, I would like her to speak about me, not badly." (December 28, 2011, Oboroceni village, field notes)

I have often heard the comparison with the pig—a domestic animal considered filthy and disgusting—expressed by the peasants in the area and especially in Oboroceni. It was mostly uttered as a rhetoric question ("But am I really pig enough to do this?") and always related to the potential non-fulfillment of a form of generalized reciprocity. In this case, the way close relationships between the villagers prevailed under the form of generalized reciprocity became obvious once again during the dense winter holidays full of events.

Another topic that came to light by analyzing the value judgments of the villagers was the social inequality in the *comună*. Although delicate and little talked about publicly by villagers, this topic was closely related to the village system of values and especially to the villagers' approach to work and its pair—play—involving entertainment and, in the meantime, a special way of relating to personhood. As Kligman and Verdery observed, inside the village world there is a pyramidal universe of social hierarchy that includes poor, average level and rich people ("hierarchical universe of peasantry itself"). In this universe, richness and poverty were equivalents of the human quality of the individuals forming the rural community:

> These categories had moral entailments. In the rural status ideology, being prosperous was considered a sign of virtue and hard work: villagers often attributed such qualities to the well-to-do even if they were lacking. Being poor indicated lack of character, laziness, or bad habits such as drinking (rather than, say, simple bad luck). Such qualities were thought to be inherited. (Kligman and Verdery 2011:91)

This perspective on the social inequalities inside the village probably became most apparent when analyzing the way *Mummers' Plays* and their performers were described by villagers. A simple situation made me aware of all this. By the end of March 2012, I joined the mayor of Heleșteni in his trip to Iași where he had a series of issues to solve for the township hall, and I was supposed to meet some professors from Alexandru Ioan Cuza University of Iași. On the main street of Heleșteni, a lady who was an employee of the *comună* hall got into the car, too, for she was also going to Iași to solve certain local administrative problems. I gave her right away the front seat next to the driver, the mayor. Without knowing anything about whom I was, the lady started talking to the mayor about the *Deer* ritual in Heleșteni and about the ones performing it. At a certain point, she stated something that perplexed me that moment: "*The Deer* is rather performed by the drunkards in the *comună*. A decent householder stays with his family for the New Year and does not walk around the village all night with the children," she stated while laughing (March 27, 2012, Oboroceni village, field notes).

Surprised by her remark, I tried to approach the same topic with my closest acquaintances in the *comună* and truest friends: Constantin, the mayor of the *comună*, and Florin, the sport teacher. They had never hesitated in talking to me freely about any topic I tried to deal with. Indeed, although not as eager to talk as usual, they gave me anyway some data about this topic. Florin tried to offer me an overall view on the general perspective of the inhabitants in Heleșteni: "About the ones performing the *Deer*, one usually says: take a look at this person, he works for his family even during the New Year while others stay home having fun" (March 29, 2012, Oboroceni village, field notes).

Constantin gave me valuable extra information on the topic: the householder's perspective, as a man used to welcome these teams year by year. He said: "Indeed, the *Deer* performers are poor people. Because a householder does not go out with the *Deer* during the New Year, he stays at home and welcomes it. Actually, this is what makes him a (good) householder—the fact that he can offer something to another one who is poorer" (April 25, 2012, Oboroceni village, field notes). From this standpoint, folk plays were not only an expression of simple generalized reciprocity (Sahlins 1974:193), but also a complex process of redistribution of community resources where wealthier people in the village offered something of their surplus to the needy ones (Idem 1974:190). The idea of redistributing the surplus within the community was confirmed to me by an event with a similar function. After the morning church service on Christmas day, people with a better economic situation from the *comună* put money together and bought oranges and sweets. All these products were offered when leaving to those who had attended the church service that day.

A closer look at folk plays shows us that they represent neither a restatement of the social inequalities in the rural world, nor a reversal of the social roles already existing like in the case of the Roman Saturnalia. Many of these rituals involve a sort of symbolic reconciliation between the poor and the rich in the *comună*, by means of staging plays. During a play, the social differences vanish because a play is the same for everybody and it responds to a universal need of the human spirit. Because of that, knowing how to have fun had become just another important human quality for the villagers, and the value judgments about mummers' plays prove that, next to work, play was part of rural communities' system of values.

Probably this was the reason why themes as freedom, playfulness, and transcendence were widely present during the entire winter holidays period. They were embodied by some other preferences, including the joy, mirth and collective exuberance that a person needs to embrace during the entire ritual effervescence, from December 24 to January 3. I deduced all this not only by observing people's behaviors, but also by analyzing their judgments laden with axiological overtones. An expression I heard among the peasants of Heleșteni and Ruginoasa, mostly during winter holidays was: "A true householder is the one who knows how to spend holidays in fun and cheerfulness!" Even the way personhood is defined necessarily includes this propensity towards play. As I showed in the previous two chapters, there are householders who spend more than 2000 lei ($500) during winter holidays. However, all this money does not only represent an investment in the community, but also an investment in the social construction of personhood within these rural communities "heavily laden with values."

CONCLUSION

Throughout this chapter, I have implemented a method of analysis in the study of rural communities and rural plays different from the classical method of the interview. It is about analyzing the actions, behaviors. and implications behind some of the assertions of the researched subjects, beyond what they explicitly say, do, and say they do. I considered this method suitable for the present analysis because it can go beyond the horizon of superficial meanings, towards a deeper cultural level—that of human values.

However, this new method is more difficult to apply than the method of the classic interview, and the explanation for this is very simple. The moments when it can be implemented are rare, they are about the fruit of chance. Fortunately, my life experience in close relation to the rural world, as well as my close relationships with the members of the studied rural communities, gave me the opportunity to put together a rich material that has been the basis of my analysis of values.

In this analysis, I applied Kluckhohn and Hartman's theories of values to the study of rural communities, and Henry Mendras's model of peasant society. Kluckhohn emphasized that human values are formed in the context of actions that take place within human communities, and Hartman has shown that values are linked to a definition of *good* that exists in the human mind which, although rarely verbalized, directs human behavior towards a set of actions in relation to oneself and other people. Thus, this chapter becomes important from this perspective, as Hartman and Kluckhohn's theories of values are applied for understanding a set of social actions within a community.

Using the model of the sociologist Henri Mendras, I analyzed three characteristics of the peasantry in relation to their *mummers' plays*. The analysis of these characteristics revealed that play is an indissoluble part of the peasants' system of values. The analysis of peasants' plays can disclose a representation of how peasant communities looked like in the past, especially several decades ago, when they were more cohesive and their values were in closer relation with the community life. Thus, an analysis of play can also be transformed into a picture that tells us how rural communities evolved from relatively closed worlds to a much larger universe represented by the permanent contact of rural communities with the urban areas. At the same time, this analysis reveals the history of the transformation of community values in their relationship with other socio-economic realities, much more dynamic than those of the past.

Another premise in this chapter was that understanding peasants' system of values might shed light on the relation between peasants and rural plays in the stirring context of the postsocialist world. The postsocialist world is troubled by rapid changes and diverse political, economic, and social challenges. Still, the peasantry system of values is not easy to dislocate. As Kluckhohn well observed, "Values are never immediately altered by a mere logical demonstration of their invalidity" (1951:400). So, we are talking about the clash between two distinct entities: on the one hand, the postsocialist world with its challenges and dynamism; on the other hand, the peasants' system of values formed over longer periods of time. "Value implies a code or a standard which had some persistence through time and organizes a system of action . . . and places things, acts, ways of behaving, goal of action on the approval-disapproval continuum," Kluckhohn also stated (1951:395), observing that the system of values of a community might become the last bastion of a rural community against mainstream culture. Thus, the analysis of mummers in some of the last cohesive peasant communities turned into an exceptional opportunity: that of revealing the dilemmas and worries of humans living in a system of values that has organized their thinking, actions, and behavior for a long time, and which is now fading away.

In this chapter, I have made it clear that play represents, alongside work, a value for peasants. Thus, I believe that studies of peasant communities might focus on their various forms of play. This focus is important because it can reveal an incredibly rich social landscape. This is mostly because, for peasants, play is a way of understanding the universe they live in, but also a filter for the realities that sometimes seems to be beyond their comprehension.

Folk plays are circumscribed by rules that are a creation of the rural communities that had produced them over centuries. Such rules do not represent reversals of the rural social order, as various authors had sometimes described them; instead, they are rather valves through which the pressures of a sometimes very monotonous daily life are released. At the same time, the play also represents a universe *per se* in which the rural community plays with its own limits and tries to understand what seems impossible to understand—a series of realities that it often encounters, including poverty, social inequality, deep social injustice, but also phenomena thought to be parallel to peasant society and therefore almost unconceivable for the peasant mind such as prostitution, homosexuality, and indecency. Finally, play represents a way of analyzing from a different perspective some universal phenomena such as old age, death, infirmity, disease. All of these appear in *mummers' plays* and become visible only during holidays—the only days when such plays are allowed.

The analysis of the relationship between values and plays revealed a history little studied—that of the small rural communities in which the life of most of its members goes on, from birth to death, between the narrow borders of a small locality. Thus, this chapter was also a journey into the heart of the communities that have formed the peasantry of Europe for centuries. Therefore, the present study proposes an alternative history of Europe, different from the grand narratives (Lyotard 1984) in the classic history textbooks. It is the history of small rural communities that have lived according to their own rules for a long time (Robb 2007). Folk plays are, in some respect, an evidence of this history because they differ from community to community, a proof that customs of these communities have been developed in autarky and have created different cultural micro-ecosystems.

At the first glance, it seems paradoxical that mummers' plays and other rural plays, too, may differ significantly from what one finds even in neighboring villages. After having researched these rural cultural forms in Mexico throughout her career, Lourdes Arizpe speaks about *micro-regions* with similar practices, but also about *contrast marks* between rituals in neighboring villages. All these are signs of rivalry between neighboring villages, and make the villagers "feel they belong to their larger cultural circle while at the same time maintaining their singularity" (Arizpe 2013). The subjects Arizpe interviewed stated about themselves: "we do the same, but differently"; their assertion speaks about the fact that such a ritual "does not fit neatly into the cultural classifications of general ethnographic grids applied by Folkloristics in many countries" (Idem 2013:28) as they are part of a "micro-regional tradition of plurality" (Ibidem 2013:28).

All these observations illustrate that an increasing number of the people in customary rural communities have spent the longest part of their life within the boundaries of their own community where they have developed their own customs, sometimes totally against the grain with the traditions of neighboring communities. Despite that, the system of values of such communities is similar because we are talking essentially about the values shared by people who had lived under the circumstances of the same mode of production—one based on small-scale agricultural labor. That could be one reason why we find strikingly similar mummers' plays separated by huge distances and time intervals. This morphologic and symbolic resemblance should not necessarily be interpreted as cultural diffusion, but rather as resemblance of cultural expressions of the customary community living within the same type of economy that shaped its system of values over time.

The study of the relation between rural plays and peasants' system of values draws our attention precisely to these local stories happened between the borders of the small communities. In this respect, folk plays are "story(s) people tell themselves about themselves" (Geertz 1972:26). Due to this reason, at a first glance, they seem absurd. This happens because outsiders can only understand all the rules and values of the community and the way these intertwine in a system after a long time. Rural plays that I described speak about the community's shortcomings but, in the meantime, they imagine a world with characters such as the homosexual, the prostitute, the transsexual, the transvestite, the pimp, all of which are normally excluded from the rigorous moral boundaries of the peasant community. During these theatrical manifestations, the rural community proves to be open to issues that in daily life would be impossible to accept or even imagine. By play, the community manages to transcend the limits it sets with its own norms and rules, but also the narrow horizon of present time and causality.

This extraordinary ability of the peasants to overcome through their plays the narrow limits of their world, but also immediate causality, led me to the Kantian theory of the sublime. The philosopher from Königsberg was the thinker who showed that, by morality or by a privileged aesthetic sense such as the sublime, human beings could exceed the iron laws of causality and earn their freedom as rational agents, placing themselves in the horizon of transcendence where they could contemplate themselves and their society as a whole (together with all its problems and pressures) independent of nature and its causal laws:

> [T]he irresistibility of [nature's] power certainly makes us, considered as natural beings, recognize our physical powerlessness, but at the same time it reveals a capacity for judging ourselves as independent of and a superiority over nature on which is grounded a self-preservation of quite another kind than that which can be threatened and endangered by nature outside us, where by the humanity in our persons remains undemeaned even though the human being must submit to that domination. In this way, in our esthetic judgment nature is judged as sublime not insofar as it arouses fear, but rather because it calls forth our power (which is not part of nature) to regard those things about which we are concerned (goods, health and life) as trivial. . . . (Kant 2001[1790])

NOTES

1. Joseph Obrebski is one of the authors who, knowing peasant life well from within, was able to give a comprehensive explanation of what I call customary communities: "In the peasant village community, which is a society of families bound into a whole by a complex network of kinship ties, spreading and developing with the growth of its families, and contracting with the splitting up of the family, the peasant home is anything but his castle. In this society, the life of each family is of public concern to the community at large. Births, deaths, and marriages [and rural plays, I would add n.a.] are events of public importance and, as a rule, the whole community participates in the ceremonies and festivities of the occasion. There is little privacy in family matters and the family home is not private. It is, of course, a material part of the family organization, a manifestation of its psychical cohesion, a center from

which all its activities radiate, and a common family value impregnated with the collective memories of the past and the sentiments of the present" (Obrebski 1976).

2. Throughout this chapter I will widely use the syntagm *system of values*. This is because the analysis of the studied communities shows that a value never exists in isolation. It is in a network of values, always in connection to other rules and principles. All of these forms a complex network that shapes the behavior of individuals in relation to the community and other members of the respective community.

3. Kluckhohn's research on values is, according to David Graeber, "the first great effort to come up with an anthropological theory of value" (Graeber 2001:5), but unfortunately "ran most definitively aground" (Graeber 2001:5) mainly because in the 1960s the science of anthropology went in two opposite directions: one looking at economics, another one looking at linguistics (Graeber 2001:22).

4. Throughout this chapter, I extensively use the concept of *value*. Following the path opened by Clyde Kluckhohn and Robert Hartman, I define value as a publicly approved belief in ways of actions and behaviors, based on the definitions and ideas people have in mind.

5. Quis enim sapiens credere poterit inveniri aliquos sanæ mentis, qui Cervulum facientes, in ferarum se velint habitus commutari? Alii vestiuntur pellibus pecudum, alii assumunt capita bestiarum, gaudentes et exultantes, si taliter se in ferinas species transformaverint, ut homines non esse videantur.

6. In the area of Moldavia, the Play of the Bear still exists in various villages. At the beginning of my research in Iași County, at the end of 2009, I had the chance to see the performance of The Bear team in the village of Bădeni, Sticlăria comună.

7. Film director Jan Rybkowski himself was a good connoisseur of rural life, too, and his movie *Chłopi* (*The Peasants*), based on Władysław Reymont's novel with the same name, represents a landmark of Polish cinematography.

8. For a more complex view on *Călușari* custom see Gail Kligman, *Căluș, Symbolic Transformation in Romanian Ritual* (1981).

9. *Clacă*: in many of the villages I have researched the custom called *clacă* still exists under different forms. Essentially, it involves the accomplishment of an extensive task that is demanding both in matters of time and intensity, and that could not be finished only by a single family's members. In this case, that particular family asks other people in the village - especially relatives, friends or neighbors—for help. This help is given without any expectation for a financial reward, but it makes the ones receiving it feel obliged to help the other ones back later by offering a similar service.

Chapter Four

Portraying of Peasantry and Rural Plays in Peasant Studies and Mummers' Plays Studies

THE REPRESENTATION OF PEASANTS IN SOCIAL SCIENCES

Using Jean-François Lyotard's postmodern theory (Lyotard 1984), this chapter focuses on how peasant and mummers' play studies have constructed their discourse over time. I examine why most studies analyzing peasants have not included a rigorous analysis of peasants' propensity to play. I also analyze the main directions of these studies, and how they were linked to grand narratives specific to modern thinking (Idem 1984), thus neglecting the peculiarities of peasant customary communities, their system of values, and their relationship with the universe of play. The first section of this chapter proposes a journey into the field of peasant studies, while the second part explores the works of authors who have analyzed mummers' plays since the end of the 19th century.

Starting with end of the 19th century, peasants represented an engaging topic for anthropology, sociology, folklore, history, political science, but also for literature, art, theater, and cinema. Today, the number of books, studies, research, and movies focusing on peasants, their life and society is impressive and impossible to sum up within a single comprehensive work. To create laws and policies necessary to address the problems of this social class, politicians on all sides of the political spectrum and across all continents were convinced that they must understand peasantry and its evolution under the pressure of the changes created by industrialism and the infusion of market economy in the rural world. Despite this special political interest and concern, it is still impossible to state that a universally valid definition of peasantry has been found; the same thing stands true for a comprehensive set of laws that could address all peasants' problems. The large number and the incredible cultural diversity of the small-scale land workers on the planet were the main reasons why defining and understanding peasantry, as well as producing universal policymaking dedicated to this social class, met a series of unbeatable obstacles, visible even now in disciplines trying to address its social, moral, economic, and spiritual profile (Halperin 1977). Besides all these, the emergence of new political movements such as socialism and nationalism, each with their own ideology, after the second half of the 19th century, as well as the formation of European national states after the disintegration of the large European empires, were also responsible for the conceptual and ideological hindering of a rigorous understanding of peasantry (Shanin 1971; Drace-Francis 2013). In this stirred and at the same time complex context we can find the explanation that most of the authors and politicians of the time who were concerned with the problems of the peasantry tried to offer holistic explanations on peasantry as a whole, being too little concerned to understand the peculiarities of peasant communities, including their propensity to plays.

One of the most influential traditions that marked the history of rural studies was Marxism. In his *A Contribution to the Critique of Political Economy*, Marx defines peasantry as a mode of economic production that determines a way of thinking and, finally, human consciousness—a consciousness defined in relation to the economic environment and the labor performed by the individual in a certain context and historical time (Marx 1904). Coming from a similar perspective, Klaus Kautsky's work *On the Agrarian Question* wonders what the political consequences of capitalist transition were for the rural world dominated by peasants (Kautsky 1988[1899]). The answer to this question concerns both the destiny of peasantry as social class, and its possible political-economic position, next to the revolutionary proletarian class or to the capital owners (including the agricultural, land related capital). Agricultural economists Alexander Chayanov and Yevgeni Preobrazhensky whose most important works date back to the first decades of 20th century, follow the same Marxist tradition. They had also tried to understand the fate of peasantry, predicting—more or less realistically—its evolution in time simultaneous to the development of capital and capitalist relations in the countryside (Chayanov 1991; Preobrazhensky 1967). This type of polemic reflections existed not only in Russia and Western Europe, but also in almost all areas around the globe that had a significant peasant class. Therefore, the list of thinkers that had defined peasantry in Marxist terms and used a *class struggle* and *a mode of production* lens to define peasantry is incredibly rich and diverse, and found all over the world.

Another orientation that analyzes peasants originates in Durkheim's work and comes from a vision based on the *modern-traditional* dualism.

It identifies the ambiguous position of peasantry, as a society that displays traditional elements and is simultaneously closely linked to the urban world (Shanin 1971:14). Due to this *half-traditional—half-modern* ambiguity, Robert Redfield named peasants using the syntagm *part-societies* (Redfield 1969) while Eric Wolf call them "neither primitive nor modern" (Wolf 1966). Obviously, this perception of peasants stems from the modernization theory built upon the positivist premise of societies evolving from simple and primitive to complex and modern.

Michael Kearney, the author of one of the most complex studies on peasantry, tells us that western anthropology discovered the peasant during the modern age of the discipline, between 1950 and 1960 (Kearney 1996:39). This was the decade when anthropologists observed a remarkable decline of tribal societies. Peasantry had worked as a comparative term to parallel modern societies and its people to something totally different, within a dual logic such as *Us vs. Others*. Thus, for a while, peasants took the place of primitives and embodied the otherness in a comparative evolutionary discourse (Wolf 1966:1). Yet, as they had always been perceived as ambiguous, placed somewhere between modernity and traditionalism, they could never completely replace the anthropology's discourse about "the primitive" (Kearney 1966:23). This could be the reason why the rich anthropological literature about the tribal societies in Africa, South America, Asia or North America, could not find correspondence in peasant studies, although this analysis would have been extremely productive for understanding and defining peasants on a basis different from the strictly economic or class dynamic. At the same time, Folklore, the science that has been most involved in the study of peasant communities, has been and continues to be dominated by nationalist ideas and a relatively narrow understanding of peasants, as a reservoir of traditions from which nation-states emerged starting with the 19th century.

The anthropological paradigms that tried to realize a general outline of peasantry after the 1960s were economic anthropology—mainly represented by George Dalton—and historical materialism—promoted primarily by Claude Meillassoux, Maurice Godelier, and Emmanuel Terray. Both schools were strongly influenced by Marxism, Structuralism, and Historical Materialist Dialectics. Adopting this vision when examining peasants had to do with understanding the economic relations of peasantry as social class, thus regarded only from the perspective of the history of its subordination by other social groups, therefore of the evolution of relations of production as result of the relationships and conflicts between social classes (Dalton 1971). From this point of view, "[f]or communities without written record, economic anthropology serves as economic history of village organization and performance before development and industrialization seriously began" (Dalton

1967). For Meillassoux, an important representative of historical materialism, the peasant relations of production "grow from the economic constraints of agricultural activities and around the need for reproduction of the productive unit" (Meillassoux 1973) which is, in fact, the peasant family itself.

Sociologists and anthropologists preoccupied with understanding peasants from a larger perspective, tried to systematize this complex landscape of tendencies and movements that centered on peasantry's problems. Teodor Shanin, one of the most influential researchers in the history of rural studies, identified at least two more distinct orientations, apart from the Marxist tradition (1971:13–14). The most visible one is represented by European ethnography and is linked to a nationalist vision related to the construction of national states in Europe. From this perspective, the peasants on the territory of various newly formed states were believed to incarnate the essence of the new nations of Europe, following the collapse of the big European empires: the Spanish Empire, the Second French Empire, the Holy Roman Empire, the Austro-Hungarian Empire, the German Empire, the Russian Empire, and the Ottoman Empire. "From the mid-19th century until the Second World War, a parallel research tradition developed in Eastern Europe. It was concerned with studying the peasants of one's own society, and was not linked to colonial empires but to emerging nationalisms," Halpern, an American anthropologist with strong interest in Eastern Europe and rural culture, stated (Halpern 1976).

Unfortunately, this direction of study has been shaded by the nationalist political ideology that conceived rituals, customs, and peasant communities' traditions by means of certain typologies and classifications that allowed little freedom of analysis. From the national Folkloristics perspective, these typologies and classifications expressed something of the essence and the spirit of a nation formed under certain geographical-historical conditions, throughout many centuries, rather than something of the culture of a local customary community born in a specific economic, political, and cultural micro-ecosystem. Guided by nationalist principles, this vision was never concerned to analyze peasants' values and peasants' plays, and their relationship with the social-economic universe, the rural communities' institutions, as well as to the cultural needs of individuals raised within peasant communities.

This orientation became visible especially in Central and Eastern Europe where the construction of the nation-states faced, from its very beginning, what was appropriately described by the frequent syntagm of *problema ţărănească/peasantry issue*. The peasantry issue went hand in hand with the development of rural studies and ethnography in this area. Shanin himself admitted that "the systematic study of peasantry originated in Central and Eastern Europe; not surprisingly, because in those societies a rapidly 'Westernizing' intelligentsia was faced by a large peasantry—the poorest, most backward and numerically the largest section of their nations" (Shanin 1971:11). Thus, this systematic study was marked by a strongly ideologized vision where the discovery of the "national spirit of people" in a certain region intertwined with the processes of rural culture's heritagisation and the creation of local folklore archives dominated by detailed ethnographic descriptions of what was considered by local folklorists as representative for the essence of rural life and the embodiment of the people's national spirit. In this respect, Romania could be regarded as a case study because, since the late 19th century, a series of cultural-political trends emerged, revolving around the *peasantry issue* (*problema țărănească*), the understanding of peasantry as social class, and its definition within a new type of political entity—namely the national state.

Poporanism (*being on the people's side*) was founded by Romanian lawyer and journalist Constantin Stere in 1890, and has taken its inspiration from the *Russian Narodniks*—a current that had emerged not long before in Russia. Stere's *poporanism* regards Romanian rural civilization as a sign of genuineness and social cohesion, a quintessential expression of the Romanian people, opposed to an urban culture considered to be imported, inauthentic and heterogeneous. Thus, the main goal of the intellectual elites was to fulfill their duty in front of the masses mostly represented by peasants and their social-economic problems.

Another trend addressing peasants' problems was *Sămănătorismul (sowing ideas)*. It was founded by the outstanding historian and politician Nicolae Iorga around *The 1907 Romanian Peasants' Revolt*. Bearing a nationalistic tone, *Sămănătorismul* asks for specific attention to national education—a process regarded as a solution for the cultivation and emancipation of peasantry. While peasants are considered to incarnate the country's traditions, the village appears as a source of traditions and customs depicting the authentic people's spirit. Besides these idyllic notes, this current embedded certain ethnic folklore-centered nationalistic elements where the peasants' migration to the city was regarded as an alienating and displacing experience. In similar terms, peasants were perceived from a Marxist perspective as an exploited class whose fruits of labor fed other social categories such as landlords, unscrupulous merchants, and venal politicians.

Finally, another trend dating back this time to interwar Romania, was *Țărănismul (Peasantism)*, with a program advocating for peasantry and its well-being. In the vision of the *Țărănism*, rural economy was distinct from the economic structures and relations generated by capitalism. Because of this, it had to be protected by the intrusion of capital that could have destroyed its authenticity and basic principles—all of which were inherently non-capitalist. The main promoter of these ideas was the economist Virgil Madgearu who explained the principles of *Țărănism* in his substantial work *Agrarianism,*

Capitalism, Imperialism published in 1936 (Madgearu 1936). Of course, all these local tendencies echoed international events, trends and ideas, given the fact that debates on peasantry and its problems were an important topic in political-economic circles by the late 19th and early 20th centuries. This brief summary of the tendencies observed in the research on peasantry in Romania is perhaps an eloquent example of the big political-ideological debates during the period mentioned above. But this is probably just a small piece of the vast landscape comprising local studies on peasantry.

Only a few decades later, on the other side of the Atlantic Ocean, in the American anthropology, authors like Robert Redfield and James C. Scott described peasants from the perspective of their values and of the moral principles they had acquired while living in small communities based on land work and reciprocal relations. Nevertheless, this vision, too, re-emphasized the idea of peasantry as a subordinated class, a fact that results clearly from Scott's assertion that "the poor had the social right to subsistence" (Scott 1977)—considered one of the principles around which peasant communities revolved. This perspective turned once again promising innovative research on peasantry into a case study for the Marxist class struggle. Thus, peasants had been mainly perceived from a class perspective, regarded as embracing the fight against exploiters whenever their essential right to subsistence had been infringed. We thus notice that even these more nuanced perspectives on peasants bear the marks of the modernization theory and of the Marxist class struggle vision.

Following this brief presentation of some of the current tendencies in peasant studies, it becomes obvious that most of these visions have neither privileged the understanding of peasantry from the perspective of their plays, nor included inside their definition the concept of *customary com-munity*, analyzing their system of values, as representative for the peasants' identity. A dimension of this often forgotten universe could be identified in the peasants' inclination towards "the play element" (Huizinga 1968) in all its forms and manifestations. This trend has been analyzed and identified in peasant communities but never fully developed in an extended research. Mikhail Bakhtin is probably the most famous name who scratch the surface of this topic in his study about François Rabelais (Bakhtin 1984). From this perspective, *folk plays* can be seen an expression of this ludic universe and is traceable throughout entire Europe and Russia (Warner 1977), Asia (Tillis 1999), Northern Africa (Ebewo 2001), Canada (Jarvis 2014), and America (Nissenbaum 1996). For all these rural communities, based on householding economies and autarky (Polanyi 2001[1944]:59), play was one of the essential elements of social coexistence, employed for expressing joy, happiness, agreement but also satire, worries, disagreement, conflicts—a meaningful way to transcend difficulties and daily problems and, in the meantime, a complex way of communicating all kind of human feelings and emotions (Gunnell 2007b).

Michael Kearney emphasized the neglect of the aesthetic values and rituals of the peasantry by most of the peasant studies, even though, he observed, such approach would be necessary for understanding a reconceptualized peasantry:

> My evaluation of peasant studies is that they tend to dwell too much on either economics or culture and as such are unable to move forward on the problems they have set themselves—for example, analysis of development, ritual, symbolism, resistance, and differentiation. All of these issues are at the same time economic and cultural, and their reconceptualization requires a theoretical synthesis as is enabled by the theory of generalized value, which allows us to query the unity and transformations of economic and aesthetic values and how they become inscribed as the identities of persons who produce, lose, consume, and transform them and who in doing so become constituted and, on occasions, themselves transformed. (Kearney 1996:12)

Unfortunately, visions that have analyzed peasantry together with its ludic dimension and its system of values are rare. Generally, peasant studies were dominated by a political-economic perspective that made it impossible to understand peasants from a totally different view that includes their propensity toward play. This is an observation Huizinga identified long ago, in the late 1930s. The 19th and 20th centuries, he stated, are known for an over-evaluation of the economic factor, turning it into a main focus both for rationalist and utilitarian philosophies, and for the bipolar couple liberalism-socialism. Together with the directions they instilled in understanding humankind, from a mainly materialistic perspective, these tendencies created the premises for the marginalization of the playful dimension in human society. Or, more often, this dimension it is seen from a narrow commercial filter that promote sport performances in mass culture to the detriment of communities' forms of play (Huizinga 1968[1938]). Thus, today we are witnessing the preservation of only a few of the multiple phenomena and manifestations of what Huizinga called *the ludic*. One of these phenomena was the competition element that gained ground in front of *the masquerade, the carnivalesque* and *the burlesque*—in one word, the spontaneous folk creativity. This creativity is what Bakhtin and other Russian linguists such as Zelenin, Jakobson, Trubetzkoy, Bogatyrev, and Propp described by means of the opposition between the lower strata of culture and the high culture dressed as official mainstream culture—authoritarian, standardizing, and leveling both socially and intellectually (Pomorska 1984). With this last remark, I move to the next section that analyzes folk plays through the work of the authors who made the greatest contribution in this field.

THE REPRESENTATION OF MUMMERS' PLAYS[1] IN SOCIAL SCIENCES

As we have already seen, building a viable representation of the peasantry, free of ideological burdens, has proved to be a difficult task for social sciences. At the same time, the analysis of folk plays encountered a whole series of major inconveniences. This field of research has been undermined over time by a high number of methodological and theoretical issues that slowed down its development over time. In the following pages, I analyze five issues that have hindered the understanding of plays practiced by the peasants.

In short, the five problems that prevented a faster development of mummers' play studies can be summarized as follows: 1) Folk plays began to be studied scientifically when rural communities that practiced them were already largely affected by the consequences of the Industrial Revolution, which drastically affected peasant customary communities. 2) The oldest documents about folk plays, being issued before the Industrial Revolution were created either by amateurs or by church authorities who wanted to suppress them and have a bias mindset toward mumming practices. 3) The third problem is related to the diversity of cultural manifestations called *mummers* or *folk plays*. This fact contributed to a series of insurmountable terminological shortcomings, the authors who studied these phenomena not being able to find a suitable concept for this high number of diverse cultural expressions. 4) The fourth issue related to the study of folk play is a subjective one and refers to the conviction of certain authors that they can found the miraculous solution to decipher once for ever the mystery of these rural plays. This subjective stance produced repeated unsuccessful attempts to find the philosopher's stone that would solve this complicated puzzle once and for all. 5) Finally, the fifth problem that arises in the research of folk plays is related to the academic diversity of the authors who studied them. We are talking about folklorists, theater historians, philologists, sociologists, and anthropologists. These thinkers used different methods, frameworks and ideas that analyzed folk plays from various points of view, without a continuity and a clear vision regarding the proposed research and goals.

The First Issue

The first problem arising when studying mummers' plays is a historical one. The rural communities performing these rituals were first scientifically analyzed at a point in history that coincided with their dissolution after being integrated into a new economic cycle specific to the industrial revolution and the great economic, political, and cultural transformations following it (Polanyi 1944). This new logic, inherent to modern times, offered human beings new experiences and a new type of world vision "which have gradually distanced people from many of the processes which affect their lives. This has been not just a distancing from their pasts, or their roots, but a distancing from the economic, political and cultural systems that influence, or even control their lives" (Walsh 1992).

Many of the authors who began to analyze folk plays lived in a time when the decline of rural communities because of the ever-growing industrialization became part of daily reality. Thomas Fairman Ordish, the first thinker who opened the doors to the scientific study of folk plays, in his 1893 lecture entitled *English Folk-Drama*, held in the front of English Folk-lore Society members, was talking about "the traditions that have utterly died out in so many districts, but in other places where they have survived they become attenuated, and show an altogether feeble existence compared with what they were only a few years ago" (Ordish 1893). He showed his audience two dresses worn by English folk-players and a few photographs, and ended up urging his colleagues "to collect together all the fragments of folk-drama and dramatic custom which remain to us" (Idem 1893:150). Feelings of emergency, together with the fear that these folk customs would totally vanish, accompanied the first scientific effort to analyze folk plays. This trend was to be present in the folk plays' literature that followed him, where the mummers were seen as some kind of survivors of bygone eras. It is an aspect folklorist Henry Glassie remarked well. Glassie was one of the first researchers to launch a well-grounded criticism against his predecessors who had studied these cultural forms, naming them with a word later adopted in later mummers' studies—"the survivalist":

> The prime concept of survivalist theorists of mumming has its source in Sir James Frazer's *The Golden Bough* and parallels the thinking of those scholars who locate the origin of all myth in ritual—an idea that fares miserably today. Once upon a time, we are told, there was a fertility ritual that efficiently structured the agricultural year by means of magical mimicry. Later day mumming is but an irrational fragment of this ritual, having drifted into modern times through the inertia of the peasant mentality. (Glassie 1975:56)

To British Folkloristics and British Theater Studies, the research of mummers meant what investigating the primitive represented for anthropology; yet, this field's outcome was far from being as successful as the works of anthropologists like Frazer or Morgan. Mummers were perceived, in general, as a kind of "primitives from home." For example, Thomas Ordish drew parallels to the dramatic tradition in Ancient Rome, Greece and even India, and concluded that English folk drama originated in pre-Christian times. But, due to innumerable influences during history—the impact of the church included—by the end of the 19th century they were presented in a form quite different from the initial one. The *Quack Doctor*, a frequent character in English folk theater, is actually a primitive shaman and magician who, influenced by modernity, finally puts on the doctor's clothes and turns from a serious and solemn character into a jester that brings about laughter. Thus, in Ordish's investigation we find a type of approach specific to late 19th century anthropology, bearing influences from both James George Frazer and the German Folkloristics represented by Grimm brothers, themselves influenced by the Romanticism nationalism that regarded folk customs as archaic expression of national literature and culture.

Following Ordish' model, the theater historian Arthur Beatty tried to give an explanation regarding mummers' plays, but limited his research to a single case study: *St. George Play* (Beatty 1906:273). Unlike previous contributions, Beatty believes that the origin of these folk theater forms should be found in the realm of faith and the ceremonial (Beatty 1906:273). Further, he focuses his attention on *St. George Play*, and analyzes dozens of versions of it collected throughout the entire England, observing their extraordinary diversity from region to region and village to village. For this reason and following the classical trend of European Folkloristics, he tries to establish a typology based on family similarities so that all these pieces could fit together, having in fact a common core (Idem 1906:276). With this scheme in mind, Beatty launches a comparative exercise where he shows that the central event of the play—the death and the resurrection of one of the characters—is spread all over Europe and could be found even in primitive societies in Africa or aboriginal tribes in Australia. All these observations make Arthur Beatty state that the origin of English folk theater plays is an initial act of *mimesis magic* that was later dramatized and then perpetuated by the conservative mentality of the peasant and the rural communities (Idem 1906:321).

Another English thinker who studied mummers plays and who belongs to the same tradition as Ordish and Beatty is Reginald J.E. Tiddy. His book *The Mummers' Play*, published posthumously in 1923, is regarded as a notable contribution to understanding the concept of mumming (Tiddy 1923). Indeed, having a good knowledge of rural life and traditions, Tiddy managed to collect diligently a series of folk plays from 33 different regions of England—a truly remarkable effort. Living for a long time in the countryside, Tiddy was convinced that the plays he collected were created only by peasants, although "the modern survival of peasantry is a fair representative of the folk that made traditional poetry and drama (Idem 1923:65)." This view on peasants made

Tiddy conceive mummers' plays as degenerate elements of older folk plays that looked completely different in the past. Taking into consideration the decline of rural rituals such as mummers' plays, Tiddy describes the plays of his time as cultural elements "surviving" in a present that is different today from the time they had been staged over the centuries.

Other thinkers from the beginning of the 20th century, like C.R. Baskervill (Baskervill 1924) and Edmund Chambers (Chambers 1969 [1933]:233) got engaged in the same heuristic exercise as their predecessors, whom they fought at the same time, being also convinced that they had found the true origin of the mummers' plays. Since the 1960s, have appeared a series of more elaborate studies on mummers' plays often based on assiduous field research. Alex Helm, for example, who was not only a great folklorist, but also a diligent fieldworker, witnessed hundreds of such mummers' ceremonies during his life. For this reason, he was one of the few researchers who understood well the reasons of the limited success that the literature about mummers had. He drew the difference between the vivid peasant culture and the heritagisation efforts designed to safeguard these forms of culture threatened by extinction. Understanding well this aspect, he distinguished between the mummers' plays performed in the street or in the people's courtyards and households, and the mummers' plays staged as a result of heritagisation efforts. Helm believed that the mummers brought on stage do not have too much to offer precisely because of the absurd elements of the plays that only become meaningful due to the interaction between actants and spectators—an interaction that disappears when the representations are transferred on stage:

> Furthermore, the use of a stage is foreign to the Mummers. They need a space, nothing more. The space is kept clear by their forming a semicircle in which the action takes place, and round them and their audience. This could be described as early Theater-in-the-Round, but nothing more. It is vital to the performance that there should be communication between themselves and their audience. . . . (Helm 1981:6)[2]

Helm is one of the few folklorists which promoted the idea that mummers' plays should be connected to other ceremonials that had been initially considered separate entities. Thus, he suggested, they could become part of a larger body where researchers should bring together related customs, tracing the borders and distinguishing between ceremonials displaying less similarities. As a result of this idea, in 1967, together with his fellows, E.C. Cawte and N. Peacock, he published a complex book called *English Ritual Drama*. This work has a privileged position in the range of studies about folk theater. The reason is that the three folklorists manage to put together an impressive number of localities in England, Scotland, Wales, Canada, Leeward Islands, and the United States, where the English folk drama were performed or it is still practiced. In case the specified ritual was extinct, the authors also offered the presumed year of its last performance in the given locality. In this meticulous and difficult exercise, the heritagisation effort becomes obvious, encouraged by the desire to safeguard these vanishing folk dramas. Another particularity of this work is that the authors discard the concept of "mummers," considering it to be too general, and replacing it with the term *English ritual drama* (also used for the book's title). Despite this unbelievable effort, Alex Helm and his colleagues still pay tribute to the theory of searching for the mummers' origins, and conclude that these rituals could be the degenerate remains of certain ancient fertility rituals (Cawte, Helm, and Peacock 1967:30).

The end of the 1960s coincides with the publication of more important works about mummers. One of them, *Irish Folk Drama*, belongs to Alan Gailey (1969). Gailey tries to fill a gap extant in the Irish folkloristics that had studied the subject too little. He proves in the meantime the richness of the ritual material as well as its irregular distribution throughout the entire Ireland. Gailey supports the specific features of the Irish folk dramas as generally compared to British ones, emphasizing the appearance of original outfits—such as the strawmen—and of the name *Hogmanaymen* appointed to the mummers' bands. However, he identifies within Irish plays the central topic of death and resurrection—a motif often observed in mummers' plays all over Great Britain. But a provocative topic he details is the relation between mummers' plays and the collection of money for these shows. The subject had also been tackled by authors writing before Gailey, but he is the first one to discuss it in detail and quite passionately. Indeed, this represented an apple of discord among the authors regarding mummers as surviving elements of an archaic culture. If this were the case, the relations between the ones performing the customs and the spectators should be shaped as a generalized reciprocity instead of balanced reciprocity (Sahlins 1974). Consequently, using examples from Anatolia or other European areas, Gailey tries to prove that there was a time when the plays used to be performed by mummers in exchange of collecting food and beverage that would later be given back to the community by means of a collective local ceremony.

Following this tumultuous history of mummers' plays literature, one cannot remain indifferent to the efforts of the thinkers fighting the mountains of archives and undertaking a painstaking searching task to trace the mummers' origin amid dusty manuscripts. All this happened because the interest in mummers' plays went hand in hand with the progressive dissolution of mumming in rural areas. Thus, the fact that the English were the first and the most tenacious examiners of the mummers' plays confirms our previous assertion. England was the first country to undergo the great transformations of the industrial revolution, and its inhabitants were the first to lose the old way of rural life. And the decline of certain forms of culture did not arrive alone; in exchange, it brought a sort of nostalgia and a concern for the past and for its cultural forms (Lowenthal 1985).

Knowing the social and historical context in which the first works on mummers' plays arose, can provide a more adequate understanding of this approach, although it cannot justify its scientific inefficiency. Many of these authors' assumptions regarding the origin of the mummers were difficult to support with indisputable evidences, mainly because of the lack of documents validating specific relations of causality between morphologically similar mummers' plays situated far away in space and time.

The Second Issue

Out of the complex landscape described above, emerges the second problem encountered when proceeding to the study of mummers' plays. I called this issue a hermeneutical one because it is related to the nature of the old documents mentioning mummers' plays before investigating them systematically and scientifically through field research. The oldest documents concerning mummers' plays were created by amateurs (resulting, for instance, in travel notes, letters, journals, etc.) or by religious authorities that tried to suppress the plays in the name of Christian dogmas. In the first chapter of this study, I talked about a letter dating back to 1656 by a Swedish ambassador called Welling, sent on a diplomatic mission in Iaşi, the capital of the Moldavian Kingdom, in which he describes the *Play of the Goat*. Besides this, I mentioned du Cange's work *Glossarium mediae et infimae latinitatis* (du Cange 1678) where he cites several documents issued by Catholic church authorities in order to suppress different forms of mummers' plays. Many of these documents could be described as nothing more than occasional notes, and therefore could not be defined as the result of a serious scientific effort or at least of careful observation. But the paradox regarding the oldest information regarding mummers' plays are still worth mentioning. Chiefly because of ecclesiastic interdictions against mumming, most of the oldest information about these folk plays we have today were able to reach us precisely because of documents issued by the authorities trying to suppress them. However, the underlying problem remains and can be summarized by two questions: could these documents provide a foundation solid enough to be compared to the ethnographic present state of rural communities? Can the origin of today's mummers' plays be revealed by comparing mummers nowadays to the ancient documents produced by religious authorities aiming to suppress these rural plays? In any case, this type of questions requires methodological circumspection.

The Third Issue

The third issue encountered in the investigation of mummers' plays is related to their enormous diversity in Europe and elsewhere. In my view, this was the main reason why none of the authors studying them was able to find a concept that would be broad enough and precise when naming the whole range of mummers' manifestations, and at the same time acceptable by most of the authors conducting research in this field. Because of this, in texts that focus on the study of mummers, we find various concepts naming such cultural manifestations, including: *Mummers, Mummers' Plays, Ritual Drama, Folk Plays, Folk Rituals, Folk Drama, Folk Theater, Folk Theater with Masks, Early Forms of Theater, Dramatic Games, Quack Doctor Plays, Forms of Caroling* or *Expressions of Masking*. Counting all these rituals and customs brings about an impressive number of social manifestations from various parts of Europe and the world that are difficult to reunite within a general picture. This was probably the main reason why, from the 1960s until the end of the 1990s, we witnessed a fierce debate regarding the choice of the correct term to name mummers' plays.

Another cause of this dispute was the confusing use of several concepts in the past that described folk plays without a prior demarcation of the conceptual sphere of the cultural forms considered under the giant umbrella of mummers. Therefore, a new paradigm emerged, aiming to find an operational definition of folk plays; it developed in parallel to a critical attitude (Tillis 1999)—quite bitter in some authors (see Millington 2002)—against the scholars of the past who struggled to find the mummers' origin in the depths of the European history.

One of the first authors to adopt this orientation in a short article called *Folk Drama* is the outstanding folklorist Roger D. Abrahams (Abrahams 1972). Ever since the beginning of his study, Abrahams speaks about the "imprecision of generic definitions" as a fact leading to a series of misunderstandings and wrong interpretations; therefore, the American folklorist proceeds to define folk drama "as a traditional play activity that relies primarily on dialogue to establish its meaning and that tells a story through the combination of dialogue and action, the outcome of which is known to the audience ahead of time" (Idem 1972:353). Unfortunately, just as other folklorists of the previous decades, Abrahams cannot see the folk plays as more than the embodiment of theater plays. This is probably the reason why his definition excludes from the start a series of mummers' activities and plays—for instance, the pantomimic mummers observed in Newfoundland Island, carefully described by Halpert, Story and other authors (Halpert and Story 1969; Jarvis 2014). In the case of these mummers, the dialogue is totally absent while the play is focused only on action and the mummers' behavior.

A more complex and more conclusive approach in this respect belongs to the folklorist Thomas A. Green in his article *Toward a Definition of Folk Drama* published in 1978. Green begins with the distinction between drama and social life—a distinction he regards as totally obscure in the previous texts. Influenced simultaneously by folklorist Roger Abrahams and theater historian Alan Brody (Brody 1971), Green pleads for understanding folk drama "as a performance incorporating mimesis and role distribution among two or more players" (T. A. Green 1978).

The idea of redefining mimesis has been of special interest among American folklorists. Anne C. Burson, for instance, in the text *Model and Text in Folk Drama* from 1980, takes up Thomas Green's vision on mimesis, reevaluates it and finally concludes that: "A folk drama is a mimetic performance whose text and style of presentation are based on traditional models; it is presented by members of a group to other members of the same reference group. A specific inherited text is not the determining factor that makes an event folk drama; rather, it is the traditional pattern on which the event is based" (Burson 1980:316).

Going through the works of these authors that I called *terminologists*, the readers are left with the same impression as the one the *originists (survivalist)* gave us—namely that the science of folk plays advances with slow and doubtful steps. Despite this first impression, it should be mentioned that in each of the categories of authors I analyzed there were also top authors who rose well above the average of the researchers in their group. One such author was Steve Tillis, a theater historian who brought an important contribution to the field of folk drama. Tillis aims to approach mummers analytically and to revise their classification, elaborating simultaneously an operational definition of folk drama. Being a researcher with a background in theater studies, Tillis is a mature writer who knows that studying folk drama and mummers' plays means swimming muddy waters that were better left still. Therefore, his behavior is cautious, and he advances slowly in the intricate network of texts about mummers, carefully analyzing a pile of studies not only from Europe, but from all over the world. Thus, Tillis reaches notable results, supported not only by the powerful conclusions of his book *Rethinking Folk Drama*, but also by his perpetual fight for understanding and analyzing a whole range of folk dramas scattered on all continents.

Tillis engages in a critical dialogue with the tradition of folk drama research, amending it from time to time. Towards the final pages, he polemicizes with certain hypotheses and theories of the area, contesting them in the light of his new research (see, for instance, Tillis 1999:193). Following these struggles, Tillis manages to provide a complex definition of folk drama:

Folk drama is theatrical performance, within a frame of make-believe action shared by performers and audience, that is not fixed by authority but is based in living tradition and displays greater or lesser variation in its repetition of this tradition; its performance, enacted over time and space with practices of design, movements, speech, and/or music, engenders and/or enhances a sense of communal identity among those who participate in its delivery and reception. (Ibidem 1999:140)

Although the folk drama definition advanced by Tillis is extremely useful and contains a series of important elements such as the communal identity between spectator and performers, this theater studies professor sees folk drama essentially as a theatrical performance and no more than that. This assumption makes him exclude a whole range of cultural expressions that could be understood and analyzed as mummers' plays. Despite these views Tillis's study still remains a foundation stone for the literature on folk drama and mummers' plays mostly because of its deep questions and the extraordinary intuitions present throughout the entire work.

The Fourth Issue

From Tillis's work we move on to the analysis of the fourth issue hindering the investigation of mummers' plays. This is related to the deep subjective belief of many authors studying mummers in the possibility of finding the *philosopher's stone* and of turning the last page in the study of mummers. Their *"Magnum Opus"* produced only a sum of texts that are worth mentioning, but finally show us another dead end that should be avoided in the study of folk plays.

   A.E. Green's article *Popular Drama and the Mummer's Play* belongs to the above-mentioned category. Starting with a case study—a custom from Cheshire region, Antrobus village, A.E. Green focuses on the elements, the symbols and the social network of a tradition called *Soulcaking Play* that is held once per year around Halloween (A.E. Green 1980). The play performed in Antrobus village belongs to the *Hero-Combat Play* category, a type of folk theater that could not be regarded, Green insists, as a relic of the rural past, but as a property of the current working class in England. In Green's words "[h]ence British working-class theater: even when rural in provenance, these plays are the property, and their performance the expression, of an agrarian proletariat, not a peasantry; and their provenance is just as often the small town or the industrial village" (Idem 1980:143). The English folklorist goes on defining his theory and suggests that "the frame of reference of the mummers' play is in some important respects a nineteenth-century one" (Ibidem 1980:143).

To support his theory, this scholar uses the following arguments: written records of the mummers' plays before 1800 are very rare, whereas the ones after this date go beyond several hundred; most of these passages do not come from the traditional and conservative British islands, but from the industrial centers situated in the heart of England; the participants to the Antrobus rituals that were interviewed have a clear conscious of the practice of tradition, but this tradition is connected to workers' communities in the cities and not to rural culture; all the characters in the local version of the Hero-Combat Play would be marginal to any type of village community and surely belong to urban culture; the progressive extinction of the mummers' plays during the 20th century has to do with the emergence of an alternative entertainment related to modern culture that led to the loss of meaning of these now obsolete plays. A.E. Green support his theory and bombastic hypothesis by means of careful revisions of the arguments that were more likely to be attacked, thus proving that he understands what the criticism would look like. In the case of the first argument, for instance, he mentions that throughout the 19th century there was a significant increase in the amount of written texts, and its accessibility for the larger population grew. More, he states that extrapolation from the fieldwork data in the 1970s to the texts of various origins—some of which doubtful—is just as difficult as an extrapolation from today's mummers to those described by the literature dating back to the Middle Ages. In other words, Green adopts a purely synchronic vision according to which the mummers' plays performed by the working-class culture in the 20th century belong to an urban world because their relation to rural universe cannot be demonstrated!

Martin J. Lovelace's article *Christmas Mumming in England: The House Visit* belongs to the same category of the emphatic. Lovelace starts from a hypothesis issued by the folklorist Herbert Halpert, stating that "the Newfoundland custom of the informal-visit, with an accompanying guessing game, might be assumed to have originated in the British Isles despite the lack of detailed reports from England itself" (Lovelace 1980). When launching his theory, Lovelace begins from a simple observation: there are nowadays two mummers' traditions that seem to be different from each other. One belongs to the mummers in England, where poor English workers find a way to earn some money from higher classes during winter holidays by presenting a theater performance in front of the rich ones' houses. The second tradition is represented by the so-called house-visit-in-disguise, performed particularly between friends, generally by persons belonging to the same social class, without money collection, only aimed at entertainment and fun. In this case, he is pointing at a pantomimic representation of mummers, followed by the hosts' attempt to guess who is behind the masks than about a theater play. This tradition is still extant today in former English islands including

Newfoundland. On these islands, communities are usually more cohesive and have thus managed to preserve a series of ancient elements of traditions that have disappeared in England or have changed irreversibly under the pressure of industrialization and modernization. Lovelace's suggestion is that mummers' plays, supposedly of ancient origins, is in fact a more recent invention derived from the house-visit-in-disguise tradition extant especially in certain British islands, but almost vanished in England and which is, actually, the older authentic tradition.

For a mummers' researcher in Romania, Lovelace's comparison is extremely interesting especially because the two traditions could be simultaneously identified sometimes even within a single locality like Heleșteni for instance or in the neighboring villages. The fascinating fact is that, indeed, in Heleșteni, the custom informal-house-visit-in-disguise has the same goal as in Newfoundland—entertainment and fun—without involving money collection. In exchange, the *Deer* or the *Goat*'s plays are morphologically similar to some folk plays in England such as the ones revolving around the figure of the masked hobbyhorse. This mask is almost identical to the *Deer* or *Goat* masks in Moldova region where I conducted my research! Well, in an overwhelming number of cases I have observed in Moldova's villages, these folk plays with a theatrical stance are being performed only for money. The first striking aspect that can be neither denied, nor easily explained, is that of strong resemblance between the Moldavian custom of mummers and the so-called informal-house-visit-in-disguise in the Newfoundland islands. These two traditions had cultural itineraries independent from each other. However, the way they look today is almost identical. The second issue emerging is the fact that, according to all the data available, folk theater traditions such as *the Deer* or *Goat play* in Eastern Romania are older than the mummers' home visiting—meaning exactly the opposite of Lovelace's statements. Anyway, all these instances that come from my research need explanations, and the model Lovelace proposed cannot provide them. Moreover, it tries to support an exactly opposite hypothesis compared to my findings based on data collected from field.

The last author that could not be omitted in this display is Peter Thomas Millington. His PhD dissertation, *The Origins and Development of English Folk Plays*, represents one of the most strenuous efforts to understand the whole realm of literature about mummers. This author's passion for mummers dates back to several decades ago, and the amount of material he analyzes in his dissertation is impressive. In my opinion the first part of the work is the most convincing. It revises critically the most important texts forming the literature about mummers, beginning with the first publications about mummers in England and continuing with the more elaborate studies by Thomas Ordish and the folklorists following him. The critical debate in the literature review tries and almost manages to be exhaustive, standing for the proficiency of the researcher who studied the issue for a long time. However, it seems that in the end, the means finally become the goal and, further on, the main topic of the work. Thus, the revision of the old literature about mummers, instead of serving a higher aim such as understanding mummers' plays, turns into a fierce battle with the previous authors who studied mummers—*the survivalists*. Unfortunately, in the end, Millington's work became a demonstration of the recent (instead of ancient) origin of mummers. Thus, mummers' plays are not the survivors of ancient or medieval times but originate in more recent times—the 18th century. This conclusion is supported by means of a series of digital and statistical techniques that offer a more detailed analysis of the texts of the plays included in the research. Based on them, Millington decrees that the mummers' origin does not go beyond the year 1750. Nevertheless, for stating this he uses a strategy: he replaces the word "mummer"—considered vague and ambiguous—with one considered more suggestive and relevant from a statistical perspective: *The Quack Doctor*. The only problem with the new concept for mummers is that it has never been used by the actants themselves when naming mummers' plays. The title was chosen for purely statistical reasons: because the *Quack Doctor* character from English folk theater plays appears most often in the texts of the analyzed plays. However, it does not appear in all of these plays, a fact mentioned repeatedly even by Millington himself!

The Fifth Issue

The fifth problem encountered in the investigation of mummers' plays is caused by the diversity of scientific orientations of the researchers dealing with these realities. The researchers that started to analyze mummers' plays come from various disciplines of social sciences such as folklore, theater studies, sociology, and anthropology. In the previous paragraphs I used the expression *folk play literature*, but it should be mentioned that this area has never been acknowledged as an independent field of research, being rather a fallow piece of land than a clearly demarcated farmland. That is why the contributions regarding mummers come from such a diverse set of disciplines. Moreover, all these separate fields have distinct methodologies, and often they have completely different agendas, goals, ideologies, and ways of defining social realities. For all these reasons, there is little dialogue between them.

Analyzing this complex landscape, I observed that the comparative, inter-regional and global research of mummers, doubled by a good knowledge of the related literature, gave the most relevant results. Works like Leopold Schmidt's Le Théâtre Populaire Européen (1965) and Terry Gunnell's *Masks and Mumming in the Nordic Area* (2007) are a good proof of this assertion. Relevant results also came out of monographs dedicated to an entire region, merging distinct perspectives and visions about the reality of mummers' plays, as proven by the 1969 publication of *Christmas Mumming in Newfoundland* edited by Herbert Halpert and G.M. Story. These successful results demonstrate that the general picture of mummers can be drawn through a painstaking exercise: a holistic view on folk plays texts accompanied by an ethnographic effort that reveal the thorough details of mummers' plays in a certain region or even community.

An assiduous endeavor to understand mummers' play was published at the end of 1960s by Herbert Halpert and George Morley Story. These researchers reached the conclusion that mummers could offer "a unique field for observation"—an opportunity "to test the assumption about the social mechanisms and nature of rural communities" (Halpert and Story 1969). It was considered that this enterprise would not only be appealing, but also necessary because certain communities with a European descent such as the fishing ones in Newfoundland Island, were completely unknown to the anthropological literature. The volume they edited together in 1969—*Christmas Mumming in Newfoundland*—became a foundation stone and an important reference in the study of mummers' play; meanwhile, the island of Newfoundland, Canada's easternmost territory, became a famous land for the research of mummers' plays in the aftermath (Smith 2007: 755–770).

Bringing together a series of anthropologists, folklorists, and ethnologists, the volume edited by the two researchers offers a detailed perspective on the mummers' landscape in Newfoundland Island, as well as many valuable ethnographic pieces of information coming from various communities on the island. Entitled *Newfoundland: Fishermen, Hunters, Planters and Merchants*, George M. Story's text seems to be only occasionally related to a proper understanding of the mummers in this area (Story 1969). The reason is that the work speaks about the contemporary history of this island and the changes in the region's economy caused by the new social-economic demands brought by the 20th century economic transformations. All these changes left a mark on the way local communities evolved in time, from fishery to logging and mining industries after World War II, and witnessing the passage to an economic cycle oriented towards commerce and modern communication in recent years. All the data are extremely interesting when related to the other articles in the volume which are explicitly focused on the mumming in the island. This way, Story's text becomes a valuable tool showing how the historic-economic processes can influence the community practices and, finally, the meaning and performance of the mummers' plays.

With his background in folklore studies, Herbert Halpert speaks about the huge number of customs that could be covered by the mummers' category

(Halpert 1969). From the very start of his study, Halpert presents relevant cases from Canada, America, England, Austria, and Germany, as well as more ancient ones—such as the ones in Thrace. Throughout the text, Halpert enriches the list with rituals from Ecuador, Scotland, Trinidad and even from Tolstoy's Russia giving the example taken from the novel *War and Peace* where a mummers' visit was described with the incredible talent of the Russian writer. Choosing fascinating details to describe the dark face of the mummers' behavior, especially their violent behavior, Halpert remarks that it is not common to all the communities on the island and cannot be generalized to all groups:

> The typology presented in this essay, it must again be stressed, is intended as a descriptive framework within which the diverse material of the whole mumming complex may be viewed. What has not, perhaps, been sufficiently emphasized is that the diversity of this material is such that any categorization is extremely hazardous, for frequently what a typology seeks to delimit is, in practice, found in overlapping areas. (Halpert 1969:61)

With such a conclusion, Folkloristics seems to understand its limits in describing and understanding mummers, opening the way for anthropology and its methods to study these rituals. Indeed, other contributors to the volume offer various perspectives and details about the Newfoundland communities that practice mummers' plays. In his paper *Mumming in Deep Harbour: Aspects of Social Organization in Mumming and Drinking*, anthropologist Louis J. Chiaramonte provides an elaborate picture of the mummers' groups that go caroling in the islands' communities during winter holidays (Chiaramonte 1969). One of the most alluring aspects related to Newfoundland mummers is the alcohol consumption—social drinking being one of the most common features of the island mummers. In fact, many of the behavioral manifestations of mummers during winter holidays are strongly connected to the community identity of the participants. Being a mummer also means strengthening certain bonds within the community where the ones performing the mummers spend their daily life and do their daily work, but also in relation to certain community members whom they have less contact with during the year.

> Mummering not only involves the community in an intriguing guessing-game; it requires identification of the people who are playing the game. The community takes stock of its members; many may not have visited any of the houses on the other side of the harbour since the last funeral or wedding; in particular, young children are named and their growth appraised. Christmas in Deep Harbour can be viewed, then, as an event in which the community reaffirms its identity. (Chiaramonte 1969:103)

Another article, reaching similar conclusions by means of a different argumentation, belongs to John F. Szwed—*The Mask of Friendship: Mumming as a Ritual of Social Relations*. Szwed adopts the classical path of a field anthropologist and tries to scan mummers from a single village on the island—Ross village, situated a few miles away from the Gulf of St. Lawrence, in one of the few fertile areas of the island. After describing the place and the village inhabitants, Szwed follows—maybe for the first time in the history of the studies about mummers—the anthropological theories about reciprocity, social structure and ritual, trying to explain the mummers' plays through these concepts. According to the observations collected on the field and to the frame provided by the theories mentioned above, the initial social hostility between mummers and the host becomes an expression of the hostility between a smaller community—based on the equality of its members and on positive reciprocity relations—and possible outsiders that could alter the fragile social balance. Therefore, the whole situation between the mummers and the host, initially hostile, as well as the game of guessing who is wearing the mask, finally leads to a "recreation and renewal of the social order" (Szwed 1969:117), the minute after the one behind the mask is acknowledged as a member of that community and not as an outsider.

> Rituals of social reaffirmation mark Newfoundland communities off from the larger part of Western complex society; whereas the urban-oriented world rejects and denies social conflicts and repressed hostility, groups such as those found in Ross are able to utilize this same material in open expression to limit the strength of conflict in the group. (Idem 1969:117)

Other articles in the volume edited by Halpert and Story approach mummers from the perspective of a social control mechanism (Ben-Dor 1969), but also as a cognitive complex that reinforces gender roles after the temporary social reversal operated by transvestite mummers—an expression of the aggressive and socially polluted alterity. After having guessed the real persons behind the masks, the return to normality could also mean a return to the community—a space of peaceful and predictable intentions and behavior compared to the outside world that seems ominous, unpredictable, uninhibited, dangerous and polluting (Faris 1969). Displaying this wide series of interpretations and descriptions of the Newfoundland mummers, the volume edited by the two North American researchers opens the way for a new research direction in the discipline.

The late 1960s were rich in publications on mummers' topic. An author who struggled hard to distance himself from the previous works on mummers and had, at the same time, a holistic approach to the incredibly diverse reality of the mummers, is the theater professor Alan Brody. He published his main work about mummers—*The English Mummers and Their Play, Traces of Ancient Mystery*—in 1969. Unlike the authors preceding him, Brody warned about the fact that mummers should be understood through the analysis of their actions rather than through their discourse (Brody 1971). Brody conducts a philological exegesis of the term *mummer*, showing that both the Dutch *momme* and the Danish *mumme* mean "to disguise oneself with a mask." Yet, the research of folk plays in Great Britain, Brody observed, proves that there are mummers that wear no mask; instead, they only paint their face with soot. Besides, many folk plays classified as mummers' plays by English folklorists are called in a completely different way by the participants (*hogmanaymen*, for instance) among whom some have never heard of mummers and any mask wearers.

Despite these extremely pertinent assertions, Brody's approach finally follows the path of the similar studies preceding it—that of discovering the origins of those folk theater forms. He states from the first pages of his work that there are two common elements for all the folk theater plays: they are all seasonal and they all contain a death and a resurrection somewhere in the course of their action. Thus, Brody, too, fits the direction of the Folkloristics looking for typologies of the versions of the folk elements collected from the people, and for a common origin. This origin, Brody says, is different for all the three plays analyzed: *The Sword Play, The Wooing Ceremony* and *The Hero-Combat*; but all of them go deep into the European history, to the fertility cults sometimes exemplified by ancient Greek drama. In the concluding pages of his book, he struggles remarkably to prove how, during the troubled European history, British folk theater borrowed Christian elements that were later covered by various tendencies emerging with the advancement of industrialization and modernization. All these left a mark on English folk theater, but also left space for the contemporaries to find "traces of ancient mystery" in it.

The 1970s mark the series of authors who try to break with the tradition of their predecessors. Henry Glassie, for instance, in his *All Silver and No Brass* (1975), approaches mummers from the perspective of their relationship with local communities and their rules. Despite he identifies himself as a folklorist, he starts with a well-argued critique of the attempts conducted by the traditional Folkloristics preceding him to understand and to explain mummers. This critique against *the originists* is not destructive; on the contrary, it is efficient and well directed. What Glassie reproaches his predecessors, is that they had paid too little attention to the intentional and emotional dimension these plays had for their performers. Precisely because of that, Glassie builds his study around the interviews of some Irish communities' members who had participated or witnessed these rituals themselves. Thus, he proves that, contrary to the originist thinkers' tradition, mummers are not the ghosts of customs once alive, but still a living tradition to the present day, as long as the communities practicing them remain cohesive (Glassie 1975:121).

Consequently, mummers could be understood from two perspectives, as parts of a larger totality (the European culture), but also as autonomous ethnographic units whose functioning is closely related to community life and could be described in relation to it (Idem 1975:59). This is one of the basic reasons why mummers should be observed in relation to the community producing them. Only this way, Glassie believes the researcher could hope to understand the social and economic changes that transformed mummers' plays from pagan fertility and agricultural abundance rites into a source of fun and entertainment (Ibidem 1975:135). Promoting this model in understanding the mummers, Glassie brings into discussion other elements contributing to the strengthening of community relations through mummers' plays. Alcohol consumption, the lack of a firm barrier between actors and spectators—the last ones turning into actants, too –, overcoming the difficulties through drama and entertainment and, finally, the controlled violence, are part of this complex landscape where communities redraw their physical and social frontiers expressing in the meantime their goodwill and hope by means of these ritual plays.

The 1970s brought a change of perspective in understanding folk plays, the search for their origins falling second and often being replaced by ethnographic exercises based on fieldwork using the methods of cultural anthropology. A comprehensive article—*The Antrobus Soulcaking Play: An Alternative Approach to the Mummers' Play*, is written by anthropologist Susan Pattison. She is one of the first anthropologists to relate mummers' plays to the impact of changes taking place in England's economy (labor migration, for instance) and their consequences on the inhabitants of a small locality, now de-ruralized. In this context of profound social-economic changes, mummers' plays performers are no longer peasants, but commuting workers who work and sometimes live permanently in the towns around Antrobus village. For them, the living tradition of mummers had become an opportunity to reinforce a sense of community that seemed to vanish because of the economic transformations the locality went through during the previous decades. Thus, *Soulcaking Play* becomes a unifying factor that gives the participants a sense of belonging and of promoting local values represented by a physical object—*the head of the Wild Horse*—one of the permanent assets of mummers, transmitted from generation to generation for more than 200 years, according to the statements of the participants. The feelings of cohesion and sense of community speak about a living tradition, still practiced by workers and labor migrants; thus, it could not be regarded as a reminiscence of ancient fertility cults, as *originist* folklorists had interpreted it. In the meantime, Pattison reaches a safe conclusion regarding mummers' plays, an option placing her among the authors who stay away from speculations and unsustainable theories that are very tempting in this sometimes very slippery topic of research:

> It seems to me that the motivation behind and the response to the Mummers' Play will vary from place to place and time to time, and that in order to make any step forward in our understanding we must abandon the impulse toward a single interpretation which will explain all examples of the play's performance. Each occurrence of the tradition must be studied in the context of the community in which it occurs and by reference to those taking part. By looking for tenuous clues to an understanding of the Mummers' Play in the past we risk missing the valuable concrete evidence available to us in the present. (Pattison 1977:11)

As I stated at the beginning of this section, there is a great diversity of those who brought important contributions to the literature on mummers, and it is very likely that an exhaustive literature review of this field is impossible to accomplish. Nevertheless, it should be included in this attempt not only English-speaking researchers, but also authors who wrote in languages little known internationally. Unfortunately, such works have never had the chance to become too visible in the mummers' field. For Romania, the 1980s coincide with the publication of two significant works on folk play topic—*Teatrul fără scenă/Theater without Stage* (Oprișan 1981) and *Teatrul popular românesc/Romanian Folk Theater* (Oprișan 1987) by folklorist Horea Barbu Oprișan. I call this relentless researcher of folk play a folklorist because he had been described as such by certain representatives of Romanian Folkloristics. Nevertheless, the term "anthropologist" or "original author" used by Ovidiu Papadima who wrote the preface of one of these books (Papadima 1981) would be more appropriate for truly describing the assiduous field research conducted over more than five decades by a man who loved with all his heart "the folk theater without stage" and spent all his winter holidays among the mummers, far from his own family. This is a fair perspective since Oprișan rejected from the beginning the pedantic discourses and the excessively typologizing inclinations of Romanian Folkloristics, and depicted the animate reality of Romanian folk plays mostly through the voice of his interlocutors. Without pretending to be meticulous, he did not withdraw from writing down funny details such as the quality of the wine offered by the hosts, his parties with mummers, as well as his childhood recollections related to the night visits of the mummers at the house of the "railway station chief"—his father. This free style writing, combining cultural anthropology and oral histories study caused him harsh criticism, as well as the "unscientific" label to all of his works on folk theater (Adăscăliței 1966:147).

However, I believe that Oprişan was the most important personality among the researchers of folk play in Romania. Had he published his works earlier and had the English researchers of folk drama known his original works, they would have avoided many hesitations, dilemmas, and meaningless fumbling on large "unexplored" territories. This is possible because, for five decades (1930–1980), Oprişan managed to gather an impressively rich material about folk plays. He collected these data in a time when Romanian peasantry went through the most dramatic transformation of its entire history that far. Peasantry transitioned from a system of natural economy to a larger economic system represented by the urban world, the development of heavy industry, the often violent engineering projects meant to systematize agriculture and small peasant households (Kligman and Verdery 2011). All of these led to the transformation of the farmer-peasant into a worker-peasant (Cole 1976). These changes were reflected into the performance of the mummers' plays, their dynamics, symbolism, and morphology. In this restless context, Oprişan was the right man at the right place, describing all the transformations of the "theater without stage" over an entire century. Due to the interviews he had taken to elder villagers—remarkable representatives of the local collective memory—this "original thinker" (Papadima 1987) managed to go back to the late 19th century, shedding light on earlier mummers' performances.

Based on this rich material, Oprişan tells us—most of the time by letting his interlocutors talk—how a series of simple genuinely peasant plays, initially connected to the village world—such as the *Play of the Goat*—changed into something different and almost unrecognizable. Living a time when these plays changed under his own eyes, he could not face the dilemmas and hesitations of English or American researchers. Therefore, it is fascinating to notice the freedom with which he narrated the folk theater plays he had witnessed. For Oprişan, folk theater had a purely peasant origin, and its contact to the urban world brought a series of inventions and adornments caused by the "lust for money" and meant to please a larger semi-urbanized audience that could offer more money to the performers. Old elements—including the *deochi*/enchantment and *descântec*/disenchantment by the body of the deceased character in view of a revival—were replaced by the physician arriving to make an injection that would bring the dead one back to life. Likewise, figures pertaining to the rural world such as the shepherd or the old man, owners of the goat or the ones disenchanting it, were replaced by clowns or by the physician with his syringe. Interestingly, for *originist* writers such as Thomas Ordish, this was exactly the reason for speculation regarding the moment and why the shaman turned into a physician. Well, for Oprişan this could not be a dilemma since he precisely recorded the moment when these transformations had taken place.

From this perspective of social change his article *Satelitul/The Satellite* (Oprișan 1965) is more relevant than the books he published in the 1980s. It speaks about a group of peasants from a mountain village in Moldova who decide to replace the traditional *Play of the Goat* with *the Satellite*, thus moving from a traditional play to an urban, even sci-fi topic. The play revolves around the construction of a small wooden satellite covered in metal sheet and painted in light yellow color. Just as the other folk theater plays, the topic of the play focuses more on action and on a series of absurd elements that generate a grotesque, comic atmosphere—a sort of opera buffa. Aliens come to visit Earth and try to communicate through sign language with terrestrials—the peasants in the audience—but communication is not easy; as a result, aliens first sit at the table and get their lunch, taking a crow, a rat, some dead sparrows, a sheep head and some onions out of the satellite, to the general surprise and laughter of the audience (Oprișan 1965:67).

The end of the 1950s—when this play was performed in the small mountain village of Cuejd in Neamț county—marks the time when the contact between the village and the urban world had become more frequent, and schooling as well as written press were already made accessible to a larger number of peasants because of the educational communist policy. All these are the influences that created the *Satellite* play together with the freedom to replace a traditional play with a new one, invented ad-hoc. Witnessing all these transformations of the Romanian village, Oprișan himself lives the changes of the Romanian rural world together with the "theater without stage's" actors. The Romanian researcher seems to offer a simple explanation to problems that seemed inextricable in the British literature about mummers. What does not matter too much for Oprișan is when and how these plays emerged, as well as how the irreversible transformations of ancient plays took place, or whether the new plays rather belonged to workers' culture than to the rural one. Finally, we are dealing with the human mind creating dramatic scenarios where it participates next to a community when that community is cohesive, and people are used to express their experiences and feelings to each other through various forms, symbols, and representations. This is because, in the end, the origin of such a folk theater play consists of something rather trivial, part of the daily existence, than of something sensational. Abandoning the classical canons of traditional Folklore studies and adopting his own style of research, Barbu-Oprișan anticipated through his works the recent orientations of the mummers' literature. These new perspectives, adapting the classical methods of cultural anthropology—interview and participant observation, aimed to understand the meanings conferred by the active participants to these cultural forms.

Perceiving mummers' plays as diverse and complex forms of human communication, just like Oprișan described them two decades before, was a fundamental idea of one of the most elaborate studies in the literature about mummers. I am talking about Terry Gunnell's work *Masks and Mumming in the Nordic Area* (2007). It comprises 840 pages representing the outcome of the collaborations of twenty-six researchers in Northern European countries including Norway, Sweden, Denmark, Estonia, Iceland, Greenland, and Newfoundland region in Canada. They all present various aspects of the mummers' plays in these countries and regions, offering a comparative perspective of an incredible diversity of cultural manifestations. Furthermore, the study Gunnell edits proves a striking isomorphism between mummers in all northern European countries, Great Britain and Newfoundland Island. Nordic countries could have offered the first British researchers of mummers the opportunity to test much more fertile comparisons. We could simply take the instance of *The Christmas Goat*, a dramatic play from Norway (*julebukk*) that is present in Sweden (*julbock*), Denmark (*julebuk*), Finland (*joulupouki*) and Estonia (*naarisokk*), England (the *hobbyhorse*), Romania (*capra*), and Russia (*коза*). It is indeed fascinating to follow the way various symbols and elements of such mummers' play are activated by certain local cultural patterns, by languages, and dialects.

Besides the structuring of all these data—a colossal effort on behalf of the editor—Gunnell's vision opens two perspectives. On the one hand, he revalidates a series of observations of authors who had investigated these rituals before him; on the other hand, he advances a new, innovative interpretation of mummers. For Gunnell, mummers' plays represent a form of communication that involves simultaneously both actor and spectator, enhancing an exchange of diverse information between the two, connecting all the human senses, "including sound (of various kinds), vision, movement, touch, smell, rhythm, tone, deep mental association, prior expectation and more" (Idem 2007:29). Because of this, one of the apparently simplest forms of theater becomes in fact "one of the most complex cultural phenomena known to humankind" (Ibidem 2007:28).

More than that, the recent evolution of mummers' plays from community ritual forms to national and global level due to their transformation in commercial heritage or embodiments of local or national political agendas, turn them into cultural forms that are even more complex than when they belonged just to the community performing them. Therefore, the research of mummers today, in their community/heritagization/marketization context, could reveal an entire series of local, national and global social expressions that would be difficult to seize if they were viewed in a different setting. This is because today's rural communities or small urban communities are not like those extant a few decades ago; today's integration into the globalization process by means of television, internet networks and radio, influences the entire behavior of both performers and viewers.

Gunnell's study aims to capture this plethora of cultural manifestations. At the same time, he describes the mummers immersed in a world accompanied by incredible challenges. It is about the recent challenges created by the advance of the market economy, of the media, and the attempts to heritagize these cultural forms. However, in some articles I still found the old directions of analysis in the research of mummers, for example the tendency of national folkloristics to find typologies and also the search for an explanation regarding the common origin of certain phenomena comprising huge diversity of cultural expressions. These small inadvertences are an expression of a long tradition that has examined the mumming from this perspective. However, they are inherent in a substantial study, which manages to bring together so many authors. The main merits of this research should be reemphasized. Firstly, the diligence of scanning a huge geographical area comprising of eight countries, and secondly the willingness for opening a door to understand the transformation of mummers' plays from the perspective of the challenges brought by globalization in communities where mummers are still an active presence.

With these last remarks about Gunnell's book, I move to the last study that I think deserves a thorough analysis. I am talking about *Masquerade and Postsocialism. Ritual and Cultural Dispossession in Bulgaria* by anthropologist Gerald W. Creed. From the start, Creed observes that the behavior and look of the mummers reveal something ancient, but rejects the hypothesis of mummers' old age that would bring him closer to Frazer's anthropology. Instead, he builds a demonstration of exactly the opposite—the mummers who lost their "potential alterity" over times, are an expression of modernity, although actually an expression of "just modernity in premodern drag" (Creed 2011:216). To support his demonstration, Creed takes a journey to a series of Bulgarian localities where mummers' rituals and folk festivals take place. The mummers' manifestations help Creed touch on many important aspects related to mummers' play, including sexuality and gender, masculinity, civil society, democracy, nationalism, and interethnic relations. They all form the lens through which Creed tries to decipher the transformations of the Bulgarian society after the fall of communism.

A valuable distinction made by Creed is between mummers' rituals in their native villages and mummers' festivals in urban areas. This distinction stands for two totally different cultural expressions and could be the key to understanding Creed's demonstration (Idem 2011:55). Unfortunately, this dichotomy is not rigorously applied throughout the entire study. Thus, from the very beginning we are told that, in some places, these practices are spreading, whereas in others they are gradually vanishing (Ibidem 2011:1). But the author does not mention which are actually the ones expanding and which are the ones vanishing. Neither do we know whether the author refers to mummers' festivals in urban areas or in village rituals. We could deduce that he is talking about the ones in the first category, and this could be connected precisely to the peasants' "cultural dispossession" of their own cultural heritage because of its exportation to the urban world and its transformation into something totally different from what it had been initially. But this idea remains pending and is not clearly expressed; it rather makes the readers believe that the dispossession is somehow the result of the postsocialist mess where the promise of the country's development and modernization are only empty hopes. These hopes were never accomplished completely during the long transition to market economy. More, the two types of rituals are regarded as being "interactive and reinforcing" (Ibidem 2011:56).

In this vaguely defined landscape, mummers would represent an alternative modernity able to replace or to feel like having replaced the aggressive modernity that eviscerates cultural practices (Ibidem 2011:216). The only problem that makes it difficult to understand such an assertion is the fact that mummers could hardly represent an alternative modernity as long as they are actually just one of the cultural realities the peasants are dispossessed of in Postsocialism. This dispossession is because of the interference of numerous consequences including the lack of jobs, the expansion of alternative entertainment forms, the demographic decline and the migration to Western European countries. So, one could wonder, how could a cultural reality—mummers—be an alternative modernity for Postsocialism when it is in fact just one of the cultural phenomena eviscerated by the stirred postsocialist transition to capitalism? The final conclusion of the study follows the same line: mummers manage to survive in front of the postsocialist corrosive modernity by means of carnivalization, displacement from the village world and commercialization—the price for losing the potential alterity they could have represented. "It is now just modernity in premodern drag" (Ibidem 2011:216), the author tells us.

Finally, moving beyond these conclusions, the most valuable direction provided by this study is the extensive field research based on participant observation and extended interviews with the participants themselves. All these prove the special meaning that joining these plays has for the villagers, particularly when the rituals happen within their own communities. The value of mummers' plays results most obviously from an interview to a villager who declared, inversing the terms of the equation between mummers and reality: he is a mummer all year long and, two days each year, during the holidays, he is a human being and a person (Ibidem 2011:63). His statement and other similar ones, excellently observed and exemplified by Creed, represent something essential for mummers' plays, something I am going to explain further in the next chapter.

CONCLUSION

Modernity could be defined as the period that came out of the overcoat of the Enlightenment which had marked the beginnings of experimental science, accompanied by the search for truth and objectivity. It came with the imposition of grand narratives with the pretense of explaining various historical events by providing meaning to seemingly scattered phenomena that it connected within a frame of universal knowledge. Criticizing the legitimacy claims of such knowledge, Jean-François Lyotard defines the postmodern condition "as incredulity towards metanarratives." Such grand narratives, Lyotard points out, marked not only the history of science, but also the ideologies of the main religions and political state constructions. If narratives are stories that have functioned over time to justify power relations and to impose a totalizing view on reality, grand narratives are a set of ideas that claim to explain certain disparate historical events through a general scheme that claims universal value. This category includes Marxism, Freudianism, the doctrines of great religions, and nationalism as the foundation of the construction of national projects. In general, a metanarrative implies a philosophy of history used to legitimize knowledge by involving certain state institutions, thus imposing that knowledge.

Briefly reviewing the main points marked in this chapter, we remember how the construction of the discourse on peasants has been marked since the 19th century by Marxism and nationalism. These currents fully subscribe to the concept of grand narratives. Imagining peasants as a great mass of people spread over all the continents of the planet, or in relation to the revolutionary idea of class struggle, as well as to the structural problems of nation-states demanding urgent solutions, is the equivalent of the denial of the cultural particularities of peasant communities. This prevents the understanding of their history as a set of cultural micro-ecosystems revolving around their own rules and gravitating around their values.

The same can be said about mummers' plays studies. The relentless search for a common origin of phenomena belonging to disparate geographical areas and times speaks of the inclination of modern thinking to build grand narratives, which can explain cultural phenomena whose functionality is provided by a supposed connection hidden in a presumed origin that became invisible in the mist of history. In fact, all these phenomena can well exist even without a grandiose idea underpinning them, due to a web of connections and local networks. This becomes clear in the case of mummers' plays and it is exactly what Lyotard states at one point in his demonstration:

> It should now be clear from which perspective I chose language games as my general methodological approach. I am not claiming that the *entirety* of social

relations is of this nature - that will remain an open question. But there is no
need to resort to some fiction of social origins to establish that language games
are the minimum relation required for society to exist. . . . (Lyotard 1984:15)

Throughout this chapter, incursions into Marxist currents, nationalist doctrines, and Folkloristics influenced by social evolution theory, have amply
demonstrated that all these domains have been dominated by the modern
view imposing grand narratives. This vision has rather legitimized certain
variants of truth, sometimes with a strong ideological substratum, rather
than explanations of how certain local cultural phenomena work in relation
to the cultural micro-universe that created them. One of the major stakes of
Lyotard's work *The Postmodern Condition* was to replace the grand narratives with a new perspective on history in which the diversity of human experience in the local cultural context came first. This was also one of the stakes
of this chapter—to break with a tradition where peasants and their propensity
for games were neither fully emphasized, nor studied enough.

Most of the peasant and folk plays studies presented in this chapter are an
expression of the tendency to construct metanarratives that legitimate certain
truths, institutions, and political actions with which many peasant communities had nothing in common. In a vast majority, peasant studies were meticulous remarks of the policies that had to be implemented to transform a social
class—peasantry—according to standards set by the leadership of modern
states. *The Agrarian question* and *the peasantry issue* are the most significant
examples in this regard. Likewise, much of the research on mummers, especially that guided by the search for a common origin and a common concept
explaining the mummers' diversity over a large area of Eurasia, is essentially
an attempt to justify the existence of certain ancient cultural forms within the
modern society, a society dominated by the industrial revolution which was
accompanied by other economic and cultural expressions, totally different
from the universe of mummers.

Of course, these metanarratives provide a holistic perspective needed in
any science, but not the necessary nuanced view required by the study of
human diversity and the heterogeneity of human communities. By the end
of the 20th century, disappointed by arrogant claims of metanarratives such
as "progress," "reason," and "truth," certain authors have turned to particular "smaller narratives" (petits récits), such as the history of everyday life and
the history of marginalized groups. One of them was the philosopher Ludwig
Wittgenstein whose concept of "language game" was taken over by Lyotard
when rethinking the role of the local context and the diversity of human
experience lived in local communities. It is about highlighting a cultural
heterogeneity whose explanation lies in its very diversity and not in a set of
prefabricated features that can be applied anytime to any community. I used

the same Wittgensteinian method and theory in the next chapter to understand rural plays. A similar approach was presented in the previous chapter when I made a journey into the cultural micro-ecosystems in which the values of the peasants took shape.

Following the path opened by Lyotard, I express my skepticism about the attempts to standardize cultural phenomena, attempts whose limits were presented in the pages of this chapter. Such visions falling into the category of grand narratives have not favored the understanding of the peasant universe neither from the perspectives of their value system and of the peasants' propensity for play, nor from the perspective of human interrelationships inside customary communities. It is also worth noting that the history of colonialism, a history based on domination, oppression, and racism, is often hidden behind these metanaratives. Not infrequently, the peasants were victims of this history. A decolonialization of this history from the rural play perspective, I think it is necessary.

The postmodern deconstruction promoted by Lyotard opens new horizons dominated by "smaller narratives" (*petits récits*) through which can be understand the individuals of rural customary communities in their full manifestations, including their propensity for violence, complex economic relationships, plays, conflicts, and tensions, far from the romantic kind of idealizations that promoted a noble savage model of Rousseauian influence or a derogatory Hobbesian perspective depicting peasants as nasty and brutish people that need to be included in the civilizing programs implemented by national states.

Unfortunately, the grand peasantry's narratives, too, tell us little about the relationships of people in rural communities. Or, folk plays were exactly that: cultural forms that gave people the opportunity to place themselves in relation to each other, to rethink their relationships of love, friendship, animosity, and conflict. That is why there is no common origin of mummers, just as there is no universal history that could explain the events happening in all rural communities over time. There is only a plethora of similarities and differences in the experiences of people who have lived inside small rural communities for hundreds of years, and who, consequently, have developed over time a set of common values and similar plays that sometimes partially overlap, so that striking similarities between them are observable.

NOTES

1. Throughout this section of the current chapter, I will use the concept of mummers' play specially to refer to the plays practiced by peasants or the proletarianized

peasantry. This is because most of the authors cited in this part of the study are English authors for whom the most commonly used concept is that of mummers' plays.

    2. The English Mummers' Play was published posthumously in 1981 by the Folk-
lore Society of England but was written a few decades earlier.

Chapter Five

The Evolution of Play/Game—
From Rural Plays to Video Games

A HISTORICAL JOURNEY INTO THE
CULTURAL EVOLUTION OF RURAL PLAYS

In the previous chapter I adopted a critical view against grand narratives that analyzed the peasantry and folk plays. Accordingly, the task assumed in this chapter is a difficult one. There are two reasons for this difficulty. Firstly, I have to explain folk plays through theories that do not threaten the diversity of peasant cultures and that could later be labeled as grand narratives. Secondly, these theories should be able to examine the peasants' plays at a time of great social, economic, and technological transformation: The Scientific Revolution. Speaking about the Scientific Revolution, the historian Yuval Noah Harari starts his analysis with an imaginative exercise that reveals the incredible transformations this revolution has produced in human societies. If a Spanish peasant had fallen asleep in 1000 AD and woke up at the beginning of the Age of Discovery when Columbus embarked on his great adventure to America, the landscape around him would not have been completely unfamiliar and foreign. If, on the contrary, a Columbus sailor had been teleported in the 21st century, in the middle of a modern city dominated by current technology, he would surely have thought that he had reached heaven or maybe hell (Harari 2015:275).

Well, what seems at first sight to be just an imaginary exercise, has actually happened to millions of peasants during the Industrial Revolution. They literally woke up from the middle of a simple world dominated by rules and values they knew well, and which have been perpetuated for hundreds of years only with minor changes, to a changing urban world produced by a new technological revolution visible in all fields, from culture and art to economy

215

and politics. The outcome of this event lies in the clash of the two cultures: the peasant one dominated by medieval values and mentalities and the industrial urban one dominated by technological inventions and a new mode of production foreign to the rural world that preceded it. This clash took place all over the planet, but it happened neither at the same time, nor under the same premises everywhere.

With the emergence of industrialism and the encompassing of rural communities into a different economic and social cycle, folk plays, like many other cultural forms belonging to peasant culture, started to feel these challenges. Many rural plays gradually vanished while others got adapted for a while to the urban environment by changing their symbols, significance, and morphology. Finally, they were replaced by new cultural forms that took the place of the rural plays inside the humans' mind. All these transformations emerged differently in various countries all over the globe. While in industrial countries like England and the United States folk plays were subjected to these challenges since the early 1800s, in the extensively ruralized Eastern Europe the same challenges started to be visible only in the 20th century.

For a while, folk plays were able to adapt to the emerging working-class culture that was also made of cohesive communities. In many cases, they turned into a rush for money or a brutal intrusion against the firm rules of urban cohabitation than into a caroling with deep meanings for the community. This new social landscape was well depicted by Stephen Nissenbaum in his research on Christmas, where he talked about "the insolent and clamorous" journeys of the mummers throughout Boston at the end of 1793, making local authorities ban them finally through the firm intervention of the local police (Nissenbaum 1996:44). In Romania, a country with a less diverse population and a substantial urbanized peasantry, the incursions of the mummers' teams in search for money is still a present phenomenon and is much better tolerated by authorities and city dwellers, despite mummers' rowdy nature.

From the analysis of this complex landscape, one thing remains certain. Although folk plays were an elaborate cultural activity in agricultural societies (Beeman 1993:385), with the Industrial Revolution, this type of play underwent major transformations or disappeared altogether in many places. The question that I aim to answer in the pages of this chapter is: how can be explained the enormous success of folk plays in agricultural societies for centuries, followed by their mass extinction with the emergence of the Industrial Revolution? As we will see, the implications of this question are profound and will lead to an analysis of the relationship between the human being and the plays/games produced by the extraordinary advancement of technology in the 20th century.

Moreover, this question has a higher stake than the previous ones. So far, we have talked about mummers' plays, a rural play form that is bizarre, to say the least, for many of our contemporaries who regard it as something specific to other times and places or as something still alive only in isolated places. I have come to the point where I stated that these plays were in fact some of the most widespread cultural forms performed by humans in agricultural societies. It is about some cultural forms that involves a whole series of social relations and, precisely because of that, they had an important role in the system of values of communities based on agricultural work. This is the reason why, throughout this study, I insist on naming mummers' plays not by the English word *play* which covers a small range of activities, but also by the Romanian word *joc* which involves a wide range of activities such as dance, theater, confrontation, competition, trick, and so on.[1]

The mummers' plays in agricultural societies involved all these features—an aspect that makes them some of the most important plays of the people living in agricultural societies. Therefore, the disappearance of folk plays cannot be considered an isolate event without any deep meaning, but a mutation produced inside the human society during industrialization, a mutation that I am struggling to explain throughout this chapter. It is, as we will see, not only a social transformation, but also a change in the mind of humans in its relation to play/game. Based on Wittgenstein's theory of language games, Ioan Petru Couliano's theory of mind games, the conceptual framework outlined by Huizinga in his *Homo Ludens* and some other more recent theories, in the following pages, I will answer the question raised above.

MUMMERS' PLAYS AND LANGUAGE GAMES

I use Ludwig Wittgenstein' theory on language to analyze mummers' play as he is one of the thinkers who, in his research on language, faced a similar problem to the one the researchers of mummers had already encountered: the incredible diversity of language games and by extension of human games/plays. The problem posed by Wittgenstein can be synthesized in one question: what is the common element of all games? This is how Wittgenstein framed this topic:

> Here we come up against the great question that lies behind all these considerations.—For someone might object against me: "You take the easy way out! You talk about all sorts of language games, but have nowhere said what the essence of a language-game, and hence of language, is: what is common to all these activities, and what makes them into language or parts of language. So, you let yourself off the very part of the investigation that once gave you yourself most headache, the part about the *general form of propositions* and of language." And this is true.—instead of producing something common to all

that we call language, I am saying that these phenomena have no one thing in common which makes us use the same word for all,—but that they are *related* to one another in many different ways. And it is because of this relationship, or these relationships, that we call them all "language." I will try to explain this. (Wittgenstein 2010[1953]:65)

According to Wittgenstein, the assumption of the common origin of some forms of language such as language games is a fiction. The similarities of language games do not necessarily speak of a common essence of them but of certain relationships built contextually during the discourse, by connecting it to everyday experience. During his demonstration, Wittgenstein discusses the concept of games, which brings his analysis in the vicinity of the subject I discussed in the previous chapter. In a passage from his Philosophical Investigations, Wittgenstein was able to offer an original perspective on games:

Consider for example the proceedings that we call "games." I mean board-games, card-games, ball-games, Olympic games, and so on. What is common to them all?—Don't say: "There must be something common, or they would not be called 'games'"—but look and see whether there is anything common to all.— For if you look at them you will not see something that is common to all, but similarities, relationships, and a whole series of them at that. To repeat: don't think, but look!—Look for example at board-games, with their multifarious relationships. Now pass to card-games; here you find many correspondences with the first group, but many common features drop out, and others appear. When we pass next to ball games, much that is common is retained, but much is lost.—Are they all "amusing"? Compare chess with noughts and crosses. Or is there always winning and losing, or competition between players? Think of patience. In ball games there is winning and losing; but when a child throws his ball at the wall and catches it again, this feature has disappeared. Look at the parts played by skill and luck; and at the difference between skill in chess and skill in tennis. Think now of games like ring-a-ring-a-roses; here is the element of amusement, but how many other characteristic features have disappeared! Sometimes similarities of detail. And we can go through the many, many other groups of games in the same way; can see how similarities crop up and disappear. And the result of this examination is: we see a complicated network of similarities overlapping and crisscrossing: sometimes overall similarities. (Wittgenstein 2010[1953]:66)

Correlated to the previous chapter about the folk plays, the excerpt I have just cited is truly striking. The reason is that, analyzing two different realities—language games and folk plays—it is easy to observe a series of similar aspects whose correspondence is amazing. And this isomorphism causes even more perplexity since, to explain language games, Wittgenstein refers precisely to human games in day-to-day reality. Because of this reason, this paragraph—often quoted in philosophy—could perfectly fit the problem I am discussing, namely folk plays. Following Wittgenstein's model, I could generate a series of similar assertions:

Consider, for example, the proceedings that we call folk plays. I mean *Hero-Combat Play*, the *Sword Dance Play*, the *Wooing Play* from England, as well as the *Christmas Goat* from Northern European countries, the *Play of the Deer* from Moldova, the *Pantomimic Mummers* with their house-visit-in-disguise in Newfoundland Island, and so on. What is common to all of them?—Do not say: "There must be something common, otherwise they would not be called 'folk plays'"—but look and see whether there is anything common to all of them.—For if you look at them you will not see something that is common to all, but similarities, relationships, and a whole series of them with similarities and differences. To repeat: don't think, but look!—Look for example at Christmas mummers, with their multifarious relationships. Now go to spring mummers like the Romanians' *Călușari*; here you find many correspondences with the first group, but many common features drop out, while others appear. When we move further to folk theater with puppets or marionettes, much of what is common is retained, but much is also lost.—Are they all "amusing"? Compare the pantomimic mummers with their house-visit-in-disguise, full of joy and amusement, with the folk theater of *Haiducii/The Mavericks*, which are serious and grave from beginning to end. Or, is there always the idea of death and resurrection in all these plays? Yes, indeed, this is a common theme for many of them but many other have never embodied this notion. Now, think of masks. In mummers' plays there are always characters who wear masks, but not all of them do. And there are some folk plays like *Haiducii/The Mavericks* where no character actually wears a mask or just one of them does, like in *Călușarii* as well. And we can identify plays where the performers have their face blackened with soot, again not wearing a regular mask. Look at the parts consisting of verbal plays and of pantomimic ones; and at the difference between oration and action. Think now of plays like the *Christmas Goat*; here is the element of amusement, action, and pantomime, but how many other characteristic features have disappeared! While the *Christmas Goat* is based mainly on action and pantomime, the *Hero-Combat Play* from England and the *Irod Play*[2] from Romania and Hungary are mainly based on dialogue and oration. Sometimes we see just similarities of details. And we can go through the many, many other groups of plays just the same way; we can see how similarities crop up and disappear. And the result of this examination is: we are seeing a complicated network of similarities overlapping and crisscrossing: sometimes overall similarities.

What we are seen when scrutinizing mummers' plays is a long series of "family resemblances" (Wittgenstein 2010[1953]:67), a complex network of superpositions, differences and complicated relations that make it impossible to produce a totally comprehensive definition or a holistic theory that could define once and for all some precise conceptual borders. Yet, what we discover in all these manifestations—ongoing or just mentioned in historic documents—is the individual's predisposition to *play* and his capacity to create simulacra of everyday experience; this happens without the realities preserving a certain pattern, but rather a variety of topics and motifs.

But, let's go back for a moment to Wittgenstein theory and analyze the relations between his discoveries in the field of language games and their implications for studying folk plays. The basic idea of his *Philosophical Investigations* is that there is no single logic of language; instead, there are multiple ones, depending on the context that produced the language. Precisely because of that, language games become a key element of human society since they often help us understand reality and adapt to its demands much better than concepts and theories could. Thus, language games are strictly connected to the contextual use of language, and language becomes a collection of practices that change at the same time with the context of talk. They represent one of the most important sources of human identity mostly because they have the capacity to create vital connections between the values, the beliefs, the ethics, and the human mind. The expressions also bring important aspects regarding the historicity of any linguistic and cultural community that uses them in daily language, thus becoming a sort of living history of the community. Therefore, knowing a language outside of its cultural context does not guarantee the access to understanding the behavior and human values of the community speaking that language. This is because there is no access to the context and the human experience that brings meaning into the expressions, besides one's own living experience in that community. When Wittgenstein speaks about these things, he also offers, perhaps not coincidentally, the example of such a cross-cultural encounter:

> One learns this when one comes into a strange country with entirely strange traditions; and, what is more, even though one has mastered the country's language. One does not understand the people. (And not because of not knowing what they are saying to themselves.) We can't find our feet with them. (Wittgenstein 1967)

This fragment sheds light on an individual's own limitations when crossing cultural barriers and understanding the context involved in the experience of other people who had lived within a community with an economic and political system different from the outsider's cultural perspective. That precise context could be expressed by what Wittgenstein called "language game," and language games are components of what he called "life forms."

Regarding "life forms," it should be mentioned that there are just few passages in *Philosophical Investigations* that talk about them. Probably this was one of the reasons why this concept generated many controversies.

> It is easy to imagine a language consisting only of orders and reports in battle.— Or a language consisting only of questions and expressions for answering yes and no. And innumerable others.—And to imagine a language means to imagine a form of life.
>
> Here the term *"language-game"* is meant to bring into prominence the fact that the *speaking* of language is part of an activity, or of a form of life.
>
> "So, you are saying that human agreement decides what is true and what is false?"—It is what human beings *say* that is true and false; and they agree in the *language* they use. That is not agreement in opinions but in form of life.
>
> Can only those hope who can talk? only those who have mastered the use of a language. That is to say, the phenomena of hope are modes of this complicated form of life. (If a concept refers to a character of human handwriting, it has no application to beings that do not write.)
>
> What has to be accepted, the given, is—so one could *say*—*forms of life.* (Wittgenstein 2010[1953])

Based on these paragraphs, we can draw some conclusions. A language is like a form of life, and language games are activities that belong to such forms of life. For this reason, the conventions we establish, and in fact all our interactions, take place on the territory of language, seen as a kind of cultural micro-ecosystem where both the confrontation and the collaboration of those who are part of a social environment take place together, in fact, with the entire cohabitation of all the individuals that give it consistency.

An ecosystem cannot exist independently of the life forms that compose it. However, in general, these life forms cannot exist outside their ecosystem. There are few exceptions to this. For example, fish in an aquarium can survive because the entire system in which they live is kept alive artificially. But they are no longer part of an ecosystem and do nothing to make it work. The same thing happens to old languages, such as Latin or Sanskrit. They no longer have an organic relationship with the cultural system that created them. That is why they are called dead languages. The metaphor has a deeper meaning. These languages are dead because the social and cultural environment that gave them vitality has disappeared. And what is valid for ancient languages is also valid for the cultures themselves. When we read about Mesopotamian culture, we do nothing but imagine a form of life based on data provided by archaeologists and historians. However, imagining a form of life is not the same as the form of life itself. For this reason, we can no longer know exactly what it means to have lived within that culture, to be born and to grow inside that living culture, which is now extinct long ago.

Experiencing the language and the culture we belong to provides us with a way of being in the world. However, language transcends people who happen to speak it at a certain moment. But, in turn, the language would not be alive without the people who use it as living speakers interacting by means of it. Latin language still exists, although there are no longer native speakers of this language who lived under the auspices of Roman culture. Probably these are the premises that make Wittgenstein conceive language as a form of life. Within a language, language games have the capacity of immersing us in a living culture, and thus in a form of life. And plays/games—which are always an integral part of cultures—can also be imagined as components of a form of life which is, in this case, a culture.

The experience of the *joc* within a culture also teaches us a way of being in the world by immersing us inside a universe with its own rules to which our minds are connected. This accounts for a fact noted a few decades ago by anthropologist Ernest Becker. Human beings have a dualistic nature consisting of a *physical self* and a *symbolic self*. The symbolic self has a kind of autonomy from its physical counterpart, and makes humans build a civilization, which is a cultural invention that can enhance humans to transcend the dilemma of mortality through heroism (Becker 1997). Humans plays/games are also expressions of this symbolic self and its partial autonomy from the world of nature from which it emerged. That is why some plays/games (*jocuri*), although they are expressions of the society that created them, sometimes seem very different phenomena from the surrounding reality and especially from nature.

Following the footsteps of Wittgenstein, we could say that to imagine a *joc* means to imagine a significant part of a form of life. This is also true for modern games such as football, rugby, handball, etc. For example, when a match is over, it can be analyzed and examined as if it were a vanished creature. But we all know that any creature had once an exuberant life in a cultural micro-ecosystem (which includes the stadium, players, fans, sports commentators, etc.). This is probably the reason why sport fans look for live broadcasts of a match and have a much lower interest in watching the recordings of that match. Analyzing a sports game from the outside, as a panoramic landscape, one can find in it both stupid mistakes and sequences of mastery and perfection, great moments of art, but also of helplessness, despair, hope, and humiliation, just as in the lives of ordinary people. That is why a sports match can be seen as an expression of a life form because it is an activity that gives rise to complex interactions between living beings endowed with intelligence. This is all true for mummers' plays since they were community plays. We can always catch there a glimpse of life, an intense and prodigious human activity—a sort of X-ray of a form of life.

In my research on mummers' plays, I had the opportunity to witness several times, at the end of the winter holidays, long discussions between locals regarding the quality of the plays performed that year. Unlike sports comments about a football game, which are primarily focused on the quality of the show offered, these discussions always included moralizing remarks about the participants and the hosts who had received them. That is why community plays like mumming cannot be separated from the history of the community and its system of values. Through them, community members interact in a complex way, so that character traits, moral qualities of community members or, on the contrary, their defects are always revealed. At the same time, the values of the community are restored or contested and those who violate them are sanctioned. All these are part of a form of life—a cultural micro-ecosystem—and mummers' plays are activities that highlight them in an eloquent way.

In Wittgenstein's view, the forms of life represent a combination of factors such as interpersonal relationships, cultural attitudes, and various forms of communication extant within the human society. They are distinct worlds and, if we want to understand them, we have to make them comprehensible by deciphering the meanings involved by language games, plays (*jocuri*) and other forms of communication that facilitate people's interactions in a meaningful way. Yet, an experienced anthropologist could easily observe that we are in front of one of the basic concepts of the discipline: the cultural relativism, which tell us that we could not hope to understand a series of cultural aspects in a community unless we fully comprehend the rules, values, and principles of that society.

Again, it is obvious that Wittgenstein talks in this context rather as a cultural anthropologist than as an analytic philosopher. One of the dilemmas this part of Wittgenstein's work caused is whether there is a single "form of life" or a series of "forms of life." The reason for this dilemma comes from the fact that Wittgenstein used the expression in both singular and plural. Jesús Padilla Gálvez, one of the philosophers who tried to find the meaning of this dispute, argued that "the language games we use in our actions are embedded in a form of life." (Gálvez and Gaffal 2011). Gálvez assumption tell us something simple: what Wittgenstein called "forms of life" are entities similar to the anthropological concept of cultural forms, this time understood from the perspective of the analytic philosophy as media where various forms of communication and exchange of ideas happen. These forms of communication are based on a routine and, therefore, on certain rules and norms inscribed in the community's traditions and history. Through their constant use, they generate speaking, nonverbal and behavioral habits, etc.

Drawing a parallel between Wittgenstein's discoveries on language games and the multifarious reality of mummers, I notice incredible similarities.

Just as language-games express the cultural context of their production, folk plays speak about their place within the cultural milieu of the customary community that produced them. More, folk plays speak about the existence of more complex communication needs between the members of the village communities where the individual's life had limited connections with the outside world. Therefore, the context of the folk plays is not a nation or a continent—as some researchers believed—but a customary community, a human group connected to a specific cultural milieu, which is not completely isolated, but always connected to other surrounding areas by means of various commercial, social, and cultural links. Thus, folk plays are just as convincing for proving the context of a form of life as language-games. Precisely because of the contextual particularities of these forms of life, folk plays cannot be explained by a single general concept, as it was repeatedly the case in the history of their research aiming to find typologies or theories designed to understand their diversity through a common origin.

Consequently, if we follow the history of small agriculture communities, both in Europe and in other areas of the globe, we see how rural plays have been used to satisfy an extremely varied array of human needs. And what Wittgenstein stated regarding the language is equally valid for folk plays. In the agricultural societies, they represented complex communication means between the individuals and their village community, at the same time being part of the way people organized their community life. These situations can range from very simple to extremely complex. For the time being, I can only enumerate a few of the human needs expressed by the rural plays: creating a connection to those members of the community with which relations are sparser throughout the year; extending the social network beyond the family circle; finding a spouse; analyzing universal problems such as death, sickness, poverty and social inequity; cementing a community identity; realizing a bridge to the community's past; creating some reference points on the collective memory map; reinforcing the sense of belonging to the community; the temporary trespassing of certain social rules that seem too rigid; satirizing flaws and personality features of certain community members; restating one's ego sometimes even violently; collecting money from the community members in a kind of reciprocal exchange; satisfying the entertainment and relaxation needs; articulating/alleviating conflicts/animosities between individuals or groups inside the community. For all these reasons, mummers' plays seem to be expressions of those entities Wittgenstein called forms of life, which I called *cultural micro-ecosystems*. Even more, mummers' plays speak about the indissoluble connection between human language expressions, always adapted to a specific cultural context, and human experience. The plays in general (*jocuri*), as well as language-games are relevant expressions of the cultural ecosystem that had produced them.

MUMMERS' PLAYS AND HUMAN MIND

Despite his emphasis on the multifarious usage of language through language-games in the complex universe of human experience, Wittgenstein was less interested in explaining the relation between these games, human mind and the power relations that have always been present in the history of human civilization. He was a pioneer in his field and he emphasized one simple thing which, for some reasons, has been ignored by many other thinkers in the history of ideas. The logic that governs the way people learn and use language-games, it is always in relation with humans life experience. This process shapes the subjects involved in it as it is a somehow superordinate phenomenon—a form of life.

What Wittgenstein did not emphasize is the relationship between the humans, their experience in a complex culture and the human mind. The human mind together with the context where it manifests are the terms that had to complete Wittgenstein's equation. The correlation of language games with human experience seems a natural process because the human mind is constructed in a way that enables this correlation. This is probably the secret of children's language acquisition. It is what Noam Chomsky called universal grammar, a set of innate abilities that allow children to acquire a language in the context of experience within a human community (Cook and Newson 1995).

Learning a dead language is not impossible, but it will always have something artificial in it. This is because the human mind will not be able to build the set of experiences that lie behind the use of that language. Things are similar in terms of games/plays (*jocuri*). The play/game has the capacity to teach us the norms and rules of a culture through active participation in a universe that seems a simulacrum of everyday experience, but actually reproduces in a symbolic form the processes present in the factual reality—what we call everyday life. In fact, the game/play is possible because it reproduces a process in the human mind. It is about a series of mental constructs which are representations of the human mind in relation to the events unfolding in the everyday world, in the so-called mundane reality.

These are what Kant called phenomena, and Arthur Schopenhauer caught the problem into a comprehensive statement in the very opening of his work *The World as Will and Representation*: "The world is my representation" (Schopenhauer 1966[1819]). But while Schopenhauer reduced the world to his own representation, Wittgenstein saw the world as a kind of interaction between humans and language in the linguistic experience. The world is an experience built on a canvas whose parts functions beyond the experiences of particular speakers - this is the language which in itself is like a form of life. And what is valid for language is also valid for game/play, a fact already observed by Wittgenstein.

The game can also exist separately from the individuals who play it. We can imagine, for example, football games, such as friendly matches that allow an unlimited number of changes of players on the field. Thus, the game that started at a certain moment with 22 players on the field can end with 22 other players than those who started it. This does not mean that it is another match; it is, in fact, the same. And, what is true for sports games is even truer for mummers' plays. Members of the rural community talk about the exuberant atmosphere of winter holidays. This atmosphere is not created by the journey through the village of teams A, B, and C, but by the fact that a number of teams composed of community members continue to perform their plays in the village within a pre-established time frame. Thus, teams A, B and C can be replaced over years by teams X, Y, Z from the same community, and the holiday atmosphere can remain the same. In fact, this is what actually happens, the teams of mummers undergoing changes from year to year, with some players remaining in the original teams, but also with many others replaced by different players. Or, all of this is very similar to the Wittgensteinian concept—form of life. These forms of life exist because human beings can conceive them through mind games and transpose them into reality as a set of skills that help us better filter the factual reality. This is what the historian of religion Ioan P. Coulianu perfectly sums up in one sentence: "A game fascinates the human mind because the mind recognizes in it its own functioning, and this recognition does not depend on the kind of game offered to the mind" (Couliano 1992:247).

Couliano is the author who was able to successfully explain the relation between factual experience, games/plays and human mind, in his work *The Tree of Gnosis*. This scholar speaks about the theological debates between Gnosticism/Western Dualism and Christianity—debates that led to the official establishment of the Christian doctrine. Unlike other historians of religion, Couliano advances a new methodology; with it, all the theological debates about the Creator of the World and of the world's principles seem to be the expression of certain "mind games people played with one another for centuries" and that almost resembled chess games and, thus, should not have affected the players negatively. The reason it that they had no rule for checkmate, so they could not be won by anybody. "Yet they nevertheless accomplished the moral and physical destruction of many, and were won by an exercise of power" (Idem 1992:267).

Couliano explains here the logic of the relation between historicity and the rules of the human mind functioning when it is guided by the game's logic. Above all these, one can observe how arbitrary aspects of existence overlap—including the historic and social contingency. Couliano talks about the institutional aggressiveness through which some of our fellows, mesmerized by the exercise of power in stratified human societies, have destroyed what was essentially something purely harmless—the human propensity for playing with concepts and ideas. In this respect, George Orwell is the author who created an extraordinary example with his well-known work *1984*. This book can also be perceived as a meditation on the consequences of totalitarian systems on free spirits and human creativity. In *1984*, Orwell imagines a society where certain expressions and concepts of the language itself become the target of censorship. Syme was a philologist at the *Ministry of Truth* who helped a totalitarian regime to develop a new language and the dictionary of *Newspeak*. He came out with the idea that some words in the dictionary must be eliminated in order to make people incapable of thinking against the dictatorship that ruled their society. In this case, it is a censorship directed not so much against language itself, as it would seem at first sight, but rather against the human mind. Through its inherent creativity, the human mind could imagine a society different from the dystopian one dominated by Big Brother. Yet, conceiving it differently means being able to imagine a different and potentially better society than the current one. But in the absence of expressions and concepts that would materialize such thoughts, any kind of construction of this kind became impossible (Orwell 1961[1949]).

If we look at recent history, we find out that various dictatorships have tried to implement the idea of controlling the human mind over time. The Maoist dictatorship and the totalitarian dictatorship in communist Romania after the Second World War, implemented in prisons experiments designed to control human mind so that it became obedient to some artificially inoculated principles. These experiments included physical and psychological torture that was believed to be able to nullify the informational baggage acquired by the individual through a normal socialization process within a human community (Coillie 1969; Bacu 2016).

Unlike Wittgenstein who describes language games in a logical and somewhat ideational dimension, the mind games presented by Couliano take place in a historical context in which the facts presented are more consistent because they embody factual realities. Maybe that is why this perspective on human historical processes presents a turbulent landscape which is not infrequently loaded with hatred, anxiety, fear, selfishness - widespread feelings in all stratified societies based on social inequalities. This is the territory where both language games and mind games unfold. Couliano tells us that, in fact, for human beings all over the planet, playing this kind of games could have been a way of understanding the complexity and diversity of other people's economic, social, and political reality. This statement has recently been confirmed experimentally by a group of researchers from McGill University and other North American universities, led by Professor Jeffrey Mogil. They demonstrated how a shared gaming experience like the video game *Rock Band* increases empathy between strangers and decreases the stress of all participants (Martin et al. 2015). The idea of freedom, empathy and cooperation is involved by many games/plays, opposing from the start the obedience of rules that had been pre-established by individuals and institutions belonging to state authority. Here is what Couliano says about this:

> Likewise, Western dualism was a mind game that overlapped with the Christian one, and used many of its elements (and characters) to implement itself. It was a game that might have yielded no external consequence, since it existed in its own logical dimension. Yet for well over one millennium it committed its players to certain destruction at the hands of those in power. Early Christian theology and Western dualism were "ideal objects" or systems in a logical dimension, having nothing intrinsically to do with the games of power that were played in their name, which belonged to other dimensions of reality. (Couliano 1992:267)

In his work, Couliano refers to a single historic example that expresses mind games—the theological-hermeneutical debates about the Bible. But he is aware that the areas standing for the use of these expressions are multiple. "Thus practically no sector of the world and human existence can not be defined as a mind game, with certain rules and often uncertain issue" (Idem 1992:267–268). I believe that one of the most convincing examples in this respect is represented by folk plays. When these plays took place within the borders of the rural communities, they embodied various human needs as well as expressions of their freedom in a certain cultural context. That is why acts that were not allowed in everyday life became possible in the world of mumming. The peasants' attachment to these forms of culture was extraordinary because the human mind in general is built to recognize in play its own principles of operation. And mummers' plays were among the most widespread and successful plays in agricultural societies. That is the reason why the church's intervention against them had little impact.

The extraordinary success of mummers in agricultural societies and their extension across all cultures where agriculture was practiced emphasize one more time the profound relation between the human mind and the human *plays/jocuri*. It is about something that lies deeper in humans and connects people deeply to plays, and that is what Couliano calls mind games. Folk plays embody various ways of approaching reality and responses to purely human problems just as language games are used by humans to express various aspects and ideas of the cultural micro-ecosystem where they live their life. Homo Sapiens is essentially a cultural being which uses *play/joc* to organize and understand a reality of very diverse symbols and representations.

For all these reasons, analyzing mummers' plays and their local cultural meaning represents an immense reflexive effort, and demands much more energy, knowledge and wisdom than the brutal attempt of subordinating them to a thinking system that belongs to another cultural ecosystem. I am stating this because the thorough understanding of the whole significance of folk plays for a community could only be possible through a long coexistence of that person with the members of the community performing them. This is because folk plays represent expressions of cultural micro-ecosystems, as it also results from the previous chapters of this study. But, in reality, if ones follow European history, he will rather see a picture of coercion and violence than one of tolerance and understanding of folk plays. The brutal ecclesiastical interdictions of these customs went hand in hand with the attempts to subordinate them by means of an official and institutionalized discourse. This process started immediately after the transformation of Christianity into the state religion of the Roman Empire, ten years after the Edict of Milan in 313 AD, and continued during the entire period of the Middle Ages. If we go far back in time, we learn that in the first decades after Christianity became the official religion of the Roman Empire, the doors were opened to a wave of enraged attacks against all forms of culture that could be identified as expressions of the demonic and the pagan. The entire classical Roman and Greek culture and especially the forms of polytheistic religion were effectively wiped out by these attacks (Nixey 2018). Therefore, it is even astonishing that the mummers' plays managed to survive in this climate loaded with hatred, especially since they were identified as being pagan and even demonic.

> The Swedish folklorist Waldemar Liungman showed in his work investigating the spread of customs among the peoples between the Euphrates and Rhine, so in the Mediterranean area too, that between our plays with masks (the folk plays on the current Romanian territory n.a.) and the plays of Byzantine mimes there are indisputable connections. Or, it is known that at a time when the church begins to impose its domination and control people's behavior, it vehemently condemns these plays as pagan. (Pop 1976:184)

In fact, ecclesiastical interdictions of mummers' plays developed in parallel with the progressive spread of the onstage theater, the emergence of professional theatrical plays and the commodification of the itinerant theater plays. The separation between actants and spectators after the spread of staged performances also represented, among many other implications, an expression of the social inequalities and progressive dissipation of the community model where humans lived most of their time as a species. Despite these outcomes, mummers' plays still survived for centuries in agriculturists' customary communities. The individual's desire to dramatize, his propensity to play, and theater prevailed against obscurantism and intolerance. This was possible mostly because there was a natural attachment of the human mind to the play/*joc*.

Language games and folk plays, both expressing the mind games and the playful/*ludens* nature of the humans, were harmless ways for the human mind to evolve inside the social, political, and economic framework of a community. All these games have permanently embodied an expression of the human spirit's freedom which does not need any stage or lights to express itself; instead, it only needs a human community. This assumption was made by few authors who had studied the topic and who, in most cases, reached the conclusion by traveling different roads (see Bakhtin1984[1968]:7; Helm1969:6; Glassie 1975:93). In Couliano's view, this tendency is not at all accidental. He compares human's speculative systems and doctrines in various contexts with the random combinations of the colorful cubes of architect Frank Lloyd Wright. Just like these colored cubes, doctrines, and theories, like "bricks" that seem to have nothing to do with each other, come sometimes together in strange shapes and create edifices that can resemble enormously between them, even if they are separated by great distances in space and time. This does not prove their common origins, as believed by Belgian scholar Franz Cumont, who struggled for a long time trying to prove that all beliefs in metensomatosis came from India and that Greek Pythagoreans brought them from Iran (Couliano 1992:56).

What political and religious authorities of the past had to suppress was precisely this freedom of human mind, since the individual with a free mind and an unrestricted behavior could neither be controlled, nor manipulated by the official doctrine and ideology. Yet, when the masses could not be controlled, it was very difficult, if not impossible, to build institutions that aimed at imposing and maintaining a set of social inequities. In the past, folk plays have always been community plays. Therefore, the history of their interdiction is, in fact, the history of the subordination of human communities by leviathan-like institutions, be they religious or statal.

FOLK PLAYS AND INDUSTRIAL REVOLUTION

The last and fiercest assault on folk plays takes place with the advent of the Industrial Revolution. With the onset of the industrial mode of production, rural plays do not have the same role as before. The agricultural communities became insular and lost their customary community features. The problems of people within these communities started to be solved rather by state-led institutions than by the communities' rules and traditions. These processes took place gradually, at the same time with a massive peasant migration to the city. Dislocated from their native places due to the development of profitable industries, these peasants became the lumpen proletariat of the great metropolises. They arrived in that world carrying the cultural baggage of the communities where they had grown up.

In his book *The Battle for Christmas*, Stephen Nissenbaum talks about the transformation of Christmas during the 18th and 19th century, from a pagan custom into a festival of domesticity and consumerism. He opens a window to the world of Boston's and Philadelphia's mummers at the end of 18th century and the beginning of the 19th century, and publishes a few documents of that time that vividly depict this landscape. These documents talk about groups of masked bands bearing various names such as anticks, mummers and belsnickels, whose presence was observed during Christmas time. Their activities ranged from playing absurd theater plays to begging, making a lot of noise, drinking and frightening householders with their aggressive behavior. The newspapers of the times published a bunch of articles including letters from ordinary citizens asking the police to act against mummers. Answering such demands, a Boston police inspector urged citizens to take troublesome mummers into custody, promising that these people would be prosecuted as criminals. The same inspector admits the extraordinary resemblance of these mummers' behaviors to Roman Saturnalia manifestations because of which, he thought, they probably bore the name of *Anticks*. In other accounts, the clothes of these carolers are described as ragged and shabby, with some members of the group wearing women outfits—two common elements of mummers, as we remember. Journalists of the time, as well as ordinary citizens, tried to explain the provenance of the mummers, attributing their behavior to the poverty and lack of education of the performers, the mummers' behavior being often described as an expression of the resentment of the poorest city dwellers against the middle class and local bourgeoisie.

From such descriptions of mummers' acts, a connoisseur of their rituals could easily deduce the old motifs these teams played. A witness of these events even mentions that he identified an old English folk play called *St. George and the Dragon*, one of the most famous plays of mummers in England, which includes the moment of death and rebirth of one of the characters—a persistent theme of mummers' plays, as we showed in the previous chapter. Other citizens described the absurd dialogue between the actors, a fact little appreciated by the audience. Nevertheless, as we learned before, this is one of the main features of most mummers' plays. These (anti) social manifestations were considered by the majority of the viewers as a form of begging, while the performers were perceived as vagabonds. The entire phenomenon was (mis)interpreted as an invention of the cities' poorest inhabitants to extort some money from the higher classes' urban dwellers during Christmas time, in a kind of Saturnalia craziness (Nissenbaum 1996).

Without devaluing these interpretations, I daresay all these phenomena embodied a series of once legitimate traditions in the village world, brought to the city by the proletarianized peasantry of the first decades after the beginning of industrialization in the United States. Carried into the cities by dislocated peasants, the mummers lost their natural and rustic charm and were soon viewed just as insolent money extortions. The urban community was dominated by other rules than those at the countryside, and there were other relationships between its members, a fact ignored by the practitioners of these folk plays. The otherwise honorable citizens of the city did not only misunderstand the hidden meanings of these plays, but also gave them other interpretations that had nothing to do with the basic themes of mummers' plays. Their performers were not familiar to the spectators either, as in the village world, and the big social distance between the actors and the spectators also complicated their relationship. All these facts have led to the rejection of the mumming phenomenon in the urban United States in the early decades of industrialization. The same phenomenon occurred under various forms in some other countries where industrialization emerged, with mummers gradually fading away in all these societies.

While mummers were gradually fading away, some other forms of plays started to rise. This is because, with the Industrial Revolution, a different kind of society took shape in those parts of the world where it emerged. These societies were very different from the agricultural world that preceded them. Because of that, the peasants who encountered the industrial world tried to use their *plays/jocuri* to make sense of an unknown universe in which they now had to live. As stated earlier, the *play/joc* can create adaptive mechanisms to societal challenges for those who perform it. The intrusions of mummers into the urban world were in fact the attempts of humans coming from agricultural societies to adapt using their own cultural levers in a society with major challenges. Probably performing mummers' plays in the American cities of the late 18th century offered the participants a momentary satisfaction, representing at the same time a release of the frustrations accumulated over the year by the members of the poorest recently urbanized class. However, this adaptation was not successful in the long run because the culture of the new industrial society and the universe embodied by mummers were different worlds.

The inhabitants of the cities conceived the world using other cultural filters. This was also reflected in the way they reimagined their relationship with the *play/joc,* but also with the market economy based on profit and efficiency. In this new world, the spectacular elements offered by the organized, professional *game/play* began to take precedence over the playful element and the community relations involved in the peasants' plays. The strict rules, the clearly demarcated perimeter of the playfield and a well-defined period during which a game take place became main elements of the plays/games developed during industrialism. If we go deeper into history, we see that the game/play has already become a spectacle beginning with the first societies based on strong state institutions and differentiated into social classes with unequal access to strategic resources, like Ancient Rome, Greece, and China.

Probably the most eloquent expression of the inclusion of the spectacular element in the game/play was represented by the gladiator games performed in the Roman Colosseum. These games expressed the inherent violence of the Roman society, but also the masses' desire to be delighted by the show of brutality. However, these games were never commodified, but sponsored by the upper classes of Rome: "So far as we know, spectators did not pay for their tickets; attendance was one of the perks of citizenship" (Hopkins and Beard 2011:109). Most of the spectators were especially members of the Roman plebs whose revolt was feared by both the Roman emperors and the members of the Roman Senate. Thus, those games became mechanisms of controlling the minds of the poor classes in an urban world marked by oppression and social inequalities, hence the emergence of the slogan "bread and circus." Being organized for state reasons, these games had a logistics superior to the community plays of the farmers. This fact was marked primarily by the appearance of the stage and the clear separation between actors and spectators.[3] This new rigidly delimited space marked the limits that the game had to fit to so that it offered a good view. This visible delimitation, as well as the disposition of the social classes in the coliseum, speaks of a society based on social inequalities where the game serves political purposes.

In contrast, community games—not only mummers' plays, but also rural plays in general like ball games—which may include the ancestors of today's football and rugby, were not initially circumscribed by precise boundaries. Probably this was the major visible difference between the plays/games of the agricultural communities and those organized by the Roman state, instead of the lack of violence which one might think of at first. On the contrary, the ball games played by peasants during Antiquity and the Middle Ages, the so-called mob football, were in some cases very violent and could result in serious injury or even the death of some participants. To have a suggestive image of the way these games were played in the past, we could compare it to the old ball games that have been preserved in some communities and that perpetuate, in a relatively similar form, a series of traditions long gone elsewhere. This category may include the so-called *Ba game* performed at Christmas and New Year in Kirkwall, Orkney Islands Scotland, and also the much better-known *Royal Shrovetide Football* which became the subject of the successful documentary *Wild in The Streets* produced in 2012. Both are variants of the so-called medieval football, a widespread game performed by the peasantry of the Middle Ages. As proof that the origin of football should not necessarily be sought in the UK, we find the community game called *Lelo Burti*, still played by peasants in the village of Shukhuti, western Georgia.

> On game day, the village is split in two—Upper and Lower Shukhuti—and men from each half compete to carry the ball back to their side of town. Once that happens, the game ends. That is it. There are no boundaries, no limit to the number of participants, no real tactics, and almost no rules. Women are not prohibited from playing but rarely do. The game typically lasts a couple hours. Sometimes it rages long into the night. One year it took less than 20 minutes. The rewards may be modest—pride, and a dumpling-shaped ball as heavy as a cinder block—but they are cherished for generations. In all corners of the world, of course, sporting victories are invoked as tributes to the deceased. In Shukhuti, such tributes have become the sole purpose of the game, and they can carry huge weight. (Keh 2019)

Mob football, Ba game, Royal Shrovetide Football and Lelo Burti display striking similarities. They all consist of chaotic fights between two teams composed of an impressive number of players. In all these cases, the core element is a confrontation between two village communities for the possession of an animal skin ball, in the absence of almost any guiding rule. Once in possession of the ball, an attempt is made to bring it to the marking point of the neighboring village, located a few miles away from the one in the first village.

This is how sports games took place in agricultural communities centuries ago, and what can be find today in the countryside are only fragments from a cultural continent of the past dominated by such events. The same landscape can be observed in the case of the Battle of Ruginoasa: unlimited number of participants, rudimentary tactics, few rules, and the ritual occurrence of the custom once per year. As we can see from the previous description of the Lelo Burti game, the boundaries of these games were the boundaries of the community. The rules of the games were in line with community values and were often connected to local rural rituals.

Interestingly, despite their well-organized character, mummers' plays were not the one to become the ideal candidate as games of the working-class culture; this role was taken over by the violent ball games of the peasantry which were organized more rudimentary, but had the potential to become spectacles for a wide audience. Thus, football and rugby, two of the most beloved sports nowadays, emerged from rudimentary, violent peasant games. Of course, they were transformed by the spirit of the new industrial society under its new rules whose firm observance was supervised by an authority imposed on the field and which all players had to obey—the referee. This new role was also an expression of firm rules on the ground that did not accept improvisations or ad-hoc changes during the ongoing game. At the same time, the presence of the referee spoke of a new principle inherent in industrial societies: obedience to authority and respect for superordinate entities. This way, the influences of the industrial society became increasingly visible in the most successful games of the working class.

When referring to the type of participants in the game, can be observed that with the institutionalization of the game, performers became professional. Thus, the main participant is no longer the whole community, but the teams specially trained for this purpose. Additionally, spectators are no longer just members of that community. The spectator becomes someone from whom the organizers of the game—the political authorities and the economic elites—demand a sum of money in exchange for attending the show. At the same time, can be observed a cultural mutation in the taste of the spectators, with a predilection for the show instead of the playful and spontaneous element of the game. If until its institutionalization, the game was performed out of passion and was an expression of the freedom of the human mind, of that ludens mentioned by Huizinga as an expression of the primordial quality of play (1968[1938]:3), afterwards the freedom of the viewer's mind became the target of certain interests. All this becomes visible even if we compare the community plays of the peasants with the institutionalization of games already operated by the great empires, especially during the period Karl Jasper called The Axial Age (800 BC–600 AD) (Jaspers 1968).

However, the industrial period brought along the implementation of a set of unprecedented changes in the dynamics and promotion of games. The game became the target of commodification. Huizinga talks about how "economic forces and material interests determine the course of the world (1968[1938]:192)" and takes over the playful nature of the play. To make commodification of the game possible, it was necessary a reorganization of its principles and rules. The perimeter of the game become strictly circumscribed to a specific area so that the spectators can watch the game from a privileged position. With the imposition of these principles, a part of the human freedom—the ludic and spontaneity the game/play still contained when it performed within agricultural communities—was irretrievably lost.

More, during the industrial period, what used to be the ancient Roman colosseum and other arenas for gladiators' games were replaced by an impressive number of stadiums. The most successful games—football and rugby—started to be played on specially built game perimeters. Working class culture became the cradle of these sports. The first sports clubs were developing in the shadow of large industrial factories. If the games played by peasants involved close human relationships at the community level where spectators and players had equal roles in the dynamics of the game, this changed completely in the era of industrialization. The professionalization of sports also led to the rise of sports stars who end up, in a rapid evolution of only a few decades, on a pedestal where they can hardly be reached by simple spectators (Andrews and Jackson 2002:4). At the same time, the positive parts of this evolution should be mentioned - the practice of inter-club competitions opened the horizon of the limited world where peasants used to live. It was about broadening the intellectual understanding of the diversity of communities in other areas and cities. Therefore, the evolution of the game was closely intertwined with the cultural evolution of human society and represented an important step in the transition from the narrow world of agricultural societies to the much more diverse and complex universe of the urban world (Hessayon 2018).

At the same time, became visible a mutation in perception of society and the world. It is not without reason that this period was called the Scientific Revolution. Science was involving not only in developing a new technology that made possible various types of games for as many spectators as possible, but also in squeezing as much money as possible from the laborers who worked in factories and desired to watch these matches. In addition, a new science developed based on the game, transforming sports events into real shows, with professional players who knew tactics and used them efficiently on the field, and whose skill and performance exceeded by far those of ordinary people. At the same time, we witness the rise of professional clubs that were accessible only after a series of pre-established stages that involved the selection of candidates, the demonstration of the sports talent and the physical qualities necessary for a good player. All these new requirements excluded from the start a whole series of possible players who were thus meant to become spectators who just watch passively the performance of these games.

If we remember the narratives of the first two chapters of this work, in the village world all community members had the chance to join community games and, in fact, everyone could perform an important part in them. However, the evolution of the game towards something different from what it used to be took place quite slowly over more than a century. The number of people who started practicing these new sports outside the stadiums was and has remained high for a long time. For many working-class culture's members, their childhood, was marked by the dream of becoming a real sports star. Even though this became reality for very few, the games were and still are intensely practiced by many people outside of sports clubs, especially in the first part of their life. Thus, human interaction, self-control, physical exercise and social dynamics remained the main components involved in these games, and followed the course of working-class culture for a long time. Even in the case of simple spectators, the attachment to and the identification with local sports clubs were still present in this stream of transformations caused by a new mode of production and its influences on the *game/play* (*joc*). Indeed, in the working-class culture many of the workers become passionate fans of their club teams and thus a cult for supporting and promoting local teams develops (Houlihan and Malcolm 2015).

From the analysis of this information, can be observed that one feature of games/plays it remains unchanged. It is the *ritual* that has accompanied them throughout their cultural evolution. As the reader remember from the first part of this study, folk plays were performed ritually, usually only a few days each year, and preparing them involved the development of an entire logistics that would secure good conditions. All these sequences were preserved in the structure of games created later in the working-class culture. The ritual was kept not only in the case of players who had to follow a certain kind of training and to respect the organization of the game and the rules on the field. It remains present in the case of spectators, too. This is because the matches take place only on certain days and at precise times set some time in advance. The activities carried out around the game—buying tickets, entering the stadium—and the rules of conduct for both players and spectators are also carried out according to pre-established rituals. Even if all this satisfies one great purpose - the desire for spectacle—it is worth emphasizing that ritual accompanies closely the game at this stage of human cultural evolution. The presence of the ritual maintains a series of principles and values for the relationship of humans with the game. Simultaneously, through play it cemented several human features of human societies such as the ability to organize social groups, the construction of social networks in relation to the daily experience, the interrelationship, the capacity of self-reflection and self-analysis in relation to society's needs. All this reconfirms an assertion related to Wittgenstein's philosophy of language games: sports games can also be seen as forms of life because they are activities that give rise to complex interactions between beings endowed with intelligence.

At this point, another important observation needs to be made. Starting with the commodification of the game, the mind games involved in the development of these activities are increasingly replaced by power games. Human creativity does not simply disappear, but is transferred to other areas which are commodified, too. In this new context, the market economy itself becomes a Wittgensteinian form of life that exists independently of the goals and interests of the players who are involved in it. The economy has a kind of independence that Karl Polanyi has already noticed in his substantivist economics when he talks about the Satanic mill. This Satanic mill sometimes grinds the souls of those who enter the game which, Polanyi tells us, happened in the first stage of industrialization especially with the proletarianized peasants who became victims of a new mode of production based on the market economy (Polanyi 1944). In turn, the market economy itself is a kind of organism with a life independent and separate from the will and interests of the players involved in it. In market economy, those who try to increase their financial capital by participating in the stock market and other ways of invest-ing money understand from the beginning that they are actually involved in a game. It is a game they can either lose or win. But in essence it is about their participation in a gearing that can be defined without hesitation as a game with an uncertain result and that can lead to the physical or moral destruction of those involved in it, maybe even more than the mind games described by Couliano in relation with religion.

At this stage, we are not only witnessing the commodification of the game, but also its secularization. Performed only a few days a year and linked to an agricultural and religious cycle, folk plays contained an aura of sacredness, which is why their performance on dates other than those established by tra-dition was strictly forbidden. With the commodification of the game, it was not only its playful element that disappeared, but its magic, too. Economy and especially its engine - money - are not only games with very strict rules, but also social convention almost unanimously accepted on all corners of the globe, beyond cultures, political orientations, religious currents, and moral visions (Harari 2015). While economy itself becomes a playground, "the real play-spirit is threatened with extinction" (Huizinga 1968[1938]:199).

A BRIEF CULTURAL HISTORY OF HUMANS' PLAYS/GAMES FROM EARLY TIMES TO INDUSTRIAL REVOLUTION

Before proceeding to the analysis of the latest evolutions of the game/play, I will clarify one of the previous statements that could cause confu-sion. Following Huizinga, I strengthen the assertion that, with the Industrial Revolution, one could witness a decline in the playful element of culture, together with a progressive loss of human freedom. This has to do with a series of elements that involve spontaneity, charm, and magic. A contradiction result from a fact already demonstrated by peasant studies: the small-scale agriculturist was far from having a free and unrestricted life within peasant societies. On the contrary, the family and the community established, based on group interests, the premises of an important series of events such as the choice of a life partner, the type of work performed in the household, the role of that person in the community. Even more trivial aspects of the individual's life such as wearing a certain type of clothing, accepting people to his/her circle of friends, and duration of going out in public were strictly regulated by family and community. Instead, the family provided the conditions that warranted the individual's survival in the rural community.

A 21st century city dweller could hardly perceive such a picture as an expression of freedom. It really took a revolution to unleash the individual from the community reins and give him the opportunity to choose his own job, lifestyle, partner, and many other aspects of his life. All these were made possible by the Industrial Revolution (Harari 2015:402–405). From this wider landscape results a great paradox that could be summarized by a question: how is it possible that in a society—the peasant society—that restricts the individual in many aspects of his private life, one could enjoy such an exceptional freedom and spontaneity when playing? To answer this difficult question, ones need to understand how the play/game has evolved and what it has meant to human society over time. This is because the play/game can be seen as a lens through which human societies are seen, and thus it is inextricably linked to the way mind is shaped. At the same time, we can understand what happens to the play/game by analyzing the economic and cultural features of a community.

For example, in hunter-gatherer societies like Bushmen communities, the game/joc played a crucial role. All members of the community were involved in different kind of plays when they were not hunting and gathering. Plays in Bushmen bands were dominated by improvisation, spontaneity and an outpouring of exuberance which represented a pure expression of human freedom. But if we look at their degree of complexity we see rudimentary forms, little elaborated and lacking in depth. Bushmen plays can be reduced to three categories: the games, the plays, and the dances. Their enumeration shows us how all these are expressions of their surrounding universe: the pantomime of some hunting scenes; the imitation of some animals in their wild life; dances in circle accompanied by clapping; throwing objects in the air and catching them in flight; practicing shooting with a bow and arrow (Doke 1936; Uys 1980). Their game represents the pure playful element that is also not regulated by any higher instance, often taking place on the spur of the moment, without restrictions, but also without too many rules.

With the Agricultural Revolution, the idea of accumulating resources resulted from the agricultural crops appears for the first time in human history. This automatically involved the idea of systematizing, calculating, counting, and sharing these goods among community members who worked together in the production process. These mathematical operations, together with the invention of writing, led to the liberation of the human mind from the constraints of nature and triggered its unprecedented development (Goetzman 2016). In addition to these aspects, the "[e]mergence of agriculture has opened the doors to the development of human communities and personal safety, thus more experiences being required for the development of self-control. At the same time, this ability became more important than ever, as a peasant had to plan much longer periods of time than a hunter-gatherer" (Spitzer 2020). Long-term economic planning led to the emergence of more sophisticated games that involved, in turn, more laborious mental activities. All this led to an elaboration of the individuals' self-control.

Let us remember from the first part of this study the elaborate planning and logistics needed to organize the *Play of the Deer* or the *Play of the Goat*. Comparing these plays with those performed by Bushmen, we see a whole series of differences, but we find similarities, too. The playful element and the involvement of the whole community remain common elements in both societies. However, in the case of the peasants' plays we saw more elaborate logistics and a more complex planning. At the same time, we observed a social stratification that appeared in the plays, with poorer members of the community, adolescents, and children more involved as actors, and richer members rather acting as hosts who received players in their yards. Besides, we observed how ritual regulates the performance of the game only during certain days of the calendar.

On the other hand, the distance between spectators and players is absent in both hunters-gatherers and agriculturists societies. In both types of games all members of the community could take part regardless of their social status. But if we compare the plays performed by peasants with those of the first great empires, such as the Greek Olympics and the games in the Roman Colosseum, we see how the latter became more elaborate and consolidated the barrier between spectators and players, consequently diminishing the playful element of the game in favor of the spectacular element. At the same time, social inequalities became increasingly visible in the games, both through the rigorous selection of those who played the game and the arrangement of social classes in arenas—those with a higher status in the best positions, and those with a lower social status occupying the positions from where visibility was lower during the match. However, these games are more elaborate and involve a well-demarcated playfield.

The professionalization of the game/play and the clear distinction between spectators and players became even more visible with the commodification of games that occurred during the Industrial Revolution. Starting with the end of the 19th century, the act of watching the game begins to be sold to spectators as a commodity. This was also possible because of a clear delimitation of the playfield and the space outside the game. The rules of the game became more rigorous, and their violation was no longer possible because they became basic components of the game itself. The playful element gradually disappeared because the spontaneity, innovation, or the involvement of the spectator in the game was now impossible. While all of this happened for now professionalized sports games, the same was not true in the case of street games. The practice of games by children of the working-class members kept that playful element that Huizinga believed to be lost. Even games with strict rules such as football and handball, once transferred to the children's culture, became more malleable, and could even accept a series of rules created ad-hoc by the players themselves. And, most often, they were also played without a referee. In addition, children's culture retains elements of the game that existed in the Middle Ages or even earlier. Spontaneous dance, the primitive dramatization of life scenes, pantomime—all of which were ubiquitous in the culture of hunter-gatherers—would still be found in the culture of children in workers' societies. However, they got a rather insignificant place in the mainstream culture of industrial societies, since they had been almost entirely commodified and professionalized in the adult culture.

Referring for a moment to the evolution of language games, can be observed that they are also the consequence of a long process that culminates with the emergence of national languages resulting from the hard work of leading intellectuals of the 19th century. Only with the development of these pragmatic and comprehensive national languages, language games such as those described by Wittgenstein could emerge. It is obvious that, for a member of the Ponca tribe or for a Bushmen, language games represent a foreign territory. This is because the hunter-gatherers' languages proceeded by describing reality in very elaborate details. The same idea that a modern language such as English would express clearly and precisely in a short sentence such as: "A man killed a rabbit," would be expressed by a Ponca Indian in a very elaborate way: "He, one, animated, standing, purposedly killed, by shooting an arrow, the rabbit, he, the one, animate, sitting . . . " (Powell 2015[1879]).

Therefore, language games were, in fact, possible only in modern, comprehensive languages. This was mainly due to their pragmatic aspect, their multiple interpretations regarding the cultural context as well as social and professional status of the person making the assertion. All these observations allow us to understand how certain major cultural changes lead to redesigning games in human cultures, while humans always find other cultural outlets to manifest their freedom and follow the natural course of their mind flow, a mind intrinsically connected to game/play. This large picture can explain how the human freedom manifested through play/game, apparently lost with the cultural evolution of humans, has always managed to find other territories to express itself. Bushmen whose freedom in play was almost unlimited had a much more limited freedom of thought because their minds did not have to calculate too many things and their language, anchored in realities that were too concrete, allowed them little speculation on more complex issues. On the other hand, the extremely restricted private lives of agriculturalists allowed them less freedom in this area, but their plays acted as a valve through which this freedom could flow. In the end, the human games/plays of industrial societies employed much less ludic elements than those of farmers, but human freedom was much greater in market economy, private life, language, and science—all of which became more elaborate during this period.

The common element that comes out of the analysis of this large picture is the fact that the freedom through play lost during the Industrial Revolution was looking for other "lands" to express itself. Another observation is that, with the development of the working culture, the highly successful games of the moment ask the spectator to be rather passive. At the same time, they are much more elaborate and endowed with more complex rules which makes it more difficult to understand their logic. However, even in this case, the ritualization, the social communication, the construction of social networks in relation to the game, the interrelation based on game, the capacity of self-reflection and self-analysis in relation to the game remained essential characteristics of the industrialism games/plays. Thus, over time, play has been a permanent companion of human communities, promoting values including those related to sociability, cooperation, and networking that have always occupied an important place in humans' lives. In the following section, I analyze the latest evolutions of the game/play, especially those that occurred with the development of television and the Internet, and I explain their implications on the human mind and their ability to eliminate pre-existing forms of play.

MODERN TECHNOLOGY—A GAME CHANGER

The road to the stadium, the interaction of the spectators, and watching the match itself at the stadium, involved a set of rituals without which the access to the games became impossible in the early stages of Industrial Revolution. By the 20th century, the entire history of socialization through plays/games took an unexpected turn. This occurred because of the mass spread of sports games and of their presentation to the general public through written press at first, then, by the 1900s—through the radio. Thus, this new step in the evolution of game/play globalized the idea of the game/play and a broader understanding of the world, now seen as a set of global interactions between teams representing clubs, countries, cities, or regions around the world. Again, the idea of transcending the boundaries of small communities and their values which used to be limited to a specific social context, was fully involved in these new technological discoveries. Nevertheless, in addition to opening the world, technical progress also brought a series of negative aspects that started to become more obvious by the middle of the 20th century.

With the growing success of television (Bruckner 2000) and the primacy of the image transmitted via television before the written word (Sartori 2005[1997]:17–21), the relation between humans and games/plays started to change radically. Gradually, play bids farewell to ritual. The spectator no longer needs to go to the stadium. The game becomes a pure entertainment that can be consumed at home as an image, without involving any form of socialization (Bruckner 2000). In other words, what once used to represent interpersonal interactions involving communities needs through play, could become a harmful addiction with the spread of television. These processes progressively led to the atomization of individual, as he is placed in front of "a box with images" through which the game can be accessed at any time, while his mind is programmed to take part in the game. Thus, problems arise when there is no longer a social-moral instance like a community, meant to restrict the continuous exploration of all these possibilities without any interdictions. At that moment, the propensity of the human mind to play and the continuous investigation of all its possibilities turns into addiction. In his book *The Temptation of Innocence: Living in the Age of Entitlement*, Pascal Bruckner observes this phenomenon when he describes how the TV box attracts humans and can destroy them just as the light bulb attracts and kills night butterflies:

> Anyone who has not experienced the atrocious, the irresistible temptation to spend the whole night frantically surfing from one channel to another, without being able to tear himself away from the ribbon of images, does not understand how strong is the magic in this little window. There is always something more interesting going on at the station than in our life. Television's hypnotic power lies in the fact that it roasts us with its light like butterflies around a lamp: it produces continuous jets of flowing colors and impressions that we suck down with a never-ending thirst. Television is an animated piece of furniture and it speaks, it serves the function of making dullness bearable. (Bruckner 2000)

The emergence of television blew up all this scaffolding composed of: game/play-ritual-human interactions, and the one fascinated by games can access them anytime. Thus, in the absence of rituals, of specific dates for watching them and of the human interactions involved by play/games, modern games could become a source of compulsive and unhealthy behavior for their viewers. In line with the same criticism, Giovani Sartori talks about the humans' imbecilitating through television. In his view, television changes the nature of *Homo Sapiens* and transforms him into a *Homo Videns* by imposing the primacy of the television image, thus predisposing to a lack of reflection:

> We are in the full and extremely fast multimedia revolution. A process with many tentacles (Internet, personal computers, cyberspace) which is characterized by a common denominator: tele-view, and thus a tele-living of ourselves. So, in this book the fire focuses on television, and the basic thesis is that the video phenomenon turns Homo Sapiens, produced by the written culture, in

a Homo Videns, in which the word is deposed by the image. Everything gets
visualized (Sartori 2005[1997]:11).

But the final brick to this set of new technological inventions would be laid
with the advent of computers, video games and, finally, the smartphone most
often connected to the Internet (Spitzer 2020[2012]), which have all created
a number of (virtual) communities that did not exist before (Turkle 2017).
All these started to change the relationship of the people with the play/
game, with their own community/society, and with themselves. In his book
Digital Dementia, Manfred Spitzer adopt a critical stance against the emergence of modern forms of technology that can negatively affect the human
mind and lead to social atomization. According to Spitzer, practicing social
skills, constructing social networks, connecting the individual mind with
community norms and values, and exercising self-control and rigor in thinking are increasingly endangered by the emergence of new technologies that
essentially change people's relationship with play and with society. Our brain
is above all a social brain. However, in social media networks self-control
decreases a lot because the individual can use various anonymous identities
protecting him from other ones' counter-reactions that he would face if the
dialogue took place in reality instead of a virtual environment. Thus, the virtual environment predisposes to violence precisely because the barriers that
exist in face-to-face communication are erased. The same is true for video
games that lead to desensitization against physical violence in the real world.
Community games like folk plays impose the idea of self-control from the
start and thus train cognitive flexibility. On the contrary, video games lead
to self-isolation and ultimately to stress because the social component—
part of any game throughout the cultural evolution of humans—is missing.
Frequently and indiscriminately used, digital media impede the development
of self-control in relation to human society, predispose to violence, cause
stress, and ultimately lead to digital dementia (Spitzer 2020[2012]).

This discouraging landscape is completed by Sherry Turkle, a sociology
professor at MIT, in her book *Alone Together*. Turkle demonstrates how
online social networking like Facebook and Twitter allow us to present
the self as we want it to be. While face-to-face conversations take place in
real time and cannot be controlled, the online medium allows people to get
immersed in an artificial environment where they get reinforcements for
their own ideas, so that they hear just what they want to hear. This creates a
kind of echo chamber where they do not learn new things as they only get
confirmations of their own statements from people who share the same ideas.
This medium creates the illusion of companionship without the demands of
friendship and leads in the end to loneliness and isolation from the real world.
Moreover, it suppresses people's capacity of self-reflection as they don't

take time for mental reflections anymore. This is indeed concerning because self-reflection is one of the most valuable characteristics that people acquire, and it is exercised only when they are able to sit with themselves and analyze their own thoughts (Turkle 2017).

Life experience has given me the chance to meditate a few times on these issues. I had such a revelation in January 2020 when, traveling from London to Nottingham and waiting for the bus at Victoria station, I looked around me and noticed that all the young people and children around were immersed in their iPhones, while older people were engaged in discussions, eating a sandwich or looking at the world around them. I thought back then that, paradoxically enough, if an unexpected danger occurred there, the best prepared to react immediately would be the elders. While I was meditating at all this, a man in his 60s approached me and started a small dialogue about the journey we were going to make and other insignificant daily issues. Starting a dialogue with a stranger in a bus station requires a dose of courage. Reactions can be unpredictable, just as the course of the discussion. However, in the end one can learn new things about the people and the realities around. Why are young people less and less tempted to do such an exercise? And in the end, what attracts them so much to their iPhones? Passing by such a group of young people, I saw that most of them accessed Facebook, Instagram, Twitter, and children were engaged in video games. That was when I started to realize something very simple: the play, the community and the story are altogether inside the iPhone today.

Throughout the entire cultural evolution of our species, until just two decades ago, our communities were not our creation. We happened to be born in a certain community and we had to make efforts to integrate better into its social life. With the invention of the iPhone and online social networks, this history ceased. Of course, it ended after a lengthy process that started long ago. It began with the atomization of tribal communities, then of peasant societies, and finally of working-class cultures that had been very cohesive from the beginning of the Industrial Revolution to the restructuring of heavy industry and the development of global capitalism in the second half of the 20th century. All these processes went hand in hand with the emergence of an increasing individualism. With the iPhone, video games and social networks like Facebook, the individualism that appeared after the industrialization has been doubled by an atomization process. The young people from Victoria bus stop were no longer present with their minds in the surrounding reality. The iPhone gave them the chance to escape from everyday life and also to live in the communities they had created themselves. These communities have the quality of being carried around inside one's pocket all the time. For what else does it mean to have a Facebook account than to be part of a tribal community sharing one's own values, rules and interests—however, in the end, a tribal community created by oneself—and at the same time a strange community whose messages and plays can be accessed at any time without going through any ritual or obeying any minimum social conventions.

I also wondered where this needs to have one's own community close by at any time come from. If we look at human history, who were the ones who always lived all the time in the midst of their own community? Weren't they hunter-gatherers? Even in the most cohesive rural communities, there were many moments when individuals carried out activities only with the family, or sometimes even individuals alone, in the field or in the vicinity of the village. The same is true for the humans of modern societies whose contact with their own community can often be extremely scarce. So, hunter-gatherers were the only people in human history who have always lived with their own community, a community in which they have always been accepted and whose plays were community plays and have always included all its members. Hence, the question of whether or not these modern technologies allowed human access precisely to a state of affairs that seemed lost forever in the mists of history, does not seem to be absurd. In his book *The Sacred and the Profane*, the historian of religion Mircea Eliade made the statement that even in modern societies that declare themselves secular or anti-religious "we can discern traces of the 'nostalgia for Eden,' the desire to re-establish the paradisal state before the Fall, when sin did not yet exist and there was no conflict between the pleasures of the flesh and conscience" (Eliade 1959). Eliade offers the examples of purely modern expressions like nudism or the movements for complete sexual freedom. But, perhaps more eloquently than the movements Eliade mentions, social media communities in the pockets of young people express not necessarily a nostalgia for the biblical paradise, but most certainly a desire to live a life in the middle of an original cohesive community, now lost in time.

FROM MUMMERS' PLAYS TO VIDEO GAMES

Meditating on all this, I also wondered if there could be certain parallels between mummers' plays and video games. This is perhaps one of the strangest and difficult questions I have raised throughout this study. The answer became even more complicated as video game is the field that has experienced the most spectacular evolution in the last two decades, a fact that I examine in the following lines. Analyzing the possibilities expressed in the question just launched, I was surprised to find that, despite obvious discrepancies, there are many similarities between mummers' plays and video games.

It is primarily about the players assuming a different identity than the current one. Let's remember from the previous chapters the way mummers changed their personality once they put on the mask. Or, assuming various roles under the anonymity of the mask is one of the oldest human activities. The Bushmen plays as well as the simplest children' plays embodied the adoption of various roles which are assumed by those who are involved in them as if they were real. The same thing happens in video games, with the only difference that those who play them no longer wear a mask. However, the phenomenon of identity change is practically the same and the realistic setting of the latest games such as *Bloodborne, Horizon Zero Dawn, The Last of Us* or *Ghost of Tsushima* make it possible today for players to easily assume the role of the character they lead through hundreds of possible paths offered by the virtual reality of the game. The versatile players of these games claim that, as in non-virtual games, these virtual creations offer the possibility of deeply human moral choices in front of the challenges posed in the game. Or, games like *Horizon Zero Dawn* really give players the chance to choose how the main character—Aloy—responds to the challenges that rise along the way: with compassion, aggression or logic. All this proves that in the case of both mummers' plays and video games, the players wear different personalities and experience various human situations during the game.

Even older video games that had a single main character and a predetermined path, benefited from the extraordinary flexibility of the human mind and its ability to naturally embrace various identities made possible by the game. I remember how, in the early 1990s, when I first saw *Street Fighter*, considered a complex video game at that time, the first question I asked a friend of mine who was playing was: *Which one is you?* And he answered me nonchalantly, pointing to the screen: *That one!*

As absurd in terms of scenario and action as mummers' plays, video games fascinate the human mind. A rational and outward reflection on some of the video games such as *Sven, Mister Mosquito, Icarus Proudbottom* or *Captain Novolin* makes one wonder about the mental health of those who created them. But at a closer look, they exploit topics such as sexuality, violence, embarrassment, illness, death, immortality, and the fight between good and evil—universal human themes that have been explored by most of the mummers' plays. Their most striking aspect is that, once one starts playing and getting involved, one gets caught up in their internal logic and, as a result, the apparent absurdity of their scenarios disappears.

Another recurring theme of video games is the main character's—the hero—overcoming of multiple barriers, often facing monsters, dragons, and demons. All these ideas appear both in mummers' plays and in many of the peasants' tales. The hero's initiating journey to a miraculous land, sprinkled with adventures and hard trials, is also found both during the mummers' wanderings through the village and in the texts of the mummers' stanzas who talk about various attempts that strengthen the hero and cement his strong character. Furthermore, the moment of the main character's resurrection—a common theme in mummers' play—appears very often in video games. In many of these video games, the hero, exhausted from fighting dragons and monsters, searches for his energy "goblet" in various corners of the virtual reality, and once he finds it, he continues his adventure with new and powerful energies. Incredible similarities, especially with the *Play of the Deer*, are observable here when the main character in the play falls as dead to the ground, and then finds a miraculous form of energy in the shaman's enchantment that makes him get up and dance with even more vitality than before. In both cases, one can notice expressions of magical thinking that make human or animal characters come to life when they hear enchantments or when they find a source of miraculous "living water."

Looking at the controversies created by video games, we find here a series of similarities to mummers' plays, too. A video game with huge popularity like *Pokemon*, for instance, has been the subject of moral dilemmas and tensions in various countries around the globe. The game has been accused of promoting cruelty against animals, by cultivating violent, occult, and anti-Christian themes, or of using symbols that contradict the doctrines of various religions such as Buddhism, Judaism, and Islam. All this culminated with the legal banning the game in Saudi Arabia in 2001 on the grounds that it promoted several themes and symbols that were against Muslim faith (www .express.co.uk, July 21, 2016). All these episodes remind about the outsiders' misunderstandings regarding mummers' plays throughout history. As some authors mentioned (du Cange 1678; Pop 1976:184), these folk plays were perceived as absurd and irrational and their practice has always awakened negative feelings and inflammatory accusations from those who had lived far from these customs, but had the power of decision in certain societies. Just as today, when powerful state institutions tried to ban the practice of certain computer games, the ecclesiastical institutions of the Middle Ages tried to stop mummers' plays through various edicts. As we know, the success of these edicts was extremely limited, just like nowadays when any severe criticism conducted by state or church institutions against computer games led to a significant increase in the global sale of those games as well as in their number of players. Moreover, in my fieldwork, my interviewees have always talked about their addiction to folk plays. The same way, video games generate dependence and sometimes addiction.

Well, at this point, the series of analogies between mummers' plays and the games produced by modern technology are breaking apart. In the past, mummers' plays were regulated by tradition and their practice was only ritualistic. Any transgression of this rule was harshly charged or even punished by the community. The community established the place and date of the performance of these rituals, and the individuals addicted to them had to wait for a full year to enjoy playing them just for a few days (Pop 1976:86). As we have seen in the first three chapters of this study, mummers' plays always involved collective action and complex sets of social relationships. They also implicate complex forms of communication between the individual and other members of the community, while in most of the video games this element disappears. Moreover, participants in video games are no longer the games' creators and the games no longer involve interaction with other people like mummers' plays used to entail.

No matter how many thousands of possible virtual paths a video game could offer, they are still circumscribed by the game designers to a model that cannot be reshaped by the creativity of the participants. That is why sometimes there are heated debates on social media between fans of the games where some of the players are harshly criticized for revealing secrets of certain video games. This shows that, in fact, the contribution of the participants in the game is and must be limited to buying and playing the game, excluding a creative involvement in the development and perpetuation of the game in the future under a more complex form. All these aspects prove that the main motivation behind the creation of such games is a financial one and has nothing to do with the wellbeing of the players and the values of a community. For this reason, the basic elements that predominate in these video games, as in the case of the other highly successful games of the Industrial Revolution, are the entertainment and spectacular ones. A video game would have no success if it presented the dull life of workers in a factory or that of peasants working the field. That's why, in most cases, video games include engaging stories that often involve fighting, violence, sexuality, mystery, action—all important ingredients that contribute to their commercial success. The marketization of the play/game has, in many cases, led to the abolition of the connection between the individual and the community, strangling human creativity, as Thomas Malaby observed:

> Further research would be needed to evaluate the nature of this ludo-capitalism, but along with the use of games to attempt to colonize creativity, we should also notice the implicit distinction here between "players" and the sponsoring institutions that create the conditions for such play. What we are beginning to see is the bifurcation of creativity, separating those who are creative within a ludic system from those game designers creatively contriving the ludic system itself. (Malaby 2009:216)

This analogy between mummers' plays and video games is meant to show that the vanishing or the dramatic decline of mummers after their long-lasting centuries old success in the agrarian societies is, in fact, an illusion. Those that have disappeared are just the folk plays in the agrarian societies, and not "the mummers" in people's minds. This statement may seem difficult to understand at a first glance. But in the light of Wittgenstein's theory, and especially of Couliano, things become clearer. The competition between mummers' plays, sport competitions and video games, is for the same "patch of land," to use a metaphor. It is about that part of the human consciousness by which humans as social beings are inextricably linked to *play/joc*, in all its forms and expressions, from theater to dance, from pantomime to competition, and from fun to logic. Humans' ways of adapting to the surrounding economic, political and social reality through games/plays are multifarious, as Couliano observed. At a certain moment, he argued that these systems tend to overlap in some parts, and maybe this could be one reason why we can find so many similarities between mummers' plays and video games.

> [M]ind games have necessarily similar mechanisms (because the way the mind works and its capacity have remained unchanged for at least sixty thousand years), and therefore systems that have been sufficiently run in time would tend to overlap not only in shape but also in substance. With complex data at hand, we should be able to demonstrate that portions of the map of the Buddhist system would overlap with portions of the Christian system with portions of German idealism with portions of modern scientific thought, because all systems are infinite and tend to explore all possibilities given to them. Accordingly, when sufficiently extended, their maps of reality would certainly coincide. (Couliano 1992:268)

As I have underscored in the paragraphs above, the human mind's tendency to theatricalize and play based even on rules that are apparently absurd, has not been replaced by the advent of market economy and consumer culture. Only the place of mummers' plays inside the human mind has been taken over by other expressions and forms, for example the video games, when society changed its mode of production and its system of values. These *games/jocuri*, accessed anytime and anywhere by means of modern technology—depleted the rigor of the ritual rules and cycles firmly imposed in the past by the agricultural communities—have quite often turned into a dangerous addiction with harmful effects on the behavior and social life of human beings. Therefore, in the absence of firm rules implemented by the community, the relation between humans and game may become addictive and pathological. This fear is shared by both psychiatrists and sociologists such as Manfred Spitzer and Sherry Turkle. But things must always be seen from multiple and nuanced perspectives. In the case of video games, there were players who said that due to video games they gained more perseverance and self-confidence, and these in turn helped them find the solution to difficult problems that at one point in their personal lives seemed overwhelming. The experience provided by video games is that of learning how to overcome obstacles in order to achieve a goal, and in this way the will of humans to move forward in their life is cultivated despite the difficulties and obstacles that arise, followers of video games say (Zaiafet 2020).

The comparison between mummers' plays, social networks such as Facebook and video games may seem to be the most surprising part of this study. But let us not forget that folk plays were among the most successful plays of the agriculturalists. Agricultural societies and their development in time eventually led to the Scientific Revolution. And the rural plays had, of course, their part in this successful enterprise. As we have seen, with the Industrial Revolution they were replaced by other, more spectacular, dynamic, and elaborate games.

VIDEO GAMES VERSUS FOLK PLAYS

If some questions related to development of new technologies would be difficult to find their answer yet, the fieldwork provided me with the opportunity to understand deeply the relationship between folk plays and video games. On the afternoon of January 1, 2015, my host in Oboroceni received the visit of several families. One of these was that of Nicoleta and Mihai Cosma and their children, Ștefan, a ten-year-old boy, and Ioana, a seven-year-old girl. Back then, they lived in Bacău, one of the most developed urban centers in Moldova region. Mihai was the younger brother of Mrs. Doina, my host. From the family's discussions, I learned that among the six children of the Cosma family, Mihai had been the most diligent at school. Thus, after finishing an elite high school and the College of Economics in Iași city, he started to work in the banking sector and, after several promotions, became bank inspector. His wife Nicoleta also worked in the financial field as accountant. In other words, they were the kind of family their acquaintances regarded as successful, and that had a very good financial situation, a rarity in the troubled and uncertain postsocialist world. However, instead of spending their winter holiday in a foreign country at a luxury resort, Mihai's family spent it in Oboroceni village every year, waiting for the mummers' visit. However, I noticed that the two kids, Ștefan and Ioana, were less fascinated by mummers than by their last generation Mac tablet with many video games installed on.

Shortly after being invited inside the house, the guests took a seat at the table of my host and started chatting in front of a glass of wine. But, just half an hour later, another family, this time from the same village, came to visit the Hâra family home. They were Roxana and Mitică Alexa, the godchildren of the Hâra family. They were also accompanied by their two sons: Robert, seven years old, and Andrei, four years old. The two children had become the undisputed celebrities of the Deer team who had participated in several folklore festivals during the previous two years. Their age and especially their stage performance as masters of the Deer, reciting the incantation in the animal's ear, probably contributed to the success of the Heleşteni band that had thus won several awards at these festivals. This was a reason of great local pride. Perhaps that was why the mayor, as host, immediately introduced the two children and their parents to the other guests. In the following moments, the two children were asked to interpret the incantation of the Deer for the present guests. Mitică seemed to have foreseen the situation, so the two children had come with their bear-leader drums. The subsequent representation was full of liveliness and exuberance, managing to cheer up the atmosphere. The scene was completed by a series of wishes and carols recited by Robert, the older one, already considered a master of the local winter traditions.

The wonderful recital performed by the two members of the Deer team won many applauses and praises. Finally, some of the guests even offered money to these two veritable tradition promoters. But I observed how the entire scene made the two children of the Cosma family watch the performance with envy. The children of the Cosma family had their own merits: Ştefan was a national champion in swimming and Ioana had good results in school, but these talents could neither compete with the skills of the Deer "masters," nor be appreciated within the caroling and mumming atmosphere of the Heleşteni's Winter Holidays. However, these moments did not last more than 20 minutes, after which the whole group of children retreated to the room nearby. About half an hour after the recital, I saw them interacting with each other. Ştefan seemed to have introduced Robert to his iPad's secrets. And Robert, who had never seen a tablet before, was so fascinated that at one point he laid his head on Ştefan's chest so that he would not lose any "event" on the iPad's display. There were video games and other apps that totally fascinated Robert. Thus, in just two hours, Robert had learned some of the tablet's secrets, and continued to ask Ştefan many questions about other functions and icons he did not understand.

However, the time had come for the family to go home. Robert's parents had already taken their clothes, and the departure was about to happen in a few minutes. Realizing that this departure meant separating from the iPad, Robert seemed very disappointed, and I think I even spotted a sense of despair on his face. Right away, I saw him going to the next room and coming back with his drum in hand. He immediately approached Ştefan and, without a word, gave him the drum. At the same time, he looked at the tablet, probably hoping he would get it in exchange for his bear-leader drum. The scene impressed me deeply. In Robert's hope, I had sensed all the aspirations of the village emigrants giving their rural world away for the brightness and fascination exerted by the lights of a modern urbanized society. Finally, I could thus catch a glimpse of the entire history of rural plays in the last decades, and of their transformation from community rituals to simple representations inside the cyber-space and among television images.

CONCLUSION

Human beings have a dualistic nature consisting of a physical self and a symbolic self, which could create confusion about their real nature. Moreover, these two realms are different from each other: the symbolic self involves imagination, beliefs, symbolism, ideologies, and freedom of thought while the physical self represents the world of nature, its determinism, and restraints, tell us, Ernest Becker, in his book *The Denial of Death* that brought him the Pulitzer Prize. The peculiarity of humans is related to the fact that they must always live between these two worlds, following the requirements and principles that come from both. For this reason, their mental health can only be kept by maintaining an adequate involvement in both realms without neglecting one to the detriment of the other. On the one hand, a distance from

Figure 5.1. Robert giving his bear-leader drum to Ştefan whose Mac tablet he was fascinated with—January 1, 2015.
Photo credit: Alin Rus

the symbolic part of the self, from ideologies and beliefs, including immortality projects, leads to depression, neurosis, and anxiety. On the other hand, being too close to the symbolic self, an unnatural attachment to the ideologies created by our minds and the idea of immortality, leads to narcissism and schizophrenia. Becker elaborates all these ideas in his most important book, "The Denial of Death." The main argument of his work tells us that the whole human civilization is only an ideological answer in front of the consciousness of death. Unfortunately, Becker analyzes the game only fleetingly when dealing with neurosis. "The neurotic opts out of life because he is having trouble maintaining his illusions about it, which proves nothing less that life is possible only with illusions" (Becker 1997:189). Becker then makes an unexpected connection between the play and the imaginary constructions of the symbolic self: "The quality of cultural play, of creative illusion, varies with each society and historical period. In other words, the individual can more easily cross the line into clinical neurosis precisely where he is thrown back on himself and his own resources in order to justify his life" (Idem:190).

In his book *Philosophical Investigations*, Wittgenstein also emphasizes the connections between the human mind and the realm of language games, which is also a significant part of our symbolic self. He pointed out that there can be no final definition of games because all of them are expressions of *forms of life* that is the way humans interact through their experience with other members of their society. Therefore, the game is a mechanism used by humans to adapt to the requirements and cultural needs of their communities.

Rural plays also represented life forms through which community members interacted with each other on the canvas of a community culture with precise rules and values. That is why it is almost impossible to subscribe games/plays to a concept. Human experience in the society and human ways of interacting with other members of the community are innumerable and, at the same time, were different from one community to another in rural Europe before the Industrial Revolution. At the limit, rural plays are coextensive with the experience of the humans living between the borders of their own rural culture.

From the perspective of Becker's work, and taking into account the arguments of this chapter, a simple conclusion can be drawn: humans are creatures of fantasy and imagination, while the diversity of human play/games (jocuri) is an expression of this peculiar nature. Play is a vital fantasy and a "necessary illusion," as Becker puts it. The illusory nature of the play becomes apparent, especially when different societies discover that the plays in the minds of their members are different from the plays in the minds of other communities. Unfortunately, what should become an effort of understanding the mind games belonging to other people different than us turns into a war to demonstrate the veracity of the ideologies on which the games in our minds are based. Thus, in history, too often, the mind games (jocurile minții) are suppressed by the exercise of power and violence. This is the conclusion reached by both Ernest Becker and Petru Couliano, following completely different paths.

In spite of this negative feature, the propensity for play has existed and will continue to live in the human mind as long as people are around. However, different historical conditions, technological innovations, major political, economic, and social transformations will always produce significant changes in people's relationship with the play. The economic, political and social conditions that led to the creation of small agricultural societies have been perpetuated for a long time in history, making rural plays the most successful plays in human history for hundreds of years. With the radical changes imposed by the Industrial Revolution, these plays (jocuri) were fundamentally transformed, being replaced in the human consciousness with other cultural forms better anchored in the new economic, social and political realities.

At the end of this chapter, I have taken a critical stance on new technologies that have changed humans' relationship with play in recent decades, eliminating the ritual component that accompanies access to play, leaving human consciousness addicted to it. My critical stance is not unique throughout history. New technologies have always created harsh criticism. Aware of all this, in the conclusion of this chapter, I will use a witticism to explain the new position of humans toward the games/plays made possible by 21st-century technologies. The question is whether modern games such as online social networks and video games will lead to a cultural evolution or, on the contrary, will move humans away from their social nature, intensifying the process of social atomization. All these questions naturally occur in historical moments when technology threatens to destabilize a way of relating to reality through already established conventions and social rules.

In his book *Dissemination*, Jacques Derrida (1981) talks about Plato's work *Phaedrus* which analyzes the dialogue between Theuth, the inventor of the writing, and the King of Egypt. Theuth argues that writing would make the Egyptians wiser and improve their memory. But the king is more skeptical and claims that what appeared to be a remedy might turn into poison. Writing can lead to memory loss, replacing its dynamic and active life with a prosthesis. The immediate consequence of this is that of eliminating the exercise of mental gymnastics and memory's extraordinary ability to memorize. "Writing" will produce an alternative reality, creating a non-authentic copy of it and making it even more difficult to comprehend (1981[1972]:96–97). Moreover, this pharmaceutical antidote for memory is actually a counter-remedy because it is essentially an artificial creation that goes against the normal processes of natural life:

[U]nder the pretext of supplementing memory, writing makes one even more forgetful; far from increasing knowledge, it diminishes it (Derrida 1981[1972]:100). . . . . Confident of the permanence and independence of its types (topoi), memory will fall asleep, will not keep itself up, will no longer keep to keeping itself alert, present, as close as possible to the truth of what is (Derrida 1981[1972]:105). . . . Letting itself get stoned [medusae] by its own signs, its own guardians, by the types committed to the keeping and surveillance of knowledge, it will sink down into Lethe, overcome by non-knowledge and forgetfulness. Memory and truth cannot be separated. The movement of aletheia is a deployment of mneme through and through. A deployment of living memory, of memory as psychic life in its self-presentation to itself. The powers of Lethe simultaneously increase the domains of death, of nontruth, of nonknowledge. This is why writing, at least insofar as it sows "forgetfulness in the soul," turns us toward the inanimate and toward nonknowledge. (Derrida 1981[1972]:100)

NOTES

1. Huizinga makes some pertinent remarks about the replacement of the term *ludus* with that of *jocus* in Romance languages, but expresses his perplexity at the disappearance of the term *ludus* in Romance languages and oscillates between a phonetic or semantic cause in explaining this mutation. Although a linguist by profession, Huizinga did not have a native knowledge of any Romance language, which would have allowed him to understand that the whole range of meanings embodied by the concept of *ludus* was transferred to that of *jocus* (Huizinga 1968[1938]:36).

2. *Irod* is a folk drama based on the biblical motif of the three Magi from the East who announced the birth of Jesus Christ. It presents a dialogue followed by a sword fight between King Herod who had ordered that all babies younger than two be killed, and the three Magi. This play, really successful among Romanian peasants, was also a symbolic weapon in the Romanians' fight for national emancipation and the affirmation of their national identity, although it seems that it was actually borrowed from other people that used to perform it, too, such as the Hungarians and the Szeklers.

3. Senators and Vestal Virgins got front-row seats (as did the emperor and his family). Wealthy equestrians sat above. Then came male Roman citizens of the middle classes and finally women and slaves at the top of the auditorium where the view was poorest. . . . This hierarchical division was achieved not only at the vertical level but also at a horizontal level . . . the most important people . . . sat closest to the emperor and his family (probably including the women) (Welch 2007).

Chapter Six

From Community Plays to Transnational Cultural Heritage

POLICIES OF PATRIMONIALIZATION
IN POSTSOCIALIST ROMANIA

In one of his aphorisms, Emil Cioran succinctly exposes the fate of Ishi, the last Native American of Yana tribe who was hidden for years in the forests for fear of the White Man. In the end, reduced to starvation, he surrendered of his own free will to the exterminators of his tribe. He was convinced that he would have the same fate as the members of his community. To his surprise, he was celebrated. This is because he was the last of his tribe and had no posterity. (Cioran 2013[1973]:121). Indeed, the last survivor of his tribe, whose life was spared by gold prospectors in that area of California, Ishi was eventually handed over to Professor Alfred Kroeber. Later, the writings of Kroeber and of his wife Theodora Kroeber told the world about the excruciating experiences endured by poor Ishi before meeting the great American anthropologist. Sometimes, an aphorism by a great philosopher has the power of catching a glimpse of a series of characteristics of humans that would otherwise take dozens of pages of scientific explanations.

Besides highlighting the brutality of colonialism, Cioran's aphorism expresses something else that is common to humans. It is the humans' curiosity about mysterious things because of their archaic perfume, and especially because these have become a rare presence within human society. If this tendency of the human spirit had not existed, most probably the previous chapter of this paper would have been the last. After observing how rural plays have been replaced by more dynamic plays/games which are more in tune with modern society, the final page of my research on mummers would have been written. However, with the growing disappearance of such plays even in the most ruralized areas of Europe, I have noticed a parallel increase in the public's interest in them. At the same time, I have witnessed the implementation of heritagization programs through the involvement of local political authorities and cultural institutions created specifically for this purpose. All these activities are expressions of modernity and especially of global capitalism. In this chapter, I will talk about the transformation of rural plays from community cultural forms to expressions of transnational cultural heritage. I will describe this process together with adjacent emerging phenomena such as *touristicization, consumerism,* and *mass-mediatization.*

In the afternoon of January 1, 2015, I was once again in the house of my hosts in the village of Oboroceni, Heleșteni *comună,* waiting for carolers and for the mummers' play teams. A good friend of the Hâra family, Mr. Gheorghiță Chelaru, and his wife, Mrs. Mariana, were the first guests welcomed that day. Like many other inhabitants of Heleșteni in their late 40s, they had migrated during communism to a highly industrialized city center, but kept being intimately connected to the world of their native village. Just like many other migrant villagers, they used to spend the winter holidays in their native village. Sitting at the table together with our host, the mayor of Heleșteni, Mr. Gheorghiță started to reveal memories dating back to the time of his youth when he used to wander with his *Deer* team through the village. The discussion reached a point where the two men began to compare the vivid world of their childhood's village to the shadow is had turned into in present times. Mr. Gheorghiță's intervention was revealing and clarified the issue in this respect. His house was located on a small street with only ten other houses in the village, just 200 meters away from my host's home. During his childhood, Mr. Gheorghiță recalled, all those ten houses would welcome the *Deer* and *Goat* teams, while now, with an "aged, impoverished and sick" population, only three of the households opened their doors to mummers. This remark made my host reply that this situation urged him, as mayor, to intervene in preventing the disappearance of local customs. That moment, as faced with a revelation, Mr. Gheorghiță stated in a manner I found memorable:

> Do you remember, Costică? In the 1970s, when we were teenagers, the mayor of our *comună* did not care at all about how we performed our winter plays and customs. On the contrary, the mayoralty collected a tax to grant us the right to herald through the village. Now, you—as mayor—and the township hall representatives, are heavily involved in organizing these activities, and encourage the young guys to engage in these winter customs, and they fuss a lot. I really don't understand how this mutation was produced! (Gheorghiță Chelaru, 49 years old, Oboroceni village, January 1, 2015, field notes)

Unaware, Mr. Gheorghiță had touched a sensitive issue that had become a central theme in heritage studies over the last two decades: how and why has the oral culture transmitted by a community (up to a certain moment without any external interventions) recently become the target of safeguarding, a process involving structures and people in connection to state institutions and international organizations. The 2003 UNESCO Convention for Intangible Cultural Heritage revolved around this important issue. The Convention was aimed at safeguarding those "practices, representations, expressions, knowledge, skills, as well as the instruments, objects, artifacts and cultural spaces associated therewith that communities, groups and, in some cases, individuals recognize as part of their cultural heritage" (UNESCO 2003 Convention for Intangible Cultural Heritage).

In many parts of the world where rural culture has occupied an important place over time, local political authorities, NGOs, folklorists, and anthropologists have become increasingly involved in safeguarding such forms of rural culture that have become increasingly evanescent with the advent of a modernity progressively accentuating the process of depeasantization (Araghi 1995). The heritagization process took various forms, as different actors understood differently the way peasant cultural forms threatened with extinction should be safeguarded. In Romania, just like in some other postsocialist countries, the heritagization policies took inspiration from late Communism. In those days, the most widespread form of heritagization was represented by folklore festivals. This process of patrimonialization through local and international folklore festivals proved to be an increasingly strong trend in the area of Moldova throughout my entire research, from 2009 to 2017. During this period, I witnessed a rich process of significant transformations that affected folk plays, especially with the rise of local festivals where many villages analyzed by me participated with their own teams. Throughout my entire field research, I managed to observe two inseparable trends whose evolution speaks about the great transformations and challenges of rural culture. Thus, while the vivid, authentic rural culture represented by cultural forms such as mummers' play has experienced a sharp decline, local and international folklore festivals in the region have expanded and become more intense.

In December 2009, when I first came to Heleșteni, there was no stage in the locality for the team of mummers to present their sketches. This simple fact gave a sense of freedom and created the premises of a continuous interaction and communication between mummers and the spectators who became actors in their own turn. In 2010, on my second visit to Heleșteni, an important part of this environment had disappeared. The township hall had erected a stage between the building of the mayors' office and the cultural house. The stage was important for organizing many cultural and artistic events in the *comună* and contributed positively to the local cultural life. But from the point of view of the carnivalesque and burlesque culture of the mummers, the appearance of the stage brought about a series of changes. The local political leaders were no longer required to descend among the mummers and thus to expose themselves to the mummers' carnivalesque plays. They could go out through the back door of the township hall, and in a few seconds they would already be on the stage from where they could control the events of the afternoon of December 31. From there, the mayor or deputy mayor would hold a speech and then introduce to the spectators the teams that were going to carol through the village. Afterwards, the teams would offer an onstage performance and then receive a diploma from the township hall representatives as a sign of gratitude "for the young people's efforts to participate in maintaining local traditions."

For me, the seemingly simple event of building a stage in the village has become a metaphor for the events I was about to witness in the following winters, events that have increased the distance between folk plays and the village culture that had created them. If in 2009 the *Deer* and *Goat* teams, as well as the *Pantomimic Mummers*, were caroling only through the village, in 2010 I observed for the first time the participation of a large team of mummers representing the Heleşteni *comună* at winter folklore festivals organized in Iaşi County. In Heleşteni, it was decided that the band meant to represent the locality would be the *Play of the Deer*. But it was not the same team of 6–7 children aged 8–14 who used to roam through the villages of the *comună* at the end of the year. The newly formed group consisted of 12–18 participants and was composed mainly of 16–30-year-old guys, highly experienced veterans of the custom who were also very resilient to the requirements of such festivals.

I observed the same trend in Ruginoasa where, starting with 2010, either the *Malanca* or the *Play of the Deer* team began to participate in various festivals in the Moldova region. In this case, too, the *Malanca* team representing Ruginoasa in folklore festivals, was no longer the same as the one I had seen in the village. The large group was rather an eclectic band consisting of: girls in folk costumes who were reciting New Year's carols, *căldărari* and *arnăuţi* from the classic *Malanca* team, a pair of professional trombone players and two pairs of fighters wearing masks and long wooden clubs. These fighters were just accompanying the team as dancers.

The pressure of joining these festivals grew proportionally to the previous success of the participating teams. Moreover, since 2009 such folklore festivals in the area have begun to grow both in number and intensity. In this context, some new festivals have been set up and the old ones have risen to an unprecedented level. Thus, if in 2010 and 2011 the *Play of the Deer* team from Heleşteni participated only in the *Festival of Winter Customs and Traditions in Paşcani* city, since 2012 three more festivals have been added to their schedule: *The International Folklore Festival of Winter Customs and Traditions of Iaşi* city; *The Festival of Customs "Start the Plough Dear Charming Princes"* of Vatra Dornei city; and the *Alexandru Vasiliu Folklore Festival* from Tătăruşi town. Between 2012–2016, other seven festivals were added, hosted by cities not only from Iaşi, but also from various counties of Eastern Romania. The cities of Piatra-Neamţ, Buzău, Tulcea, Suceava, Târgu-Frumos, plus the *comune* Liteni, Moldoviţa and Suceviţa—all of which were hosting winter Folklore festivals—welcomed the *Deer* team from Heleşteni among their participants.

A brief look at the geographical position of these localities shows us that some of them, such as Târgu-Frumos and Paşcani, are just 20 kilometers away from Heleşteni *comună*, while cities like Buzău and Tulcea are situated more than 300 kilometers away. Finally, a settlement outside Romania—Chernivtsi (Cernăuţi) in Ukraine—was added to the list in 2016. Either way, the trip to these urban centers involved high costs and more elaborate logistics to ensure the participation of a team of 20–22 members in these events. I observed a similar situation in Ruginoasa, too. The team organized by the Ruginoasa township hall has missed neither an edition of the *Festival of Winter Customs and Traditions in Paşcani* city since 2009, nor *The Festival of Customs "Start the Plough Dear Charming Princes"* of Vatra Dornei city since 2010.

Figure 6.1. The deer team from Heleşteni comună, participating in the Festival of Winter Customs and Traditions in Paşcani city—December 30, 2014.

Photo credit: Alin Rus

Of these folklore festivals, the oldest ones—including those of Iaşi and Hârlău cities—were established during the Communist Era, beginning with 1967. However, a few others were founded after 1995, and after 2009 many others began to develop quickly, benefiting from the participation of numerous and better organized teams. Moreover, with the multiplication of such festivals, a competitive system between them has been generated. The organizers tried to provide the most attractive accommodation and prizes to attract folk teams from the *comune* that were interested in joining these cultural events. The pressure to take part in the events began to increase, too, given the incredible growth of the festivals after 2009. The pressure came from multiple directions: from the county culture committees that were in touch with the mayors of *comune*; from the organizers of the festival who sent invitations to those localities that had organized folklore teams in the past; from the local and national TV stations that produced full broadcasts and shows based on the recordings of the festivals; from local politicians who built symbolic capital through these events; and even from locals who wanted to see on the TV screen their own representatives on the festival stage. Despite this pressure, bands that were already well-established such as the Heleşteni's *Deer* had an overloaded program at the end of the year; consequently, they had to reject at least few of the offers received and to follow only those considered the most important.

Compared to each other, all the festivals shared common characteristics, but they also had features that distinguished them. The common attribute of all these events was represented by two key elements. The first was the presence of the participating folkloric teams usually consisting of 12–25 members. The second one was the staged winter folk traditions, ranging from carol singers to dancers, mummers' plays, or resulting in a combination of all of them. In terms of morphology and deployment, most festivals proposed two basic elements: the bands' parade on the city streets and the stage performance of these bands according to the order established by the organizers. Although these festivals resembled each other from the point of view of the performance, and generally received the visit of similar bands enacting the same kind of winter traditions' repertory, they were somewhat different in terms of the targets they pursued.

For tourist cities such as Vatra Dornei or county residences like Iaşi, hosting winter festivals also had the purpose of attracting tourists. From this point of view, the large number of people present on the streets of these cities, the groups flowing from the gates of local hotels immediately after the events started, and especially the numerous cars with plates issued in various other counties of Romania, demonstrated that the purpose had been probably achieved. While this was the case in such localities, in others like Paşcani and Târgu-Frumos, the festivals were smaller, with fewer bands participating, and their purpose seemed to be rather cultural, media-related and political. A ubiquitous fact supported this hypothesis. Local politicians, mayors and deputy mayors would usually take the floor at the opening of these festivals, declaring therein that through these festivals they showed respect and appreciation to their fellow citizens, struggling to offer them an "attractive cultural and educational spectacle." Likewise, every time, at least several local TV stations broadcasted news and reportages on the events.

All the dilemmas that I have had at various stages of my research concerning the distinction between village rituals and stage performances, were related not only to the issue of safeguarding, but also to a series of important questions about the heritagization process: what aspects of rural culture are being patrimonialized, by whom, by what means, and especially how this is done. In heritage studies this topic has become a classic one in recent years, with technical discussions on the issue of national identity involved in the process of festivalisation of rural traditions (Cash 2011).

Other issues were related to the external intervention required to safeguard the customs, the genuineness of the cultural product resulting from the safeguarding process, the economic and political stakes surrounding the cultural elements on which *the intangible cultural heritage* label had been placed (Skounti 2009). Last but not least, an apple of discord appeared over the process of safeguarding and the relationship of this process with several forms of "invented tradition" (Hobsbawm and Ranger 1992). From this perspective, the question was whether traditions invented or reinvented during the safeguarding process—such as the folklore festivals I had witnessed—could still be considered authentic and genuine, or were they just the fruit of recent interventions that could no longer be included in the category of rural traditions such as mummers' plays?

INTANGIBLE CULTURAL HERITAGE—FESTIVALISATION, URBANIZATION, MASS-MEDIATIZATION

In the light of my research on rural plays, I wondered if the folklore festivals I analyzed could somehow reproduce a part of the rich universe of meanings and expressions that these cultural forms embodied when played in peasant communities. During centuries, these plays were ways of designing and redesigning a rich social universe, manners of addressing the problems of the village, expressions of the social networks created in the village by the peasants themselves, ways for people to relate to each other, means of transcending temporarily the daily burdensome realities and, finally, "story(s) people tell themselves about themselves" (Geertz 1972:26). Folklore festivals not only made it impossible to preserve these features of the customary community culture, but sometimes seemed to turn into a different stream eroding the foundation of a rural culture that, despite being moribund, was still alive in some villages in the county of Iași. In my view, this situation was accomplished through three processes: *festivalisation, urbanization,* and *mass-mediatization.* What I call *festivalisation* and *urbanization* represent the changing nature of the folk plays under the influence of local or international folklore festivals and the urban environment where these festivals take place; further, I define *mass-mediatization* as a process through which rural plays, as well as other rural traditions, were recorded by professional team of reporters and transformed into news during winter holidays.

The three cumulative processes led to the peasants' alienation from their own culture and rituals, since the increasingly predominant medium of relating to them became the TV broadcast, a different environment compared to the face-to-face interaction that used to mediate the creation of human relationships in the past. I started to understand this phenomenon when I interviewed a 63-year-old lady from the village of Oboroceni. In April 2012, I inquired the elderly lady if she had been visited by the *Deer* team the winter before. She lived in a remote area of Oboroceni village that—I had learned from the head of a team—the *Deer* bands had little motivation to visit. Houses were far from the main roads and mainly populated by elders who gave little money to the artists or did not receive the mummers' bands at all. The answer of the elderly lady was quite astonishing: "Usually the *Deer* teams don't come to our house. They are not so interested in caroling two old ladies (she and her mother). But I saw on TV our *Deer* team performing at the festival in Pașcani city and I enjoyed it a lot" (Voicu Cornelia, Oboroceni village, April 29, 2012, Interview). Thus, especially for poor people and elders, the heritagisation activities and their broadcasting through local TV stations became the new medium through which they remained in contact with their own cultural heritage.

In addition, the investment of human effort and capital to prepare the team that participated in the festivals was sometimes detrimental to rural culture. Villages with a declining population such as Oboroceni felt it very acutely and, to my surprise, the phenomenon had been observed even by the vigilant eye of locals. This came out in one of the last interviews I had conducted in the winter of 2014, right before leaving the area after an intensive field research. The interviewee was Mitică, whom I mentioned already throughout this study, the father of two little boys who were current members in the Play of the Deer team that participated at many festivals in different cities from Moldova region. In spite of this, Mitică raised a critical voice against folklore festivals:

I had an argument with the cultural representative of the mayoralty. I told him: How is this possible? We send our Deer to the folklore festivals in cities for city-dwellers to see it, and people in our village don't have any chance to watch the team performing in their village? But he replied to me, We have no choice! We have to send our Deer to the local folklore festivals! Then I got angry and I talked to a neighbor who worked in Italy throughout the year. I asked him to help me make our Deer team in the village. This is because here in our village it is a local pride to have your own Deer that comes to your house to play in front of you—the householder. Finally, I made a team with my neighbor, my children, plus two more boys from the village. With this Deer team, I was able to go through our village at least to a few houses and in front of the village hall on December 31. (Mitica Alexa, 32 years old, Oboroceni village, January 3, 2015, Interview)

Paradoxically, the safeguarding processes that should have stimulated the village communities to preserve their rural customs, have eventually contributed, just like many other forces of modernity, to erecting the mummers' plays funerary stone. Through these three cumulative processes—*festivalisation, urbanization and mass-mediatization*—mummers' plays were exported to the urban world, one that was more anchored in the realities of the modern world of the 21st century and endowed with more financial and institutional resources than the impoverished and aged Romanian villages. Just like the peasants who migrated to a better world, rural traditions took the road to cities that proved to be a powerful magnet against which any resistance was almost impossible. Besides these processes accompanying the culture of patrimonialization, in my fieldwork I managed to identify other influences coming from the modern society which marked the rural culture and mummers' plays. One of the events that strengthened my conviction that peasant culture and its values are under siege took place on January 2017 in Chernivtsi (Cernăuți), Ukraine.

THE INTERNATIONAL FESTIVAL OF CULTURAL TRADITIONS—BUCOVINA'S MALANCA

When I started my field research in the winter of 2009, in Heleșteni and Ruginoasa, I would not have imagined, even for a single moment, that my last days of fieldwork would end on the streets of a big city, in a foreign country. Back then, I was thinking that my study would be one about the cultural heritage of the peasants, particularly their rural plays, and that meant it would be strictly related to the geography and history of their own localities where winter plays were part of a complex social network. My vision of the peasants' cultural heritage had been influenced not only by Romanian Folkloristics, but also by some of the classics of the anthropological literature about peasants such as Eric Wolf, Oscar E. Handlin, and Paul Stirling.

Handlin, for example, defined the regular peasant as a person who "temporarily mixes his sweat with the soil" (Handlin 1967:456), while the peasant community's social life gravitates around the narrow borders of the village and the firm rules imposed by the clan's network: "within the village, every family had its place, and in the family—every individual" (Idem 1967). From a similar view, Wolf saw the peasants' ceremonies as a means of validating a social and moral order only wider than the familiar household, and in which the hostilities were "contained and constrained" (Wolf 1966:97). Stirling, too, stated that peasants "have little to do with these people who control their existence, and see only a tiny proportion of them" (Stirling 1965:266). From all these perspectives, the cultural heritage of the peasants was intimately linked to a territory, a locality, and the community occupying it.

Moreover, my fieldwork in a relatively isolated community such as Heleşteni, but also in other villages nearby such as Cucuteni and Sticlăria, confirmed my conviction that the cultural heritage of the peasants, as well as their system of values were formed in a cultural micro-ecosystem. But the same research has shown me that, at the beginning of the 21st century, even in the most isolated rural areas, the new peasantry (Ploeg 2009) is no longer the same as the old one whose only economic resource was the land. This fact could be noticed when analyzing the decline of the peasants' system of values that also talks about the radical transformations of the peasants' cultural heritage. Just as the peasants migrating in search of a better world, their plays also follow the way to urban centers, and sometimes even to foreign countries. The most eloquent case in this regard was the team of *The Deer from Heleşteni*. In 2016, this team crossed not only the borders of the native village, but also those of its country, to join an international folklore festival.

In January 2017, I did not resist the temptation of accompanying the members of this team during their international trip to the city of Chernivtsi in Ukraine. My friend Florin from Heleşteni *comună*, who had in the meantime become cultural referent of the *comună* hall in this locality, was now the leader of the *Deer* team and one of the organizers of the trip. The festival was scheduled for the afternoon of January 15, 2017. The crew of the Heleşteni's *Deer* was accommodated at *Hotel Oasis*, located at the city's entrance.

As early as 8:00 a.m., from the window of the hotel, I began to see platforms carried by trucks entering the city. On these platforms, gigantic constructions such as a rooster, a pair of reindeer and a bunch of Santa Clauses had been placed. They came from the villages neighboring Chernivtsi, and headed to the city center where their parade would later take place. Compared to all these gigantic platforms where dozens of artists dressed in extravagant costumes were dancing, the team of the *Deer* in Heleşteni seemed small and insignificant. This impression became stronger when we got to a central square of the city, called Sobornaia (Mitropoliei). Right there our *Deer* team got off from the microbus directly into the street, among the people. Immediately, there was an ad-hoc performance right in front of the plaza's Christmas tree, to the delight of the large audience gathered there. During this first street performance, I noticed a fact that would become the most frequent occurrence during the following hours spent on the streets of Chernivtsi: the hundreds of iPhones, photo and video cameras in the hands of the bunch of people on the streets of the now overcrowded urban center were heading, as if attracted by an invisible magnet, straight to the festival participants.

Thereafter, the representative of the *Bucovina Art Center for Conservation and Promotion of the Traditional Romanian Culture Cernăuți (Chernivtsi)*, made way through crowd waves for the members of the *Deer* crew from Heleşteni, so that they could join the whole *Malanca Festival*'s teams who were already coming in a line to the Mitropoliei Square, on the roadway now closed to traffic. Some of these *Malănci* were folklore ensembles dressed in traditional costumes and accompanied by groups of musicians, similar to the Romanian bands that participated in the festival. As in the case of the folklore festivals I had seen in Romania, each participating team had a representative in front of the group, with a placard in his hands where the viewers could read the name of the locality his team came from. In addition, there was always a distance of a few meters between two bands. Others so-called "Malănci" had nothing to do with the rural custom they had taken their name from. It was actually the same kind of platforms that I had seen that morning from the hotel window. These "Malănci," too, had written the name of the locality their members came from on a banner on the front or side of their platforms. Except for that, there were big differences between the two types of teams.

However, for the sightseeing tourists the most impressive were the "Malănci" on the platforms. These were in some cases only large statues made of cardboard, silicone, wood and various other materials. Some of these were giant, reaching a height of over three meters and occupying almost the entire road. Impressive in its size was a Trojan horse surrounded by Greek soldiers and on whose back was Odysseus himself dressed in an antique Greek soldier's suit. However, this impressive horse was pulled by a banal agricultural tractor that made a lot of noise and made it clear that the convoy was also the creation of rural craftsmen. Of the same size was a Sphinx smartly built on the cabin of a truck whose form and brand could no longer be seen because of the polystyrene carcass artificially build above it. There was also a pirate-ship filled with frightening figures, followed by a platform with Mexican singers impossible to mistake because of their large *sombreros* and long mustaches. Immediately after—an improvised tram full of "striptease dancers" who were actually men dressed in hideous costumes representing ugly fat bodies of nude women. I also managed to identify monsters, and a three-headed dragon, a Batman, a Frankenstein, Devils, Kazak dancers, "Russian soldiers" satirized as demons, a camp of Romani people, Santa Claus and his cheerleaders of American inspiration. In the end I could glimpse even "Charlie Chaplin" and "Donald Trump" among the participants. In all this panoply of representations, there were also symbols of Romanian and Ukrainian folklore. Thus, the main character—the rooster of the story *Punguța cu Doi Bani* (*The Bag with Two Pennies*) by the classical 19th century writer Ion Creangă, was also present among the festival participants, being three meters high and carried on a motorized platform. It was actually the same rooster I had seen that morning entering in the city. Likewise, I was able to see at one point the "Saint Melania" from which the name of the *Malanca* is believed to come from.

All these bands made Chernivtsi resemble a Rio de Janeiro carnival of folk cultures. But at a closer look, there was rather a combination between the *Rio Festival*, the *Philadelphia Mummers' Parade* and *Romanian Folklore Festivals* like those in the cities of Iași or Vatra Dornei that I had observed in previous years. Obviously, it was an unexpected encounter between the capitalist cultural industry (Horkheimer and Adorno 2002[1944]) and the rural traditional culture escaping into the realm of show and entertainment.

Figure 6.2. A Malanca team of Santa Clauses, carried by a truck on the streets of Chernivtsi. On a banner on the top of the platform the viewers could read "Зеленівська Маланка" (The Green Malanka)—January 15, 2017.
Photo credit: Alin Rus

"The whole world passes through the filter of the culture industry," Horkheimer and Adorno wrote in the middle of the 20th century (Idem 2002[1944]). I noticed that the desire to museificate the folk culture of all Romanian folklore festivals had almost disappeared in Chernivtsi. Still, the eye of an expert could spot the rural culture in many features of the festival, for example in the title of the event, in the costumes of the few bands who stubbornly wanted to preserve their rural spirit, and in many symbols carried by Malanca teams' members. Rural culture has been immersed in the cultural industry specific to capitalism that had permeated all the pores of the festival. Everything around seemed to be made for consumption. From the candy bars, sausages, barbecue, sugar cottons, balloons and ornaments sold in the city's main squares, and the restaurants and bars around that were full of people, to the hotels that had been fully booked the day of the festival, everything was destined for the urban audience to consume in its rush to experience the "rural savory."

CANNIBALIZING FOLK PLAYS

Indeed, more than anything else, it was all about cultural consumption. All the bands wandering through the streets of Chernivtsi passed immediately in front of the "eyes" of the cameras of local and national Ukrainian televisions and from there they instantly entered the online space or even the direct broadcasts of news departments. At the same time, the images taken during the festival would appear in the next few days in television programs and articles of the written press. But more than anything, every iPhone and camera in the hands of the spectators would bring the thousands of images taken during the festival into their homes. These images would go directly to the personal pages of Facebook, Hi5, Twitter, as well as YouTube and other social media sites, reaching out to even more viewers. Walking alongside the *Deer* team in Heleşteni, I noticed how every few minutes a group of 2–3 spectators came out of the crowd, stopped the members of the *Deer* team from Heleşteni for a few seconds and took a picture with them. The same was true for all the teams in front of and behind our group, so the parade slowly moved like an earth worm with frequent stumbling blocks. At the same time, the gendarmes on the sidelines were too few and totally ineffective in stopping the continuous incursions of the spectators from the sides who wanted to take photos with the members of the *Malǎnci* teams.

Finally, the folklore teams reached the festival stage where only the *Malǎnci* prepared for this part of the competition had arrived. The trucks with platforms carrying giant statues and dancing teams continued their way across the other streets of the city. Part of the viewers followed them with their iPhones and photo cameras, while another less numerous public remained in the Philharmonic Square to watch the folklore competition. Here, things happened the same way as in the festivals I had seen in Romania. The teams that had managed to transform folk culture into an exciting and dynamic amalgam, combining in an attractive way various elements such as songs, dances and folk plays, were those that received the appreciation of the public and later on the prizes offered by the jury. More traditionalist teams such as the *Deer* of Heleşteni, aiming to transpose a fragment of authentic rural culture on stage, received only a few anemic applauses instead.

Not long after the stage performance of the *Deer* team from Heleşteni, the *Malanca-Fest* came to an end. Many spectators were already leaving in small groups, heading to the parking lots to withdraw as quickly as possible from the overcrowded city. Other tourists, following a different strategy, went to the hotel rooms and rented apartments where they hoped to be able to leave only the next day, avoiding the big crowd on the festival day. Being among those who had to leave the same day, the members of the *Deer* team were now walking towards their microbus, situated more than one kilometer away. But along this road their colorful costumes, the beaded helmets, and especially the *Deer*'s mask with huge horns and mobile jaws, were constantly attracting the attention of the numerous groups of tourists still on the city's streets. Unavoidable, the most daring of them asked the team to stop for a few seconds to take pictures of them. So, until reaching the microbus, the band made at least twenty more stops.

In the end reaching our car, Florin, dressed in a bear-leader suit and visibly tired after that full day, sighed hard saying: "Done! The pictures with the monkey are over!" Surprised by this statement whose full sense was just beginning to emerge in my mind, I asked him what he had really meant. Florin smiled slyly, and said: "What? Haven't you ever taken pictures with the monkey at the seaside?" This response brought back to me a memory from the times of my adolescence. Going with my family to Eforie Nord, a seaside resort at the Black Sea, I took a picture of me and my brother next to a monkey. Professional photographers from the Romanian seaside resorts used to come to the beach accompanied by their small monkeys that walked next to them in a leash. The monkeys were trained to climb on the shoulders of tourists who wanted to be immortalized with an animal brought from a distant land. Considered an exotic animal, the monkey immediately attracted the attention of curious tourists who paid twice the price of a normal picture, only to be photographed together with the animal coming from remote areas. Remembering all of this when I got home later, I found my photo with the monkey, in fact an old rhesus macaque, dated July 1987. At the age of 13, I was also the kind of tourist wishing to be near an exotic being, without knowing anything about its habitat and behavior.

Figure 6.3. The deer team from Heleşteni comună performing on the streets of Chernivtsi—January 15, 2017.

Photo credit: Alin Rus

Extrapolating, I started to look around and ask myself how many of the hundreds of people who had photographed the *Deer* from Heleşteni knew or wanted to know something about this play and the cultural micro-ecosystem that had created it. Apart from the fact that the cultural heritage of the Heleşteni *comună* had become transnational, entering the houses and computers of the Ukrainians, was this an appreciation of peasant values and of the culture that gave rise to this cultural form? Or was it rather a kind of consumption of momentary pleasures made possible by cultural industry and modern technology?

In any case, following the observation of the *International Festival of Cultural Traditions—Bucovina's Malanca*, my conclusion was not that the participating teams, even those on the truck-transported platforms, would lack creativity or would be inferior to the *Malănci* produced in the rural universe. On the contrary, these participants also demonstrated an exceptional inventiveness, involving energy and time for the completion of cultural products with ephemeral existence. But they were meant to survive only during the few hours of parading the streets of the city and being offered to an audience that, in many cases, knew nothing about the symbols and history behind the masks and costumes; however, this audience could easily consume them if it had the financial resources to visit Chernivtsi during the festival. In my opinion, this type of festivalisation represented in fact the death of those theatrical performances incarnated by mummers' plays where spectators became participants and participants became spectators in a burlesque rural culture based on community memory. Through this collective memory, such interactions and communication were possible because the rural customary communities represented that system of vessels through which this exchange took place. For a researcher of the rural culture like me, the entire show represented not only a sort of urbanization of traditions, but also a form of exporting them to the world of entertainment, show, mass consumerism and global tourism.

GLOBALIZATION, INVISIBILITY, SYMBOLIC VIOLENCE . . . AND ALSO HOPE

Festivals such as the *International Festival of Cultural Traditions—Bucovina's Malanca* in Chernivtsi and *Mummers' Parade* in Philadelphia bring on the stage symbols and representations that come from the peasant culture that gave birth to all mummers' plays. However, few spectators attending them are aware of this, can and want to understand rural culture by participating in these parade type festivals. Despite its posting in the spotlight of the modern world, peasants' culture has become even more invisible than before (Smith 2015). It is an invisibility designed by stratified societies and more recently by all those global entities that Van der Ploeg called the *Empire* (Ploeg 2009:269). This designed invisibility is in fact an active process that leads to the marginalization of the peasants and deny their economic and cultural rights. All this sum of factors is a subtle form of violence that Bourdieu has well circumscribed through the concept of symbolic violence (Bourdieu and Wacquant 1992). From all these processes, a kind of blindness toward peasant culture results, and it is not only present in the minds of tourists who come to these festivals in search of cheap fun, but also in the minds of many scholars in the field of social sciences.

Perhaps better than ever, I realized this when, between 30 April and 1 May 2017, I attended an international symposium entitled *The Role of Heritage in Migration and Displacement*. I made a presentation there entitled *Global Depeasantization and Peasants' Intangible Cultural Heritage*. The basic idea of my presentation was that with the process of depeasantization in recent decades, the cultural heritage of the peasants suffered a continuous process of deterioration and disappearance. Because of it, I argued, in the UNESCO list of Intangible Cultural Heritage, a great number of customs and traditions belong to peasant culture. Of all the participants in that symposium, I was the only one who used *the peasant* concept to refer to this social group and its cultural heritage. This happened even though, when some of the participants talked about "refugees," "displaced people," "migrants," and "unemployed youth," I could clearly distinguish the sensibilities, behaviors and lifestyles belonging to peasants.

I understood the mystery behind this problem when, in the break after my presentation, an Australian researcher asked me if the peasants really existed and were not just a concept invented by a particular orientation in social sciences at a certain historical moment. Another Professor from England asked me how I could figure out which of the customs in the UNESCO list of Intangible Cultural Heritage belonged to peasants. These questions made me meditate deeper on my position as researcher of Eastern Europe's rural culture. For me, the reality of the peasant world has become something undisputed. And since I had been in contact for years with this culture, through all the senses and pores of my being, it had become something self-obvious that did not require much explanation. The smell of freshly cut hay and of the smoked pork or beef in the attic of the house; the taste of the fresh cheese that has just been taken out of the barrels by the shepherds; the noise of the herd of cows that leave in the morning to the pastures outside the village, run by the cowman of the village; the fine unmistakable texture of lambs' fur only a few hours after they were born; the picturesque image of the haystacks placed from place to place on a hilly field and the shepherds' wood stall surrounded by the flock of sheep; last but not least, the mummers with their specific noise of bells and rattles, and the vivid colors of their costumes on the white snow background; all these are things I once perceived and that remained deeply impressed on my soul. But it would be hard for me to explain to anyone who had never had a contact with them. More, a mere fugitive glance at the UNESCO list of *Intangible Cultural Heritage* could not make me believe that "Albanian folk iso-polyphony," "Azerbaijani carpet weaving," "The Chinese Hua'er," or "Oxherding and oxcart traditions in Costa Rica" belong to a social class different than that of the peasants.

Unfortunately, for a long time, peasants have been viewed just as underdogs (Shanin 1971:15), a social class whose capacity to organize, defend and promote their own interests was very low. Moreover, in the last few decades, under the influence of globalization, everything related to peasant society, from economic to social and cultural aspects, seems to enter an accelerated decline, which made Hobsbawm state the death of peasantry (Hobsbawm 1994:289). But, as the great religions of mankind and at the same time the principles of biology and genetics teach us, where the principle of death stands, there is also revival and resurrection. Even mummers' plays, with the sequence of death and resurrection of the animal by the hand of his master, talk about the same very simple principle.

Globalization brought with it the birth of the world's most impressive peasant organization. *Via Campesina* or *The Peasants' Way* was founded in 1993, bringing together peasants' associations from several countries and continents. Today, this organization is one of the largest in the world. It is a coalition of over 164 peasant organizations spread around the globe and with more than 200 million members who advocate for the rights of this social class that has suffered severe infringements by food corporations and intergovernmental organizations such as the World Trade Organization. In relation to the motivations and goals of *Via Campesina*, Christophe Golay, Research Fellow and Coordinator of the Project on Economic, Social and Cultural Rights at the Geneva Academy of International Humanitarian Law and Human Rights (Geneva Academy), wrote a document entitled *Negotiation of a United Nations Declaration on the Rights of Peasants and Other People Working in Rural Areas*. This document created the basis for serious negotiations with the United Nations for the recognition of the rights of this social class, rights that have often been violated or ignored. This document also talks about the peasants "social and cultural rights" (Golay 2015) even though its main objectives are those related to peasants' economic rights. Perhaps in the near future, the peasants' cultural rights, including the right to recognize their property on intangible cultural heritage forms in the UNESCO list, will be promoted.

In recent years, people interested in rural traditions have increasingly considered the online medium as an extremely effective way to promote them. Practitioners of rural oral traditions and those interested in these cultural forms are getting together more and more often in the virtual space of the Internet to discuss and promote the customs of their own communities. In 2017, the Heleșteni's mayor made a Facebook page where he posted photos taken during the cultural events organized in his village. In just a few months, the webpage was visited by several thousand people, gathering appreciation not only from people in Romania, but also from Israel, Belgium, France and England. Ethnologist Bogdan Neagota also drew attention to this phenomenon, noting that in recent years more and more peasants whose rituals and customs are being studied by his ethnological association, *Orma Sodalitas Anthropologica* are requesting that the videos made by *Orma* members be posted on YouTube.

YouTube itself became a form of patrimonialization. It is a form of patrimonialization through which the performers of a ritual/ceremonial complex assert their community identity in front of other local communities. But, at the same time, this form of patrimonialization contributes to the emergence out of the isolation state of certain customs, and to the awakening of peasants' comparative consciousness, if I may say that. Villagers from isolated localities begin to realize that their customs are not singular, but they are part of a sort of network of such habits. (Rus and Neagota 2016)

Besides all this, many of the sons and daughters of the peasants who had left their village, guided by higher aspirations, and became something more than simple rural workers, have not forgotten the traditions of their native lands and have promoted them in their travels around the world, sometimes at the highest levels and among people who have very little in common with the rural culture today. Mihai Alexa, the current technical director of the *Dacia—Renault Group* in Piteşti city, left Hărmăneasa, his native village, at the age of 14, to attend high school in the city of Roman, and university at the Polytechnic Institute of Bucharest. Being *comoraş* in the *Play of the Goat* team in his village four years in a row during his teenage, he told me that it is very likely that many of his qualities as good organizer and manager had been acquired or perfected during adolescence when he has made use of all the logistics necessary to achieve such teams and the rituals associated to them.

I am happy to come home to the village every year, especially during the winter holidays, because there I feel the best. However, I can no longer say I am a peasant, because I have never made a living from agricultural work. But I am a peasant's son, and my origin is in the countryside. I say this with pride. Precisely because I grew up in the countryside, I have a good education, based on strong principles and values. All these helped me later in all the challenges of my life. Even though today Romania is going through a period of deep agitation and unrest, I believe that true values will never disappear. These values, at least in the case of our country, are indissolubly linked to the peasant world. I have always kept in touch with the life of my village, and even if I live in another city and travel a lot to foreign countries, I have always promoted the authentic traditions of my village in all the places I have been. I also talk to many of my interlocutors about my childhood and the rural world where I spent it. Childhood and adolescence are part of my identity, and of every human being, I believe, and they always have a sacred place in the consciousness. (Mihai Alexa, 58 years old, January 24, 2018, Phone Interview)

In 2012, immediately after having finished the documentary *Behind the Masks*, made by Monica Heintz, my colleague, and myself, with the support of the Paris Ouest Nanterre La Defense University and the French University Institute, Mr. Mihai Alexa asked us to send him a few copies of it with French subtitles added. At one of his meetings with his French colleagues from *Renault* Company, Mr. Alexa offered them a copy of the documentary. One of these colleagues, Mr. Alexa remembered, even stated in one of the subsequent meetings that "only then could he fully understand what the true spirit of the winter holidays was and, especially, why his Romanian employees want to be free during the end of the year, in order to spend their winter holidays within the family and community."

All the ways and means made possible by globalization, have in turn become forms of heritagization of the rural culture that has become transnational in the meantime. Perhaps more than through official channels, peasants' culture becomes known and promoted despite the processes that have led to its erosion. The story, the play, and the recourse to memory (the one that makes any story and play possible) are phenomena that have always accompanied human beings throughout their journey on this planet. Those who have lived in the rural culture and who have been in contact with rituals of the world such as the mummers' plays, will always carry them in their souls, for these have been landmarks on the community memory map and have decisively marked their personality traits as human beings. As long as these people are alive, working and living in other countries or cities away from their native villages, stories about rural plays will circulate and will be heard in the most unexpected places of the world. And, if one day in the future folk plays disappear completely from the rural universe and everyone who was ever involved in their practice is gone, those interested in the village world and the values that governed it will find all these plays, customs and traditions anytime in the virtual space of the internet, and will thus, with some efforts, be able to find out what these had meant for the rural communities that begot, performed and promoted them over time.

CONCLUSION

The end of the 20th century marked one of the most bombastic theses on peasantry. Eric Hobsbawm decreed the death of peasantry and thus the cessation of a way of life that had marked the cultural evolution of humans over a long period of time. Meanwhile, authors such as Farshad A. Araghi (1995), A. Haroon Akram-Lodhi (2009), Cristobal Kay (2009), Deborah Bryceson (2000), and Van Der Ploeg (2009) have thoroughly analyzed and reformulated this statement. The most valid conclusion that emerges from this research is that, rather than disappearing without a trace, the peasantry adapts to the new conditions of the market economy and globalization, becoming something else than it has been so far. With this process, their plays undergo significant transformations. By analyzing their transformations, we can understand the great challenges that this class has faced over the last decades. This is, in fact, one of the major stakes of this study.

Van Der Ploeg is the author who used a relevant concept when explaining the major transformations peasant societies had recently encountered: *the new peasantry*. The new peasantry is represented by a critical mass of people who carry out small-scale agricultural work and is defined by their struggle against the *Empire*. The *Empire* is composed of global food corporations, agribusiness groups, large retailers, state apparatuses, scientific models, and technologies that together form the tentacles of a transnational reality spread across the planet. In these new economic, political, and social conditions, it is obvious that peasant communities suffer radical transformations. These transformations are not only economic and social, but also axiological. The system of values that has guided the peasant's life for centuries has begun to fall apart, being replaced by other ways of being and seeing the world. And these, in turn, have also affected the cultural heritage of the peasants of which the rural plays are an important part.

Authors such as Robert Redfield (1969), Katherine Verdery (2003), and Katy Fox (2011) have observed that in recent decades we have been witnessing a process of crumbling of the peasant values under the pressure of multiple causes. In particular, economic, political transformation and legislative factors have been highlighted among the most important agents of the erosion of the peasant system of values (Verdery 2003; Fox 2011). From my perspective, as researcher of the Romanian countryside at the beginning of the 21st century, labor migration proved to be one of the phenomena that contributed most to the undermining of those values formed in the cultural micro-ecosystems of the rural localities studied. The emigrant is the one who has brought other images of the world even to the most isolated Romanian villages, in strong disjunction with the values of the rural world, through channels such as the phone and the internet.

All these trends have attracted the attention of many people interested in maintaining and promoting rural traditions, and especially in their long-term fate. Unlike in the past when these rural plays were performed by customary communities within a complex system of social relationships, now it is increasingly necessary to intervene from the outside to safeguard them. However, one of the most acute problems that arise is whether or not these interventions cause an alteration of the authenticity of these cultural forms. The issue has long been debated in heritage studies, and the conclusion of many researchers was that, through state-run institutions, programs, and even international organizations, the process of patrimonialization produced substantial changes to the safeguarded culture, sometimes transforming it into something different than what it used to be.

In Romania, a country whose dictatorial past was closely intertwined with the phenomenon of patrimonialization of rural traditions, these patrimonial practices of the past have strongly influenced the present-day safeguarding activities. Stage folklore festivals and folk team competitions have become the most widespread forms of safeguarding oral rural culture. Essentially, these festivals have become processes of museification of the rural culture, increasingly resembling a set of frozen cultural forms subsequently presented to the public, rather than living cultural forms that could speak about the current dynamics of rural communities. These transformations are due not only to the fact that they are "exported" to cities through folklore festivals, but also to the presence of prizes that make the competitions even more bitter and intense, and to the media that instantly transfers them to the homes of hundreds of thousands of lovers of peasant traditions.

Three visible processes such as *festivalisation, urbanization,* and *mass-mediatization* accompany these patrimonialization practices. Paradoxically, they create another type of culture than the one aimed to be safeguarded, one whose life is parallel and autonomous compared to the rural world and peasant culture. Transported to festivals stages, mummers' plays are no longer ways of addressing communities' problems and "story(s) people tell themselves about themselves" (Geertz 1972:26), but lifeless artifacts in a sort of open-air museums of the peasant culture. Sometimes, all this leads to the peasants' alienation of their own rituals, such as mummers' plays, while the TV becomes the increasingly favorite medium of relating to them.

The end of my field research did not take me to Heleşteni or Ruginoasa, but outside Romania's borders, to Ukraine. I got there following the *Deer* team in Heleşteni at the *International Cultural Traditions Festival—Bucovina's Malanca* in the city of Chernivtsi, located in the south of Ukraine. In the 21st century, the cultural heritage of the peasants sometimes born in small villages, leaves behind these borders, even along with the borders of the country where they had been living for a long time, becoming transnational and changing their regime property.

Indeed, my presence at the *International Cultural Traditions Festival—Bucovina's Malanca* in Cernăuţi has shown me that this festival's morphology and organization is more like the *Rio de Janeiro Festival* and the *Philadelphia Mummers' Parade.* This type of cultural event in which the "Malănci" are carried on truck platforms to impress thousands of tourists coming from all over Ukraine and Romania, is a perfect embodiment of the concept of cultural industry coined by Max Horkheimer and Theodor Adorno in the middle of the 20th century, rather than an attempt to safeguard rural culture threatened by extinction. In such festivals, mummers' plays are just "consumer items," and the symbols put on stage no longer tell anything about the rural culture that gave birth to the plays. Thus, rural culture becomes exoticized, only to be later consumed as a form of entertainment.

Although it is placed in the spotlight, peasants' culture is even more invisible than when it was living between the borders of the cultural micro-ecosystems that produced it. As Van der Ploeg has well observed, it is about an invisibility created by those entities, individuals and institutions that have contributed to the subordination and marginalization of peasants in recent decades: global food empires, agribusiness groups, large retailers, state apparatuses, scientific models and technologies. But this type of fabricated invisibility is in fact an extremely active and subtle process that Bourdieu circumscribed well through the concept of symbolic violence (Bourdieu and Wacquant 1992). Unfortunately, the type of invisibility and symbolic violence accompanying it have moved from the economic to the academic sphere where the peasant is seen more as an invention of thinkers in a certain historical-political context than as a reality of our times.

However, globalization has brought about not only an acute process of depeasantization, but also the dissipation of this massive social class in all corners of the planet and in all major urban centers. In this context, international organizations that advocate for the rights of peasants have gathered under the umbrella of one of the world's largest existing organizations: *Via Campesina*. In addition to this type of militancy with overwhelming economic purposes, those who have lived under the auspices of peasant culture and have spent their childhood in the countryside will carry the rural plays in their souls, together with all the other traditions that marked their childhood and adolescence. Thus, they will become ad-hoc patrimonialization agents of a type of safeguarding that is little discussed and even mentioned in heritage studies, but which has accompanied the life of human beings for millennia—the story. Through these involuntary and invaluable safeguarding agents, folk plays will become stories told in the most unexpected places and situations in the world. These people who will always be tied with invisible threads to the culture where they had spent a significant part of their lives, will find their "place of meeting" and communication in the virtual space of the internet, through social media sites such as *Facebook*, *Twitter* and, above all, *YouTube*. In addition to the state-led patrimonialization, through formal institutions and complex international organizations such as UNESCO, the type of safeguarding emerging from the globalization overcoat will prove to be extremely persistent and effective in the future. Patrimonialization through state institutions often proves its limits and effectiveness in safeguarding rural culture. This is a lesson demonstrating that institutions created by states or transnational organizations in just a few years or, at most, a few decades, cannot replace certain cultural forms created by customary communities that have proven their efficiency over the centuries.

Afterword

Now, at the end of this approach, it is perhaps time to meditate for a few moments on the title of my book: *The Globalization of Rural Plays in the Twenty-First Century*. If we define globalization as a sum of connections and networks between people, communities, organizations, countries and socio-cultural systems, this work presents exactly a part of this landscape: the way rural customary communities departed from their relatively narrow and limited world, entering the almost unlimited universe of connections, networks and relationships represented by the global society. All these processes were seen through the filter of rural plays whose transformations speak of identity, cultural, economic, and social changes. Although the word globalization did not appear too often in the pages of this paper, it has always been present between the lines. This work presented the effects of capital infusion in the Eastern European rural areas, mainly as a result of labor migration, market economy and consumerism. In addition, it presented the media's intrusions into one of the most genuine parts of the rural world: its winter customs ritually practiced by village communities. Finally, this study presented in ethnographic detail how heritagization, a process designed to safeguard intangible cultural heritage, has in fact become an additional source for the dramatic transformations of authentic rural culture, this time represented by the rural plays created by peasants during their millennial existence within their small customary communities. The advent of market economy in the countryside, bringing about consumerism and commodification, led to capital accumulation and social inequalities at a level never seen before, and has thus brought irreversible changes in the peasants system of values. So, the crumbling of the last bastion represented by the peasant values drove to a torrent of changes that have visibly affected the dynamic and development of rural plays in the countryside. All these streams described in detail throughout the pages of this book are globalization guises that appear in all corners of the planet. However, rivers of ink have already tackled globalization. The uniqueness of this study comes from its focus on peasants from the perspective of their plays (*jocuri*), caught in the grids of globalization—an aspect far too often ignored by social sciences.

Coincidentally, I wrote the last lines of this study a few months after the global crisis caused by the coronavirus pandemic had begun. One of the first questions I asked myself concerned the fate of rural plays in relation to the pandemic. Globally, the coronavirus spread has disrupted many economic and social relations, with numerous businesses and other human activities going bankrupt, with others declining in intensity and, finally, some other blossoming on the brink of the pandemic. "How did the pandemic affect the rural plays in the villages I studied?" was the first question that aroused my curiosity. Although I did not manage to reach Heleșteni and Ruginoasa in December 2020, at the peak of the pandemic, by the end of 2020 I was still able to talk via WhatsApp to my friends in these villages, and to get information about the organization of rural plays during the global coronavirus outbreak. Unfortunately, traffic restrictions from countries such as England, Spain, and Italy—some of the hardest hit Western nations during the crisis—have prevented the arrival of many immigrants to their home villages. Some of these immigrants were fervent supporters of such traditions and their absence in their native villages was visibly impacting in a negative way the organization and development of rural plays. In addition, Pașcani police patrols "who had nothing in common with the custom," according to my friends, turned the mission of the audacious mummers' plays organizers into one full of obstacles and risks, including threats of being arrested or getting big fines. Last but not least, even among the young people there were some who were afraid of coronavirus contamination and stopped organizing traditional mummers' teams around the New Year. The same was noticed by some householders who were anxious to open their doors of carolers' teams. However, the venturesome guys who managed to defeat all these obstacles were rewarded better than usually by householders sick of isolation and restrictions, and glad to see groups of carolers in their courtyards. Thus, each member of the only Goat team that roamed the villages of Heleșteni *comună*, managed to earn 2000 lei ($500) in the two days of the journey through the village. The members of the two Deer teams were able to earn about 1500 lei ($375) per person as well.

By the end of December 2020, during my trip from Boston to Bucharest and then to the city where my parents live—Vulcan, in the south of Hunedoara County, I obtained other valuable information that completed my initial puzzle. First marked by the extreme fear of getting infected, my trip went better than I had initially anticipated, without incidents and unforeseen events, with less crowded airports and planes that took off on time and arrived without delay at the destination. Arriving on the evening of December 24 at the North Railway Station in Bucharest, I met a 12 members team of the *Play of the Bear*. They had come from a village in Suceava County, in the north of Moldova and were going to perform in Craiova, one of the largest cities in the south of the country, after they have caroled through Bucharest for two days. I met a similar team a few days later, this time representing the *Goat play*, on December 28 in the city of Vulcan. Such teams managed to defeat the restrictions and rigors of the pandemic, but especially the personal fear of coronavirus infection, sometimes traveling more than 500 kilometers from their home villages, to play under the windows of the urban apartments. The most convincing sign that their performances were successful was their continuous presence, from Christmas to January 1, on the streets of larger cities. Their success was measured in the fact that an appreciable number of urban dwellers gave them smaller or larger amounts of money, and watched them from balconies and windows.

In this formula, rural plays were reduced to an intense but short dance under apartments windows where the expected effect was obtained by loud noises created by drums and trumpets, but also by a short wish meant to arouse the curiosity and interest of the tenants: *"Scoateți capul la fereastră/Să vedeți căprița noastră/Să vedeți cum vom juca/Să vă veselim așa/Să trăiți ca merii/În mijlocul verii/Să înfloriți ca perii/Să fiți sănatoși ca zeii."* "Head to the window / To see our little goat / To see how we play / To make you glad / May you live like apple trees / In the middle of summer / May you bloom like pear trees / Be healthy like deities." When I approached this team asking them to perform a sketch for me, a guy who seemed to be the leader of the group warned me from the beginning: "Sir, don't you see, we are so many?!" meaning that they deserved a nice reward. Of course, the target of the play had become a purely financial one, in the purest spirit of market economy. But the perseverance and the strong motivation to face the pandemic restrictions, the risk of being questioned or even fined by police patrols, and at the same time the exposure to the coronavirus, is worth being emphasized.

For me, all this was a proof that rural plays overcame the pandemic, managing to bring out many residents at their windows and balconies, all happy to see a drop of vitality and joviality in a world of uncertainty and unrest following almost an entire year overshadowed by draconian restrictions and strict rules that prevented a whole series of shows, games and other cultural activities from taking place. The pandemic has negatively affected rural plays as well, but it has failed to annihilate them. The simple fact that ordinary people supported mummers, despite financial means drastically diminished by the restrictions of the pandemic, was a proof of their vitality in the minds of peasants transformed into city dwellers during socialism and postsocialism. Humans' connections with play thus transcended the narrow and rigid boundaries dictated by the pandemic. I was going to understand this right at the end of the journey I made at the peak of the coronavirus pandemic. Arriving at the Bucharest airport on January 8, I was glad to discover that the souvenir shops were still open. Inside, I saw a whole series of rural-inspired artifacts sold as Romanian identity brands to tourists. But what caught my attention the most was a chic corner with a huge mask that attracted attention from afar. Around it, a collection of wines entitled "Folklore" was on display. The collection comprised five different wines, each with labels representing various images of rural origin. When I got closer, I was surprised to find out that the names on the labels were in fact those of the most popular rural plays in Romania: "The Goat (Capra)," "The Bear (Ursul)," "Călușarii," "Malanca," "The Small Horses (Căiuții)." Immediately accessing the website of that wine company, I found that, in addition to the names and related representations, they also described pertinently in a few sentences those specific customs. This closing event of my journey once again demonstrated to me the power of rural plays' adaptability and their transformation into something different than what they had been before—something that ensured their survival in a world different from the one where they appeared and existed for a long time.

Another thing that came to my mind, giving me a comparative perspective on the universe of mummers, was the relationship between the pandemic and the facial mask. Since the beginning of the pandemic, it has been proved that the face mask is a good protection against the spread of the Covid-19 virus. Most governments on all continents of the planet have understood this simple fact and have tried to impose a series of rules and even laws related to wearing a facial mask. Overnight, we have all became mummers against our own will. These measures had to face many citizens' hostility and sometimes it resulted in violent confrontations between insurgent demonstrators and law enforcement, mostly in the countries considered the most democratic in the world: Germany, France, and the United States. It has been repeated a countless number of times that the mask is a violation of individual freedoms, drastically limiting the ability of people to manifest themselves in various social contexts. Many citizens have resorted to the most inventive methods of criticizing government measures related to the imposition of the face mask. The most common criticism was expressed by wearing masks imprinted with various anti-government slogans, Nazi swastikas, vampire mouths, or demon faces. The face mask was called "the muzzle" referring, once again, to the dictatorial policies of the governments trying to find various measures to stop the spread of the virus. This situation gave me an opportunity for unexpected comparisons.

In rural societies, wearing a mummers' mask was an occasion for joy and satisfaction. The mask was an expression of human freedom, of eroticism, of playfulness, and represented a way of transcending the social constraints of peasant communities with strict rules. Thus, in two different political and social contexts, the same artifact—the mask—proved to be both an expression of human freedom and of the censorship. The meaning of this unforeseen event is that generalizations about the purpose of a mask such as those stating that it embodies "the taste of man for mimicry" (Caillois 1961 [1958]), can often be hasty.

In a way, the world of mummers described in the pages of this study tells us about the evanescence of the grand narratives regarding various aspects related to humans in the relations with their own plays. Paradoxically, to this day, one of the most influential studies of the game is, at the same time, the one including the most fanciful generalizations. I am talking about the study of Roger Caillois, *Man, Play, and Games* (Caillois 1961 [1958]). Demonstrating an extraordinary scholarly erudition, the French sociologist tried, and some of his supporters would say that he succeeded, to offer a taxonomy of the game by subscribing it to six basic features, four play forms and two types of play. Despite this erudition, Caillois does not discuss the games played by peasants at all, and when he refers twice to mummers, he talks about the carnivalized versions of these plays, already exported a while ago from the rural to the urban world. From this point of view, Caillois's study has a stereotypical character which is also found in many other influential research on game/play written since then. Although he devotes important pages to games/plays in tribal societies, and modern games occupy a central place in this work, the plays of the peasants are omitted altogether. Caillois defines the game "as an activity which is essentially:

> *Free:* in which playing is not obligatory; if it were, it would at once lose its attractive and joyous quality as diversion; 2. *Separate:* circumscribed within limits of space and time, defined and fixed in advance; 3. *Uncertain:* the course of which cannot be determined, nor the result attained beforehand, and some latitude for innovations being left to the player's initiative; 4. *Unproductive:* creating neither goods, nor wealth, nor new elements of any kind; and, except for the exchange of property among the players, ending in a situation identical to that prevailing at the beginning of the game; 5. *Governed by rules:* under conventions that suspend ordinary laws, and for the moment establish new legislation, which alone counts; 6. *Make-believe:* accompanied by a special awareness of a second reality or of a free unreality, as against real life. (Caillois 1961: 9–10)

A closer look at the rural universe and at mummers' plays would have given the French sociologist more to think about when defining the game. This is because play/game is not always an activity in which humans are necessarily involved by means of their own free will. The rural world with its strict rules and dominated by the dense social networks that made mumming possible proves that in this cultural environment the pressure on the individual is often very high, making him participate in some games/plays even against his own will. In this respect, there is an eloquent saying in the village world: *"Odată intrat în horă trebuie să joci!"* *"Once you enter the choir, you have to play!"* This saying precisely demonstrates the coercive power of the game in the context of dense social networks. I am also wondering if one could consider the "victims" of the mummers (those unmasked inhabitants caught walking on the streets of the village during the winter holidays and harassed on the spot by 5–6 masked guys) to be players, too? I think the answer is yes. But, then, could one state that they took part in this game through their own free will? Another relevant example in this regard would be that of gladiators who used to participate in those Colosseum's games of death. I am wondering again if they did this because of their own free will or constrained by unfavorable circumstances. More recently, an example taken from the modern world are the pranks that sometimes have a huge television success. In this case, the comic effect stems from the fact that the victims are involuntarily caught in the game. Could it be stated in this case that the victims of pranks are not actors of the play in which they were involuntarily caught?

Regarding the second characteristic of the game, that of being separate from reality, "circumscribed within the limits of space and time, defined and fixed in advance," it is obvious that the French sociologist refers especially to modern games, developed mostly after the Industrial Revolution. Let us remember the Ruginoasa Battle with Sticks, Ba game, Royal Shrovetide Football and Lelo Burti that we have talked about in this study. All these games were little limited to a certain space and time, and could last a few minutes or a few hours, while their playground could sometimes, depending on the circumstances, be very restricted or, on the contrary, extremely vast, with a virtually unlimited expansion.

Looking at the third feature of the game discussed by Caillois, namely the uncertain nature of the game whose course can neither be determined, nor anticipated in terms of results, I can provide, once again, solid counterexamples from the world of mummers. Let us remember the journey of the Deer Play or of the Goat Play teams from Heleşteni. Their route was predetermined by the *comoraş* (the head of the team) together with the members of his band, and the play was always the same. Even the sums of money offered by the villagers could be easily anticipated from the experience of previous years, and the good knowledge of the householders in the village could also enhance the anticipation of their interaction with the team members. Therefore, the uncertain nature of these games was not necessarily a feature that accompanied these plays.

Concerning the fourth feature of the game, namely its unproductive nature, the same Play of the Deer and Play of the Goat show that the financial motivation was important for the members of the respective teams. The end of the game brought a significant amount of money for the team members. This happened even though the plays included an important social component, in addition to the financial motivation that stimulated players to get involved in such activities.

As for the fifth characteristic of the game, that of being governed by rules that suspend common practices and temporarily replace them with something different, one of the basic arguments of this book militated precisely against this aspect. Far from being a reversal of the social order, mummers' plays were only a necessary component of the rural world without which it could not function at its normal parameters. In other words, the game/play does not represent a parallel universe of the rural world, but a basic attribute of it that ensures its proper functioning in an organic ensemble that includes both elements: work and play.

Finally, the last feature of the game mentioned by the French sociologist is also the most complicated to analyze. In many games, the player is indeed clearly aware that the game really involves types of rules different than everyday reality. However, a scrutiny of several games shows that the process of becoming aware of a second reality is very porous in terms of boundaries and consciousness, which does not necessarily coincide with a specific temporary moment; instead, it is blurred and sometimes very unclear. Consider, for example, the whole ritual involved by the Play of the Deer. What is the moment that makes the player become aware of a reality of the play distinct from everyday life? Is it when he performs the actual play in a householder's yard, when the team walks through the village from one house to another, or during the entire duration of two and a half days of this play? On the other hand, let's think about children's gambols that start out of nowhere and end just as abruptly few minutes after their debut. Is there always a consciousness that accompanies these sudden transitions from the state of play to that of non-play? Additionally, if we refer to the training of athletes, outside the official games when they are not dictated by the whistle and the presence of the referee, the same problem as before arises: when exactly does the player's awareness of the presence of a secondary reality begin, making the game a reality parallel to that of everyday life? In this indistinct landscape, isn't it easier to assume that play is an essential part of life, inextricably linked to the way humans conceive their relationship with the social universe where they live?

The attempt to find a series of fundamental features of the game or to pour the whole universe embodied by games into a series of categories starts from the assumption that the game/play has an essence, and that this essence can be captured by a heuristic exercise. In fact, for humans, the game is only a way in which they approach certain social, political, economic, psychological, cultural, and philosophical realities. That is why the game/play is nothing but a way of being in the world in relation to the events of life. For the same reason, games/plays are always cultural expressions of the societies that have created and performed them for years. So, they can function as barometers of the societies that perform them, and the changes within them tell us about a series of profound challenges in the values of the society that produced them. In this sense, the first part of the present study was revealing because it presented the challenges of the postsocialist period through the lens of the plays performed by a social class in the process of transformation and re-evaluation of its own values: the peasantry. The first part of the study is therefore relevant because it shows how plays are influenced by social phenomena such as the migration, the political and economic change, the social inequalities, and the media intrusions within them. All this led to a change of values in society, and the values always become explicit in the game.

So, if the game is such a volatile territory, the question is why have so many thinkers fallen into the trap of trying to find a definition of the game? I found at least two pertinent answers to this question. First of all, many of the thinkers who approached the problem of the game were subordinated to the positivist thinking of the modern times, starting from the assumption that the game/play has an essence, and this can be circumscribed by a definition. Secondly, all these thinkers assumed that it was more productive to understand the essence of the game than humans' propensity to play.

In my opinion, a thinker who explained well the humans' inclination towards the game/play was Couliano when he stated that "a game fascinates the human mind because the mind recognizes in it its own functioning, and this recognition does not depend on the kind of game offered to the mind" (Couliano 1992: 247). It seems that Couliano understood something very simple: the game/play is a product of the human mind, thus related to storytelling, drama, fantasy, myth, and religion—all of which are works of imagination in a specific social context. In his existence, the individual needs all these or at least a part of them because his mind functions according to the pattern offered by the principles provided by these works of the imagination in various social, political, and cultural circumstances.

Another thinker who managed to open a new window to a different understanding of the game is Wittgenstein. He outlined the idea that the game cannot be defined because it is an expression of the life experience acquired by members of a society over time. Trying to define the game is impossible because it always leads to logically inadequate definitions. And this happens not because there are no extraordinary thinkers who could accomplish this task, but because the limits of the game are coextensive with those of the social and cultural reality of humans across all times and spaces. From this point of view, it is rather interesting to observe how various cultures activate certain patterns of the human mind. The same model can be applied to moments of the individual life because the games/plays the individual plays in childhood are no longer the same as those of maturity or old age. The short poem of the Romanian poet Lucian Blaga, entitled *Three Faces*, is very relevant in this respect:

> *Copilul râde:*
> *"Înțelepciunea și iubirea mea e jocul!"*
> *Tânărul cântă:*
> *"Jocul și-nțelepciunea mea-i iubirea!"*
> *Bătrânul tace:*
> *"Iubirea și jocul meu e înțelepciunea!"*
>
> The child laughs:
> "Play is my wisdom and my love!"
> The young one sings:
> "Love is my play and my wisdom!"
> The old man remains silent:
> "Wisdom is my love and my play!"

Having reached this point, the reader of the book might ask, in the light of this new information, what the role of mummers and of their performers—peasants—is in the rather complex landscape related to the game/play. In this regard, two important purposes of this study could be highlighted: the construction of a new conceptual framework through which folk plays can be understood, and the rethinking of a social class—the peasantry—about which an enormous number of works were written over time. However, despite this, anthropology has never examined it through the lens of its plays.

Many of the scholars who studied folk plays got seduced by mummers' masks and costumes and could not see behind them. That is why some of them saw in *mummers' plays* only several surviving cultural forms of eras long gone (Chambers 1969 [1933]). With this research, I tried to see beyond the charming masks of mummers. There, I saw human beings and their attempts to respond to problems of the world they lived in, including capital shortages, social inequalities, the challenges of a new economic and social system, as well as universal human problems like illness, death, eroticism, pride, identity, marriage, and love.

Rural plays and peasants were the main concepts of the present study, but they should finally be put aside as they were just a pretext for a deeper understanding of humans and of their great existential dilemmas related to life, illness, freedom, sexuality, love, violence, and death or their little passions, hopes, needs, aspirations, problems, and daily worries, whether their life was lived between the borders of small agricultural communities, or in the globalized society of the 21st century. By understanding these aspects, we should now abandon the concepts that have accompanied us all along, and take a look beyond them. Following Wittgenstein, I could say that they were just a ladder we can throw away once we climb it: "he who understands me finally recognizes them as senseless, when he has climbed out through them, on them, over them. (He must so to speak throw away the ladder, after he has climbed up on it)" (Wittgenstein 1922: 189).

Appendix I

DOCUMENTS FROM DU CANGE'S GLOSSARIUM, MENTIONING THE PLAY OF THE DEER AND THE MUMMERS' PLAYS IN MEDIEVAL EUROPE

Cervula (par C. du Cange, 1678), in du Cange, et al., Glossarium mediae et infimae latinitatis, éd. augm., Niort: L. Favre, 1883–1887, t. 2, col. 277c.

Cervula, Cervulus, Ludi profani, apud Ethnicos et Paganos: solebant quippe ii Kalendis Januarii belluarum, pecudum, et vetularum assumptis formis huc et illuc discursare, et petulantius sese gerere: quod a Christianis non modo proscriptum, sed et ab iis postmodum inductum constat, ut ea die ad calcandam Gentilium consuetudinem privatæ fierent Litaniæ, et jejunaretur, ut observare est ex Concilio Toletano IV. can. 10. S. Isidoro lib. 1. de Offic. Eccles. cap. 40. Concilio Turon. II. can. 17.

The Deer [Cervula], the Little Stag [Cervulus], profane dance at barbarians / pagans and peasants[1]: indeed, at the calends of January, taking the appearance / shape of wild animals, cattle[2] or old women / old maids, [they used] to run around and to behave rudely / shamelessly / with no shame: it is clear that this thing was not only forbidden by Christians, but they even decided / introduced that in that day, in order to eliminate / suppress the pagans' custom, one should make private litanies and fast, as it turns out / one observes in the Toledo Council . . .

S. Augustinus Serm. De Tempore 215:

Si adhuc agnoscatis aliquos illam sordidissimam turpitudinem de hinnula, vel Cervula exercere, ita durissime castigate, ut eos pœniteat rem sacrilegam commisisse.

If you know other people that perform this sordid and disgusting custom / a spurious and despicable thing that has to do with *the deer (hinnula)* and *the little stag (Cervula),*[3] scold them harshly so that they repent for committing a sacrilege / they did a unlawful thing.

Vita S. Eligii lib. 2. cap. 15:

Nullus in Kalend. Januarii nefanda et ridiculosa, vetulas, aut Cervulos, aut jotticos faciat.

Nobody should in the calends of January do spurious and ridiculous things, such as *The Old Women*[4] or *The Little Stags* (Cervulos) or *plays (superstitious).*

Concil. Autissiod. can. 1:

Non licet Kalendis Januarii vetula aut Cervolo facere, vel strenas diabolicas observare, etc.

It is not permitted at the calends of January to feast with the [custom of] Old Woman / old maid and the Little Stag,[5] nor to keep / respect the custom of the devilish / cursed gifts.

Halitgarius in Pœnitent. cap. 6:

Si quis in Kalendis Januarii, quod multi faciunt, et in Cervulo ducit, aut in vetula vadit, 3. annos pœniteat.

If at the calends of January someone, as many do, walks with *The Stag* or behaves as *Old Woman* [in Cervulo ducit, in vetula vadit], he should repent for three years.

Ita apud Commeanum in lib. de mensura pœnitentiarum cap. 7. Burchard. lib. 19. cap. 5:

Fecisti aliquid tale, quod pagani fecerunt, et adhuc faciunt in Kalendis Januarii in Cervolo et vetula: si fecisti 30. dies in pane et aqua pœniteas.

Did you do something such as pagans did and still do at the calends of January, with the [play of] the Little Stag and the Old Woman: if you did that, then you should repent for 30 days, with bread and water.

Meminit præterea Cervuli S. Pacianus in Parænesi ad pœnitentiam. Denique S. Ambrosius in Psalm. 41:

Sed jam satis in exordio tractatus, sicut in principio anni, more vulgi Cervus allusit.

St. Pacianus then mentions the *Cervulus,* in *Paraenesis,* at the penitence. St. Ambrose also mentions it in Psalm 41:

But from the beginning already [the topic] was enough treated / exposed, that in the beginning of the year, following the people's custom, the *Stag* [*Cervus*] was performed.

Faustinus Episcopus Sermone in Kl. Jan.:

Quis enim sapiens credere poterit inveniri aliquos sanæ mentis, qui Cervulum facientes, in ferarum se velint habitus commutari? Alii vestiuntur pellibus pecudum, alii assumunt capita bestiarum, gaudentes et exultantes, si taliter se in ferinas species transformaverint, ut homines non esse videantur.

For what wise man could believe that there are sane people who would want to change [their appearance] to wild animals / beasts, making / feasting the Cervulus? Some dress in cattle skins, others wear animal heads above, feasting and jumping so that, had they turned into wild animal species, they would not seem to be human anymore.

Maximus Taurinensis in Serm. in Kal. Jan.:

Nunquid non universa ibi falsa sunt, et insana, cum se a Deo formati homines aut in pecudes, aut in feras, aut in portenta transformant.

Isn't all that false and crazy, when people created by God turn into cattle or beasts or monsters.

Bonifacius Episc. Moguntin. Ep. ad Zachariam PP. cap. 6:

Affirmant se vidisse annis singulis in Romana urbe, et juxta Ecclesiam S. Petri, in die vel nocte, quando Calendæ Januarii intrant, paganorum consuetudine choros ducere per plateas, et acclamationes ritu gentilium, et cantationes sacrilegas celebrare, et mensas illas die vel nocte dapibus onerare, et nullum de domo sua, vel ignem, vel ferramentum, vel aliquid comodi vicino suo præstare velle.

They state that every year they saw in the city of Rome, and close to St. Peter's Church, in daylight and at night, when the calends of January begin, dances and incantations as with the unfaithful ones, and profane songs are celebrated, and tables are full day and night with banquets, and nothing from the household is given to the neighbor, neither fire, not iron instrument, nothing [that could be] useful.[6]

NOTES

1. The term *ethnicos* is used for naming ethnic groups, folks, barbarian populations unconverted to Christianism, pagan. The term *paganos* refers to peasants, the rural population that has been superficially christianized and had a deeply syncretic trait.

2. Here, the term *cattle* is used generically (cf. it. *bestiame*, en. *cattle*), naming both small cattle (sheep, goats) and bovines (cows, oxen).

3. The two terms, *hinnula* and *Cervula* stand for the mask play, not for the animals.

4. The reference is to *Old Women.*

5. This is a free translation, given the particularity of the syntactic structure "facere + Abl." In other versions of the text, we have *vitulo* (eng. calf) instead of *vetula*.

6. Translation from Latin by Carmen Fenechiu, revised by Bogdan Neagota.

Appendix II

THE OLD INCANTATION OF THE DEER

The incantation of the deer collected by Professor Ion H. Ciubotaru from Ştefan Paul, 16 years old, in the village of Oboroceni, *comuna* Heleşteni, in 1970s, and published in the book *Traditions on the Iaşi land*, Pim Publishing House, Iaşi 2010. Translation by Mirona Palas. Source: Heleşteni Community.

Descântecul Cerbului	The incantation of the deer
Foiliţî de-on bujor,	Leaflet of a peony,
Vin'la tata puişor,	Come to pappy, lil' one,
Cerbu tati cu cercei	Pappy's deer with eardrops,
Spuni-i tati ci mai vrei?	Tell yer pappy what more you want?
Ori ţî-i foami,	Are you hungry,
Ori ţî-i săti,	Are you thirsty,
Ori ţî-i dor di codru verdi?	Or you long for the green forest?
Codru verdi l-ai văzut,	The green forest, you have seen,
Cî într-însu-ai fost crescut,	In it you were born and reared,
Aşa, Jănic,-aşa!	That's the way, son, that's the way!
Ia mai dă tu ochişorii roatî	Come and cast your eyes around you
Şî ti uitî-n lumea toatî,	And look into the whole wide world
Cî di cinci anişori di zâli,	Cuz for whole five years 'n a row
Di cînd umblu eu cu tini	Since I've been wandering with you
Tu nu mî cunoşti pi mini!	You still haven't known me, have you!
Eu sunt bulibaşu Stănicî,	My name's Stănicî 'n I am a gypsy king
Cari discântî la ulcicî,	Who breaks spells in a pipkin
Cu lingura, cu cusâtura,	With the spoon and with the stitch
Cu barosu şî cu gura,	With the mallet or the lips
Cu lingura ti hrăneam,	With the spoon I used to feed you,

Cu pila ti pileam,	With the file I used to file you,
Cu cusâtura ti cosâtoram,	With the stitch I used to stitch you
Cu barosu-n cap dădeam,	With the mallet I'd hit heads
Di la răuri ti scapam,	From the evils I had saved you,
Măi botosule uăăi!	Oh, you morose, you!
Eu pi tini te-am găsât	I found you
Într-o păduri,	Right in the woodland
Înnodat î fragi şî mure,	Tangled in berries and bramble
Înnodat şî susţânat	Tangled and propped
Şî di coarni agăţat.	With your horns all gibbeted
Eu fragi şi mure le-am tăiat	And I cut through wild berries and
Şi te tine te-am scăpat.	bramble
Te-am adus din codru verdi,	And I set you free.
Te-am scăpat în sat la feti,	Took you out of the green woods,
Fetili când te-au văzut,	In the village among the damsels,
Tu pi loc ai şi căzut	You broke loose.
Si-o cordică roşie mi-ai pierdut,	When the damsels spotted you,
Măi tătucă uăăăi!	You fell down right on the spot
	And you lost me a red rope,
	Oh, you little one, oh!
La leliţa la cerdac	There, on the dame's porch,
Frumos creşte-on liliac	Nicely grows a lilac bush
Şi mă-ntreabî di ci zac;	Asking why I lie around;
Ori di cori,	Have I measles,
Ori di varsat,	Have I smallpox?
Ţî la dracu, ţî dalac,	To hell with it! Damn you,
Nu eşti bolnav di dalac,	*Devil-in-a-Bush*!
Cî mai ai ş-un rost în sat!	You're not sick of anthrax
Ş-am zâs verdi de-on bujor,	You're still of avail 'n 'tis village!
Hai la tata puişor,	So I say, green leaf of a peony
Şî te-apleacî frumuşăl,	Come to pappy, lil' one,
Ca frunza di pătrunjăl,	And lean over nicely,
Aşa tat,-aşa!	Like the leaves of the parsley
	That's the way, son, that's the way.
Băi ursari,ursari voinici,	Ye bear-leaders, fine 'n sturdy
Di când stati pi la potici,	bear-leaders,
N-aţi văzut vrun grec pe-aici?	Ever since ye hovering about these tracks,
Grec bătrân, cu punga plinî,	Have ye seen a Greek walking 'long these
Ci sî duci la hodinî	paths?
Şi pândeşti	A Greek old man, with a bagful,
Ca pi mini sî mă prindî	Going to have a loll
Iar pi tini sî ti vândî,	But lurking
Sî ti ducî la abator,	To catch me
Sî-ţi facî cărniţa ta rasol,	And to sell you,
Iar din corniţele tale,	Take you to the butchery,
Albe şi strălucitoare,	Cook jelly of your meat

Umerare la cucoane,	And make of your little horns,
Nu vrai tată,nuu!	White and glossy ones,
	Hangers for the missies,
	You wouldn't want that, baby, no!
Mă duceam pe o cărare,	I was walking down a path
Di nimenea umblată,	Trodden by nobody,
Di nimenea calcată,	On which no one set foot yet,
Numai di furnici pişcatî	Beaten by little ants only
Şî de-o babî fermecatî.	And charmed by an ol' judy
Văzui şerpi cu nouă colţi de fier	I saw snakes with nine iron fangs,
Cu nouă de oţel,	With nine of steel,
Cu nouă umblătoare,	With nine rovers,
Cu nouă plimbătoare,	With nine hoofers,
Cu nouă fermecătoare,	With nine soothsayers,
Aşa, tatî,-aşaa!	That's the way, son, that's the way!
Măi,Jănică,puişor,	Hey, little Jănică, baby mine,
Di ţ-o fost di mini dor,	If you missed me
Di ci n-ai luat tu	Why did you not kiss
Guriţa ta cei cu amor,	With your little loving yap
Într-o frunzî di bujor	The leaf of a peony,
S-o trimeţi la mini-n zbor,	And then wing it to me?
Sî mă rog lui Dumnezău	To God Almighty I pray
Sî-ţi facî mai binişor,	To keep you alive and hale
N-ai vrut,tatî, nuu!	You didn't want it, sonny, did you!
Băi, la fântâna lui Adam,	Hey, at the fountain of Adam,
La izvorul lui Iordan	At the spring of river Jordan
Sunt doi dardări di jidani,	There are two yids
Care dau bani peste bani	Who'd pay lots of money
Şi mie peste mie,	And thousands of dibs
Ca pe mine să mă prindă,	To catch me,
Iar pe tine să te vândă!	And to sell you!
Hai răspunde mai curând,	C'mon, sonny, answer now,
Cî-ţi zbor crierii în vânt,	Or I'll blow your brains out,
Şî ti sparg cu-acest ţăpoi,	And I'll thrust you with this pitchfork
Cari-mpart fânu la oi,	That gathers hay for the sheep flock
Ş-am o ghioagî ţîntuitî	And I also have a stick
Pentru capul tău gătitî,	Ready for your head to hit,
Aşa,tat,-aşaa!	That's the way, son, that's the way!
Ia mai fă tu ochişorii roatî	Cast your eyes around once more
Şî ti uitî-n lumea toatâ;	'N look into the whole wide world;
Cî eu răul di pi chelea ta	Cause the evil on your fell
În veşca dobi l-oi lua	I will hide in the drum frame,
Şî-n Marea Caspicî l-oi arunca.	Into the Caspian Sea I'll throw away.
Tu sî rămâi curat	You shall remain pure
Şî luminat,	And bright

Ca Iancu din sat,	Like that old man John in village
Cari nu mai ari	Who ain't got no more left
Nici un par la gard!	No more stakes to his fence!
Pusei traista-n cui,	I hung the purse on the hook,
Făinî-ntr-însa nu-i,	Flour in it there is nary.
Pusei oala la foc,	I put the pot on the fire,
Lemni nu sunt diloc,	Firewood there is not any.
Aşa, tatî,-aşaa!	That's the way, son, that's the way.!
Frunzuliţî stuh di baltî,	Reed leaflet, down by the lake,
Lasî vântu sî ti batî,	Let the wind blow you,
Şî soarili sî ti ardî,	And the sun burn you,
Dac-ai fost tu blastamat	If you were cursed
Di mini sî fii discântat,	I shall free you from your spell,
Aşa,Jănic,-aşaa!	That's the way, Jănic, that's the way.!

La vatra cu doi tăciuni,	In front of a fireplace with two cinders
Undi fac fetili rugăciuni	Some gals say their prayers,
Sâmbata,duminica,	Saturdays or Sundays,
Sî să poatî mărita.	To be able to get spliced.
Da cini dracu sî li ia,	But who the deuce would wanna
	wed them?
Cî-s bătrâni ca mama	Cuz they're old as my mamma,
Şi cărunţi ca tata!	And as grizzled as my ol' papa!
Da nici mama nu-i bătrânî,	Mamma either's not that old,
Cî mai ari-un dinti-n gurî,	Got one tooth in her mouth hole,
Ari-un dinti ş-o măsă	She's got one tooth and a grinder
Şî îs pusî-n lopoţă;	One is here 'n one is yonder;
Când mânâncî molfăeşti,	That's why when she eats, she mumbles,
Când be apî mă stropeşti,	And when she drinks water, she sprinkles.
Aşa,tat,-aşaa!	That's the way, son, that's the way!

Băi ursari, jos ti puni
Şî din gur-începi-a spuni,
Cît mânâncî borş cu peşti
Şî discântî ursăreşti.
Eu ştiu multî discântăturî,
C-am mâncat multî fripturî
Şî di multî ce-am mâncat
C-un ciolan m-am înecat.
Părinţî, cân au aflat,
Di mânî m-au luat
Şî afarî pi uşî m-au dat!
Ş-am luat-o pi-nsarati,
Şî m-am însurat măi frati,
Aşa, tat,-aşaa!

Auleu şî vai de mine,
Cân credeam cî ţî-i mai bine
Tu ti-mbolnăveşti cu zile!
Măi Ioane, Ionele,
Adî cuţâtu cu stricnele
Sî-i ieu sângi cerbului
Din piept,
Di sub piept,
Din sprânceana ochiului drept,
Din rărunchi,
Di sub rărunchi,
Din sprânceana ochiului stâng!
Din codiţa lui cea mică
Sai în sus tu, măi Jenică!
Şî sî sai o datî-n sus
Ca sî nu ma faci di râs,
Şî sî sai o datî bini,
Ca sî nu ma faci di ruşâni
Într-atâta amar di lumi!

Sai, Jănică,
Recunoaşte-ţi locu
Şi urmează iarăşi jocul!
Frunzuliţî de-on harbuz
Sî ţâi minti ci ţ-am spus,
Sî mai sai, Jănică-n sus!
Foai verdi lămâiţî
Zi-i din trişcî măi bădiţî!

Bear-leader, hey, seat yourself down
And start out to mouth,
While they eat borsch with fish
And break spells, like bear tamers do.
I know how to break many spells,
Cuz I ate a lot of steaks
And because I ate that much,
With a bone I choked and such,
When my parents this found out
They took me by the hand
'N through the door they kicked me out!
While the night was dawning, I went
    farther
And I got married, my dear brother,
That's the way, son, that's the way!

Alas and woe and misery!
When I thought you're better still
For many days you're taken ill!
Hey, dear Ioan, oh Ionică blade,
Bring me that sharp bleeding blade
To bleed the deer
From its chest,
From under its chest,
From the eyebrow of the right eye,
From the reins,
From under the reins
From the eyebrow of the left eye!
From its little tail
Up you jump, dear Jănică boy!
And jump once up
Don't put me to shame,
And jump up high once again
Let me not embarrass myself
In front of that many people!

Jump, Jănică, jump,
Take your place
And follow up the game!
Leaflet of a watermelon
Now remember what I told ya.
Jump up and again, oh Jănică!
Green leaf of the thyme,
Blow the penny trumpet, boy!

Appendix III

Table A3.1. The Demography of Heleşteni Comună's from 1912 to 2011

Year 1912			
Comună	Village		
Heleşteni	Heleşteni-Hărmăneasa	Oboroceni	Movileni
1973 inhabitants	1037 inhabitants	750 inhabitants	186 inhabitants

Year 1930			
Comună	Village		
Heleşteni	Heleşteni-Hărmăneasa	Oboroceni	Movileni
2098 inhabitants	1073 inhabitants	830 inhabitants	231 inhabitants

Year 1956			
Comună	Village		
Heleşteni	Heleşteni	Oboroceni	Movileni
3250 inhabitants	1692 inhabitants	1132 inhabitants	426 inhabitants

Year 1966				
Comună	Village			
Heleşteni	Heleşteni	Hărmăneasa	Oboroceni	Movileni
3393 inhabitants	847 inhabitants	1023 inhabitants	1124 inhabitants	399 inhabitants

Appendix III

Year 1977				
Comună	Village			
Heleşteni	Heleşteni	Hărmăneasa	Oboroceni	Movileni
3424 inhabitants	891 inhabitants	1086 inhabitants	1106 inhabitants	359 inhabitants
Year 1992				
Comună	Village			
Heleşteni	Heleşteni	Hărmăneasa	Oboroceni	Movileni
2600 inhabitants	740 inhabitants	762 inhabitants	859 inhabitants	239 inhabitants
Year 2002				
Comună	Village			
Heleşteni	Heleşteni	Hărmăneasa	Oboroceni	Movileni
2654	809	772	827	246
Year 2011				
Comună	Village			
Heleşteni	Heleşteni	Hărmăneasa	Oboroceni	Movileni
2626	815	760	825	226

Credit: Adapted by Alin Rus from the Archive of Heleşteni comună, and Iaşi City Bureau of Statistics (The National Censuses).

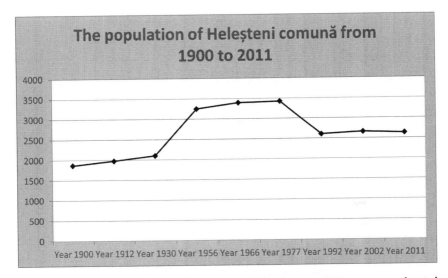

Figure A3.1. The population of Heleșteni comună for the year 1900 was approximated as 1864 people. Before 1912 this comună had a different administrative–territorial structure and did not include Movileni village but included Volintirești village, which is now part of Cuza comună.

Credit: Adapted by Alin Rus using data from two sources: the Archive of Heleșteni comună, and Iași City Bureau of Statistics (The National Censuses)

Bibliography

Abrahams, Roger. 1972. "Folk Drama." In *Folklore and Folklife. An Introduction,* Edited by Richard M. Dorson, 351–62. Chicago: The University of Chicago Press.

Adăscăliței, Vasile. 1966. "Varietatea Teatrului Popular Haiducesc." *Revista de Folclor* 1: 147–52.

———. 1968. "Jocul Cerbului În Moldova." *Revista de Etnografie Și Folclor* 5 (13): 421–38.

Akram-Lodhi, A. Haroon, and Cristóbal Kay, eds. 2009. *Peasants and Globalization: Political Economy, Agrarian Transformation and Development.* London and New York: Routledge.

Andrews, David L., and Steven J. Jackson. 2002. *Sport Stars: The Cultural Politics of Sporting Celebrity.* London and New York: Routledge.

Araghi, Farshad A. 1995. "Global Depeasantization, 1945–1990." *Sociological Quarterly* 36 (2): 337–68.

Arizpe, Lourdes. 2013. "Singularity and Micro-Regional Strategies in Intangible Cultural Heritage." In *Anthropological Perspectives on Intangible Cultural Heritage,* 17–36. Cham; New York: Springer.

Bacu, Dumitru. 2016. *The Anti-Humans.* 1st edition. Helsingborg: Logik Förlag.

Bakhtin, Mikhail Mikhaĭlovich. 1984. *Rabelais and His World.* Bloomington: Indiana University Press.

Baskerville, Charles Read. 1924. "Mummers' Wooing Plays in England." *Modern Philology* 21 (3): 225–72.

Beatty, Arthur. 1906. *The St. George, or Mummers' Plays; a Study in the Protology of the Drama.* Madison, WI.

Beeman, William O. 1993. "The Anthropology of Theater and Spectacle." *Annual Review of Anthropology* 22: 369–93.

Ben-Dor, Shmuel. 1969. "The 'Naluyuks' of Northern Labrador: A Mechanism of Social Control." In *Christmas Mumming in Newfoundland,* 119–27. Newfoundland: University of Toronto Press.

Berdichewsky, Bernardo. 1979. "Anthropology and the Peasant Mode of Production." In *Anthropology and Social Change in Rural Areas,* 5–42. Bristol: Mouton.

Blaga, Lucian. 1919. *Poemele luminii (Poems of Light).* Sibiu. Biroul de Imprimate Cosînzeana

Bourdieu, Pierre. 2008. *The Bachelors' Ball: The Crisis of Peasant Society in Béarn*. Translated by Richard Nice. Chicago: University of Chicago Press.

Bourdieu, Pierre, and Loïc J. D. Wacquant. 1992. *An Invitation to Reflexive Sociology*. 1st edition. Chicago: University of Chicago Press.

———. 2004. "Symbolic Violence." In *Violence in War and Peace,* edited by Nancy Scheper-Hughes and Philippe Bourgois. Oxford: Blackwell Publishing Ltd.

Brody, Alan. 1971. *The English Mummers and Their Plays: Traces of Ancient Mystery*. Philadelphia: University of Pennsylvania Press.

Brown, Stuart. 2009. "Play Is More than Just Fun." *Ted Radio Hour*. Boston.

Brown, Stuart, and Christopher Vaughan. 2010. *Play: How It Shapes the Brain, Opens the Imagination, and Invigorates the Soul*. Reprint edition. New York: Avery.

Bruckner, Pascal. 2000. *The Temptation of Innocence: Living in the Age of Entitlement*. New York: Algora Publishing.

Bryceson, Deborah Fahy. 2000a. "Disappearing Peasantries? Rural Labour Redudancy in the Neo-Liberal Era and Beyond." In *Disappearing Peasantries? Rural Labour in Africa, Asia and Latin America,* edited by Deborah Bryceson, Cristobal Kay and Jos Mooij, 299–326. London: Intermediate Technology Publications.

———. 2000b. "Peasant Theories and Smallholder Policies: Past and Present." In *Disappearing Peasantries? Rural Labour in Africa, Asia and Latin America,* edited by Deborah Bryceson, Cristobal Kay, and Jos Mooij, 1–36. London: Intermediate Technology Publications.

Burson, Anne C. 1980. "Model and Text in Folk Drama." *The Journal of American Folklore* 93 (369): 305–16.

Caillois, Roger. 1961. *Man, Play, and Games*. Urbana and Chicago: University of Illinois Press.

Cantemir, Dimitrie. 2016. *Descrierea Moldovei*. Iași: Litera.

Caraman, Petru. 1997. *Descolindatul în orientul și sud-estul Europei: studiu de folclor comparat*. Iași: Editura Universității "Alexandru Ioan Cuza."

Cash, Jennifer R. 2011. *Villages on Stage: Folklore and Nationalism in the Republic of Moldova*. Berlin: London: LIT Verlag.

Cawte, E. C., Alex Helm, and N. Peacock. 1967. *English Ritual Drama: A Geographical Index*. 1st edition. London: Folk-Lore Society.

Chambers, Edmund. 1969. *The English Folk-Play*. Oxford: Oxford University Press.

Chayanov, Alexander. 1991. *The Theory of Peasant Co-Operatives*. Ohio: Ohio State University Press Columbus.

Chiaramonte, Louis J. 1969. "Mumming in Deep Harbour: Aspects of Social Organization in Mumming and Drinking." In *Christmas Mumming in Newfoundland,* 76–103. Newfoundland: University of Toronto Press.

Chirot, Daniel. 1989. *The Origins of Backwardness in Eastern Europe: Economics and Politics from the Middle Ages Until the Early Twentieth Century*. University of California Press.

Cihodaru, C., I. Caproșu, and N. Ciocan. 1980. *Documenta Romaniae Historica. A.Moldova*. Vol. Volumul III (1487–1504). București: Editura Academiei Republicii Socialiste România.

Cioran, E. M. 2013. *The Trouble with Being Born*. New York: Simon and Schuster.

Ciubotaru, Ion H. 2010. *Datini de Pe Meleagurile Ieşene*. Iaşi: Pim.

Clark, John. 2015. "'Playing the Stag' in Medieval Middlesex? A Perforated Antler from South Mimms Castle—Parallels and Possibilities." In *Deer and People*, edited by Karis Baker, Ruth Carden and Richard Madgwick, 208–15. Oxford: Oxbow Books.

Coillie, Dries van. 1969. *I Was Brainwashed in Peking*. Nederlandse Boekdruk Industrie n.v.

Cole, John W. 1976. "Familial Dynamics in a Romanian Worker Village." *Dialectical Anthropology* 1 (3): 251–65.

Cook, Vivian, and Mark Newson. 1995. *Chomsky's Universal Grammar: An Introduction*. 2 edition. Oxford, OX, UK; Cambridge, MA, USA: Wiley-Blackwell.

Couliano, Ioan P. 1992. *The Tree of Gnosis: Gnostic Mythology from Early Christianity to Modern Nihilism*. 1st HarperCollins edition. San Francisco: Harpercollins.

Crăciun, Boris. 1969. *Ruginoasa*. Iaşi: Casa Judeţeană a Creaţiei Populare Iaşi.

Creangă, Ion. 1978. *Memories of My Boyhood: Stories and Tales*. Bucureşti: Minerva.

———. 2010. *Fairy Tales by Ion Creangă: Harap Alb, Ivan Turbinca, Danila Prepeleac, the Goat and Her Three Kids*. General Books LLC.

Creed, Gerald W. 2011. *Masquerade and Postsocialism: Ritual and Cultural Dispossession in Bulgaria*. Bloomington: Indiana University Press.

Dalton, George. 1967. *Tribal and Peasant Economies*. 1967: Second University of Texas Press Printing.

———. 1971. *Economic Anthropology and Development: Essays on Tribal and Peasant Economics*. Basic Books.

———. 1972. "Peasantries in Anthropology and History." *Current Anthropology* 13 (3/4): 385–415.

Deletant, Dennis. 1999. *Communist Terror in Romania: Gheorghiu-Dej and the Police State, 1948–1965*. New York: Hurst.

Derrida, Jacques. 1981. *Dissemination*. London and New York: Continuum.

Doke, C. M. 1936. "Games, Plays and Dances of the ǂKhomani Bushmen." *Bantu Studies* 10 (1).

Dosoftei. 1974. *Psaltirea în versuri*. Iaşi: Mitropolia Moldovei si Sucevei.

Drace-Francis, Alex. 2013. *The Traditions of Invention: Romanian Ethnic and Social Stereotypes in Historical Context*. Leiden; Boston: Brill.

Du Cange, Charles du Fresne. 1678. *Glossarium Ad Scriptores Mediae et Infirmae Graecitatis*. Paris: J. Posuel et C. Rigaud.

Ebewo, Patrick. 2001. "Satire and the Performing Arts: The African Heritage." In *Pre-Colonial and Post-Colonial Drama and Theatre in Africa*, 48–58. South Africa: Africa World Press.

Eliade, Mircea. 1959. *The Sacred and the Profane: The Nature of Religion. First American Edition*. Translated by Willard R. Trask. 1st American edition. New York: Harcourt, Brace & World Inc.

Eretescu, Constantin. 1968. "Măştile de Priveghi Origine, Funcţionalitate." *Revista de Folclor* 1 (13): 37–44.

Eretescu, Constantin, and Florica Lorinţ. 1967. "'Moşii' in Obiceiurile Vietii Familiale." *Revista de Folclor* 4 (12): 299–307.

Faris, James C. 1969. "Mumming in an Outport Fishing Settlement: A Description and Suggestion on the Cognitive Complex." In *Christmas Mumming in Newfoundland*, 128–44. Newfoundland: University of Toronto Press.

Fox, Katy. 2011. *Peasants into European Farmers?: EU Integration in the Carpathian Mountains of Romania*. Zurich: LIT Verlag.

Frevert, Ute, and H.G. Haupt, eds. 2002. *Omul secolului XX*. Iasi: Polirom.

Gailey, Alan. 1969. *Irish Folk Drama*. Cork: Mercier Press.

Galtung, Johan. 1990. "Cultural Violence." *Journal of Peace Research* 27 (3): 291–305.

Gálvez, Jesús Padilla, and Margit Gaffal. 2011. *Forms of Life and Language Games*. Frankfurt: Ontos Verlag.

Gennep, Arnold van. 1909. *The Rites of Passage*. Routledge.

Giddens, Anthony. 1991. *Modernity and Self-Identity: Self and Society in the Late Modern Age*. Stanford, California: Stanford University Press.

Ginzburg, Carlo. 1993. "Microhistory: Two or Three Things That I Know about It." *Critical Inquiry* 20 (1): 10–35.

Goetzman, William. 2016. *Money Changes Everything*. New Jersey: Princeton University Press.

Golay, Christophe. 2015. "Negotiation of a United Nations Declaration on the Rights of Peasants and Other People Working in Rural Areas." Geneva Academy of International Humanitarian Law and Human Rights.

Graeber, David. 2001. *Toward An Anthropological Theory of Value: The False Coin of Our Own Dreams*. First Edition edition. New York: Palgrave Macmillan.

———. 2011. *Debt: The First 5,000 Years*. 1st edition. Brooklyn, N.Y: Melville House.

Green, A.E. 1980. "Popular Drama and the Mummers' Play." In *Performance and Politics in Popular Drama*, 139–66. Cambridge: Cambridge University Press.

Green, Thomas A. 1978. "Toward a Definition of Folk Drama." *The Journal of American Folklore* 91 (361): 843–50.

Groos, Karl, and Elizabeth L. Baldwin. 2012. *The Play of Man*. Ulan Press.

Gunnell, Terry, ed. 2007a. *Masks and Mumming in the Nordic Area*. Uppsala: Kungl. Gustav Adolfs Akademien för svensk folkkultur.

Gunnell, Terry. 2007b. "Introduction." In *Masks and Mumming in the Nordic Area*, Edited by Terry Gunnell, 27–43. Uppsala: Kungl. Gustav Adolfs Akademien för svensk folkkultur.

Haja, Gabriela. 2003. *Structuri Dramatice În Folclorul Românesc*. Iași: Alfa.

Halperin, Rhoda. 1977. "Introduction: The Substantive Economy in Peasant Societies." In *Peasant Livelihood, Studies in Economic Anthropology and Cultural Ecology*. New York: St. Martin's Press.

Halpern, Joel. 1976. "Introduction." In *The Changing Peasantry of Eastern Europe*, 1–7. Cambridge, Massachusetts: Schenkman Publishing Company Inc.

Halpert, Herbert. 1969. "A Typology of Mumming." In *Christmas Mumming in Newfoundland*, 34–61. Newfoundland: University of Toronto Press.

Halpert, Herbert, and George Morley Story. 1969. *Christmas Mumming in Newfoundland; Essays in Anthropology, Folklore, and History*. Toronto: Published for Memorial University of Newfoundland by University of Toronto Press.

Handlin, Oscar E. 1967. "Peasant Origins." In *Tribal & Peasant Economies*, edited by George Dalton, 456–78. Austin: University of Texas Press.

Harari, Yuval Noah. 2015. *Sapiens: A Brief History of Humankind*. 1st edition. New York: Harper.

Harper, Krista. 2006. *Wild Capitalism: Environmental Activists and Post-Socialist Ecology in Hungary*. Boulder, CO: New York: East European Monographs.

Hartman, Robert S. 1969. *The Structure of Value*. London and Amsterdam: Southern Illinois University Press.

Heisig, James W. 1977. "Bruno Bettelheim and the Fairy Tales." *Children's Literature* 6 (1): 93–114.

Helm, Alex. 1981. *The English Mummers' Play*. Woodbridge, Suffolk; Totowa, NJ: D.S. Brewer.

Hessayon, Ariel. n.d. "From Violent Peasants to Multi-Million Pound Megastars: The History of Football." Goldsmiths, University of London. Accessed January 16, 2020. https://www.gold.ac.uk/news/comment-the-history-of-football/.

Hobsbawm, Eric. 1994. *The Age of Extremes: A History of the World, 1914–1991*. New York: A Division of Random House, Inc.

Hobsbawm, Eric, and Terence O. Ranger. 1992. *The Invention of Tradition*. Cambridge University Press.

Hopkins, Keith, and Mary Beard. 2011. *The Colosseum*. Profile Books.

Horkheimer, Max, and Theodor W. Adorno. 2002. *Dialectic of Enlightenment*. Stanford: Stanford University Press.

Houlihan, Barrie, and Dominic Malcolm. 2015. *Sport and Society: A Student Introduction*. California: SAGE.

Huizinga, Johan. 1968. *Homo Ludens: A Study of the Play Element in Culture*. Boston: Beacon Press.

Ibraileanu, Garabet. 1966. *Memories from Childhood and Adolescence*. București: Editura Pentru Literatură.

Ioanid, Radu. 2008. *The Holocaust in Romania: The Destruction of Jews and Gypsies Under the Antonescu Regime, 1940–1944*. Chicago: Ivan R. Dee.

Iordachi, Constantin, and Dorin Dobrincu. 2009. *Transforming Peasants, Property and Power: The Collectivization of Agriculture in Romania, 1949–1962*. Central European University Press.

Iorga, Nicolae. 1928. *Istoria Românilor Prin Călători*. Vol. 1. București: Editura Casei Școalelor.

Jarvis, Dale Gilbert. 2014. *Any Mummers 'Lowed In?: Christmas Mummering Traditions in Newfoundland and Labrador*. Newfoundland and Labrador: Flanker Press Limited.

Jaspers, Karl. 1968. *The Origin and Goal of History*. Trade Paper edition. Yale University Press.

Kaneff, Demma, and Pamela Leonard, eds. 2001. *Post-Socialist Peasant?: Rural and Urban Constructions of Identity in Eastern Europe, East Africa and the Former*

Soviet Union. 2002 edition. Houndmills, Basingstoke, Hampshire; New York: Palgrave Macmillan.

Kant, Immanuel. 2001. *Critique of the Power of Judgment*. Revised edition. Cambridge: Cambridge University Press.

Kautsky, Karl. 1988. *The Agrarian Question*. London: Zwan Publications.

Keh, Andrew. 2019. "A Wine-Soaked Ball Unites a Georgian Village, but Only After Dividing It." *The New York Times*, May 7, 2019, sec. Sports. https://www.nytimes.com/2019/05/07/sports/georgia-ball-lelo-burti.html.

Kideckel, David A. 2008. *Getting By in Postsocialist Romania: Labor, the Body, and Working-Class Culture*. Bloomington: Indiana University Press.

Kligman, Gail. 1981. *Calus: Symbolic Transformation in Romanian Ritual*. Chicago: University of Chicago Press.

———. 1998. *The Politics of Duplicity: Controlling Reproduction in Ceausescu's Romania*. Berkeley: University of California Press.

Kligman, Gail, and Katherine Verdery. 2011. *Peasants under Siege: The Collectivization of Romanian Agriculture, 1949–1962*. Princeton, NJ: Princeton University Press.

Kluckhohn, Clyde. 1951. "Value and Value-Orientation in the Theory of Action." In *Toward a General Theory of Action*, edited by Talcott Parsons and Edward A. Shils, 506. New York: Harper & Row Publishers.

Knuts, Eva. 2007. "Mask and Mumming Traditions in Sweden:A Survey." In *Masks and Mumming in the Nordic Area*, edited by Terry Gunnell, 107–88. Uppsala: Kungl. Gustav Adolfs Akademien för svensk folkkultur.

Kundera, Milan. 1999. *The Book of Laughter and Forgetting*. Reprint edition. New York: Harper Perennial Modern Classics.

Lahovari, George Ioan, C.I. Brătianu, and Grigore G. Tocilescu. 1899. *Marele Dicționar Geografic Al României*. Vol. I–V. București: Stab Grafic J.V. Socecu.

Leibniz, Gottfried Wilhelm. 1999. *The Monadology and Other Philosophical Writings*. London: Oxford University Press.

Leustean, Lucian N. 2008. *Orthodoxy and the Cold War: Religion and Political Power in Romania, 1947–65*. 1st edition. Basingstoke England; New York: Palgrave Macmillan.

Lommel, Andreas. 1972. *Masks: Their Meaning and Function*. New York, Toronto: McGraw-Hill.

Lovelace, Martin J. 1980. "Christmas Mumming in England: The House-Visit." In *Folklore Studies in Honour of Herbert Halpert*, 271–81. Newfoundland: Memorial University of Newfoundland.

Lowenthal, David. 1985. *The Past Is a Foreign Country*. Cambridge: Cambridge University Press.

Lyotard, Jean-Francois. 1984. *The Postmodern Condition: A Report on Knowledge*. Translated by Geoff Bennington and Brian Massumi. 1st edition. Minneapolis: University of Minnesota Press.

Madgearu, Virgil. 1936. *Agrarianism, capitalism, imperialism: Contribuțiuni la studiul evoluției sociale românești*. București: Institutul de arte grafice "Bucovina."

Malaby, Thomas M. 2009. "Anthropology and Play: The Contours of Playful Experience." *New Literary History* 40 (1): 205–18.

Martin, Loren J., Georgia Hathaway, Kelsey Isbester, Sara Mirali, Erinn L. Acland, Nils Niederstrasser, Peter M. Slepian, et al. 2015. "Reducing Social Stress Elicits Emotional Contagion of Pain in Mouse and Human Strangers." *Current Biology* 25 (3): 326–32. https://doi.org/10.1016/j.cub.2014.11.028.

Martin, Rachel and Sean Carberry. 2014. "Buzkashi: Like Polo, But With A Headless Goat." Radio *Npr.Org*. Boston.

Marx, Karl. 1904. *A Contribution to the Critique of Political Economy*. Charles H. Kerr.

———. 1994. *The Eighteenth Brumaire of Louis Bonaparte*. New York: International Publishers Co.

Meillassoux, Claude. 1973. "The Social Organization of the Peasantry: The Economic Basis of Kinship." *The Journal of Peasant Studies* 1 (1): 81–90.

Mendras, Henri. 1976. *Sociétés paysannes: éléments pour une théorie de la paysannerie*. A. Colin.

———. 2002. "The Invention of the Peasantry: A Moment in the History of Post-World War II French Sociology." *Revue Française de Sociologie* 43: 157–71. https://doi.org/10.2307/3322761.

Neagota, Bogdan. 2000. "Dacismul si fenomenul originar' in studiul culturii populare." *Anuarul Institutului de Etnografie și Folclor "Constantin Brăiloiu"* 11–13: 117–32.

Neagota, Bogdan and Ileana Benga. 2011. "Niveluri Explicative În Căluș. Între Narativitate Și Ceremonialitate." *Orma. Revista de Studii Etnologice Si Istorico-Religioase* 15, edited by Alin Rus: 121–64.

Nissenbaum, Stephen. 1996. *The Battle for Christmas*. New York: Alfred A. Knopf Inc.

Nixey, Catherine. 2018. *The Darkening Age: The Christian Destruction of the Classical World*. Boston: Houghton Mifflin Harcourt.

Obrebski, Joseph. 1976. *The Changing Peasantry of Eastern Europe*. Cambridge, MA: Transaction Publishers.

Oișteanu, Andrei. 2012. *Grădina de dincolo. Zoosophia*. Iași: Polirom.

Oprișan, Horia Barbu. 1965. "Satelitul." *Teatrul* 9 (10): 64–69.

———. 1981. *Teatru Fără Scenă: Evocări Ale Unor Spectacole, Personaje Și Interpreți Ai Teatrului Popular Românesc*. București: Meridiane.

———. 1987. *Teatrul Popular Românesc*. București: Editura Meridiane.

Ordish, Thomas. 1891. "Folk-Drama." *Folk-Lore* 2 (3): 314–35.

———. 1893. "English Folk-Drama." *Folk-Lore* 4 (2): 149–75.

Orwell, George. 1961. *1984*. New York, NY: Signet Classic.

Papadima, Ovidiu. 1981. "Preface." In *Teatru Fără Scenă*, 5–10. București: Meridiane.

"Play Is More than Just Fun." 2009. *Ted Radio Hour*. Boston.

Polanyi, Karl. 1944. *The Great Transformation: The Political and Economic Origins of Our Time*. Beacon Press.

Pomorska, Krystyna. 1984. "Foreword." In *Rabelais and His Word*, vii–xi. Bloomington: Indiana University Press.

Pop, Mihai. 1976. *Obiceiuri Tradiţionale Româneşti*. Bucureşti: Institutul de Cercetări Etnologice şi Dialectologice.

Powell, John Wesley. 2015. *On the Evolution of Language*. Prabhat Prakashan.

Preda, Marin. 1957. *The Morometes*. New York: Foreign Languages Publishing House.

Preobrazhensky, Evgeny. 1967. *The New Economics*. Translated by Brian Pearce. Clarendon Press.

Rachel Martin. 2014. "Buzkashi: Like Polo, But With A Headless Goat." *Npr.Org*. Boston.

Redfield, Robert. 1969. *The Little Community: And Peasant Society and Culture*. University of Chicago Press.

Reid, Nick. 2017. "Atherstone Ball Game: The Story behind England's Ancient Sport." *Coventry Telegraph*, 2017.

Retegan, Gheorghe. 1957. "Dracii Din Valea Ţibleşului." *Revista de Folclor* 4 (2): 27–54.

Reymont, Władysław Stanisław. 1925. *The Peasants*. London: Alfred A. Knopf.

Robb, Graham. 2008. *The Discovery of France: A Historical Geography*. New York: W. W. Norton & Company.

Robben, Antonius C. G. M., and Marcelo Suarez-Orozco. 2000. *Cultures Under Siege: Collective Violence and Trauma*. Cambridge: Cambridge University Press.

Robinson, William I. 2014. *Global Capitalism and the Crisis of Humanity*. New York City: Cambridge University Press.

Rosetti, Al, Mihai Pop, and I. Pervain. 1964. *Istoria Literaturii Române. Folclorul. Literatura Română În Perioada Feudală (1400–1780)*. Bucureşti: Editura Academiei Republicii Populare Romîne.

Rus, Alin. 2003. *Valea Jiului: o capcană istorică*. Petroşani: Realitatea Românească.

Rus, Alin, and Bogdan Neagota. 2016. "Patrimonializarea—Procese, Tendinţe, Curente Şi Aspecte." *Sinteza* 33 (Octombrie): 106–17.

Sahlins, Marshall David. 1974. *Stone Age Economics*. Transaction Publishers.

Sartori, Giovanni. 2005. *Homo Videns. Imbecilizarea Prin Televiziune Si Post-Gandirea*. Bucureşti: Humanitas.

Schmidt, Léopold. 1965. *Le théâtre populaire européen*. Paris: Éditions G.-P. Maisonneuve et Larose.

Schopenhauer, Arthur. 1966. *The World as Will and Representation, Vol. 1*. Translated by E. F. J. Payne. 5844. 1st edition. New York: Dover Publications.

Scott, James C. 1977. *The Moral Economy of the Peasant: Rebellion and Subsistence in Southeast Asia*. New Haven: Yale University Press.

Shanin, Teodor. 1971. *Peasants and Peasant Societies: Selected Readings*. Penguin Modern Sociology Readings. Harmondsworth: Penguin.

———. 1990. *Defining Peasants: Essays Concerning Rural Societies, Expolary Economies, and Learning from Them in the Contemporary World*. B. Blackwell.

Skounti, Ahmed. 2009. "The Authentic Illusion: Humanity's Intangible Cultural Heritage." In *Intangible Heritage,* edited by Laurajane Smith and Natsuko Akagawa, 74–92. London and New York: Routledge.

Smith, Kimbra. 2015. *Practically Invisible: Coastal Ecuador, Tourism, and the Politics of Authenticity*. Vanderbilt University Press.

Smith, Paul. 2007. "Remembering the Past. The Marketing of Tradition in Newfoundland." In *Masks and Mumming in the Nordic Area*, edited by Terry Gunnell, 755–70. Uppsala: Kungl. Gustav Adolfs Akademien för svensk folkkultur.

Sorokin, P.A., C.C. Zimmerman, and C.J. Galpin. 1971. "Rural Economic Organization, Europe, 1930." In *Economic Development and Social Change*, edited by George Dalton, 412–24. New York: The Natural History Press.

Spitzer, Manfred. 2020. *Demența digitală: Cum ne tulbură mintea noile tehnologii*. București: Humanitas.

Stahl, Henri H. 2008. *Traditional Romanian Village Communities: The Transition from the Communal to the Capitalist Mode of Production in the Danube Region*. Translated by Daniel Chirot and Holley Coulter Chirot. 1st edition. Cambridge: Cambridge University Press.

Stirling, Paul. 1965. *Turkish Village*. London: Weidenfeld and Nicolson.

Story, G.M. 1969. "Newfoundland: Fishermen, Hunters, Planters and Merchants." In *Christmas Mumming in Newfoundland*, 7–33. Newfoundland: University of Toronto Press.

Tiddy, R. J. E. 1923. *The Mummers' Play*. Oxford: Oxford University Press.

Tillis, Steve. 1999. *Rethinking Folk Drama*. Westport, CT: Greenwood Publishing Group.

Turkle, Sherry. 2017. *Alone Together: Why We Expect More from Technology and Less from Each Other*. Expanded, Revised edition. New York: Basic Books.

Uys, Jamie. 1980. *The Gods Must Be Crazy*. Comedy.

Verdery, Katherine. 2003. *The Vanishing Hectare: Property and Value in Postsocialist Transylvania*. 1st edition. Ithaca: Cornell University Press.

Vissarion, Ion. 1987. "The Pale Oxen." In *Reading Textbook for the 4th Grade*, 43–45. Bucharest: Didactică and Pedagogică Publishing House.

Vulcănescu, Romulus. 1970. *Măștile populare: Monografie*. București: Editura științifică.

Walsh, Kevin. 1992. *The Representation of the Past: Museums and Heritage in the Post-Modern World*. London: New York: Routledge.

Warner, Elizabeth A. 1977. *The Russian Folk Theatre*. Hague-Paris: Mouton.

Welch, Katherine E. 2007. *The Roman Amphitheatre: From Its Origins to the Colosseum*. Cambridge University Press.

White, Bowen Faville. 2000. *Why Normal Isn't Healthy: How to Find Heart, Meaning, Passion, and Humor on the Road Most Traveled*. Center City, Minn: Hazelden.

Whitehead, Neil L. 2004. "On the Poetics of Violence." In *Violence*, 55–78. Santa Fe, New Mexico: School of American Research.

Wittgenstein, Ludwig. 1922. *Tractatus Logico-Philosophicus*. Harcourt, Brace, Incorporated.

———. 1967. *Zettel*. Berkeley and Los Angeles: University of California Press.

———. 2010. *Philosophical Investigations*. Malden: John Wiley & Sons.

Wolf, Eric. 1966. *Peasants*. Englewood Cliffs, NJ: Prentice-Hall.

Wolf, Eric R. 1990. *Europe and the People Without History*. Second Edition. Berkeley: University of California Press.

Zaiafet. 2020. "De Ce Jucăm Jocuri Video?—YouTube." 2020. https://www.youtube .com/watch?v=1KCueTn0Bus.

Index

Page references for figures and tables are italicized.

About the Author

Alin Rus is a cultural anthropologist interested in social movements, traditional customs of rural communities, and the relation between local rural rituals and global capitalism. He earned a PhD in philology from Babes-Bolyai University, Cluj-Napoca, Romania, in 2007 and a PhD in anthropology from the University of Massachusetts, Amherst, in 2018. He is the author of two books: *The Jiu Valley—An Historic Trap* (2003) and *The Mineriades (miners' social movements)—Between Political Manipulation and Working-class Solidarity* (2007). Over time, he has also published articles in various collective volumes and journals in Romania, England, Poland, France, and the United States.

Besides his activity as a writer and cultural anthropologist, he is also interested in visual anthropology. He has produced seven documentaries so far, three of them in cooperation with two other anthropologists. His movies were screened at international film festivals, international conferences, and television. His last movie, "Malanca—a time machine," is the result of a long-term project in Krasnoilsk, a southwestern Ukrainian village, where the author filmed a winter ritual for four years. This ritual is used as a lens to analyze a rural community for which the event works as a mark for promoting its ethnic identity in the last six decades despite the oppressive policies of the dictatorial Soviet state and the economic downturn, political tensions, and war during postsocialism.

Alin Rus is currently an adjunct lecturer of anthropology at Franklin Pierce University, New Hampshire.